The Great Rebellion

The
Great Rebellion
1642–1660

Ivan Roots

Senior Lecturer in History, University College
of South Wales and Monmouthshire, Cardiff

B T Batsford Ltd   London

First published 1966
© Ivan Roots 1966

Made and printed in Great Britain by
William Clowes and Sons Ltd, London and Beccles
for the publishers B T BATSFORD LTD
4 Fitzhardinge Street London W1

For my parents
with love and honour

Preface

My aim in this volume has been a modest one. I wanted to write a fresh narrative of a lively period in our history, one which stirred my imagination when I was at school and has challenged my appreciation ever since. At the same time as I have sought to see events through the eyes of actors in them, I have been conscious of the need to re-appraise the age in the broken light of my own researches and of those of many other workers in a crowded field. If I have garbled their notions it would be charity to put it down not to malice but to my want of understanding.

Stress is on political and constitutional matters, though I hope I have given indication here and there of my awareness of other considerations. Much play is made of the interaction of personalities and of the interposition of chance. But I feel no desire to rob this great catastrophe of any connexion with ideas and deeper issues. Some of these, like 'the general crisis of the seventeenth century', have left little impression not because I am convinced they did not happen but because I am not yet persuaded that they did. The civil war was a mystery to many gifted contemporary observers and participants, who were I believe as intelligent and thoughtful as any historian now studying the period. They were puzzled by the answers they got to the questions they asked. I know that I am puzzled by much that is turned up by the questions asked today.

Some explanation needs to be given for the weight I have put on the sixteen-fifties. It seems to me that this decade is too readily brushed aside as a mere tottering obstacle to the inevitable Restoration of 1660. Perhaps monarchy in the old line was bound to come back. Certainly many within and without the British Isles thought so and waited for it to happen. Others worked positively for it. Yet others pushed against it. Some of these were buoyant in confidence that England had other purposes to consider than cutting short the reluctant travels of young Charles Stuart. The activities or lack of them of all these men make these ten years, too long for some, for others too brief, a period of deep interest, worth studying again and again for its own sake.

I am grateful to Professor Geoffrey Barraclough for suggesting to me, so long ago he has probably forgotten, the writing of this book, and to Mr Samuel Carr of Batsford's for keeping me at it. Without his enthusiasm and gentle chiding it would, I fear, have been an endless project. It is a pleasure to record at last my thanks to Mr R. J. Bates, the Librarian of the University College of South Wales and Monmouthshire, and to his staff, particularly Dr F. G. Cowley, now of University College, Swansea, for getting me so many of the books I needed. Mrs Margaret Bird deserves both gratitude and congratulations for turning my painful scrawl into an intelligible type-script. Mr Douglas Matthews, of the London Library, besides taking a great deal of pains with the Index, has kindly prevented me from making a number of slips. Miss Mary Scriven has been very helpful in seeing the book through its final stages. I owe a lot to my students who have over the years, mostly with courteous patience, submitted to the verbal expression of many of my views.

The biggest debt is to my wife, who has for so long affectionately concealed her just exasperation at the chaos of books and papers out of which this book has slowly emerged. She has helped with the proofs, too.

University College of South Wales
and Monmouthshire
Cardiff

Ivan Roots
1966

Contents

Prologue

The Great Rebellion sprawls across the two middle decades of the seventeenth century. It was the outcome of immediate political circumstances and personalities and of the interplay of a variety of accidents and misunderstandings. But it was also the crisis of a complex of issues that had been straining the fabric of State, Church and society for at least half a century. The Tudors, a talented and well-served dynasty, had ruled with a tough but sensitive hand. Though hampered by practical and constitutional checks upon their authority, they had effectively brought England, and themselves, through a distracted century. Each monarch had managed to die a natural death. Throughout they had had the support, or at any rate the acceptance, of the bulk of their politically articulate subjects, a few thousand families in a population of some three millions, a tiny segment of the whole people, but large enough for their purpose. In tackling the problems left by their predecessors they had used methods apt for their situation, copying what was best in the brief Yorkist triumph. Clear-sighted but not visionary, the Tudors were opportunists, very mundane politicians, who grappled with the difficulties as they cropped up and were not ashamed to be satisfied with something less than perfection. Because they deserved it, politician's luck often came their way.

By the end of the long reign of Elizabeth I it seemed as if their main tasks were done, done well enough. The realm was orderly in some degree, lip-service was ostentatiously paid to ideals of discipline and authority like those set out in *The Book of Homilies*, and gathered together by tidy-minded literary historians under 'the Elizabethan World Picture' or some such title. Faction certainly thought it expedient to put on a fair mask of concern for the community. The nobility, a small, only slowly growing group, may or may not have been in absolute decline, dependent upon royal gifts and the fawning patience of their creditors. They still had a huge grip upon land, basis of all wealth and strength, but their independent military power was broken and their interests more and more intertwined with those of the crown. Wisely the Tudors had a place for them, if only they would settle themselves in it. Essex's rebellion in 1601—in so many ways a dark episode—is clear on one point: the day was past when the magnate who wanted everything could hope to encompass it. If the crown was in danger from below, it would be a threat of a different kind from that which produced the dynastic wars of the fifteenth century. James I was not being especially perceptive when he foretold an eclipse of the nobility if the crown toppled.

Another old-time rival lay low. The Church, free of papal entanglements that may have been more irksome than inhibiting, had in the fear of God abjectly submitted itself to royal supremacy. Bishops calmly organised their sees to revere the king as much as to worship the Almighty. Elizabeth I found it difficult to sort out Church and State funds. Some bishoprics were kept vacant for decades, displaying for profit the reality of royal control, but sapping spiritual vigour. There was also, alongside apathy, religious dissidence born of Lollardy, continental protestantism and recent English experience. The Reformation in England as elsewhere made theology a 'nose of wax'. But in 1603 there seemed little prospect of the sort of politico-religious wars that had savaged France for 40 years past, while the monarchy was feeble and the nobility inordinately ambitious. Though the English protestant critics—vaguely labelled 'puritan'—spoke up forcibly enough in press and pulpit, they were a mixed batch, mostly content to be within the Church of England, contemplating what should be considered minor changes. As for the catholics, they were possibly numerous, but as a positive, homogeneous force in politics they were dwindling, fast becoming a bogey to be ruthlessly exploited by others. Apart from a few great magnates and their clients at court they lived their circumspect lives far from the mainstream, lingering in the remoter corners of the realm, the north and Wales, less assimilated to central authority. Restlessness in these regions was now less frightening, though they were still subject to special jurisdictions. Spain, undefeated in the war of attrition after the destruction of the Armada, was, however, unlikely to invade again, whether through Ireland, Wales or the north. A friendly France under the anti-Hapsburg Henry IV and the joining of the Scottish and English crowns in the pacific person of James VI made a revival of the old anglophobe alliance improbable. Elsewhere the international scene seemed equally bright. The new-born United Provinces would be inveterate commercial rivals, but the two sea-states had already entered upon that puzzling love–hatred that ran through their relations during the whole Stuart era.

All this favoured Elizabeth I's optimistic successor, who by concluding (at once) a peace (the treaty of Hampton Court, 1604) with Philip III delighted those of his new subjects who saw more to be gained from legitimate trade with Spain and the Mediterranean than from freebooting on the Main. But it was a drawback, too. Enmity for Spain had bitten deep into many English emotions, defying reason perhaps. The desire to please the Spaniards, which was shared by both James I and Charles I (apart from an aberration in the sixteen-twenties), was a source of discontent that outlived them. It was a promoter of faction at court as well. Moreover, Elizabeth by thumping on the drum of foreign peril had drowned criticism on other topics. James would have to look elsewhere for a gag. Worse, in a way, was the peaceful succession, confounding the gloomy expectations of realists like Bacon, who had long been hearing ancestral voices prophesying civil war on the demise of the last Tudor. The open succession had been in fact Elizabeth's masterpiece. It was a sure instinct that prompted her to name no heir until the very end. Her long-preserved virginity had been an adamantine shield. But James I was married, had sons, and could not claim that the country's survival and his own were co-terminous. Yet he continued to fear for his life, padding about his sleazy court in shapeless garments quilted against cold steel. His cousin, Arabella Stuart, whose offence was to combine royal blood with political naiveté, was treated with calculated cruelty. But the main Stuart line was too fecund to encourage pretenders.

A problem solved often means a new one born. The very successes of the Tudors were a test for the Stuart kings. Although much of what we associate with Elizabethan England—notably the literary effulgence—was in fact a part of the Jacobean age, it is true that a whole new era was in the making. The old queen herself had had an inkling of how the vitality of her kind of rule was fading. The political scene at the end of the sixteenth century had dark corners hidden by the splendour of light in the foreground. Peering into those areas it is possible to observe that something was happening among those strata of the ruling class that lay beneath the peerage, among the landed gentry, and to a degree among the professional, trading and industrial classes whose most successful members were forging close links with the gentry. All had stakes in the country and might be described as 'men of substance', varied though that substance might be. Of necessity the crown had called upon men of this sort to help in the campaign for stability. On the whole they had responded, often working hard. As a result they had grown, some of them, in confidence, prestige, capacity and ambition. Even those who failed to get on had the urge to improve their prospects or to stop the rot in their fortunes. Rising, declining or perdurable gentry—all three have been uncovered—were active, straining the shape of society, disturbing traditional policies, producing friction by their movements, up and down or along the one plane. Historians have argued whether a rise or a decline of the gentry brought about the long crisis of the seventeenth century. Others have judged the controversy sterile. Yet there was a rebellion, which had something revolutionary about it, and gentry were in the thick of it. They must be taken seriously.

The gentry formed a good part of the government, especially in the vital local dimension. The peerage was recruited from them. Others were clients, not always supine, of magnates whose way of life impressed them and which they imitated, often with fidelity. They were crown officials, members of satellite councils like that in the marches of Wales, deputy-lieutenants, justices of the peace. They had lately 'invaded' the parliamentary boroughs, swamping the seats which had hitherto been the little-regarded preserves of townsmen. In the process they had started to transform the House of Commons. They were educating themselves at the universities and the inns of court and stacking their shelves with books and pamphlets. What they did or did not care to do, what they thought, said or wrote had repercussions. They had contributed to and partaken of the economic changes of the past two centuries, which, though subject to upsetting fluctuations, had brought growth in agriculture, trade and industry. Men who had gained or lost by these rather mysterious developments found themselves concerned about royal policies directed towards economic activity. There was room for disagreement about what was best to be done. Certainly some regulations which at an earlier period might have been thought helpful or nugatory were now felt to be frustrating. Niggling about them might turn into resistance and that in time could come to a questioning of the very prerogatives upon which they were based. Whether they knew it or not some men by the reign of Charles I had started to shuffle along the road to rebellion. There were other incentives to nudge them on their way.

Religion was one. James I and, more uncompromisingly, Charles I, whose upbringing was entirely in the Church of England, set their faces against further 'purification' in religion. Those who wanted it—they included many gentry and their associates—encountered a royal supremacy that took no account of their sentiments and which favoured aspects they deplored in a 'high' Anglicanism regarded by its well-placed advocates as God-sent, no longer the by-product of a hasty compromise. Critics, met with this aggressive resistance, extended both their requirements and their sense of grievance. Objection to paying

4

tithes may serve as an example. It sprang from a variety of sources, but, with sabbatarianism, zeal for a preaching ministry, hatred of the ecclesiastical courts, came to a focus in impugning the existing frame of the Church. Given the avowed intimacy of hierarchy and the secular government, hard words about the former could take in the latter. Obviously many puritans were only lightly affected by these extra steps. But others pushed on in all ways open to them. Of these parliament was the chief, and so religion took its place with foreign policy and questioned taxation in the debates of the early Stuart meetings. Its protagonists were hardly revolutionaries. If constitutionalists imagined some golden age of political harmony in Anglo-Saxon times or thought that Magna Carta really was an efficacious fundamental law, puritans hankered after pristine days of purity with the Bible as the all-embracing unanswerable authority. In each case the inclination was to haul in the past to shore up the future.

All this meant in every sphere a hunting for precedents to assail or defend positions. Inevitably, one might feel, the dusty quest palled for some impatient, present-centred men. They gradually accepted the need for new laws, rather than for historical investigations followed by petitions for putting into effect what could with some effort be shown to be the existing law. Ultimately even this was not enough. There followed a period of competition in power, in which ill-defined groups of men, sieved by events and under leadership flung up by them, were shaken into armed conflict with the King. Charles I by standing as a symbol of order and establishment attracted many, though, significantly, not all, of those who left or got left behind by the more enterprising 'opposition' phalanxes. The result was the Great Rebellion.

PART ONE

The Road to
Nottingham

I 1629

On the morning of 2 March 1629 the third parliament of Charles I reassembled at Westminster after a brief recess. Weary of rebuffs and expecting further obstructions, the King decided on a further adjournment until 10 March. When the Speaker reported this to the House of Commons there were shouts of dissent. At once he rose from his chair to prevent a debate. Whereupon two members rushed forward and held him down, swearing 'by God's wounds he should sit still until they pleased to rise'.[1] Other members locked the chamber doors. It was an operation carried out with suspicious smoothness. Sir John Eliot then produced a protestation against tonnage and poundage and innovations in religion. The tearful Speaker refused to put it to the vote. Eliot, never in sure command of his temper, flung his 'paper' to the floor. A lively debate ended with John Selden's motion that the Clerk of the House should be commanded to read the protestation. Eliot now confessed he had burned it, but Denzil Holles was able to recite it from memory. It was carried by acclamation over the noes of embarrassed moderates and courtiers. The House then adjourned itself until 10 March, the doors were unlocked and in a babble of talk the members drifted out. A little later the indignant King came down to the Lords. Addressing them and the few M.P.s who had gathered at the bar, he blamed the Commons for the dissolution he had now resolved upon, not all of them, but 'the undutiful carriage of some'. 'I know', he went on, 'there are many there as dutiful subjects as any in the world; it being but some few vipers amongst them that did cast this mist of undutifulness over most of their eyes. ... Those vipers must look for their reward of punishment; so you, my Lords, must justly expect from me that favour and protection that a good king oweth to his loving and faithful nobility.'[2]

Charles did not expect to be long without a parliament and was already playing his favourite sport of divide and rule, setting if he could Lords against Commons, and some of the Commons against the rest—a policy he pursued until the abrupt end of his days. Ineptly

Eliot and company had passed the ball to him. Few could have whole-heartedly approved of what had just happened and there was a revulsion in favour of the King. Charles pursued his initiative by a declaration plausibly defending his action. He also imprisoned some of the seeming ringleaders in the Commons. They included, obviously, Sir John Eliot, who was to die and be buried in the Tower, quite unforgiven, three years later, and Benjamin Valentine, who was not released until just before the summoning of the next parliament, 11 years later in 1640.

Meantime cloth merchants, assuming from recent experience that there would soon be a new parliament, and caught between the threat contained in the protestation against those who paid tonnage and poundage and the immediate wrath of the King, ceased to trade. Loss of profits and the calculation after a time that the little finger of a present King was heavier than the loins of a future parliament brought them round. Even so the stop of trade had caused widespread unemployment and distress. If the merchants had stuck it out there might have been so much disorder the King would have had to call a parliament for the means to put it down. As it was, the merchants had guessed correctly about a long intermission. In the light of what followed, 1629, which ushered in the somewhat ill-named 'Personal Government of Charles I', marks a definite stage in the political and constitutional crisis of the seventeenth century.

It had been sad experience of three parliaments in four years that had brought Charles I to his present enmity for them. The years 1625–9 had confirmed his father's prediction that he would live to have his belly-full of them. The first two, very brief, and the opening session of the third had met in the shadow of the young King's painful infatuation for George Villiers, Duke of Buckingham, the dynamic favourite he had first shared with and then inherited from his pre-decessor. Buckingham by his monopoly of office and advice, his frank enjoyment of it, and his crude nepotism had alienated a good section of the peerage. His flamboyant foreign policy, which produced war with Spain and France at the same time, disturbed the Commons. War with the Spaniard was welcome in some quarters, but Buckingham's strategy was disputed, and though the disasters that attended his expeditions were perhaps not entirely deserved, he became an object of scorn and hatred. His nearness to the King made it difficult to disentangle criticism of him from carping at the crown itself. Charles would argue later that 'the Duke was not alone the mark these men shot at'.[3] He may have been right. To label the favourite 'the grievance of griev-ances'[4] was an easy way out of a difficulty. To have fitted all the upsets of the reign to the procrustean bed of even his inflated personality was impossible, though it was tactically desirable to try it. His untimely death soon exposed the realities.

The first parliament (June–August 1625) failed to grant Charles tonnage and poundage for life, unseasonably busying itself with a scheme to set state revenues on a stable footing. Taking the traditional vote to be a mere act of manners, and the revenue, which he genuinely could not 'want', to be his of right and due inheritance, Charles levied it as if it had been duly made. His view was not accepted and the argument grew fiercer over the years. This parliament also raised matters of religion, attacking the 'innovations' of Arminian divines, like William Laud, the bustling bishop of London, who, much favoured at court, cried up in press and pulpit extreme views of royal authority and the duty of utter non-resistance. Puritans of most sorts regarded them as 'the spawn of papists', but they were in fact strongly anti-Roman.

The significance of this parliament was two-fold. It exposed the inability of the King and duke to manage it, but also tested the capacity of the Commons leaders, notably Sir Edward Coke, former lord chief justice and the 'Sir Oracle' of the common law, and Sir John Eliot, of Cornwall, a former follower of Buckingham. Both were passionate men. Their deficiency was that, though they could collect abuses and suggest remedies, they could devise no way whereby they could secure the continuance of a parliament long enough to have them effected. (A less demonstrative parliamentarian, however, John Pym, was already quietly learning his profession, not so much in the big debates as in the committees, which he had grasped had a vital function in constructive politics.) The second parliament (6 February–15 June 1626) had a similar history. Pinpricks on Buckingham, whose elaborate raid on Cadiz was a flop, culminated in an all-out assault in the shape of an impeachment (a recently refurbished medieval device of limited utility) for crimes as extensive as his areas of activity. After weeks of worsening relations Charles once more packed off the parliament to save his favourite. Eliot had compared the latter with Sejanus, thus making, whether intentionally or not, Charles the tyrant Tiberius. It was an insult he never forgot.[5]

Twenty months passed before King and minister could bear another election. During them England was committed to even more expensive operations. Money was to be raised by whatever means could be hit upon, all unparliamentary, rendering solider returns of animosity than of cash. What there was of the latter was poured away in shameful fiascos, this time in a war with France in which no obvious national interests could be discerned. Loans on privy seals failed to materialise and so Charles turned to forced loans. Many refused to pay, big men, little men. The small fry were bullied at the council table or had soldiers, by definition dissolute persons, billeted upon them. More important personages were imprisoned. Five of them, all knights, asked for a writ of *habeas corpus*. Unwilling to have the legality of the loans tested in open court, Charles instructed the jailer to return a general answer that the knights were there 'by His Majesty's special command-ment'.[6] The King's Bench accepted this as an adequate justification for a remand. So the grievance of arbitrary imprisonment was added to that of arbitrary taxation.

The third parliament met on 17 March 1628. At once it started to consider how it might speedily redress the most outstanding of recent abuses, as they were, in spite of legal decisions to the contrary, widely regarded. After excited discussions within and between the two Houses, both anxious to do things as much by precedent as might be, a strange device was hit upon. It was the child of Coke's legal imagination, the conversion of an individual petition of right into a Petition of Right, a supplication from the entire nation that right should be done in certain areas, a sort of statement of fundamental rights to which the King should give his assent 'by a record and in particulars'.[7] Charles was naturally uneasy about it. All the things complained of—arbitrary direct taxation, arbitrary imprisonment, forcible billeting and com-missions of martial law—had some basis in law, and in any case ought in an emergency to come within the precept *salus populi suprema lex*. But in the Petition the precedents such as they were were construed against him and the matter of reserved powers ignored. By a clumsy form of words he tried to answer in such a way that his prerogative was left entire, but pressure was built up by another massive onslaught on the duke. The King capitulated, giving his assent—*soit droit fait comme il est désiré* [8]—in an acceptable phrase. He confessed that he himself could see no difference between this and the original unavailing reply. But there was a moment of elation in the Commons and many felt a great sense of relief at what they imagined was the happy inauguration of a new era.

Almost at once they were proved wrong. The anti-Buckingham crusade hotted up and other grievances in Church and State were hustled forward by the Commons managers. They took in unparlia-mentary tonnage and poundage, which in fact had not been covered by the financial clause of the Petition. To avoid receiving impossible remonstrances Charles abruptly ended the session.

In the recess he shewed by word and deed that he held the Petition of Right to be no check upon his freedom of action. Indeed, from the start the Petition was of little practical importance. The fine guarantees it uttered and supported by copious appeal to precedent would have to be secured by later legislation and practice. It had little more relevance to the actual circumstances than that other fundamental law to which seventeenth-century Englishmen so reverently appealed— Magna Carta, which really was 'decrepit' in spite of all the magical properties ascribed to it.[9] The recess was notable, too, for major changes in the personnel of Charles's government. Buckingham, in accordance with notorious prophecies, was assassinated, on 22 August 1628, by a crazy lieutenant with a private grouse, John Felton, who became something of a popular hero. The passing of the great duke ought to have cleared the air. At a blow the barrier between the King and the hearts of his subjects should have tumbled down. In fact, relations deteriorated, for in a curious way Buckingham had stood as a shield. A little earlier Sir Thomas Wentworth had entered the King's service as President of the Council of the North. Wentworth, a rich, proud, able Yorkshireman, had played a somewhat ambivalent role in recent parliaments, especially in the debates that led on to the Petition of Right. (He would have preferred a bill.) Some thought him an apostate. But he seems to have been more concerned with efficiency than with constitutional niceties. The sheer factiousness of the Commons in the post-Petition weeks disgusted him. He turned, naturally enough, in his view, to the King, the traditional guarantor against anarchy. For Charles it was at first a great accretion of strength, but in the long run Wentworth proved to be a man with a trail of fire, bringing himself to destruction and almost ruining his master.

The new session began on 20 January 1629. At once the pent-up emotions of the past six months exploded. The King made no personal gesture to improve relations but left the Commons to their own devices. With initiative theirs by default they embarked upon a catalogue of miscellaneous griefs of the commonwealth, rushing incontinently from one uncompleted topic to another. Resolutions were proffered which were increasingly upsetting to the crown, yet the courtiers and middle-of-the-road men could make no impact. On 25 February 1629 the King ordered an adjournment. His purpose is not clear. If he hoped to lower the temperature he certainly failed. What happened when the Commons re-entered their chamber has already been described.

II Personal Rule

By 1629 the problem, though most men could not descry it, was fast
becoming one of sovereignty: where lay final authority in English
government? Was England an 'absolute' or a 'mixed' monarchy?
That it was a monarchy was indisputable—but advocates of an absolute
one were scarce. There was more room for argument about what made
up the mixture and in what proportions the elements were poured in.
If they could not fuse together, how was it possible to avoid an ex-
plosion? These, though not so explicitly stated, were some main issues.
To meet them the medieval constitution—or what men took to be that
constitution—was ransacked for precedents and examples, which were
newly interpreted to meet what were in truth new difficulties. Their
irrelevance was already being shewn, and before long political expedients would have to replace them. In some ways the personal government is a grudging recognition of this process. Its ultimate inability
to make a working combination of old and new claims made a case for
more forthright approaches to what must be judged a grave constitutional crisis. Charles, professing an anxiety to meet scruples, based his
actions on law and history. In a carefully-phrased speech, Wentworth,
at his installation as the last President of the North, unfolded the ideals
and principles of kingly government as he saw them:

> '... to the joint individual wellbeing of Sovereignty and of sub-
> jection do I here vow all my cares and diligences through the whole
> course of this my ministry. I confess I am not ignorant how some
> distempered minds have of late very far endeavoured to divide the
> considerations of the two; as if their ends were distinct, not the
> same, nay, in opposition; a monstrous, a prodigious birth of a
> licentious conception; for so we should become all head or all
> members. But, God be praised, human wisdom, common ex-
> perience, Christian religion teach us far otherwise. Princes are to
> be indulgent, nursing fathers to their people; their modest liberties,
> their sober rights ought to be precious in their eyes, the branches

of their government be for shadow for habitation, the comfort of life, repose, safe and still under the protection of their sceptres. Subjects on the other side ought with solicitous eyes of jealousy to watch over the prerogatives of a crown; the authority of a king is the key-stone which closeth up the arch of order and government, which contains each part in due relation to the whole, and which once shaken, infirmed, all the frame falls together into a confused heap of foundation and battlement, of strength and beauty. Furthermore subjects must lay down their lives for the defence of kings freely, till those offer out of their store freely. Verily these are those mutual intelligences of love and protection descending, and loyalty ascending, which should pass, be the entertainments between a king and his people. Their faithful servants must look equally on both, weave, twist these two together in all their counsels, study, labour to preserve each without diminishing or enlarging either, and by running in the worn, wonted channels, treading the ancient bounds, cut off early all disputes from betwixt them. For whatever he be which ravels forth into questions the right of a king and of a people shall never be able to weave them up again into the comeliness and order he found them.'[1]

Royal aversion to branching out from 'the worn, wonted channels' of legality was marked by frequent resort to the judges privately and in the courts. Charles had good reason to expect comforting replies. It was not only that the Benches held during royal pleasure and that some of their members might be servile or venal, but that they were disposed to construe law in such a way as to enable the crown to fulfil its duty of protecting society, if need be from itself. But critics could also find, at least to their own satisfaction, ample justification for their positions in the medieval arrangements that had been desultorily worked over by the Tudors. In these conditions there were many points of agreement, and it would be a gross error to hold the arguments in the period before the civil war as the product of completely irreconcilable viewpoints. Men who would fight for the crown in the civil war opposed ship money and voted Star Chamber down. Men who had stuck out for the Petition of Right served the King loyally during the personal rule. Not all were conscious of being renegades. For the supreme instance, Wentworth, biographers have been able to put a good case for consistency and constitutional probity. A very vocal parliamentary leader in the 'twenties, active among the unruly local governors of Somerset during the sixteen-thirties, Sir Robert Phelips, had once exclaimed with tears in his eyes that if it be a crime to have loved the King too well, then 'we are criminous'.[2] Even Sir John Eliot, mouldering in his living tomb in the Tower, could still write feelingly of those monarchical principles under whose actual application he was suffering.

It was common ground that God appointed and anointed Kings. But then, what? Most men would take it that the Lord's lieutenants were limited by the laws—of God, of nature, of the realm. But how far? And when, if ever, was a King released from any of these bounds? At once agreement brushed the ragged hem of discord, for to such hard questions there was no simple answer. (In another age this sort of inquiry might never have been made, even hinted at. That it was and was by some pushed to a reply tells us something about the character of the early seventeenth century.) Clearly a King made by God in his own image must be just as God is just. Some men might take his justice as they took their own maker's, passing all understanding. Others wanted justice to be seen, understood, confirmed. Again, it was conceded that divine rights mingled with divine duties. But friction came from any attempt to fix an exact relationship. Could Kings be arbiters in their own cause? The subject was under the King and under the law. Was the King, under no man, yet subject to the same law? God pours with a lavish hand on monarchs the qualities of competence expected of rulers. Could they for their part delegate that competence? Men who strove against monopolies might judge them to be an unwarrantable transference to a private hand for private gain of the indubitable royal competence to see to the common weal. This opinion had been mumbled under Elizabeth I. By the end of the personal government, because the issue had become an even more practical one, it was being shouted aloud.

Such tension, sprung from initial accord, could in the circumstances of the reign of Charles I become intolerable. The controversies were not only material for clever academic treatises, but were very matter-of-fact, touching raw private or group interests. Thus supporters of German protestantism in the Thirty Years War would probe the royal prerogative to form foreign policy when they found their views traduced or ignored. When royal control of economic life picked the merchant's pocket, he responded at last with constitutional queries. The tax-payer, finding his obligations increasing, moved from muttering to complaining, from petitioning to blunt demands for reform. Each found others carping away in other areas. What more natural than a drift to a loose, wobbly alliance with them? Met by executive intransigence the relations might become tighter. The royal case, put at its highest in word and deed during the personal rule, tended to integrate what might otherwise have been inchoate. The effect was the initial unanimity of the Long Parliament of 1640. That did not go very deep, perhaps, but deep enough to undermine 'thorough'.

It is worthwhile pursuing this theme of conflict born of general agreement a little further. The King is accepted as father of his people, a seventeenth-century father, given by the law of nature all original authority, whether economic, political or whatever. But—there is always a 'but'—how does he exercise that paternal control? By mere acts of will? or along specified paths? This is a matter of procedure. Whatever else it was about *Hampden's case* (1637) was about that. It enquired how does the King provide security in a national emergency. Such procedural disputes are rarely trivial, as the history of post-war international conferences has shewn. Success is often the result not so much of what you do but the way that you do it. The very shape of a convention table, like the position of an altar, may determine an era. There was this much to be said for the costly, elaborated procedures of the common law courts: they were checks upon arbitrariness. From this point of view one of the vaunted advantages of the prerogative courts—that their procedure was flexible—would be a prime defect.

Part of the King's agreed paternal authority was a discretionary power. He must have it to preserve the common weal. But when and how was it exercised? It came to this: what is the proper association of King's prerogatives and subjects' liberties? Both certainly existed, as Wentworth pointed out. The same law that smiled on prerogative had an eye to private rights, especially property rights, without which men might as well be slaves. The stress that men of property put upon its liberties is at any time comprehensible. It was abundantly so in an age in which the European situation, of which educated Englishmen, perhaps not so insular as they are sometimes made out, were much aware, was depressing. 'We are the last monarchy in Christendom that retain our original rights and constitutions. Let them not perish now. Let not posterity complain that we have done for them worse than our fathers did for us.'[3] (Property was regarded in this largely familial society as a trust. Heads of families were always conscious of their descendants peering over their shoulders.) It is fair to say that in spite of some spectacular 'royalist' decisions, notably during the sixteen-thirties, Stuart courts of law wanted to preserve property rights. Even in the ship money case five out of 12 judges could not find for the King, mainly on technical grounds. But in the same period the conciliar courts began to take on causes involving property, partly because calls on them for settling breaches of public peace were dwindling, leaving time for other business. But the King's fiscal needs were an added incentive. The consequences are patent: a dislike that would have puzzled Tudor Englishmen. Attorney-General Heath revealed that he shared something of this unease, when, commenting on the 'regulating' of the Privy Council in 1641, he admitted that he had favoured it 'having long been of opinion that ... that honourable board ... should not have meddled' in cases of *meum* and *tuum*.[4] (Heath was, of course, a common lawyer.) Unfavourable comment on the ecclesiastical courts was also connected with their attempts under Archbishops Bancroft and Laud to interfere in tithe disputes. Tithes were commonly regarded as coming within the purlieu of the common law courts.

Matters of controversy, then, ranged a whole field from principle to earthy interests. Arguments were buttressed by subtle or perfunctory reference to law-books, history, the Bible, political thinkers, ancient, modern, English, continental. They were picked out with sophistry and imagination. Once it began to become clear that the disputes could not be resolved to universal satisfaction by precedent or right reason, a role for political pressures, and ultimately military power could be envisaged, though at all times many would not let themselves be driven so far. By the sixteen-thirties it could be seen that little was to be gained by trying to pull the ripe fabric of the old constitution over the angular frame of seventeenth-century circumstances. The personal rule—an orgy of antiquarianism—clinched that.

In these times of strain it is not surprising that men should look to parliament. From the reign of Elizabeth I at least a concept was forming of it as an institution, broadly representing national interests, capable of changing the law in those interests. (The view held of parliament at the same time as an institution concerned with resisting change from elsewhere was not inconsistent with this.) It was but a pace forward, not a leap into the air or a change of direction, to imagine parliament as a guardian of public welfare alongside the King. Even before 1629 it was suggested that it was some sort of public trust, pushing it to something of the same paternal status as the King. This gave a further twist of meaning to the 11 years without a parliament. 'No parliaments' meant going against a trend. The fact that 'abuses' occurred while there was no sitting was a further advertisement for frequent parliaments. So in 1640–1 parliament emerged as benign physician of the state, though soon enough for some men the remedies prescribed took on a bitter tang.

The dozen years or so before rebellion—or revolution or whatever it was—broke out in 1642 were a stage in which limited adjustments were tentatively made under a tattered screen of legality. The effort failed. But few were ready to admit the need to exploit policy and power. Even in 1642 when parliament took up arms it did so 'For King and Parliament' and maintained this fiction well into the war period. Yet legislation by ordinance—a revolutionary step in spite of the cloudy examples the antiquaries conjured up—had come in. Men cling to their fables as long as they can. Before then, in the sixteen-thirties, Wentworth and Laud, with their grave insistence that less than thorough would not do it, were halfway to admitting the unlikelihood of maintaining full constitutional propriety. In their campaign to preserve an organic society they looked to the crown, considered to be above and free of particular interests, as the vital instrument. They were ready to go a long way, in what they had no doubts was an emergency, to allow Charles I something like absolutism. Unfortunately their approach was really negative, checking change where change had already occurred. Claiming to stand for a genuine national welfare, they could not bear to have it discussed. They denied parliaments, inflicted censorship, and handed out harsh exemplary punishments. Yet it was obvious that there were solid grievances even under their patriot King. Wentworth himself was modestly corrupt, while Laud, proclaiming that private interests were *ipso facto* anti-social and therefore blasphemous, refused to cast his piercing eyes on his only ally's feet of clay.

'Thorough' was based on emergency powers (as we have seen) generally recognised to exist. But 1629–40, except perhaps at the very end, was not obviously a period of crisis. Indeed the royalist writers like Clarendon praised its prosperity and tranquillity.[5] The major modern study of its closing years, by Dr C. V. Wedgwood, is entitled, without irony, *The King's Peace*. It seems that Charles and his advisers wanted the best of both worlds, making a great deal about the crown having to have freedom to cope with 'urgent and weighty matters of state' at the same time as they stressed the normal legal nature of what they were doing. In consequence they got the worst. The Long Parliament in its phase of cohesion set about reducing both the scope of emergency action (together with its advocates) and the routine legal powers of the crown. Moreover, collapse of personal rule spoke of incompetence. Men may well have been more distressed that a King unhampered by parliaments could not beat the Scots than that he aimed to suppress them at all. For such a crown to be the keystone of the arch of government might in 1640 be more alarming than comfortable.

What has been spoken of above is the inadequacy of personal rule. Clearly it is not the whole tale. An unprejudiced observer in 1636 might have forecast an indefinite continuance of 'unparliamentary' government. It needed the test of 1637 onwards to prove it. Before the

Long Parliament, for all the constitutional disputations, there were no clear principles of anything like parliamentary sovereignty. Parliament might have faded away like the French States-General. By faltering, the personal government changed all that, and was in itself an argument for a more searching consideration of parliament's role. Without a parliament sitting, 1629–40 was in fact a positive period in parliamentary history, leading to an appreciation of a problem of sovereignty, imbuing significant groups of men with a will to solve it in a parliamentary way. 'The 11 years' tyranny' was the last chance for royal absolutism—if that was intended—in England. Never again was there any real prospect of it, whatever may be said about the aims of Charles II and James II. How seriously Charles I himself sought in those years to justify the claims and ideals of monarchy by sheer practice remains a question. He certainly had assets. The instruments of propaganda were his. With Buckingham in an early grave, he could have a more moderate foreign policy and retrench financially. The courts were generally amiable. Laud organised the Church for kingly policies, even though in his scheme of things they were incidental to the true worship of God. Wentworth was moulding the north and Ireland, and Bridgewater more quietly was coping with Wales and the marches. There was some economic rehabilitation and opportunity to woo the 'have-nots'. Besides, the crown was the traditional and actual head of the executive and could call upon the services of some able ministers. But the disadvantages were substantial, too. Criticism was not extinguished, merely damped down. Now and then warning signals broke through. Essential economies were provided by a policy of friendship with Spain, unpopular even with many at court, and stirring primeval fears of popery, reinforced by the giddy proceedings of Charles's queen, Henrietta Maria, of whom he had grown inordinately fond, and by well-publicised conversions. The proceeds of financial expedients, niggling, obsolescent if not obsolete, were increasingly hard to collect. Social policy, expression as much of a need to keep the meaner sort of people quiet as of any large ideas of social welfare, irritated powerful and articulate interests, and was smeared, more obviously to contemporaries than to some modern historians, by what R. H. Tawney called 'a trail of finance'. Support of the Church was encouraging but was marred by the prying archbishop's patent inability to make little Lauds out of even the most sympathetic to his version of the Church Triumphant. It also meant making enemies of his enemies. By welcoming secular affairs as the business of the Church, Laud allowed critics of both to merge together. As for Wentworth's spectacular progress in Ireland it was got at the price of upsetting every group over there and alarming almost everyone back home. Finally, there was little that was really experimental in the personal government, and the energies that directed it were fitful. It only lasted long enough to ensure an insistence that it should not come again. Thus when events outside England flared up into a conflagration, as they did from Charles's almost unknown northern realm, little support for him was forthcoming and the flaws in the régime's foundations were starkly exposed.

III The Scottish Business

Near neighbours often make good enemies. A tradition of hatred built up over centuries of misunderstandings and contempt still coloured the relations of England and Scotland, disparate countries, which James VI and I had fondly imagined joining in wedlock through himself. His blithe plans for union had foundered on the adamantine rock of English suspicions. Indeed, even under Charles I there was little more than sharing a King to give any affinity at all. Like those of Aragon and Castile the crowns were quite separate. Scotland, poor and tetchy, remained obstinately herself. James had got on well there the hard way before he came to the softer—as he thought it—south. He had appreciated Scottish peculiarities and framed his policies accordingly. His son lacked all that experience and could command no instinctive understanding of the North Britons. In any case, their bleak and sparsely-peopled land was always secondary among his interests. The best policy he could devise was to make it as like his ideal of England as was possible. That was not much.

Highland and lowland skins had this much in common—they were thin. Within a dozen years of the opening of the new reign irritation had been rubbed into an open wound. Predictably religion brought the issues to a focus. The Reformation in Scotland had gone its own way, largely against the inclinations of the monarchy, which found in fact that its position was weakened by it in favour of the truculent nobility. James VI had tried to adjust the balance by maintaining episcopacy. In Scotland, as later in England, no bishop might mean no King. His plan seems to have been to let bishops become not too obtrusive but eventually familiar features of the landscape, then to make them prominent, and, at last, dominant. He was quite patient about it. At his death no startling advances had been made but there were grounds for assuming that a moderate conjunction of bishops with presbyteries and synods, under a General Assembly, might prove feasible. But the bishops were not enthusiastic and had made little impact upon Scottish life generally. On the other hand they did not provide useful information about what was going on in their sees to the Scottish Privy Council which stood in for the absent King. Charles I, who had a deeper attachment to episcopacy than his father, had no mind to wait long for the Scottish Church to improve itself. From the very onset of his reign the pace quickened. The first effort was to provide that economic backbone without which bishops, however dedicated, could not hope to bring the Church to stand firm for God and King. The problem as in England antedated the Reformation, which in this respect was but a more unedifying stage in several centuries of spoliation and neglect. The 1626 Act of Revocation tackled flaws in title to former Church lands. The principal landlords affected were noblemen, magnates like Mar, Morton, Roxburgh and that 'old cankered gouty man', Hay. In spite of James VI's inspired handling they were still, in potential at least, overmighty subjects in a way that the English peers, even the most exuberant, obviously no longer were. These men had a long tradition of banding together, or against one another, to get their own way. It had often worked. In a country in which such confident men were still invested with heritable jurisdictions, giving them control even of life and death over their vassals, their discontent meant perturbation of the spheres. Charles tried to placate them by offering compensation for voluntary surrender of illicit holdings. There was a derisory response. The next step was to let disputed lands stay with their present holders on payment of specified rents to the crown and with some rather complicated changes in the levying of tiends, or tithes. As in England the latter were a potent source of contention. It was felt that tithepayers would have found in the new arrangements a little easing of the elephantine burden of the titheholders and so might shew a little gratitude to the King. Crown and Kirk would have benefited materially and politically, too, but the scheme faltered because those entrusted with it were negligent or remiss. (The parallel with some of the financial schemes of the personal government further south is an obvious one.) In any case the nobility chose to be aggrieved and started to exploit ill-will stirred by other features of royal policy.

The critical year was 1633. For the first time since early infancy Charles set foot in his native land, coming tardily for his Scottish coronation. There might have been a chance to enlist popular support against a demonstrably greedy and uncommandable aristocracy. The common people certainly gave their stranger King a cordial welcome. But in his train was that most tactless of courtiers, William Laud, about to become Archbishop of Canterbury, member of the English Privy Council and, before the visit was over, of the Scottish one as well.

Laud was not there as a tourist but a participant. In particular, he brought the bishops out of obscurity, in which though some question might be made how he pleased the Scots, he certainly pleased the King. The bashful prelates were given state positions, thereby robbing laymen of means of profit, prestige and influence. (Again a parallel with England may be noted.) Then the ritual at the coronation, in which Laud fussily took part, and the flavour of all services conducted in the King's presence, awakened suspicious of popery and revived a slumbering anglophobia. When Bishop Forbes of Edinburgh prayed for one liturgy, one catechism, one confession of faith, a true-blue Laudian programme seemed presaged, especially as Forbes went on to beg Charles to be that good Samaritan who would give the Church the helping hand it needed to ward off those who for private gain robbed it of the substance which alone could maintain its unity.

Soon, with Laud's probing encouragement, a Scottish Service Book was being drawn up. Its compilers claimed to be very jealous of any dependence on the Church of England. In their fashion they did try to meet the more obvious Scottish susceptibilities, using, for example, the term 'presbyter' for 'priest'. But they could hardly avoid being influenced by the English liturgy. Such contacts were traditional. The earliest Scottish reformers, not excluding John Knox, who had an English intonation, had used the Book of Common Prayer without distaste. But it was known that the new work had been looked over by the King and his English advisers. That was a blunder. In 1637 the book came out on the authority of the King alone, together with canons of uniformity, which made, as Bishop Juxon of London shrewdly forecast, more noise than all the cannons of Edinburgh Castle. The object of the blast was to bring some sort of order to the Scottish clergy, who, 'uncouth, unlearned and unenlightened', as somebody said, swarmed immodestly over the land. At the same time a fresh effort was made to effect the Act of Revocation, still languishing in spite of a formal confirmation by the well-managed parliament of 1633. Here was material for a bonfire.

A spark was put to it by a riot in St Giles's Cathedral in Edinburgh on 23 July 1637. As the bishop stood, in obedience to the provisions of the new service book, facing the holy table, members of the congregation, apparently from among the meaner sort, clamoured that the mass was come amongst them. Similar sentiments had already been expressed from many a pulpit, even before the order enjoining use of the book had been issued, but active resistance had needed something violent like a stool aimed at a bishop to set it in motion. (The providence of God actually diverted it from the good man's head.) From that moment all the strands of Scottish animosities seemed to wind together —patriotism, protestantism, property and privilege. Many of the nobility, whose enthusiasm generally for genuine presbyterianism had never been much remarked, hastened to put themselves in the van of a movement which, with a certain amount of prodding, sprang up to embrace all classes under the plausible claim of being national, Scottish. Religion bound up all the other emotions. 'They began at religion as the ground of their quarrell, whereas, their intention was only bent against the king's majestie and his royall prerogative',[1] asserted a critic, echoing Wentworth's argument that men like Henry Burton and John Bastwick sniped at the Church of England so that they might have free access to the State. Certainly adhesion of the nobility and gentry to the cause meant a powerful sweep against recent royal policies in every sphere. For his part Charles shewed that he meant to be obeyed. It was said of Laud, who was, of course, deeply involved, that 'he will breake ere he bow one inche'.[2] Wentworth advised the use of force to push Scotland as surely under England as he was himself trying to drag Ireland.

Meanwhile with suspicious alacrity the dissidents threw up an organisation—the Tables—which in effect usurped the government and brought pressure, including violence, on individuals and communities reluctant to join in. Representatives of the nobility, the gentry, the clergy, and, a poor fourth, the burgesses, strove to keep the movement united. It was a glorious story and a sordid one. 'If the tree of British liberty arose out of the Scottish Covenant its roots are in a dunghill'— the best of manure, perhaps. Out of a hot-bed of faction bloomed the Scottish National Covenant (February 1638), to be taken by all 'in defence of the true reformed religion, and of our liberties, laws and estates', thereby combining the traditional 'band' with the dynamic concept of a personal contract with the Almighty.[3] Many took it gladly, others had reservations. Some needed to be intimidated. The getting of signatures was put on an organised footing. The bishops, their name as 'odious as the devil', began to slip away, though it was not until nearly the end of 1638 that episcopacy was formally condemned, 'cropt and root'.[4]

By then the whole nation was awry. 'Our country is now at the point of breaking loose; our highlanders are making ready their arms, and some begin to murder their neighbours.' Iconoclasm was rife. Simple country folk, stunned by uncouth alterations, were puzzled whom to obey. The Tables made up their minds for them by vigorous, confident action. The Scottish Privy Council, which had witheld the service book following the St Giles's riot and had failed to enforce Charles's peremptory order to have it put into use in every diocese, continued to advise their absentee master to be conciliatory. They were much better informed than he could hope to be. But Charles looked at Scottish affairs through different eyes. He felt that it 'concerned him to carry this business *a haut luict*, as a brave prince should when matters come to such an extremity . . . whereupon depends not only the keeping of this unhappy kingdom, but both the other two, who will not fail to bestir themselves, when they see such beggarly snakes dare put out their horns; besides (that which a generous prince should prize most) the hazard of his reputation all Europe over'.[5] Here are the keys to Charles's policy—it was not, could not be, a local but an international one. Particularly important were likely English reactions. With the Covenanters 'greater puritans' than any in England, his subjects there might disdain to enter into any correspondence with such 'giddy-headed gawks', such 'brutish bedlamites.' They might, but it was a risk. In the circumstances Charles decided to take a step back to move two forward. A General Assembly of the Kirk (with lay participants) and a parliament should meet to look into alleged grievances. At the same time he was pressing on with preparations for war, convinced that in the end the rebels would understand no other language but what came from the mouth of a cannon. Unfortunately Bishop Juxon's thrifty administration of the English treasury provided enough for a short campaign to be mounted, if English peers, with suitable followers, served at their own expense and drafts of the militia were summoned. It was a poor basis for a war. Laud and Wentworth lamented to each other the 'want of thorough' in a time of opportunity. But they would have been hard put to it to explain just what that opportunity had been.

The Assembly gathered at Glasgow in the autumn of 1638. It declared itself next to the King of Heaven the most competent judgment seat for individual bishops who were impugned for horrible and unlikely crimes. With less unanimity it went on to assail the entire order. Hamilton, the King's commissioner, a timid, rather equivocal man, took fright at this and declared the Assembly dissolved (24 November 1638). He was ignored. The representatives, now in full stride, abolished episcopacy entirely, supported by many of the nobility who were pleased to see a royal *bloc* in parliament swept away. They went on to accept what Laud mildly called 'many strange acts'. Presbyterianism was asserted to be the 'official' religion of Scotland and those ministers who could not stomach the fact were to be put out of their livings. When, defiant to the last, the Assembly dismissed itself, it set up a permanent commission to keep a look-out. In the face of such blatant insubordination, Charles felt he must go on the offensive.

But his situation was worse than it had been a year before. Even Laud was having doubts. 'The greatest fear is want of money and minds of men are mightily alienated'—he means in England. 'I fear you will see the King brought on his knees to a parliament—and then farewell to Church and ship money and no help but too late.'[6] For him as always spiritual and secular matters were totally indivisible. Anyway, it was a sober forecast. The King went north and war sped near. Scottish professional soldiers, blooded in the Low Countries and Germany, came back to take commands and make fortunes. Others, taking the Covenant, stayed on the continent to help gather supplies of men and arms. That old, little crooked soldier, David Leslie, who had fought famously under the experimental Gustavus Adolphus, slipped home in a small sloop, for fear of interception, and put a military spine into the cause. They were soon busy preaching, praying and drilling.[7] Propaganda, morale and self-help, these three were the fundamentals. At this stage the officers were grateful for the efforts of churchmen and the tight organisation of the Kirk. Fiery sermons on the holy text of pike and gun would shake out purses, stimulating righteous contempt for the vain 'braggs'[8] of the English army. Those who called for a way of peace to by-pass the club law of 'bloody and cruel preachers' were insulted or ignored. Anything that would serve the cause took on a godly shape. Thus there was an appeal to the catholic king of France. He was informed that the Covenant was no danger to monarchical government but was a means to extract a nation from the passions of a foreign prelate aiming to rule them like a conquered province, such as Ireland. Louis XIII was urgently reminded of the old and faithful alliance between the two kingdoms. Nothing came of this unlikely gambit. But it points to the strongly nationalistic bias of the rising. It ought to have been a warning to English puritans of the dangers to come of meddling in Scottish affairs.

Charles's military movements, aimless and dilatory, merely exposed the rawness and 'untowardness' of his troops and soon dribbled to a stop. By the treaty of Berwick (June 1639) he was compelled to take stock, though he still imagined that time and himself would be a match for the rebels. Time could be bought by money. Wentworth, who, though by no means a monopoliser of influence, was emerging as the King's chief councillor, urged him to summon an English parliament and to present it with a ringing appeal for patriotic aid against an old and insolent foe. If, God forbid, that went unheeded, then his subjects would leave themselves 'without excuse and (he) might have the wherewithal to justify himself to God and the world that in his own inclination he desired the old way' of parliaments, but could not let 'the peevishness of some few factious spirits' destroy his government.[9] To keep the King solvent meanwhile leading councillors made him private loans. The Earl of Strafford, as Wentworth now became (January 1640), made his on the security of northern recusancy fines, which his own agents were collecting very assiduously. (Hence the reluctance of some papists to work up an enthusiasm for the royal cause in the civil war.) It may be said that beside his political programme, Strafford's personal future and fortune was tied to the survival of Charles's régime. In defending the one, he was securing the other—or so he reckoned.

Writs for an English parliament went out early in March 1640, while Strafford himself, on fire with gout, made a whirlwind trip to Ireland to force a supply through the compliant Irish Commons and to levy several thousand more troops for his army, that dangerous disciplined force which turned out to be the unwitting instrument of his downfall. 'Sound or lame', he wrote to Secretary John Coke, 'you shall have me with you before the meeting of the parliament. I should not fail though Sir John Eliot were still living.'[10] Mention of a parliament at once evoked that fearsome ghost.

In the late 'sixties Clarendon remembered the writs as coming most welcome to the entire kingdom. But Thomas May, writing nearer to the event, noted a lack of appreciation of what was going on, with the people 'almost amazed, so strange a thing was the name of parliament grown'.[11] The elections have not been thoroughly investigated but the usual mélange of local politics, mostly competitions for prestige and influence among the aristocracy, prevailed over the broad national issues. But these were not entirely overlooked:

> *Choose no ship sheriff or court atheist,*
> *No fen drainer nor church papist,*

was one rhymster's blunt advice, fusing politics and religion as firmly as ever Laud had done. Sir Roger Twysden, a keen observer, noted that Kentish voters were very averse to courtiers. Down in Cornwall only one of ten duchy-backed candidates got a seat. Men who had stood out against the 1626 loan—evidently still an issue in some minds—were readily supported. The surviving 'opposition' leaders of the late sixteen-twenties were back in force. Though the bulk of rank-and-file members were parliamentary tyros, they seem to have had no disinclination to follow direction by the older men.

Lord Keeper John Finch, whose last parliamentary role (as Speaker of the third parliament) had been so embarrassing, though generously compensated for, presented (13 April 1640) the King's demand for copious supply and added a bill for tonnage and poundage to be made legal from 1625. With these first things done, he proposed, grievances —if any—might be discussed. This tailored programme made no appeal in either House. The King's misfortunes were considered to be too good an opportunity to be missed for doing things in a parliamentary way. In the Commons the first question asked was how was it possible that in 1639 a Spanish and a Dutch fleet could fight one another in English waters without intervention. The King's bland profession of ignorance was unconvincing to men who knew that their 11-year vacation was partly the result of payment by Spain, a more obvious enemy than Scotland, for dubious services rendered. From there on complaints and putative remedies, taking in every aspect of state business, were churned out by popular orators. Harbottle Grimstone, whose outré name concealed an eminently moderate personality, expressed the mood. For him invasions of the liberties of Englishmen were in more urgent need of rebuttal than Scottish incursions over the northern border. But it was John Pym, his pudgy features giving little hint of his extraordinary political qualities, who summed it all up. His capacity for organisation was shewn in the way in which he brought under a few convenient heads the sprawling mass of grievances amid the mutterings of less articulate men. He went on to request a parliamentary solution, such a remedy as would make the King great and the people happy. He meant not subsidies but new legislation.

Committees, Pym's speciality, were at once named to cope with particularly important topics. In a matter of days the Short Parliament— for such it was to be—had entered into almost the whole legislative programme of the first session of the later Long Parliament. Charles, turning back to the old tactic of divide and rule, worked on the Lords well enough to get a solid majority vote in favour of some supply before redress. But the Commons calmly ignored his promise to give up ship money in exchange for an immediate grant. In their House all eyes were fixed on liberties. Soon rumours reached the King that this recalcitrant assembly would present him with a petition against carrying on his war with the Covenanters. He already felt he had grounds to suspect some of them of having made a 'band' with the rebels. All he could think of now to thwart them was to revert to the sixteen-twenties pattern of abrupt dissolutions. They had sat a bare three weeks (5 May 1640).

The King's exasperation is excusable, but he had acted rashly. A few ostentatious gestures might have got a generous reward—so at least it was claimed afterwards. But Charles's whole experience told him that appeasement brought nothing but further trouble. Clarendon talks of

THE SCOTTISH BUSINESS

a 'great damp' that seized upon men's spirits with the dismissal, but many politicians were not distressed, arguing with some cogency that things must get worse before they would get better. The hearts of the critics were hardened and the King had done nothing to encourage mugwumps to jump down on his side. Meantime, defying tradition, Convocation sat on for a while, framing a set of far-reaching canons, which have been well described as reaching 'the high-water mark of Laudian Anglicanism'.[12] Certainly they suggested that the Church as at present constituted was grafted to the State as that was at present constituted. The clergy also voted, as in 1614 and 1624, a free gift of a few thousand pounds. Such a gesture had little practical value when set against the King's actual needs and only irritated those who deplored the servility it demonstrated. For the rest, a few M.P.s were arrested and their papers confiscated; bullion, lodged, ironically, in the Tower for safe keeping, was appropriated; and a cargo of pepper was compulsorily purchased, against tallies on the Customs, and resold at a profit. This last quasipiratical venture upset the East India Company and provides a striking instance of Charles's inept handling of potential supporters. Normally the Company, conservative and monopolistic, would have backed him complacently. More ship-money writs were also sent out and sheriffs hauled before the Council for not pushing collection hard enough. By now local government was veering between apathy and actual resentment. Constables and bailiffs in Somerset when ordered to distrain upon the goods of non-payers retorted that 'they had rather fall into the hands of his Majestie then into the hands of resolute men'.[13] A few loans were got up in the City, mostly from men already heavily committed to the survival of the régime. Ominously they were on double interest. Feelers were put out to Spain and even to the Pope for loans and military aid, sources the least acceptable to a raw public opinion, already inflamed by bruits of Spanish troops landed in southern England. (Later there would be reports that Danes were disembarking near the capital.)

Nothing was won by these thrashings about in deep waters. When Strafford got back from Ireland he groaned that never came a man to so lost a business. He had miscalculated the reliability of English patriotism. In June a Scottish parliament met, without a royal Commissioner, and declared that its votes could become acts even without the King's assent, an example to be followed within two years in England. Soon a covenanting army, hardly opposed by Charles's demoralised troops, moved over the border and invested Newcastle upon Tyne. For a moment it seemed an old English spirit might catch fire, but the indignation of the north at this revival of old border conflicts was not matched in the south. There, at a safe distance, the rebels' appeals for solidarity met with verbal responses at least. 'We are brethren.' 'Your grievances are ours.' In August 12 peers—the list is worth examining—drew up and allowed to be published a petition for a parliament. They were working in accord with John Pym, who was by now willing to make use of popular agitation over a wide field. Several thousand Londoners, hardly spontaneously, produced a similar petition. Still the King, smarting from the intransigence of the Short Parliament and the downright insolence of the recent Scottish session, held out. He rolled back the centuries and summoned a sort of medieval great council, an assembly of notables, lay and clerical, to confer with him at York (24 September to 28 October 1640). But before it met he felt compelled to issue writs for a parliament and only asked its advice on what might be done pending a parliamentary supply. The main work of the Council, or rather of a commission of it, was to negotiate a pacification with the Scots at Ripon. The advantages lay with the invaders, whose possession of the northern counties included the Customs of coal and salt at Newcastle, a thing of no small importance. The concessions they obtained tied Charles hand and foot. In particular he agreed to pay the Scots £850 a day pending a permanent settlement. Without credit in the City, where there were mass demonstrations for a secure parliament, Charles found this a huge sum. The first month's instalment was obtained on the personal bonds of north-country gentlemen, but further payments would only come on the certainty of parliamentary supply. By now the reluctant writs were trickling out and the elections were being held in the knowledge that the King did not really want them at all. 'It was King Charles's perpetual fault to grant the people's desires by bits and so late he ever lost his thanks.'[14] He was to get none now. In November 1640, its continuance pretty well assured by an alien armed force, the fifth and last parliament of the reign assembled. If there was a revolution in the seventeenth century, it had surely begun by now.

IV A General Doomsday

Seventeenth-century communications were bad and the bare 40 days between the issue of the writs and the meeting of the parliament (3 November) gave scant opportunity for organised electioneering on a national basis. John Pym may, perhaps, have stumped the country on behalf of his friends but the evidence for it is slight. As usual, national issues were tacked on to local rivalries—'carpet-baggers' failed if they were not backed by some 'interest' prominent in the district. But there was of course, plenty of outside interference—from the royal administration and individual magnates. Official efforts had few notable successes. Sir Henry Vane, Snr., Comptroller of the Household, could tick off only three on his list of 12. In Lancashire, the Duchy secured a few seats but failed to elect both burgesses in every borough. The Chancellor of the Duchy of Cornwall saw the bulk of the inflated representation there fall to private members of the local squirearchy, men living in most cases close to the constituencies. In Kent, Canterbury turned down the two safe men put forward by the archbishop. The peers, whose territorial influence was often strong, were luckier. In the south-west Bedford returned a group including John Pym and his own eldest son at Tavistock. Francis Rous, Pym's strongly puritan half-brother, sat for Truro—his family had had close links with the Russells from the reign of Elizabeth I. In South Wales the 'royalist' Herberts were as energetic as the Earl of Essex, more critical, was in Staffordshire. In the county of Essex, where the revival of the forest courts had been strongly resented, the Earl of Warwick, later commander of the parliamentary fleet, pushed to some purpose, notably at Maldon, where an Irish adventurer, Sir John Clotworthy triumphed. (He was to play a big part in directing Irish animosities in the onslaught upon Strafford.) Lord Saye and Sele put his son Nathaniel Fiennes in at Banbury. In Huntingdonshire the ancient rivalry between the Greys and the Hastings was deepened at the polls and was to continue into the civil war itself, when the two families divided pretty sharply into parliamentarians and royalists, 'fighting the public quarrel with their private spirit and indignation', not, it must be said, a unique circumstance. In some areas (e.g. Oxfordshire), to save the considerable expense of a contest, the various interests made pacts among themselves. Ties of kinship and common interest could be as compelling as rivalry. In Devon and Dorset the return of a group associated with the Dorchester colonial schemes—Sir Walter Erle, William Pole, the 'martyr' William Strode and the cousins Denis Bond and Edward and John Ashe, 'the richest clothier in England'—was surely not accidental. The Providence Island Company was also well-represented.

Seats were sometimes fiercely contested, though here again local issues seem to have dominated. At Maidstone the two successful candidates came to blows because each wanted his name at the head of the official return. Five candidates fought for the two shire seats of Kent, and six for two burgesships at Wigan. At Reading, with five contestants, Sir Francis Knowles and his son, both of whom had sat in the Short Parliament, were elected 'in open hall, without any contradiction, but with great alacratye', no vote being given for the other candidates. The hint of sharp practice here swelled to open accusations in 30-odd disputed cases. The complaints were typical of those made after any Stuart election—chiefly of the 'undue' supply of beer, tobacco and meals. (Eventually most of the disputes were resolved on local political lines.)

Many of the most vocal members of the Short Parliament, some of them with Commons experience reaching back to the days of James I, got in again, but the majority were men new to St Stephen's Chapel. Yet it should not be thought they were entirely devoid of a political background—some had been sheriffs, justices, collectors, deputies, commissioners of sewers, militia officers. Even the members for Herefordshire, the most 'clownish' county of England, were likely to have some notion of the public problems of the age. This parliament was not an assembly of 'mere' country gentlemen or of a 'mere' anything—commercial, industrial, legal, and religious interests were in the natural course of things there in force. It may be taken not unfairly to represent a brittle political nation.

Charles was back in London for the opening of Parliament. It was a quiet affair without ceremony, a mistake, thought the Venetian ambassador,

'for it shews more clearly than ever to his people that he consents to the summons merely from compulsion . . . and not of his own free will to please the people. Thus instead of conciliating their good will at which he ought to aim particularly just now, he alienates

33

them over a matter of outward show which is of no real importance, while at the same time he increases the admiration at the steps taken by the rebels, to whose bold resolution they do not tire of publishing their indebtedness for the re-establishment of liberty and religion alike.'[1]

Certainly circumstances were very different from those in which the Short Parliament had met. The King's political grasp was slackening and he was now committed to payments which he could never hope to make without parliamentary supply. The Scottish army would move south if it did not get its pay, or if Charles attempted a dissolution. Nothing stood between it and the capital. Worse, he was soon shewn that there was something like unanimity at Westminster on many big issues. Charles could not hope to refuse his assent to early bills produced in this mood, negative though it was. By the end of the first session the machinery, particularly in its local functions, of 'thorough'—what has been called an 'expanded executive'—lay in ruins. Financial expedients which had given buoyancy to personal government were cut away. A harsh vengeance struck at 'the chief incendiaries', the leading ministers. Initiative in all these matters lay with parliament and would remain there all the while 'the lads about Newcastle' were on terms. Inside the Houses control would pass to those bold enough to grasp it. Without hesitation John Pym, backed in the Lords by men like Bedford and Brooke, and in the lower House by Denzil Holles, John Hampden, Oliver St John, Walter Erle and, at this stage, essentially moderate men like Benjamin Rudyard and Edward Hyde, took it. To keep it demanded courage and skill and tenacity. Pym lost more than one division. He had to wheedle and cajole, explain and explain away. But he was by far the most able parliamentarian in the Commons and in his case at least experience had been an education. Moreover, from the start he sensed the energy that lay dormant in public opinion. He saw it must be kept informed of what was going on inside the Houses, and equally that the Houses and their multifarious committees, of which he was a prime manipulator, must be made aware of what was thought outside the walls of the palace of Westminster. To the arts of the parliamentarian, already highly professional, he had to add those of propagandist, pollster, even agitator. Just what his relations were with the mobs that milled around the palace has never been fully resolved, but he certainly had close contacts, commercial and otherwise, with men of influence among the 'commonalty'. Luck and intuition, too, played their parts.

The prison-gates creaked open. William Prynne, his grim features split by a grin stretching from ear-stump to ear-stump, made a triumphant entry into London, his way strewn with flowers. Lilburne, Burton and the other victims of 'Thorough' found November warm with affection. But there was no drop in the prison population, merely a change in personnel. Laud, Strafford and many others were arrested and 'caged' on the orders of parliament, though some like Finch and Windebank skipped off in panic to the continent to escape this general doomsday. Of all those in custody Strafford was the most hated and the most feared. Malice alone cannot explain this animosity. Strafford's enemies had every reason to suspect a reaction. Could they be sure this parliament would last? If it were nipped in the bud, there would surely be harsh reprisals for what it had done or tried to do. Strafford, with his autocratic impatience, his savage tongue and, above all, his Irish papist army, would be there to direct the storm. He was a practical man, happiest and most dangerous in action. Pym, well-versed in the Lord-Deputy's character and notions, had no doubts about his intentions. He was ready to believe that he had advised the King to use, in the last resort, that army 'loose and absolved from all rules', and to use it to 'do all that power would admit' in England.[2] For months Strafford had been living on the jagged edge of his nerves. His tortured features argued panic measures. 'Stone dead hath no fellow',[3] growled Essex. He ought, said someone else, to be taken out and knocked on the head like a wild beast. There is evidence which can be read to show Strafford working to impeach the parliamentary leaders for treasonable contacts with the Scots. 'Black Tom Tyrant', then, must go, and go quickly. Support for his destruction could be expected from the Covenanters, and from Ireland, where his ruthless and self-aggrandising administration had set every substantial interest against him, a delegation supplied a mountain of evidence for the prosecution. So he was impeached for 'endeavouring to subvert the fundamental laws and government . . . and to introduce an arbitrary and tyrannical government against law'.[4] It was a sweeping political charge whose connexion with legality was slight but convenient. (What were the fundamental laws? A member of this very parliament once asked this tactless question and was told that if he did not know he was not fit to sit in the house. Yet no one attempted a definition. Well might Pym say Strafford's treason was beyond the reach of words.) Here was a puzzling view of treason—to advise the King to policies which 'robbed him of the hearts of his subjects' and 'set a difference' between them.[5] Rushworth's thick folio report of the trial brings out every niggling detail but glosses over the big essential issue. Yet there was nothing vague about Strafford's defence, spoken passionately, without notes, and, for one timeless moment, with tears. His fellow peers were judge and jury, but they were also, he argued, the accused. 'You, your posterity be at stake.' Could any peer ever again advise the King if he himself were condemned? Was it not a peer's bounden duty to advise without fear or favour? 'Do not, my lords, put such difficulties upon ministers of state that men of wisdom, of honour, of fortune, may not with cheerfulness and safety be employed for the public. If you weigh and measure them by grains and scruples, the public affairs of the kingdom will be waste. No man will meddle with them who hath anything to lose.'[6] These were telling arguments, both to men already in the peerage and to those who might come to be raised to it. They drove the anti-Straffordians to wilder efforts. The Irish army was still on foot and Charles had declared he would not disband it until 'these businesses now in agitation' were resolved. Rumours of plots among the half-catholic royal army in the north flew to Pym. On 6 April 1641 a curiously-worded resolution passed the Commons asking the King to make no military moves without parliamentary consent. Fear was on the brink of becoming terror. Four days later the Lords adjourned the impeachment *sine die*. Had Strafford won? The King laughed—too soon.[7]

'The inflexible party'[8] had come too far to let their necessary victim go. If one medieval weapon could not destroy him, another might. The Commons must join the jury. So, against the wishes of Pym, a bill of attainder was brought in to get round the obstacle that there was 'no law yet in force whereby he [could] be condemned to die'.[9] The second reading produced a significant minority of 'Straffordians'. But the Lords, delighting the King by their show of independence, bungled things by insisting that the impeachment must go on. Pym and his entourage, fearing an acquittal, now swung round behind the attainder, opposed by George Digby, who could not urge death by a law made *a posteriori*, but supported by the mild Falkland. Both were future royalists. On 21 April the bill passed a third reading in the Commons. Charles gave Strafford the word of a King that whatever happened he would 'not suffer in life, honour or fortune'[10]—an empty gesture.

The last days of April were hectic. The King had ordered loyal army officers to their posts, but at the same time consideration was given to a dubious scheme put forward by Bedford, Pym's patron. Bedford was to become Lord Treasurer and in exchange for more moderate ecclesiastical policies some leading parliamentarians were to take office. Pym was to be Chancellor of the Exchequer. How far Pym was committed is uncertain. Surely while the Irish army was in quarters, and army plots were bruited about, while Charles negotiated with catholic powers and, above all, while Strafford lived, Pym could never feel or be safe. As it happened Bedford died unexpectedly and this plan died with him (9 May 1641).

On 1 May Charles let it be known that he was ready to put Strafford out of his service for ever, but ruined the effect by an unsuccessful attempt to reinforce the Tower guards with 'reliable' officers. By now great crowds, not the dregs of society, but merchants, shop-keepers, apprentices, howled for the blood of 'the grand apostate'. Golden-voiced preachers devoted their long sermons to the same godly cause. Religion, as always, sharpened attitudes. On 3 May the Commons took 'a protestation' against popery and sedition.[11] Next day the protestant Lords joined them and it was circulated in the City. On 5 May, a tense House swallowed Pym's revelation of Sir John Suckling's army plot. A fat man—not Pym—shifted awkwardly in his seat, a board creaked sharp as a pistol shot under him, and members jumped to their feet certain that some new Guy Fawkes was working down below. The Lords were hardly less emotional, and the bill of attainder gained support. A bill against dissolving the present parliament without its own consent went through without opposition. This was primarily a short-term measure designed to ease the raising of loans in the City, but it is at least possible that other possibilities were seen by some.[12] Meanwhile the mobs from the City and suburbs kept up pressure on the Lords and on 8 May a poorly-attended House finally accepted both the 'no dissolution' bill and the attainder. Everything now rested with the King.

Strafford had just released him from his vow. Even so, Charles wanted to avoid assent. But his friends pressed him until, exhausted by the strain, and driven almost to distraction by fears for the security of his Queen, against whom the agitation in the streets was violently directed, he gave way. A last appeal by the infant Prince of Wales was spurned by parliament. On 12 May Strafford went, like many another in an age of men who knew how to die, with moving dignity, to the block at Tower Hill. 'I thanke God', he said, 'I am no more afraid of death, nor daunted with any discouragements rising from any feares, but doe as chearefully put off my dublet at this time, as ever I did when I went to bed.'[13] With the death of this bold, possibly bad, certainly great, man, something dropped out of the struggle. Laud's ordeal was of a different order. This poor old man of God, hated though he was, could never be the danger that Strafford undoubtedly was. Not until 1645 was the case against him pushed to a decision. By then Pym, too, had gone and the rebellion, as rebellions will, had flung up new leaders.

Strafford's trial and attainder were more than an episode. The excitements of bringing him to 'justice' fed emotions, quickened suspicions and aroused aspirations which might otherwise have faltered and died. No individual or group involved in the mordant struggle was ever quite the same. Men are changed by the way they live—and in revolutions, as Macaulay observed, men live quickly. In a few weeks Lords and Commons had undergone a political experience which might otherwise have taken years, if it had come at all. And an inescapable pattern of violence and sudden change had been set. Blood cried out for blood. Charles had done nothing to convince the more outspoken critics of his past policy that they could trust him in the future, while his irresolution and shiftiness hardened their hearts and encouraged them to keep pressing him. They knew he was toying with the idea of using force, even foreign force, but with Strafford gone, would probably bungle his chances. At the same time the radical actions taken by 'the inflexible party' and their occasional allies had already shaken moderate and conservative men, who wondered what further shocks lay in store. Their unease stimulated Charles into fresh divide-and-rule tactics too soon. At this stage M.P.s were reluctant to move at all either to 'left' or 'right'. They deplored the willingness of men like Pym to listen to—or connive at—popular agitations, but they could be intimidated by them. If in fact there was material for future royalism, as yet Charles's support was disorganised and inarticulate. Moreover, there was still agreed work to be done on old abuses—as they were genuinely regarded by moderates as well as more radical men. Thus, although Pym might lose support for this or that measure, as he had certainly done in the Strafford business, he was still capable of pulling the right rabbits out of the right hat at the right time. So, for instance, at the height of the attainder crisis he had won almost unanimous support for the 'perpetual parliament' bill because he could point to an appealing programme of remedial legislation.

So in the spring and summer without much difficulty a whole string of measures designed to prevent a recrudescence of 'personal rule' got through the Houses. These were to check not merely *coups* of the kind suspected of Strafford but the operation of what had once seemed the normal machinery of the state. Long intermissions of parliament, symptoms and causes, men thought, of abuses, were to be prevented by the Triennial Act to which Charles, though he protested at its reduction of his sovereignty, had to give his assent. A parliament of at least 50 days' duration every three years[14] was ensured by careful gradations operating in the event of the failure of various authorities to issue the writs. In fact the measure never came into operation, since its provisions were inapplicable to the present parliament, and the next regular one—the Cavalier Parliament—at a hint from the throne in

1664 profoundly modified it. Nevertheless it marks a turning point in the recognition of parliament as a more or less permanent feature of the political process. More immediate impact was made by robbing the crown of some useful institutions and powers. In July Star Chamber, fallen to degradation from the high favour of Tudor times, was abolished, and the judicial functions of the Privy Council were 'regulated' so that it was unable any more to touch upon—'invade'—the property rights of the subject. The council of the North, ruined by its association with Strafford, was wholly wiped away by a clause introduced by the common lawyer, Edward Hyde. Yet even the severest critics of the council knew that it had done a good job in trying to assimilate that complicated and not yet understood region to the rest of the country. Very soon the freeholders of Yorkshire would be moaning about its loss, and during the Protectorate there would be proposals for setting up provincial courts at York, one at least fostered by that staunch northerner Major-General John Lambert. But nothing was done and 1641 was certainly a turning point in the development of the north country, the new direction being marked out by personal and professional rivalries and short-sighted local patriotisms. So, too, were the judicial powers of the council in the marches of Wales clipped away, though there was a brief revival of some parts of its functions between the Restoration and the Revolution of 1689. The Court of Requests, another prerogative court, which had had some social utility, was not specifically mentioned in the legislation, but with the outbreak of civil war it faltered to a full stop. The Court of High Commission, whose 'enormities' on examination do not really amount to very much, was also abolished—and an assertion made that nothing like it was ever to be set up again. (To many men in 1686, some of whom were forming their political views at this time, James II's Ecclesiastical Commission was to look alarmingly like this defunct court resuscitated. Their uneasy reaction helped to bring on the Revolution of 1689.)

Whatever else they meant, measures like these signalled the victory of the old courts of common law over what their proponents regarded as upstart rivals, usurping cases, diverting fees and offering suspect justice in an unprofessional way. It was not to be an unmixed blessing. Swiftly and cheaply prerogative justice had sometimes tackled social ills for which the common law courts had no remedy. Its destruction exposed its fee-ridden, dilatory rivals to valid criticism. The Interregnum would be a period of intense controversy about legal reform. Largely over professional protests, some useful advances were made, more advocated, only to be ripped up at the Restoration. But in 1641 itself most eyes were on the tarnished conciliar courts and their removal

4

may be fairly adjudged a popular step. Falkland, Hyde and Selden were as energetic as Hampden and Pym in the onslaught upon institutions that were not the invention of Charles I but were, in fact, very characteristic of those spacious days of Elizabeth I, to which so many looked back with proud nostalgia.

General approval was given, too, to sweeping away a pile of the financial expedients of the late 'personal government. 'No part of the king's government but was inveighed against by one or other'.[15] In June 1641 a tonnage and poundage act settled a long altercation in favour of the subject. To rub it in, the grant which Charles I had claimed in 1625 for life and which the Commons had proffered for one year only was now put on a bi-monthly footing. Impositions, which had never in fact been parliamentary at all, though claimed as such, were covered by the same derogatory act. Farmers of the Customs, who for exploitable privileges had enabled the crown to anticipate some of its revenues and had helped to collect the impugned duties, were assailed at the same time. Their leases were sequestered, their estates threatened and only by the payment of substantial composition fines were they able to escape worse penalties. The multiplicity of decisions in *Hampden's case* and the continued refusal of so many to pay or collect ship money had weakened the royal case for legality. A political solution in the shape of a new enactment was unavoidable and the hated charge, whether inland or maritime in its incidence, was declared both retrospectively and prospectively illegal. The business of 'no-knights', another over-rated money-spinner, was settled in favour of landowners who objected to being either saddled with a burdensome dignity or forced to compound. Its passing marked another pace away from the path of precedent.

The Forest Courts, cunningly revived on the initiative of the renegade Attorney-General William Noy and Archbishop Laud to make things awkward for Lord Treasurer Weston, were now put down again. By employing them at all the crown had advertised itself as a clog upon the proper exploitation of the nation's land resources. For a few paltry sums powerful men like the Earl of Warwick, whom Charles would have done better to have conciliated, were exasperated. During the Interregnum royal forests—and often the woods on confiscated royalist estates—were cut down and the land given over to agriculture. This was a process, for which there was always an argument in a land-hungry society, that was not much impeded by the Restoration. The consequent dearth of shipping timber and fuel would help to bring on industrial revolution. The whole matter of the forests is a telling example of the way in which personal, financial, legal, constitutional, economic, social and strategical considerations, not excluding even religion, are inextricably bound up in this complicated period.

Another grievance with a long reach was the lavish issue of royal patents of industrial monopoly. With solid backing a new monopoly act superseded the inept one of 1624. The effort to regulate industry by prerogative, intended to reap financial[16] and constitutional advantage, had been pushed hard to the distress not only of the domestic but of the industrial consumer and of work-people and rival producers. Expensive muddling by patentees often totally unequipped to cope with the demands of the market had caused economic and social dislocation, and perhaps more outspoken criticism than on any other aspect of the past decade. Already in 1639 Charles had felt compelled to rescind many patents but more than this grandiloquent gesture was demanded. So by statute rather than the royal word of honour the parasites were driven out and exploitation given only to genuine inventors and innovators for a limited period. The Patent Office, that mundane repository of dreams, is the hardy offspring of these sensible arrangements. (Yet not all monopoly was cut away. The great trading companies kept their hard-won charters, though in the face of bolder carping. But they had members and friends in both Houses to ward off attack. The day of *laissez-faire* had yet to dawn.)

This new industrial measure meant a substantial loss of state revenue, soon felt in the civil war by King Pym's rebel government. The excise of 1643 may be considered a direct substitute. Monopolies did not come back in the baggage of Charles II in 1660 and the crown had to look elsewhere for some form of 'outdoor relief' for friends and supplicants. No longer could an Endymion Porter be kept going on the proceeds of white writing paper or a Lord Buckhurst on the profits of starch. It was all an argument for bringing in a proper civil list. A further comment may be made: one objection to the prerogative courts had been their more willing response than that of the common law courts and the local authorities to directives to implement the terms of the grants. This 'enlargement' of the council table was a piercing argument for its regulation. Thus, in the summer of 1641, a stop was put to moves which, if successful, might have led to a system of state manufactories in England somewhat akin to that suggested by Barthélemy Laffemas to Henry IV of France and ultimately operated by Colbert under Louis XIV.

Monopolies had been a grievance for generations. So too had purveyance, the privilege of the crown to feed and keep its court warm at bargain prices. If Salisbury's Great Contract of 1610 had been sealed, the crown's rights would have been bought out. But purveyance, though commuted to an annual subvention of £50,000, remained a chronic fount of resentments, especially as it was well known that in this as in so many other of the crown's financial activities a good part of the cash lodged in the maws of courtly cormorants. Predictably a bill for the abolition of purveyance was introduced in the first session of the Long Parliament. Its provisions were generally acceptable, but it had failed to get through all its stages at the adjournment and so was lost. In December 1642, by resolution, not ordinance, it was suspended *sine die*. No new steps were taken to regularise the position until the establishment of the Protectorate, with the re-appearance of courtiers, however unlikely, compelled a glance backward. An abolition bill faltered in the first Protectorate parliament, but the second completed a new version in June 1657. Significantly no part of the compensation was to come out of a land tax. This attitude was shared by the Convention Parliament of 1660. The demise of purveyance, along with that of wardships, was a characteristic feature of the Restoration financial settlement.

The remedial legislation of 1641 was both popular and permanent. It tolled in cheerful tones the knell of 'personal government', whether as conceived by Strafford or actually operated by Charles I. 'Thorough' indeed was through. But all this was the product of a brief, precarious period of concord, unique in the era. Soon the fragile unanimity was shattered. For moderate and conservative men the work of destruction had gone on long enough. All this heady stuff upset them. They wanted to draw back to normality. With fluctuating enthusiasm others pressed or let themselves be edged on. The result was a conflict within the ruling class of nobility and gentry, with their mercantile and professional associates, that shot them into civil war, making of some malignants, others rebels.

v A Rift Opens

Few members peered far ahead. Most could recognise an immediate threat—a Strafford, for instance—and associate it with the past just gone that might, if things went awry, be yet again. That some of the buffets dealt out were deadly was the effect of time, helped by the clarity of vision and the rare intuition of such as Pym. Soon the back-benchers were feeling exhausted by the spate of bills and resolutions. By late summer their zeal was reduced to a trickle. Enough had been done for unadventurous men. So when there were moves to enact more positive measures, and in particular to consider the future of the Church, the fine cracks that had already appeared on the surface of unanimity could be seen to go deep. They might go deeper yet.

There was no simple, sharp-edged division of opinion. Indeed, there were still whole areas of agreement. No one was willing to speak up for 'those innocent canons'[1] passed by Convocation last spring. Almost everybody had something nasty to say about Laud's campaigns, whether in ceremonies, tithes, visitations, High Commission or secular offices. Most members felt, or found it prudent to express, a loathing of popery. (It is strange how men, who back home obviously jogged along reasonably well with catholic neighbours would, when they got to-gether in parliament, swallow the wildest nonsense about the popish peril.)

But these matters of accord were emphatically negative. Laudianism must go. But what should replace it? To put the question was to invite disputation. A Commons resolution of December 1640 blasting the canons as contrary to law and tending to sedition was the first and last religious proposition to get unanimous backing. A proposal in April 1641 for the exemplary fining of members of the late Convo-cation perished for lack of support. This was a minor issue. The organ-isation of the Church was a big one. That parliament should have some say in its running was generally accepted, but there was no agree-ment on how it should be provided and how far it should go. Contro-versy milled around episcopacy, reform of which many took as the

43

prime end of their meeting. Had not this parliament been called, continued, preserved and secured by the immediate finger of God as it were for this work? What was that finger writing? No reform could avoid reference to the relations of Church and State. To consider control of the pulpit merely was to 'ravel' into such matters as the forming of public opinion, the dissemination of information and the purposes of education. Tithes affected payers, patrons, incumbents and the hierarchy, beating the bounds of lay and clerical property. In such mundane things genuine religious sentiments, always difficult to gauge, always dangerous to ignore, lay embedded. Yet spiritual zeal could also be an apt means of gaining support for other projects. To serve ends religion was turned to all shapes. Even if it were possible there was little will to segregate religion and politics. Moreover, the abrupt demise of Laudian censorship had released a flood of verbal agitation by a diversity of advocates of change. Their exuberance deflated moderates and conservatives who saw what reformers took to be iron chains as simply 'the golden reins of discipline'. Queasiness grew when the radicals in parliament itself shewed a readiness to inflame the turbid emotions of the *mobile*, to whom, in the conventional view, 'the mystery of government must be denied'. George Digby, for one, was not prepared 'to flatter a multitude'.[2]

This sort of thing came out in discussion of numerous petitions for 'root and branch' lopping of episcopacy. These charged the bishops with contributing to every grievance of the realm, not excluding industrial monopolies. They were branded as instigators of the policies which had brought on the Scottish wars. (Ought they not, then, to have been thanked for ensuring the summoning of this present parliament?) Low-born, they had encouraged the despising of temporal magistracy, nobility and gentry. About these accusations the Venetian ambassador noted in February 1641 'the parliamentarians waver to and fro'.[3] Prelates, for some false symbols of security and order, were for others ancient landmarks without which the nation might get lost. Sir Henry Vane, Jnr., and the as yet obscure member for Cambridge, Oliver Cromwell, were vociferous for abolition; Lucius Cary, Viscount Falkland, Sir John Culpepper and George Lord Digby—all three future royalists—wanted the order to stay, while being willing to concede some changes. Digby implored his fellow-members 'not to be led on by passion to popular and vulgar Errors. . . . Wee all agree upon this; that a Reformation of Church Government is most necessary . . . but . . . [not] to strike at the Roote, to attempt a totall Alteration. . . . I am confident that instead of every Bishop wee put downe in a Diocesse, wee shall set up a Pope in every Parish.'[4] Sir Benjamin Rudyard asked members to bethink themselves 'whether a popular Demo-craticall Government of the Church . . . wilbe either sutable or accept-able, to a Royall, Monarchicall Government of the State . . . especially in so great a Kingdome as this . . . where Episcopacye is so wrap'd and involv'd in the Laws of it'.[5] For Edmund Waller, who had a curious political career in front of him, bishops were an outwork which must be held against the assault of the people. For every example, he said, of an abuse by a bishop 'you may be presented with a thousand in-stances of poor men that have received hard measure from their land-lords'.[6] Men of property, lay or clerical, ought to stick together. Edward Hyde does not seem to have been just then a rigid episco-palian, but he understood well enough that hammering away at their spiritual lordships would widen the gap between King and parliament, and endanger the generally agreed but as yet uncompleted remedial work of the session. John Pym, never wedded or glued to any particular form of Church rule, wanted only the assurance of practical lay review through parliament. To make that effective he was for dislodging the bishops from the upper chamber, where they could defend their order *jure divino* and equally provide a reliable royal *bloc*.

An exclusion bill did in fact go up from the Commons in March 1641, backed by an imaginative list of reasons. Episcopal expectation of translation to places of greater dignity and profit was, for instance, held to be a bar to genuine independence of judgment. Moreover, 'their being lords in parliament letteth too great a distance between them and their brethren, which occasioneth pride in them, discontent in others and disquiet in the Church'.[7] The Lords decided not to be convinced. Perhaps they suspected with John Selden that 'to take away bishops' votes is but the beginning to take them away; for then they can be no longer useful to the King or State'.[8] But the King's credit was rising anyway among the Peers, buoyed up by new creations and offers of privy councillorships. Strafford's lordly call for solidarity was having its effect, too. Attempts from below to alter their compo-sition might conceal a bid for supreme power by a Commons backed— or pushed—by popular allies. Lay peers might be willing to snip away temporal authority from the clergy as a whole, but to the delight of the King, who glimpsed in quarrels between the two Houses a way of deliverance, they threw out this exclusion measure (8 June 1641).

By then, in a fit of absence of mind, soon regretted, Sir Edward Dering, a smug Kentish antiquary, had brought in a 'root and branch' bill, 'very short and very sharp'. Hyde and Falkland attacked it from the start, but Pym, who probably saw it as a screw upon the Lords to accept exclusion, was not unsympathetic. A committee under Hyde, however, tore into its provisions and it was automatically lost when uncompleted at the end of the session. The arguments had been revealing. Lukewarm though the defence of the present episcopal bench was, there was real heat in support of the actual institution. To clip wings might be desirable, to dismember the whole bird was not. Outright expropriation of Church lands—which seemed the inescapable concomitant of abolition—would be a fatal precedent. Holders of impropriations who had ignored Laud's moral suasion were in no mood for enforced surrenders. Besides, with bishops out of the way who would keep the clergy in their place? Writing, a little slow on the uptake, in 1643, Henry Oxinden put into bitter words what must have been sensed by many a member of the Long Parliament two years before. 'I thinke it ... high time for all gentlemen to cast about with themselves, and endeavour rather to maintaine Episcopall government ... then to introduce I know not what ... which will upon the matter equalize men of mean condition with the gentrie ... whom naturally they have ever hated.' Root and branch, he went on, would 'set up a teacher greater then a bishop in every parish who ... [would] study more to enslave his parishioners then to save their souls'.[9] Supporters of the bill obviously intended no weakening of traditional social leadership, but suspicious critics would now begin to see that the King, with his well-advertised devotion to episcopacy, might be a proper bulwark for their kind of world against innovators at best naive and possibly conspiratorial. Long afterwards a Cornish M.P. recalled it was 'fear for the established liturgy' that brought many of his countrymen to follow the crown.[10] That liturgy was something more than a noble form of words.

Reaction quickened when it was seen that further hacking away at royal prerogative was intended, with the bits transferred to parliament, a parliament dominated by men not afraid to experiment. The latter were egged on by the knowledge that Charles was parleying with the Scots to relieve pressure in the north and to improve his position at Westminster. So far the Scots' terms stuck in his gullet. They wanted to push their frontier south and to introduce their Church system into England, both as a thing good in itself and as a warranty of its survival at home. Impossible conditions like these suited Pym. Rejection of them would mean the Scots staying on foot. But terms could change. More moderate groups among the Scots, clustering around Montrose, no zealot, were thinking hard how to meet Charles. This was well known, and when Charles announced an imminent visit to his second kingdom it was a signal for Pym and his henchmen to formulate stiffer constitutional demands, one eye on their own personal security, the other on the future of parliaments. They had reason to be worried. The English army was restless for want of pay and from jealousy of the Scots' guaranteed £850 a day. The Irish army, officially disbanded, remained in being while dilatory arrangements were made to enlist the regiments in the service of Spain—itself an unpopular and suspect scheme. Charles's persistent dabbling in foreign intrigue was distasteful even to the 'well-affected'. Anxieties were fed by reports of 'the Incident', a deep plot to kidnap Argyll, that arrogant symbol of the covenanting cause. It failed—providence rarely had a smile for royalist conspiracy—but sounded an alarm bell in the night. If the King once got the initiative his pent-up vengeance would be terrible. Strafford could not be put together again, but the men who had harried him could be made shorter by a head, too. So in the Ten Propositions Pym pressed for a government they could trust. Charles was to stay in England and put away his evil advisers. But he spurned these insolent suggestions and calmly went on with his own plans. So Pym, skilfully prodding the majority in the Commons along his way, got a committee of defence 'to take into consideration what power will be placed in what persons for commanding the train bands and arms of the kingdom' and to keep surveillance over the King's dealings with the Scots.[11] It was a new stage. Competition for military power had begun. Lord Keeper Littleton refused to put the Great Seal to these instructions. With only a flicker of embarrassment, both Houses gave the committee authority by their own ordinance—the first tentative use of what would become the standard form of legislation during the Interregnum.

The session was now dragging to a close. Accord could still be had on this or that, but evidence of divergence was palpable. 'The sickness', at its height in a London summer, was thinning attendance. A recess was therefore voted on 9 September 1641. Just before that the Commons, without reference to crown or Peers, issued orders for placing the communion table and observing the Sabbath. The Lords took it ill and meant to come back on it, but by the time they re-assembled and the autumn session got under way disturbing events elsewhere had overrun their resentment. But in both Houses individuals, for there was nothing like an organised party, were drifting constitutionally, religiously, politically away from Pym and his tireless committee-men. It was inevitable they should find themselves in the proximity of the King. Perhaps it would be more exact to say that these men stood still while the radicals, driven on by a logic they hardly understood themselves, staggered towards rebellion.

News came in these weeks of the destruction by Spaniards of the

Providence Island settlement in which Pym was closely involved. It left him financially hurt and exasperated by a glaring instance of the inadequacies of Stuart national policies. It must have whet his political temper just at the time when the King, offering extravagant concessions, came to terms with the Scots. In particular Charles let wither an hereditary flower of the crown by agreeing to submit his government to approval by a Scottish parliament bound to be run by Argyll and his grim cronies. Views at Westminster were mixed. Hyde saw it— so he said afterwards—as an 'unspeakable encouragement' to 'the factious party' in England,[12] and certainly there were reports that they were jocund at this welcome evidence of Charles's weakness. But perhaps after all they were only putting a brave face on it. Scottish pressure had driven Charles to an English parliament. Relaxation might give him the opportunity to get rid of it. Disbanding the armies would cut taxation and that might confuse public opinion. There was only a precarious discipline among the shifting groups in the Commons. At almost any time the leaders could find themselves isolated. Yet they had to go on. Whom could they carry with them? In spite of assiduous committee-work and eloquent speeches on the floor of the House they could never be really sure. Sir Simonds D'Ewes could be relied upon for anti-episcopal moves, but, unsure of the precedents, hesitated at demands for parliament to choose the King's council. Every other man had his own set of inhibitions, by no means all revealed as yet. The confused politics of the civil war period were already becoming apparent. The incipient royalist party was still merely a few groups of drifters or foot-draggers, and its potential leaders were not as clear in their own minds as they would afterwards have liked to have thought. Much the same might be said of the parliamentary majority. But there was a difference, summed up in one man—John Pym. He was working all the time to control events. So we hear of 'meetings att Chelsey att the Lord Mandeville's house . . . to consult what is best to be donne at their next meeting in parliament.' Sir Edward Nicholas, who was regularly reporting all this to the King, believed 'they will . . . fall on some plausible thing, that may redintegrate them in the people's good opinion, which is their anchor hold and only interest'.[13] The standing committee during the recess, of which Pym was chairman, was another means of consultation. Whatever they may have decided was within a few days of the opening of the new session swept aside by an unlooked-for stroke. The Ulster Rebellion was breathlessly reported to a stunned House by a servant of Sir John Clotworthy, the egregious Irish adventurer who had acquired something of the reputation of an expert in Irish matters.[14]

The Stuart Englishman's attitude towards Ireland was a harsh and unremitting one. Intense concern for his own liberties was quite compatible with indifference if not blank hostility towards the claims of Irishmen. For all the violence of the condemnation of Strafford's policy little had been said of its meaning for the natives. They were papists and barbarians with only exiguous contacts with real humanity, literally beyond the pale. Existing prejudices hardened under impact of gross tales of atrocity and revenge. Even in sensitive men a blind hatred welled up, fed on the parliamentary side in the coming civil war by Charles's impolitic readiness to turn Irish troops loose in England. The most telling charge against that unfathomable Leveller William Walwyn, was that he counted Irish as equal to Englishmen. Now in the autumn of 1641 politicians could not grasp that the revolt was a natural consequence of long-pursued policies, stepped up but hardly changed by the ruthless drive of Strafford, Alva to Charles I's Philip II. All they could see was an immediate danger—to the English ascendancy and to their protestant religion. Their kin were being slaughtered or mutilated. The first successful English colony was being snatched away. Was Ireland, denied under the good old Queen Elizabeth to the Counter-Reformation, to be let go now? The fate not only of English protestants but of their continental co-religionaries was at stake. The Thirty Years War had not yet run its savage course. Its outcome might yet be a triumph for the house of Hapsburg and popery.

So the rising must be crushed and Ireland brought under subjection again. Military force would do it. But could the King—who was reported to have hoped that this ill news of Ireland might hinder some of the follies in England—be trusted with a great army? Perhaps he had with foreign encouragement even connived at the revolt. A few months ago a crack Irish army might have landed in England to subvert the parliament. An English army could do that, too, without giving itself the trouble of crossing the pirate-infested Irish sea. Thus the issue of military power, already, as we have seen, tentatively raised in the summer, became a burning question. If radicals would not allow a truly royal army, moderates and conservatives could not contemplate a parliamentary one. They felt that men who had courted the London mobs were not above employing an army to reach their ends, particularly now that Scottish pressure on the King was relaxed.

The Ulster Rising, then, widened the cracks in the Long Parliament. It did not create them. The few optimists who imagined that a common danger would close the ranks were soon disillusioned. On 8 November 1641 John Pym put forward an 'additional instruction' for the parliamentary committee with the King in Scotland. They were to ask of him what amounted to control of the executive, otherwise, though parliament 'would continue in that obedience and loyalty to him which was due by the laws of God and this kingdom, yet we should take such a course for the securing of England as might secure ourselves'.[15] D'Ewes extracted its true inwardness at once: 'by such an addition, we should as it were prevail the king'.[16] 'The constitutional royalists' were even more convinced of this and indicated their determination not to allow a wedge to be driven into the arch of government to ease entry for further encroachments on the established Church and social order. Nicholas wrote urgently to Charles to give them 'some notice ... for their encouragement',[17] but the King was inclined for the time being to look to the Lords for their vocal reaction.

The poverty of the majority by which the new instruction went through the Commons was no deterrent to Pym but a spur. He responded by stepping up consideration of a remonstrance which should record in detail the whole range of past abuses and list the thoughtful remedies so far applied. This huge document, hinted at during the first session, revived under different auspices on 1 November and formally introduced a week later, concluded with some specific guarantees for the future of Church, State and armed forces. It was now a clever piece of politics, designed to lead members along the paths of past accord, pointing out comforting landmarks, so they would hardly notice until too late that they had arrived in a strange land. It almost worked. As Nicholas told the King 'if there had been nothing but an intention to have justified the proceedings of this parliament'[18] only a handful would have resisted. Moreover, Charles was helping Pym—as he would do again and again—by dallying in Scotland, ignoring his advisers' promptings to stimulate support by appearing in his capital. It was lucky for the King that a few members, some of them persuasive debaters, had decided that with him or without him the revolutionary caucus must be thwarted. So the Grand Remonstrance, as it came aptly to be called, had a rough passage from the start, blown by 'a fresh gale from the coast of loyalty'.[19]

While in Ireland a stunned administration let revolt spread almost unchecked and while reports of bloody murder inflamed English opinion, the Commons pushed on with the Remonstrance, consoling themselves that in an Irish winter there could be no great progress made either way. Pym's offensive was met by the inevitable trio of Culpepper, Falkland and Hyde, now joined by Dering, anxiously sloughing off his 'root and branch' aberration.[20] He exclaimed that he 'did not dream that we should remonstrate downward, tell stories to the people and talk of the King as of a third person'. Hyde was not against a remonstrance *per se*, but could not support this version which, looking so far back, could only reopen old wounds and inflict new ones. Its tone was needlessly bitter. It had disturbing ambiguities. It threatened harmony while it talked of establishing it. The backing of the Lords was unlikely when it so patently set out to appeal over the head of the sovereign to the people themselves. It was both exasperating and dangerous. Culpepper cleverly stroked the fears of men who felt they were being taken too far into the dark. Disquiet of this kind is liable to arise irrespective of the social class, economic standing, education and intelligence of the individuals concerned. It would be unhelpful to analyse motivation here solely in terms capable of rationalisation.

For Pym, now for the first time being labelled 'King', this Remonstrance had to go through—to force home to an indifferent King and an ignorant country the perils that must come of a malignant party, riddled with popery, plotting tirelessly against them all. 'But if this king will join with us we shall set him upon as great grounds of honour and greatness in that all the world shall not be able to move him.'[21] Some upsetting expressions might be thrown out but the main clauses must stand. At midnight on 22 November 1641 the Grand Remonstrance passed the Commons by the plurality of 11 votes (159–148). It had been a long sitting, 'a tedious debate beyond all example and Precident'[22] and the vote was likened to the decision of a 'starved jury.'[23] The more determined 'noes' managed to prevent the immediate printing and publication, the member for Stamford, Geoffrey Palmer, upbraided the majority as 'a Rabble of inconsiderable Persons, set on by a juggling Junto',[24] words which should have delighted Charles I. If Pym had given notice not to mark time, a powerful minority had left him in no doubt that he could not take them with him. Through no real effort of his own the King was getting a sort of party. In the Lords he could look for a majority. In the Commons there was an amorphous group, which, taking a lead from men of integrity and parliamentary skill, might grow larger and more tightly knit.

What Charles must do was to come forward as the candid warden of the constitution and upholder of the social order. His legal position was strong and looked stronger daily. Scotland lay quiet. The City Aldermen, under a new, strongly royalist Lord Mayor, Sir Richard Gurney, and disgusted with the turbulence they associated with deliberate action by the 'faction', were anxious to demonstrate their loyalty and respect. Charles, a constant debtor, keenly aware of the City's financial potential, did his best to retain their affection. In September he had reminded them that in the recent tonnage and poundage act 'the

51

lower House forgot to reserve the advantage to the merchant . . which I have usually granted. . . . Though their own burgesses forget them in parliament, yet I mean to supply that defect . . . so that they may see they need no mediators to me, but my own good thoughts.'[25] On his progress southward during November he went out of his way to appear gracious to the people to offset 'any thing that hath bene donne for them this Parliament'.[26] Then on 25 November he entered London in triumph and with a planned exhibition of loyalty was lavishly entertained at Guildhall.

The King's glowing speech of thanks promised to give back the plantation rights in Londonderry taken away a few years earlier. He would govern always by law and maintain the protestant religion as established by his noble predecessors. 'Former tumults and disorders' he blamed on 'the meaner sorts of people', and assured himself of the affections of 'the better and main part'.[27] The latter were flattered by honours and favours, the former distracted by copious free claret. Pointedly the King made no visit to his parliament until 2 December. Indeed, his next step was to remove the special guard which had been set since the agitations of the previous spring. He told the two Houses that he himself was now their best protection. Ungratefully the Commons preferred to look to a special force provided by local justices. Charles took up residence not at Whitehall but out at Hampton Court. There on 1 December he received the Grand Remonstrance and its companion petition, promising darkly to give them the consideration they deserved.

News from Ireland kept up the demand for parliamentary action, and, incidentally, stirred the suspicions of the King's complicity. Pym pressed the Lords for consultations, stressing that if they failed to join in sorely needed measures, they must expect the Commons to go it alone. (Thus was the question of '*par ordre ou par tête*' raised. Not until 1649 was the answer finally given.) It was a bold assertion to make with so tiny a majority. But need was urgent. The King was considering a proclamation to order all absentee members back to Westminster. If obeyed, this might swell the loyalists. In the Lords the royal *bloc* was moving. On 6 December they rejected a clause in the impressment bill which would have taken away, except in actual invasion, the King's power to compel men to serve outside their counties. The Common's riposte was immediate. A militia bill was brought in by Sir Arthur Haselrig, already notable among 'inflexible men' and a future republican. This would simply have transferred control of the armed forces from the crown and lodged it in a Lord General appointed by parliament. It was read with alarm by professed moderate men like

Culpepper, who took it to place an arbitrary power in parliament. But by 158–125 it passed its first reading, as a warning to the King, who with half an eye to the moderates was trying to tighten his grip on the City of London. Unfortunately Gurney and his associates were becoming more and more isolated from the citizenry. Economically distressed, religiously dissident, alternatively warmed by pamphlets and wildfire sermons like those of Stephen Marshall, 'the trumpet', and frozen in dark homes made cheerless by lack of sea-coal from Newcastle, there were many in London who would not hesitate to back Pym. Charles's order that the Book of Common Prayer must be used throughout the realm and his appointment of new bishops kept the atmosphere tense. Petitions to parliament called for public fasts, national synods, the deprivation of bishops and catholic peers of their voices in the Lords.

The failure of the King's efforts was laid bare when the elections for the Common Council, after a skilled campaign by Venn, a hardworking City M.P., returned a majority prepared to back Pym. At about the same time the Grand Remonstrance was circulated in print. Charles made an exasperated bid for control by handing over the Tower to Col. Thomas Lunsford, a venal desperado, whose appointment was unwelcome even to convinced royalists (21 December 1641), and by adding to misgivings about the King's intentions unsettled the public and the private quiet. A little later (23 December), Charles indignantly rejected the Remonstrance, stressing his own intention and capacity to defend all established order in Church and State. At this Pym, supported by a minority in the Peers, saw nothing for it but to press on with the militia bill, and to get parliament to pledge itself to maintain the safety of the kingdom. Convinced at length by Gurney that Lunsford's promotion was unnecessarily provocative, Charles replaced him by Sir John Byron, a more respectable but certainly no less loyal supporter. Lunsford, however, stayed in Town and was soon involved in an armed affray at Westminster, in which the future Leveller leader John Lilburne was prominent.

Recruiting among suspected men of volunteers for Ireland, whence news remained grim, fostered fears of a *coup d'état*. Mobs, on holiday, surged around the Lords' House, reviling papists and bishops, who drew up (27 December) a declaration that since they were not able to vote freely, the whole House must be considered under restraint. This rash assertion, the work chiefly of Archbishop Williams of York, who was never the astute politician he imagined himself to be, brought a majority of the Lords into the arms of the Commons. Impeachment of the bishops was voted and they went off to prison—a welcome reduction of the royal *bloc* in the Lords.

A new rumour spread: Pym was drawing up articles of impeachment of the Queen. To head this off, Charles, still not convinced that Pym could not be bought, still interpreting his intransigence as 'playing hard to get', apparently offered him again the Chancellorship of the Exchequer. His rejection convinced Charles that he had entered upon a design to be really 'King Pym'. The King must work fast. Egged on by George Digby (a former 'out', now very much an 'in', almost, indeed, a royal favourite) Charles sought to beat Pym at his own game by impeaching him, four other M.P.s and one peer for treason. Articles were read out in the Lords on 3 January 1642—the villains had broken those ubiquitous indefinable fundamental laws, tried to alienate the subjects' affections, worked to seduce the army and even to invite in a foreign power. They had raised tumults—indeed, they had actually levied war on their sovereign. It was a formidable catalogue. The Lords, though disturbed, could not bring themselves to accept the Attorney-General's demand for immediate arrest. They wanted, it seemed, to be sure that the procedures indicated were truly legal. But Charles would not be held up by technicalities. Guards went to the Commons to take up the accused, but were sent away empty-handed.

The King was now awkwardly placed. He had angered the Lords, who stood by their claims to control impeachments, while the Commons had sent instructions to the city trainbands—whose command they were already disputing with the King—to be ready to turn out. The Queen, not unnaturally terrified on her own account, pushed her husband into further blunders. The Lord Mayor was told to keep order—even if it meant firing on the people, and on the night of 4 January Charles came to the Commons in person, with an armed retinue, to take his victims. But his 'birds had flown' by then and he had to withdraw with irate cries of 'Privilege! Privilege!' ringing in his ears.

The Common Council—swamped by the newly-elected members who were constitutionally not yet entitled to attend—over-rode the Lord Mayor, refused to give up the members, who had gone into hiding somewhere in the City. Inevitably, a petition was devised—to the effect that the cause of the persecuted statesmen was clearly just. This day of great trouble and deep danger drew to a close with the distraught Lord Mayor admitting he had quite lost control of the situation. Sir Simonds D'Ewes went straight home and made his will.

Sergeant-Major Philip Skippon, an ex-ranker with continental experience, was chosen, illegally, by the Commons to command the City Militia, an appointment that less than a year later bore fruit in the fields around Turnham Green. On 10 January, 1642, Charles, who perhaps felt at this point that all was lost, hastily took his family to Hampton Court, where their unexpected arrival put the domestic staff into a pother. The beds were damp and everything at sixes and sevens. Next day Pym and his friends re-appeared in the Commons. It was a triumph—initiative lay with them. But could they sustain it?

VI The Paper War

Pym could have had little cause for satisfaction—unless he was deliberately plotting war. In the panic some of the differences between the two Houses had been patched up and control of the City had passed to the 'popular' elements. But it was uncertain if the latter would last, and to reconcile all the viewpoints in parliament was clearly impossible. Moderate puritans believed that the City insurrections '. . . (as all ungoverned multitudes) are of very dangerous consequence'.[1] Pym could persuade *them* for a while that 'God, who works miracles, can, out of such violent actions bring comfortable effects',[2] but episcopalians, conservatives, royalists would not believe that. Besides, there was still no solution in sight to the problems of Ireland, the militia and the Church. If Charles had lost a round and lost it badly, he was still in the fight, and must be expected to start at once to work for a come-back.

The King was certainly already negotiating with Ormonde in Ireland, and the slippery Digby was now in Holland up to who knew what. But Charles understood that outside force would not be enough. He must have a party to represent a spectrum of political attitudes, and be backed by enough English power to bring the rebels—as he now regarded them—to heel. Sooner or later, Pym must make a mistake and provide Charles with a party. In the meantime the King would offer a bid for the armed forces and the fortified places of the the realm. So he tried to get Hull, where the arms for the northern campaign were stored, and Portsmouth. Their strategic value was equally obvious to Pym. The King's gambits were thwarted, but provoked a majority in the Commons into recommending parliamentary nomination and control of the Lords-Lieutenant, in effect, the whole militia. The Lords demurred. Already the drift apart had begun again. To step away from Pym must surely mean to slide towards the King. Charles took heart.

At the end of January agitation in London reached a peak, with thousands of women besieging the Houses, clamouring for bread. In

February the Queen went abroad for safety and to negotiate for aid. Charles was now free to move about the country, meeting people, seeking support for an inescapable trial by combat. Confident that in happier times to come he would be free to repudiate them, he gave his assent to the last few acts of his reign, among them Bishops' Exclusion. Assent was accompanied by words of conciliation, the effect of which was, however, dissipated by the prompt exposure of intercepted letters which revealed that, though he had taken constitutionalists like Culpepper and Falkland into his counsels, he was still intimately associated with advocates of naked will and force. As a result the militia bill, though hotly contested, passed both Houses—only to get a denying answer from the King, who certainly had history on his side. By this time Edward Hyde had come secretly into his service, drafting subtle replies to the petitions and proposals that proliferated in the months to come. His skill helped to speed up the formation of 'a King's party' out of men, not all of them M.P.s, who while still valuing the earlier work of parliament were increasingly uneasy about the future. Hyde showed them the crown as a shining symbol of legality and stability. The actions of Pym and some who went beyond him, as in the harsh punishment of Alderman George Benion for whipping up opposition to the claim to control the militia, reinforced suspicions.

Charles, who was maintaining himself largely through the generosity of the catholic Earl of Worcester and Lord Herbert, now began, over the protests of the parliamentary majority, a slow progress in a northerly direction, hoping by his presence in the localities and the well-publicised pathos of his situation, to increase his party. On 2 March the two Houses voted to put the country into a posture of defence and assumed control of the Navy. On 5 March the militia bill was converted into an 'ordinance', enforceable by proceedings for contempt. By this parliament usurped the legislative function, a revolutionary step, even if Sir Simonds D'Ewes, a man who 'troubled himself much in relics and records', hoped to find precedents. Asked at Newmarket to grant the militia for a time Charles replied, 'By God, not for an Hour; you have asked that of me in this which was never asked of a King, and with which I will not trust my Wife and Children.' As for letting parliament cope with Ireland, '400 will never do that Work, it must be put into the Hands of One'.[3] (In fact, in spite of all his negotiations with Irish groupings, Charles never did anything positive or effective to settle that most distressful country.) As for ordinances, he sneered, whatever their contents they were not law and every loyal subject would reject them. This snappish reply was voted a breach of privilege, and those who advised it were adjudged enemies of peace, rightly suspected to be

57

favourers of the wicked Irish rebellion. What parliament declared to be the law of the land quite simply was so. Sovereignty was being grasped.

On 19 March Charles arrived in York. He was warmly greeted but who could be sure if the enthusiasm would last long enough to bring him into 'his own again'? What, in any case, was his own? A war of manifestoes began. Official parliamentary declarations—there were dozens of them—were extended by pamphlets, such as those of Henry Parker, asserting the dependence of government on the consent of the governed, and appealing to the law of nature as the true basis of all law. This extension of claims from the technicalities of common law demonstrates the practical recognition that in 1642 precedent, however construed, was not enough to solve problems which, at least, seemed new. War shuffled nearer.

To eradicate the damaging slur that at heart he was a papist, Charles ordered the stiff enforcement of the penal laws on the recusants. A couple of priests, one a harmless old man of 90, were hanged. No doubt some support was won by this, but it revealed the King as a cold man. It was, indeed, less Charles's own actions than those of his opponents that worked for him. The parliamentary majority pushed on with a scheme for resolving the religious question by an assembly of divines, a project very objectionable to yet more men who were coming to see that perhaps there was more to be said for episcopacy and personal royal supremacy than they had thought in 1640. This attitude informs the Kentish Petition drawn up by a number of gentlemen, including a repentant Sir Edward Dering, at the Maidstone Assizes in March 1642. Parliament was urged to strive tirelessly to come to terms with the King for the peace of the nation, and, in particular, to be very wary in approaching the ticklish ecclesiastical problem. S. R. Gardiner adjudged the petition as marking the moment when civil war became inevitable.[4] It need not have been. The petition seems more of an appeal for heading off disaster than a spirited encouragement to the King to go ahead. In all its demands a recognition of a place for parliament tempers zeal for prerogative.

But parliament's reaction was unimaginative. Ringleaders were arrested and the petition burned by the public hangman. Divisions deepened. Many members and peers no longer came to the Houses. But not all of them found their way north to join their perambulating sovereign. Many men were uncommitted and remained so. Others, some very reluctantly, did allow themselves to get caught up in the irrepressible conflict. Charles might not have Hull, but he had more and more a party. Yet so had Pym.

On 12 May the King formally asked the Yorkshire gentry for advice and assistance. The response was gratifying—he was able to form a body of guards for his royal person. But even now he was pressed not to break with parliament. More ominously, leading county notables, including Sir Thomas Fairfax, stayed ostentatiously aloof. Orders sent to the London militia to come to York were predictably ignored, but gave the excuse for a parliamentary resolution that since the King, seduced by wicked counsel, aimed at making war on his subjects, he had broken his trust. His present actions were, it went on, tending to dissolve all government. By the fundamental laws anyone who assisted him was a traitor. Undeterred by the implied threat, the Lord Keeper fled on 1 June to York, taking with him the Great Seal, symbol of executive authority. Soon afterwards, Edward Hyde, convinced that there was little point in hanging on at Westminster, followed. At the same time parliament sent 19 miscellaneous propositions to the King, demanding control of practically every aspect of State activity, including foreign policy, a mystery always jealously guarded by the crown. The Nineteen Propositions, desultory and disorderly, do not amount to a written constitution, but they point to the determination of some clear-sighted men to tip the balance of the State away from monarchy.

Charles, of course, spurned the proposals, as leaving him but the picture, but the shadow of a King. His reply also gives a moderate statement of his ideal of monarchy, or perhaps what he was willing to let his more constitutionally-minded advisers persuade themselves and others was his ideal. For his part, John Pym may have had no desire for Charles to accept the propositions, but wanted the onus of rejection to bear down on the King, dampening his growing support and allowing himself to extend his control of the Commons and its multifarious committees. His success was indicated a few days later when the Commons put it on record that 'the King's supreme and royal pleasure is exercised in this High Court of law and council, after a more eminent and obligatory manner than it can be by personal act or resolution of his own'.[5] In short, parliament's will was the King's will. It was a bold claim, too bold for those who looked upon the practical sovereignty of a junto of rash, if not malicious, men as hideous beside the traditional authority of monarchy. But Pym was just then willing to lose half-hearted support if it would stiffen the others.

War was just around the corner. A rash of trivial incidents indicated the deepening malaise. Parliamentary ordinance called on all to back the cause—what exactly it was remained, in spite of all the words spat out by both sides, something of a puzzle—by bringing in plate, horses and arms. Of over 250 M.P.s asked to set a good example, 50 refused point-blank and 30 wanted time to consider. Real enthusiasts were rare. Charles answered the militia ordinance by commission of array enjoining trained bands to submit to the orders of officers named therein. This issue was now beyond legality, even if Charles produced, as he certainly could, better precedents for commission than parliament for ordinances. Most men would obey either, or reject both, less on grounds of law than on their own assessments, which might or might not be intelligent, of their own best interests. In April a private member had urged the Commons to undertake an inquiry into opinion in the localities since it was not the exacting of a law which made it of force, but the willing obedience to it. Historians would give a great deal to have the results of such a poll, and it might have been useful—or de-pressing—to both sides. As it was, neither King nor parliament had any certainty of the degree of support they might find in the 'countries'.

A start was made with commissions of array by the Hastings family in Leicestershire. They found it like an enemy country. Their traditional rivals, the Stamfords, as staunch for parliament as they were for the King, no more, no less, had already set about implementing the militia ordinance. In Northamptonshire the magnates, persuaded by Charles's declarations, vouched for by his peers and parliament-men, that he had no intention of aggressive war, were more amenable. Decisions were no doubt influenced, too, by parliament's preparations to raise a national army to supplement and stiffen the militia. Its commander was the Earl of Essex, a dour and rather colourless per-sonality, but a soldier of some experience and—more important per-haps at this juncture—of considerable territorial and political in-fluence. (The humiliation of his enforced 'divorce' from Lady Frances Howard must have bitten deep into his character and given a nasty personal tinge to his political opinions, but time was to show that he was hardly of the cloth from which revolutionaries are cut.) So both sides spent the summer, partly in raising in the localities regiments under volunteer officers, often more numerous than private soldiers, and partly in increasing the barrage of mere words, accusing each other of warlike preparations and wicked intentions.

On 19 July Charles, whose hopes of help from Scotland and the continent were cooling, said that he was every-ready to discuss matters in a proper parliamentary way. But four days earlier the first serious skirmish had come off at the prosperous clothing-town of Manchester—'that nursery of rebellion'—an early demonstration of the undoubted fact that what Manchester does today, the rest of the country does to-morrow. Early August saw parliament earnestly denying that it was seeking arbitrary power, 'it being . . . most improbable that the

Nobility and Chief Gentry of this Kingdom should conspire to take away the Law by which they enjoy their Estates, are protected from any Act of Violence and Power, and are differenced from the meaner Sort of People, with whom, otherwise, they would be but Fellow-Servants'.[6] The awkward truth that a good many of the gentry and nobility were in opposition or were neutral was ignored. As for Charles, he was stamping around the North and Midlands looking for partisans and trying to grab the strong places. Hull yet again ignored his orders to surrender and at Leicester he failed to get his hands on the county magazine. Instead he had to look helplessly on while the arms were distributed among the citizenry, some of whom were not likely to use them for him.

All over the country, enthusiasts were coming into the open, probing for local advantage. But many had no stomach for war, with its train of sudden death and swollen taxes. Some, indeed, were ready to act to keep the fighting out of their borders, a positive neutrality that was a clog to the contestants throughout the war. It was not enough to stop the conflict. By the middle of August Charles had made up his mind. There must be an immediate trial of strength, a rallying of his forces and resources. To delay a little longer might be to leave it too late. Autumn was on its way and soon Colonel Winter might assume his wayward independent command. To raise the royal standard and have it defied might persuade waverers to join the King in indignation.

The big question was—where to set it up? Lord Strange put the claims of Warrington, in the heart of the tough northern counties, where the peasants made good soldiers and where like a feudal baron he could call on the obedience of thousands of retainers. But enemies of a Stanley ascendancy—there were cross-currents on the King's as well as on parliament's side—worked on the wavering King to reject this probably sound advice. As a consequence, says the eighteenth-century historian of the Stanley family, 'many gentlemen in the north, who were well-affected to his Majesty's cause ... either remained neuter, or revolted to the Parliament with all their dependencies' ... while 'the ill affected in Lancashire grew proud, and the meaner sort of people thought it a fine thing to set up against the great ones'.[7] In the event Charles settled on Nottingham, where the drawback of some division of loyalties was outweighed by its apt position nearer to London and to the west and South Wales where he hoped for massive support. There on the blustery evening of 22 August the standard was unfurled. Civil war had begun.

VII The Line Up

Civil wars are seldom tidy affairs. During the Great Rebellion there seem to have been no sharp dividing lines between the contestants, and between them and the (more numerous) neutrals. Each episode winnowed the activists by deaths, changes in or total abandonment of loyalties for reasons often far to seek. Men unfortunately do not always express their motives adequately or honestly, nor even grasp them themselves. The absorbing kaleidoscope of allegiances in this troubled period takes in, at the least, religion, social standing and aspiration, economic outlook, education, intelligence, imagination and moral fibre. Some men, one might say, were born royalists, others were made. When they deplored, as they did, tediously, that these were 'unnatural wars', wars 'without an enemy',[1] what they were really doing was admitting their own inability to understand what they were about. The heat of controversy ever since about the issues in this crisis of the seventeenth century, though owing a good deal to present-day attitudes, is a tribute to the complexity of the original situation. As a result of the researches and intuitions of generations of historians we probably know more about some aspects of the rebellion than any one taking part in it; regrettably about others we know rather less.

When war actually broke out, the north and the west of England, with Wales, seemed to stand mainly by the King, with the south and the east backing parliament. This was in part an accident. Parliament by meeting in London already had a grip upon the south-east and to gather support the King had had to look far afield. There is also a suggestion here of economic divergence. The most backward parts of the realm were falling to the King, the richest and most economically advanced to the rebels—with obvious advantage since they also had a stronger tradition of good order. At a glance from a religious viewpoint, the most staunchly protestant, even puritan, districts such as East Anglia look parliamentarian, while the outer reaches, where catholicism often lingered, were royalist. But within the broad division there were everywhere diversities. Kent, vital to London for food supplies, lines of communication with the continent, and as a bastion against short-route invasion, harboured many royalists besides those already in arms with the King. There was a rising in 1643, another, more serious, in 1648. Each movement was the effect not only of national problems but of local politics. In Cornwall zeal for either side was notably lacking at first, both in town and country. It was only after fighting had actually started that the 'quietness' of the county was disturbed by a shuffling to choose sides. If the struggle could have been kept on the other side of the Tamar many would have rejoiced. This unmartial spirit was shared in Cheshire, Staffordshire, Yorkshire and other counties where pacts of neutrality only slowly gave way to shifting *blocs* of royalism and parliamentarianism, sliding back into neutralism.

In Lancashire the puritan clothing towns had long gone out of step with the more catholic rural areas. The latter were prodded into support for the King by the house of Stanley, but their simulated royalism was soon dissipated by the indiscriminate plundering of royalist troops. At no time was popish support for Charles absolute. In the West Country clothing districts more positive backing for parliament's war effort was sometimes forthcoming, as it was in northern towns like Bradford and Halifax with their radical religious outlook stemming from the days of the Lollards and with fierce rivalry with local country gentlemen, who inclined to royalism. Like the Lancashire clothing areas they had suffered particularly from hard times in the last two or three decades. The north of England, indeed, would provide both sides with forces, commanders and notions. (A member of Cromwell's second parliament asserted that most of the dangerous ideas disturbing the community were bred up there.[2]) Farther south, Nottinghamshire dallied in defining its attitudes, in spite of the rallying presence of the King at the commencement of hostilities. In the event a majority of the truly substantial county families turned out for Charles, sometimes nominally, and not always uniformly. But a few others of about the same standing took the leadership of an uneasy blend of lesser gentry, yeomen and the middling sort of the towns, who leaned at varying angles towards parliament. Even in Wales, where both north and south demonstrated loyalty, the enduring zeal of a few hard-headed men like Philip Jones could be engaged by the rebels. In every district there were men of all classes and religious persuasions who 'laid low'. They included papists who had a long experience of that sort of thing.

Under its skin London itself was at odds. Victory for the radicals in the 1641 Common Council elections had not expunged royalism there. Lord Mayor Gurney had at last to be pushed out for trying to implement the King's commission of array. City royalists were thereafter disinclined to do much more than mutter their opinions and read clandestine newsheets from Oxford, but they would surely have been bolder if Charles could have thrust his way into the environs and stayed there. Even after final defeat in the field he might still have spurred them to action by the magic of his presence. There were further complications in that the anti-royalist front was always breaking up and re-forming. Throughout the Interregnum London had to be watched and nursed, as often a distraction as an asset to a prevailing party.

There is much about the geographical cleavage, whether broad or fragmentary, to suggest there was a social basis to the rebellion. But this plausible notion, though strongly supported by literary sources, has yet to be clinched. Consideration of the affiliations of members of both Houses of the Long Parliament might be helpful here, since the war was certainly the outcome of shifts within that institution, which remained, even when it was not sitting, close to the heart of things all through the tergiversations of the next two decades. (When parliament did nothing it was rather like the failure of a dog to bark in the night—significant.) It is apparent that the fissures already appearing among M.P.s there before the fighting began did not closely follow major social differences. In this respect the war itself did not open up a new period. What was new was the more rapid export of arguments into the localities, where they were deepened, diluted, distorted or ignored. How far Westminster was at any time a microcosm of the whole political nation remains a problem. The county committees of presumed supporters of parliament were, like the Houses, always in a state of flux. They were purged or purged themselves to meet particular situations. Some of their internecine conflicts certainly were responses to national issues—the struggle between the advocates of aggressive war and the appeasers, for example—but they were never empty of local personalities and politics. If they did mirror the centre, it was in a cracked, flawed glass. Among the committee-men rising, falling or perdurable gentlemen are to be found, just as they appeared among those who worked in a less organised fashion for the King in his localities. More suggestive perhaps is the emergence of men who in normal times would not have had entry to the circle of county influence, but who by their drive, efficiency or enthusiasm for the cause worked their way in. Evidently service brought adequate rewards, but just what they wanted and just what they got requires specific examination. One further generalisation may be ventured. Where the middling and meaner sort of people tended to take up an independent political line—as distinct from one dictated or manipulated by their betters—they were rarely royalist. The Levellers and the Diggers are the prime examples. It is a point that directs critical attention to the claims made for Charles's 'personal government' as protector of the poor and helpless against the rich and indifferent.

Among the Peers—dissidence among whom had helped to bring on a parliament in the autumn of 1640—that group which stayed on at Westminster was a dwindling, though at the outset valuable, minority. Yet the majority itself was not made up of rampant royalists. Many were neuters all along. In time others joined them, from both sides. Among the declared loyalists there would be some who would actually change sides, or at any rate toy with the notion. Recent creations ought to have stood by their benefactor but their decisions were not always swayed by gratitude. Holders of more ancient titles were split, too, some of them pulled toward parliament by resentment of the Stuart inflation of dignities, which spoiled the public image of the whole estate. To have been kept 'out' when by rights he ought to have been welcomed 'in' might incline a magnate to rebellion, but in practice not all the 'ins' were royalists, nor all the 'outs' inimical to the King. Bounty withheld might yet flow in the right direction. Peers were individualists and much of their motivation must be sought in their personalities and prejudices. But as a social group they were fundamentally conservative and few among the parliamentary peers at any time called for radical measures. Complaints about the untowardness of Essex and Manchester started early. Essex went to war with his coffin and winding sheet ready, a symptom of gloomy lethargy rather than of determination unto death. Abolition of the House of Lords came in 1649 less as revenge for the activities of avowed royalist peers than from exasperation at the *vis inertiae* of the whole order.

Alignment of the members of the Commons has been closely studied. On the available evidence and from the questions so far asked, division into royalist, parliamentarian and neutral cannot be confidently correlated with social class or economic outlook. Both sides found room for substantial and lesser men, old and new families, some of whom were divided among themselves. Those with mercantile or industrial interests were likewise shot through with discord. The only obvious sharp distinction is that the royalists were younger than the parliamentarians by an average of ten years. This may mean that royalists were less experienced than the others in the ways of the Stuart kings, or less prejudiced, less eager to survey current problems in the light of parliamentary struggles long ago, in the 1620s or even earlier. Or it may mean simply nothing at all. One possible line of demarcation is that parliamentarians seem to have embraced rather more men who had played an active part in the proceedings of the present House, not always in the debates, in which future royalists had been eloquent and assiduous, too, but in the comparative anonymity of the committee-rooms. The importance of the latter is only now coming to light, but analysis of the composition of the numerous standing and *ad hoc* committees, of the frequency of their meetings and their management already hints at a better understanding of the politics of the Long Parliament.

The Great Rebellion has sometimes been called 'the Puritan Revolution', and religion ought perhaps to have proved a safe guide to reactions. Charles protested volubly his devotion to the prayer book and summoned Anglicans to join him on the known *via media*. Parliament was increasingly influenced by more argumentative protestant opinions. But the muddled attitudes of mind and spirit, labelled 'puritanism', were too volatile to be caught within the confines of Westminster. Advocates of liberty pulled away leftwards, the promoters of authority flying rightwards, some of them unerringly toward the King. As for high-flying churchmen, not every one was an out-and-out royalist. The King, they agreed, was a man of parts, but not all of those were attractive. Some potential supporters were perhaps put off by propaganda that he favoured the catholics above all. Papists, who might in fact have expected more from Charles than from parliament, sometimes found it prudent to keep out of the conflict, or even in appropriate circumstances cleave to parliament. Religion was only one of a number of jumbled priorities. Even Oliver Cromwell had to admit that religion was not the thing at first contested for.

PART TWO

The Road to
Whitehall

VIII King Pym

War found parliament with little or no experience of an executive, an administration and military command. It had to learn fast by waging armed conflict in which at any time victory might go to the King, or which might decline into a demoralising war of attrition. What was needed was some co-ordination of the activities and talents of M.P.s with those of parliament's supporters in the regions, including the capital. Charles must be brought to regret his sneer about a committee of 400 running a campaign. Men of contrasting outlooks must be kept together well enough to keep things ticking over until peace was won or bought on favourable terms. This was difficult, particularly in the opening months of the fighting when the King seemed to be poised for a kill. But there was a method and it was found by John Pym—in himself. Just as he had managed men and turned events in the fuddled pre-war months, so now in the time of first taking of sides and the beginning of hostilities, he dominated at Westminster, not by a blanket dictatorship—such a thing was not possible—but by sheer hard work and political capacity.

Pym knew the material he had to work with. Lacking his urbanity most members were prey to the elations and depressions of swiftly changing political and military situations. They needed sensitive yet firm handling to get them to accept measures which would provide effective prosecution of war while leaving ajar the door to negotiation. Pym had to get his own way while letting a couple of hundred snappish members imagine they were having theirs, too. Leadership was never an outright gift; it had to be won again and again. In practice the greatest bar to achievement was the belief, born of hope mingled with fear, that the fighting could not last long and that without much effort on anyone's part the King would come to terms. Edgehill (23 October 1642) was a whiff of cold reality, but ironically Charles's success was made an asset by Pym. While a group of faint-hearts, led by Denzil Holles, called for abject proffers to the King, another of irreconcilables, including that violent talker, Sir Henry Marten, demanded bolder military strokes. Between the two sprawled a middle party—or rather agglomeration of 'parties'—prepared to wait a little on events. They could be moved and Pym, by inspired interventions on the floor of the House and calculated nudging in the committee-rooms, got things in train. Never piqued by rebuffs, but learning from them, seizing opportunities as they came, or as he made them, he inclined the whole House —or what was now left of it—to accept measures to secure themselves. Charles's obvious intention in 1642–3 to win the war outright undermined the peace party, kept the middle party mobile, while Pym's patent abilities as 'director of the whole machine'[1] gave the war party no excuse for pressing major changes. By the time he died in December 1643 King Pym had built up a central administration closely linked with local government and organising armies in the field. He had wooed an ally and above all sustained a brittle morale. It had been a brief but formative reign, without glory but stamped with success.

Money was the first big desideratum. A start had been made in late 1641 and early 1642 by a mixture of financial measures along traditional lines. Then in March 1642 it was decided to settle various charges connected with 'the late Scottish business' by raising a fixed sum— £400,000—to be levied on the counties according to specified proportions. Henceforward many taxing ordinances would be based on 'the rule of £400,000', which was supposed to bear some relation to the true distribution of wealth in the country. For each shire a committee of local men was named to see to the assessment and collection of the monies. In these committees can be discerned an element of continuity between peace and war, in that, in some counties at least, they derived from the petty sessions with the professional staffs (treasurers and clerks) which J.P.s had been forming well before 1640. They may also be associated with the elaborate arrangements made by Charles I for implementing his ship money writs. They are a good example of Pym's Tudor-like capacity to give a little extra to something that already existed. What he gave, together with what they themselves took, was enough to make them useful at once and, before long, indispensable in the day-to-day running of the provinces. They became indeed the norm of Interregnum local government and the forgotten ancestor of the modern county council.

Beginning with an assessment of London imposed just after the scare of Edgehill, Pym got the taxing of non-voluntary contributors extended to the whole country—so far, that is, as parliament's warrant ran. This 'weekly'—later 'monthly'—'pay' was collected by the county committees which were supposed to send the proceeds direct to the parliamentary Treasurer, Sir Gilbert Gerard, at the Guildhall, to be applied to the purposes of 'the State'. In fact a good deal of the money never left the counties, where subordinate commanders competed with the county treasurers for it. Sometimes garrison officers collected the pay in person to meet the needs of their own troops. They rarely had anything left over for the treasurer and out of his own resources he had little enough to send up to London. In 'frontier' regions, like Staffordshire, county treasurers might find that areas from which they were expected to extract funds were actually under the power of the enemy. Then there were places controlled completely by neither parliament nor the King's agents, sometimes compelled to pay both the weekly pay and the unsystematic levies of the royalists. At all levels raising money was a fortuitous business.

Parliament also sought funds by loans from its friends and confiscations from its enemies. Cash, but also weapons, food, plate and horses (much in demand) were from June 1642 raised from volunteers in the localities on 'the public faith' at eight per cent, 'according to the propositions of parliament'. By mid-1643 this had been extended by ordinance to compulsory levies, which if paid or provided in a given time were to have the same terms for repayment as the initial voluntary contributions. Throughout the war the county committees found a local use for these loans in cash or kind, and sometimes had it found for them by self-helping subordinates. The state also expected an income from the sequestration of the goods and estates of known royalists, an expedient which Pym eased through the Houses with the timely assistance of Charles, who by rejecting the peace proposals put to him at Oxford tipped 'the middle party' towards energetic reprisals. By this measure county committees could seize all property— real and personal—of 'delinquents' and two-thirds of that of convict recusants (even though not in arms), and must administer it for the benefit of the State. The profits were, once again, earmarked for the Guildhall, but in practice much stayed in the hands of the county committees or of their agents, who allowed themselves a wide discretion in interpreting the rules laid down in the ordinance and often drew up their own. By the time Westminster was ready to detach repentant royalists from action by allowing them to compound for their estates, some of the county committees had of their own initiative devised composition schemes, treating with wives, widows and, in some instances at least, the delinquents themselves. The intervention of a central Committee for Compounding was unwelcome. It stood for outside, uniform control which offended long-standing localisms in the way that Charles had done during the 'eleven years' tyranny'. It meant a grave drain on local revenues, to the maintenance of which 'wanton and insolent' state assessors accorded no priority. Moreover the central authority, ignorant of local conditions and opinions, might allow individual malignants to compound who would not have stood a chance of favour from the county committee itself. Such men, once discharged, might come home and, secure with their certificates, stir up trouble. In this as in so many ways the interests of Guildhall and Shire Hall were incompatible.

Supplementing the multifarious items of direct taxation introduced or extended in this expensive period was the excise, an indirect charge developed from Dutch models and akin to a scheme considered and prudently discarded by Charles I in 1627–8. It was, of course, unpopular. It still is. But it proved to be so lucrative, elastic and convenient that it became a permanent legacy of the rebellion, judged to be a valid substitute for the lost income of monopolies and the fiscal feudalism that the landed classes were not willing to have back with a King in 1660.

The profits of all these general taxes, together with a pile of special levies, ought perhaps to have been enough to pay for the war. They certainly exceeded the incidence of taxation under the peace-time monarchy. But in fact they could not cope with the mounting costs of winning either war or peace. So men who had once so indignantly resisted royal forced loans and billeting now found themselves subscribing with mingled feelings of embarrassment and defiance to free-quarter, organised seizure of chattels and, even, frank looting. Every régime of the Interregnum added to the burden of expenditure, and disposed of assets, like the royal and Church lands, without making much impression on the legacy of debts. The need of money was at the root of many of the worst evils of the Great Rebellion.

But as Pym saw it parliament wanted not only money, and administration and an army—but allies and some kind of national covenant equivalent to that of the Scots to evoke enthusiasm and consolidate it by giving men a sense of dedication to a great cause—the civilian version of the fighting spirit which dynamic commanders like Oliver Cromwell were trying to instil into their troops. Some such impetus was needed to keep men firm in the times of adversity which Pym knew must be gone through before the full effect of his constructive measures was felt. Before he died Pym had edged a way through opposition to pull both proposals—for an ally and for a 'band'—through the Houses. There is no greater tribute to Pym's superb parliamentary understanding than this. He died before he saw the harvest for which he laboured. Like Moses, who took pains for Israel for 40 years, he was not permitted to bring the host into Canaan. The men who took up where he put down were not of his calibre. The war was won, but in some ways the way was lost.

IX The First Year

When Charles raised his standard at Nottingham he was aware that he could not at once mount an all-out assault on London. His forces were tiny. Between them and the capital there was to be expected a considerable army under Essex, well equipped from the stores raised for the Scottish war and based on Hull. (Here lies the significance of the royal attempts to seize Hull earlier in the year. It was, in addition, a fortress of strategical possibilities; it could be a centre for the reception of aid from the continent, especially from the United Provinces where Charles's agents had been busy all through the summer.) The time for getting together great bodies of royalist troops had not yet come. The harvest was being gathered in and the big moment of the farmers' year was more vital to them than military adventure. So early in September Charles began to move south and west towards Wales, which he saw as one of his most likely recruiting grounds, and where it might be feasible to land troops from Ireland. In the counties through which he marched —Staffordshire, for instance—an uneasy neutrality was to persist even into early 1643, but as hopes of an early peace faded in the face of determined activities of a few enthusiasts on either side, something like an alignment of forces began to show itself.

On 23 September the royalists, well led by Prince Rupert, scored their first success, when at Powick Bridge, near Worcester, a cavalry charge dispersed a larger force of parliamentary troops. They were part of Essex's army covering the King's moves westward. Up to this point they might have made things difficult by seeking a large-scale engagement. With Powick Bridge and the royal successes under Hopton and Grenville in the south-west, initiative dropped from Essex's fingers. Charles picked it up. With winter coming on he felt he had to make at least an impressive gesture before the campaigning season petered out. Luck favoured him. He was able to by-pass the parliamentary army at Worcester and the morning of 23 October found him occupying the ridge of Edgehill, near Kineton, to the south-east.

The way seemed open to the capital, but Charles felt he had to strike a blow before moving on. In the battle that followed the two sides were about equal in numbers and it is difficult at any stage of the fighting to trace a clear trend of victory, in spite of the preachers' exhortations of the parliamentary troops. A fine cavalry charge by Rupert using 'new' Swedish tactics broke the parliamentary horse, but it was an advantage thrown away when he and his men dashed off the field in reckless pursuit. Their absence may well have robbed the royalists of clear-cut victory. Even so, the latest military historians of the war are no doubt right to find the weight of advantage going against Essex, who had failed to get back between the royalists and the capital.[1] But Charles was less certain of the effectiveness of his achievement, and, moreover, was visibly shaken by the horror of his first experience of war. He could not find it in him to push on to London as a blood-stained victor and instead settled in what were meant to be temporary headquarters at Oxford. As it happened that mellow city became the centre of his activities for the rest of the war. Meantime Essex, not at all put out by his lack of success, made his way by easy stages to London. There peace proposals were being drawn up which would wear out the winter in futile negotiations. At the same time steps were taken to raise men and money for future campaigns. Pulpits and pamphlets thundered out against the King and his high hand of 'iniquity and blood' stretched out against the parliament. Notions of resistance to a King were justified in this propaganda by appeals to the law of nature, and a path was being beaten down towards more and more radical political thinking. In monthly fasting days the support of God was invoked. Such activities as much as military manœuvres ensured that the war would be more than a passing episode.

In November Rupert, who could never sit still, made a sudden dart down the Thames Valley and took Brentford. Royalist hopes of taking the capital flared up. But the alarm was up and the City trained bands, traditionally by far the best equipped and disciplined local militia, marched out to join Essex under Skippon, apparently full of zeal and exaltation. At the appropriately-named Turnham Green 24,000 men faced the cavaliers. One look determined the King to withdraw to fight for London some other day (13 November). It never came. Still, even now, there was a chance to continue the discomfiture of London by crossing the Thames at Kingston and making for Kent, where the King could expect considerable and already active support. But as at Edgehill he hesitated, and lost. The campaigning season which had begun too late could be extended no longer. The winter was taken up by each side consolidating its positions. Oxford was fortified by massive earthworks and an outer ring of garrisons, including Banbury,

Burford, and Wallingford (which also protected communications between Oxford and Reading, the royalists' strong-point nearest to the capital). Soon Cirencester and Marlborough were taken to open up direct relations with the royalists in the west country.

The new year opened brightly there for the King. At Braddock Down (19 January 1643) Hopton's victory gained by volunteer troops rid him of the enervating localism of the county militia. Now Cornwall was firmly in the hands of King's men and the way was clear for wider enterprises all over the west. In the north, too, royalist forces under Newcastle seemed to be making headway. But elsewhere the bitter weather saw little but time-wasting and incoherent local struggles which had little or no impact on such grand strategy as was being evolved on either side. The civil war in Staffordshire has been characterised as 'shewing as little co-ordinated purpose as ducks on a pond'.[2] It is a comment that might apply to most subsidiary campaigns throughout the war. But no doubt the moves had a real meaning for the ducks.

The improvements in the King's position in the north and west encouraged in the spring of 1643 a three-pronged thrust towards the capital—from the north and from the west, cutting London off from the Channel, while the central (and main) army mopped up Essex's forces between Oxford and London and then launched a final assault. It was a good plan. Parliament's defensive positions around London were strong and moves were under way to co-ordinate activities by the formation of an Eastern and a Midlands Association, but the armies still lacked cohesion and a sense of common purpose. Moreover, as Edmund Waller's plot (May 1643), though a failure, revealed, there was the makings of a 'fifth'—in this case fourth—column within the parliamentary lines. In the City itself there were grumbles and distress caused, for example, by the cutting off of coal supplies from Newcastle-on-Tyne. But the King's plan called for immediate and uniform successes among the three armies. They did not come. Newcastle certainly moved forward, getting as far as Lincoln, but his Yorkshire levies hung back all the while Hull threatened their homes, and behind him Thomas Fairfax was beginning to turn into an able and energetic commander very ready to harass his lines of communication. Soon he was disputing with Newcastle the entire control of the north. In the west, things went better for the royalists. Hopton, tough and tireless, did things in threes. Stratton (16 May), Lansdown (5 July) and Roundway Down (13 July) helped Rupert's splendid capture of Bristol, second sea-port of the Kingdom and nucleus of a vital knot of communications, and led on to the overrunning of Dorset by the Earl of Carnarvon.

75

But in the centre the advance hung fire. Essex shook himself and took Reading. After mopping up Sussex and Hampshire, Sir William Waller, inevitably labelled 'William the Conqueror', a name not very attractive to the more radical of parliament's supporters, took command of a western association, and barred the way to South Wales (April). Oxford was in a weak position until Roundway Down and the capture of Bristol relieved the pressure. But June found Essex, keeping himself in 'fast' places, slowly tightening the ring around the King's headquarters. In an effort to break it, Rupert led a dashing cavalry raid up the Thames that reached a climax in an unexpected engagement at Chalgrove Field (18 June). This broke Essex's hold and opened up the Chilterns to royalist sallies. It also saw the death of John Hampden, a serious blow to morale, played down by parliamentary commentators, and to John Pym's political control. Hampden had been a thoroughly reliable link between Pym and Essex. Within a month of his death Essex was under attack from the City and irreconcilables in the House of Commons, who saw in his sluggish tactics something worse than incompetence.

Rupert's enterprise was not followed up. In the west Hopton found his men were not so flushed with victory that they would march farther eastward while parliamentary garrisons, like Plymouth, lay unreduced in their rear. Charles himself turned west not east, striking at Gloucester (August) in the confident hope that its commander Edward Massey would seize a chance to change sides. (Many men did change sides, even in the midst of battle. An analysis of their motives might shed a good deal of light on the issues at stake in the civil war.) Massey, as it happened, was not a turncoat, and his garrison continued to menace the royal lines of communications up the Severn and into South Wales.

In London John Pym found the need of every resource of talk and toughness to maintain his hold on parliament. The way the war was going encouraged two contradictory forces—those who saw nothing but arguments for coming to terms with the King, and those who urged a more ruthless prosecution in the field and drew nourishment from hot-heads and bugle voices in pulpit and press. Criticism that would have penetrated the hide of a rhinoceros pricked Essex into offering his resignation. To keep Essex and work with the Commons was difficult, but Pym knew that they could not cope with the royalists without Essex, especially as the Earl had a loyal band of officers who would live and die with him, but hardly with anyone else. So Essex stayed on and Pym made use of the panic to push through measures which in the long run would do more than a few isolated victories in the field to serve the cause. The surest ways to the restoration of morale and the will to win in the army were to provide more money more regularly for soldiers' pay, to secure an ally to stiffen military strength and, in particular, to strike at the enemy from the rear, and to evolve something more systematic for recruiting. In July 1643 ordinances designed to provide these passed the Houses. The assessment ordinances were renewed almost without discussion; the excise was broadened in scope; and a parliamentary committee, including the younger Sir Henry Vane, a brilliant diplomat, was sent to Scotland to work for the covenanters' intervention in England. Their negotiations were supplemented by a supplication of English ministers to the Scottish General Assembly that reveals something of the gloom that darkened parliamentary efforts at this time. 'If ever a poor nation were upon the edge of a most desperate precipice . . . we are that nation. . . . God hath sent a fire into our bones and it prevails against us. Oh, give us the brotherly aid of your re-enforced tears and prayers'.[3] The result was the Solemn League and Covenant of 17 August 1643. A few days before, an impressment ordinance marked the first long step away from county militia and voluntary levies to a professional army, towards the New Model, in fact, which, well after Pym had died, did finally win the war. These legislative successes meant that Pym was once again on top of things, an achievement symbolised in the expulsion of Sir Henry Marten, leader of the rabid war party, who, almost constantly opposing and jerking at 'old Pym', went too far when he roared that it were better that the whole royal family should perish than that the kingdom should. His departure left the war party high and dry, and Pym dominated the Commons for the rest of the year until his death in December.

Meantime in the field prospects were better. Soldiers and civilians alike were tinder to each little spark of hope. Essex, with the promise of supplies and reinforcements, shook off his torpor, began to march and on 8 September relieved Gloucester, and moving back with unwonted speed defeated the King, who had been racing towards the capital, at Newbury. Newbury meant the end, for 1643 at any rate, of the three-pronged royal lunge at the capital. Charles might retake Reading, but he was held up once again by the dead weight of Essex's forces. In the north Newcastle had won at Adwalton Moor (30 June), but a plot by the Hothams to give him Hull was scotched by the citizens. Fairfax became governor of this vital garrison and began to raise new and mobile troops. Successes, nothing much in themselves but piercing the gloom, were brought off by Oliver Cromwell, by now a deeply experienced commander, whose energy and enterprise were catching. Newcastle invested Hull at the beginning of August and found

77

himself bogged down. It was his opponents who were on the move. The Earl of Manchester took King's Lynn and moved north to raise the siege. Near Boston he was joined by Fairfax and Cromwell and at Winceby (11 October) their joint forces overran a royalist force and pushed on to take Gainsborough and Lincoln. Newcastle had no option but to turn away from Hull.

In the west, too, the tide turned against the King. Rupert's less able but still useful brother, Maurice, took Exeter and Dartmouth (4 September and 6 October 1643) but was held up at Plymouth, a more formidable and important enemy stronghold. If a southerly prong were to impinge on London, there would have to be some special army formed which could afford to forget about Devon in its rear. In October a new force was placed under Hopton's command with orders to drive through Dorset, Wiltshire and Hampshire, and on to the capital. Money, as always on the King's side, was tight, but Hopton did manage to get together a considerable force, including two regiments from Ireland, where Charles had in September made the 'cessation' that stuck in the gullets of so many enthusiastic protestants. However, parliament had in its turn created a new association under Sir William Waller, now eager to come, to see, to conquer after the summer's reverses. The fact that his old adversary Hopton confronted him was an additional stimulus. In November he failed to take Basing House and Hopton mocked him by seizing Arundel Castle (9 December). But the royalist forces were too thin on the ground to maintain their long lines and on 13 December Waller caught up with a part of them at Alton, near Farnham, and thrashed them soundly. Early in January 1644 Hopton lost Arundel and was only saved from worse disasters by the winter weather which brought the 1643 campaign to a standstill. Even this was only a temporary respite.

It is not too much to say that the King's failure in 1643 to bring off his grand plan determined the outcome of the war. There would be plenty of royalist successes to come and failures, both military and political, on the part of his enemies, particularly as a result of the discordant counsels which followed the death of Pym at the end of 1643. But never again would there come a military opportunity such as emerged from the initial successes of the three armies heading towards London. In addition, the dead Pym had left a living legacy of achievement that might falter but was surely capable of development. As we have seen, he had given parliament an administrative machine, the means of raising money, and had pointed the way towards a fighting army and an ally, strong in arms and strategically placed. Scottish armies probing from the north could break up any strategy that took in the whole country. Of course a price had to be paid for this new asset. The Scots would give brotherly aid and comfort if the English shewed themselves truly brethren by obliterating prelacy and accepting for the Church of England something like the Scottish system. The phrase was 'according to the word of God and the example of the best reformed Churches'.[4] The Scots never doubted that theirs was the best reformed church and no other example was called for. In addition they had demanded a joint command that should be political as well as military. Pym, who in 1641 was certainly no strong advocate of the extirpation of episcopacy, was yet ready in 1643 to pay the Scots' price. It did not mean that he had become a thorough-going presbyterian, but that he recognised that the Scots would not come in for less, and that if they did not come in, the war might be lost. We might otherwise be destroyed, he pointed out to a member who had conspicuous scruples about conniving at a belated root-and-branch destruction of bishops. Pym was, after all, a firm believer in politics as the art of the possible. It might be desirable to continue some kind of mild episcopacy in the religious organisation of England. It was certainly necessary to have the Scottish alliance. Desire clashed with necessity. Necessity won.

Pym did not believe in annihilation. Compromise was his very nature. What he wanted was to bring about a situation in which the King would abandon the appeal to force which smeared him, and genuinely reach out for reasonable terms with his people. Pym was not a republican, nor even a radical. What he wanted was an England in which King and parliament, trusting each other, worked as one for the common weal. At the moment the King could not be trusted. Very well, he must be brought to see that he must prove his trust and maintain it. That happy realisation would never come if he won the war. He must not win it. It must be won by men of Pym's inclination, men who could work together, give a little here and take a little there, and keep moving down the middle of the road. If there were obstacles, you could move round them, either to left or right, whichever was most convenient, and then carry on down the middle again. With such an outlook it is easy to see why Pym was not afraid to meet the Scots' immediate terms. Once the difficulties of the immediate situation had been resolved, there would be, he never doubted, room for manœuvre. Unfortunately his death meant that the Scottish alliance was implemented under different auspices, and the unity he had drawn out, not imposed, was dissipated. The real burden of the charge that can be made against John Pym is not that he was ruthless, deceptive, malicious, but that he did not train up a successor who could do what

79

he had done with the same grasp of political realities. There was, in fact, no King Pym II. Perhaps there could not have been.

Rifts, political and religious, were opening up among the 'rebels'. Diversities of opinion, and therefore of intended action, had been apparent long before the death of Pym, but it had been his peculiar genius to stop them breaking into too active life. He had fostered sufficient unity to work for peace and at the same time prosecute the war with energy and intelligence. Negotiation from a position of strength was essential if the King were ultimately to consider himself seriously bound by obligations. Among the out-and-out war men were some whose chief concern was for religion, even for religious toleration; others were developing something like a secular republicanism. They were, in fact, a very mixed bunch. Again, the 'peace party' was made up of almost contradictory groupings, but their religious outlooks were chiefly conservative, certainly not moving towards toleration. Their political and constitutional aims were guarantees for what had been so far achieved by the Long Parliament and for their own safety. In the middle groups variety was likewise the keynote, with perhaps a cooler secular outlook in general. Pym was a puritan of sorts—his half-brother, Francis Rous, to whom he was close, was a prolific puritan publicist and advocate of a 'preaching' ministry—but he was never in any way a fanatic. He approached religion empirically. Thus the Westminster Assembly of divines was given a wide field for manœuvre. Pym was ready to agree with the Scots on the introduction of some kind of presbyterianism in England. But neither he nor any major grouping in the Long Parliament was committed to a full-blooded Scottish system. The root-and-branch bill was a negative measure; against bishops, to be sure, but not for anything in particular and certainly not for setting up a church which would control the whole life of the community by high moral claims and would organise itself unchecked by the State. Root-and-branch was essentially Erastian. Nevertheless the hopes of the Scots had been puffed up by the alliance and they fully expected to bring their English brethren along their own straight and narrow path to God. But already—in fact even before the Long Parliament met—there were hopes in some circles of a kind of Independency, of a loose national church with a 'preaching' ministry in which a large, though perhaps not a complete, autonomy rested with the congregations, and in which some, even considerable, religious toleration was to be acceptable. This did not mean anarchy. The Independents were not sectaries, and it has been conclusively shewn that some of their appeal was to men more influential than 'tub preachers'. Certainly by 1644 men of substance like Sir Henry Vane, junr., Oliver Cromwell and Oliver St John were counted among them, and they could hope for some sympathy at any rate among members of parliament and, especially, army officers. Pym's alliance with the Scots they supported as essential from a military point of view, but they were alive to its likely religious and political defects. They, therefore, worked to maintain the league while mitigating the impact of the presbyterianism the Scots thought was written into the covenant. It was with this aim in mind that Vane had pushed for inserting the phrase 'according to the word of God' into the covenant. That word was open to a variety of interpretations. If nothing else, discussion would buy time. Moreover, if the formulation of a Church system was ostensibly in the hands of the aggressive divines of the Westminster Assembly, in fact they had to 'deale with the Houses of Parl(iament), upon which the Assembly doth altogether depend in their order of proceiding, and in taking particulars to their consideration'.[5] The critics of presbyterianism, though like Selden they baffled and vexed their opponents, might lose in the Assembly, but the final decisions would be taken elsewhere in Westminster and when in the end it was intended to implement presbyterianism, it was too late, even for what Baillie labelled 'a lame Erastian presbyterianism'.[6] (It is worth remarking that it was not only Independents and Erastians like Selden, but many of those labelled 'presbyterians' who contributed to the frustration of hopes of imposing a rigid calvinistic organisation.)

The evidence would suggest that following the Scottish alliance the Independents in the Parliament, together with those in the City— where it was reported that Hugh Peters, 'a very imprudent and temerarious man' fresh from Amsterdam, was 'ruling the roost'[7]—came more emphatically into a 'war party'. They knew that any accommodation with the King to which the Scots were a party would not bring toleration, unless the advocates of toleration were in a very strong position indeed. So Independency must grow not only in parliament and in the City, but also in the army. Men like Cromwell wanted soldiers under their command who knew what they fought for and loved what they knew. 'The State in choosing men to serve it takes no notice of their opinion: if they be willing faithfully to serve it, that satisfies'.[8] It meant encouragement of enthusiasm and a readiness to tolerate diversity. The withdrawal of many presbyterian army chaplains to comfortable livings and to wars of the voice and pen in the Westminster Assembly left the way open to men of a more Independent, tolerant turn of mind. It is, no doubt, easy to exaggerate the extent of liberal ideas, political and religious, held by these men, but the fact remains that under the pressure of some of them, directed by energetic and intelligent officers, the army was by 1644 becoming a force to be reckoned with, not only in the field by the royalists, but in the realms of political and religious decision by parliament itself.

These developments in the army would lead to greater problems by and by; but even now there were acute tensions on the anti-royalist fronts. The Lords, for instance, were very suspicious of the Commons and of the proposal to set up a Committee of Both Kingdoms. An ordinance prepared in the Lower House proposed to hand over to such a committee, in which the Lords considered they were inequitably represented, the right to order and direct all military operations. Up to now the Lords, like the Commons and even such lesser institutions as the county committees, had interfered with all manner of military details, and they were reluctant to let slip their vestiges of power. But under pressure the ordinance setting up the committee for an initial three months did pass in February 1644. This can be considered a victory for the 'war party', especially set against the widespread desire for peace. In winter the burden of taxation seemed heavier. Chill winds, some of them economic, and empty grates upset civilian stomachs. But March brought daffodils and a sharp victory at Cheriton (29 March). The sap and hearts began to rise. The King, his own worst enemy in war as in peace, helped by further dabbling with foreign powers, trying, for instance, to get Dutch aid by pushing a match for the Prince of Wales. His non-too-delicate probings brought him as usual nothing but the renewed suspicions of his opponents, strengthening the hands of those who shouted that he could not be trusted. And this time he confirmed them by dubious proffers in Ireland. There he had to consider giving in to the demands of the catholics and those of the protestants. Most of his supporters in England would not agree to any Irish agreement that left the protestants there unsafe, while the catholics would not support him unless they felt themselves secure. Negotiations were handed over to Ormonde to gain time. They did so in Ireland, but the King's opponents could point melodramatically to his apparent readiness to give England over to bloodstained rebels, papist and Irish, and therefore scarcely human. The sentiment which supported the Cromwellian and later the Restoration settlements in Ireland was growing in this period. Thus Scotland and Ireland made in a variety of ways an urgent contribution to English developments during the Interregnum.

x Without Pym

On 19 January 1644, a little more than a month after John Pym was carried to his grave in Westminster Abbey, a Scottish army under the veteran Leslie (with Argyll as president of a mixed army committee) trudged through the snow into England. It was well trained—many of the officers were fresh from service in Holland, France and Germany. The morale of the 20,000 men (including 3,000 cavalry) was reported to be high, based as it was on a promise of regular English pay and the feeling that they had come in more or less on their own terms, at a time when intervention might be decisive. Six months before that army might have been merely a desperate shot in the arm to revive the flagging spirits of discontented and defeated English forces. But now prospects were brighter and the two sides better balanced. Perhaps the Scots could swing things in favour of parliament, helping themselves by helping their English brothers. Spalding, a fierce anti-covenanter, commented,

> 'Ressone wold say we had gottin oure willis, and thairfoir we might leive in rest and peace. No, no, it must go utherwayes. England has gottin oure turne done, and we must help to sie thame get thair turne done also in all thingis both in kirk and pollecielyke unto our government, quhairin if England happnit not to prevaill, then oure groundis so surely establishit wes to be "feirit" and the king micht cum bak upone ws and rovock all what he had done'.[1]

The King condemned the League and Covenant as soon as he heard about it, writing that even had the Houses of Parliament been in a more full and free condition than they now were they would still have no right to send commissioners to negotiate anything, nor could anyone in Scotland receive them. 'But what is the mater, no obedience!', remarked Spalding.[2] Charles went on to protest that he had 'religiously' maintained the articles he had undertaken with the Scots; any breach was their responsibility. Taking a leaf from parliament's book, the Scots claimed they were marching not against the King himself but a malignant, papistical party in arms.

Once over the border Leslie moved on the old target, Newcastle, and raised the Londoners' hopes of warm homes for the rest of the winter. But the royalist governor refused to surrender to an army bent on offensive war against a natural sovereign in the bowels of another kingdom, and conniving with the pernicious counsels and acts of a 'close committee', the English parliament. About the same time the royalist peers at Oxford appealed to the Scots to retire before there was an effusion of blood and which 'all the Englishmen must interpret as a design of conquest and to impose new laws upon us'.[3] These sentiments were an ironical echo of the fears of parliamentarians who in 1641 had condemned Strafford for aiming precisely at that. There is no evidence that they felt embarrassed in 1644.

Even before the coming of the Scots the King's hopes of a dash southwards by his northern armies were fading. A new army formed under Lord Byron, chiefly from troops released from Ireland by the cessation there, had done well in the autumn of 1643 in Cheshire, but had been destroyed at Nantwich by a joint force under Fairfax, and the energetic local leader, Sir William Brereton. The situation was so serious that Rupert was sent north to stiffen morale and to plan to meet the Scottish threat. Rupert achieved some stability in the Midlands by relieving Newark (21 March) which had been closely invested by Sir John Meldrum. Consequently the Marquis of Newcastle was able to move up to Durham to harry the supply lines of the Scots who had now reached South Shields. He won a few skirmishes, but early in April Selby fell to the mobile Fairfax and the Marquis had to retire from Durham. On 18 April he entered York. Four days later an Anglo-Scots force under Leven and Fairfax sat down around him. Rupert, ever-ready, started to march to his relief, but was called back to Oxford to give advice in the ticklish problems arising for the King there. With the start of the campaigning season in the south and west, a cavalier army under the Earl of Forth and Hopton had come upon William the Conqueror's army in Hampshire, this time reinforced by a couple of thousand cavalry from Essex, who himself still sat astride the Thames Valley between the two capitals.

The two sides, eager and energetic after a winter rest, came to blows at dawn on 29 March at Cheriton, near Alresford. The royalists did well but their cavalry, too enthusiastic, weakened a strong position by indiscipline. After a hard day's fighting they were forced to retreat towards Oxford. The whole of Hampshire was now in Waller's hands.

The King's forces could no longer hope to get to London *via* the west and south. Weakness in the centre meant that the three-pronged fork was bent and buckled. But the King did not intend to waste time clinging to prepared positions and letting too many of his men get restless and indolent in the enervating atmosphere of garrisons, especially now there were signs that this spring even Essex intended to stretch his legs. So in April Charles began to get together a field force. It meant drawing in troops from the army defeated at Cheriton, and as we have seen, the recall of Rupert from North Wales. The prince, certainly the best strategist on the King's side, wanted to maintain for the present as strong a defensive ring as might be around Oxford, to keep Essex uncertain and therefore, perhaps, immobile, while Rupert's brother Maurice mopped up the west and he himself pushed forward his scheme for the relief of York. This must be done quickly since Newcastle had indicated he would surrender unless help came by 4 July.

Charles thought these proposals sound enough and Rupert hurried back content to Shrewsbury to mount his campaign. But as soon as his back was turned, other counsel, as so often, worked its way with the King. Clean contrary to Rupert's plan he withdrew troops from Reading and Abingdon, vital in the ring of garrisons. Essex promptly took them over and, elated at the prospect of further easy pickings, started to march. What followed was too complicated to be told in detail here. Charles, tired of being cooped up in Oxford, made a sudden sortie into the Cotswolds. From three directions Essex (Thames Valley), Waller (Hampshire) and Denbigh (Worcestershire) moved towards him. It looked as if they might catch the royal force, but Essex turned aside to relieve Lyme, fearing that if it came into the hands of Maurice it might effectively protect the main supply routes of the King's armies. A decision there, he felt, might determine the whole fate of the west. Perhaps he was right, but the timing was unfortunate. Lyme was saved (15 June) but by then the King had slipped through the net and was on his way back to Oxford. The Committee of Both Kingdoms—over the protests of the Lords, who still saw Essex as a favourite son—rebuked Essex for his ineptitude and ordered him to step back quickly towards Oxford. His sharp reply shews all the traditional impatience of the plain military man plagued by ignorant civilians. 'Pardon me, if I make bold to order and direct my own Major-General', he wrote sarcastically.[4]

At Cropredy Ridge, near Banbury, Charles made contact with Waller (29 June 1644). It was a fierce engagement in which for a time Charles himself was under fire. Narrow victory went to the royalists, who now slipped unmolested back into Oxford.

The inability of the parliamentary armies to check the insolent meanderings of the King threw into even clearer relief the need for some effective central command and for forces with the willingness as well as the capacity to move anywhere in pursuit of a co-ordinated intelligent plan. There were too many masters in the field, and at Westminster the Committee of Both Kingdoms was finding how easy it was to run into trouble and brawls when the political arts and tactics of a John Pym were lacking. The Committee—the first formal expression of Anglo-Scottish union before 1707—was made up of seven nominated English peers and 14 M.P.s, with four Scottish commissioners. The English members included the principal commanders—Essex, Waller, Manchester and, significantly, Oliver Cromwell. But these men were commonly in the field and it was unavoidable that the deliberations of the Committee should be chiefly those of the civilian members, such as Sir Arthur Haselrig. A quorum of eight (including two Scots) met regularly at Derby House 'to advise, consult, order and direct, concerning the carrying on and managing of the wars for the best advantage . . . and the keeping a good intelligence between the three kingdoms, their forces, committees and counsels', including negotiations with foreign states, a field in which Sir Henry Vane was particularly adept. Vane and St John, who had been instrumental in the setting up of the Committee, were in effect leaders of 'a war group', given their head by the death of Pym, but still up against the dead-weight of a peace party, strongly entrenched in the Commons, and more so in the Lords. Vane and his friends were able to insist that any negotiations with the King must be made through the Committee of Both Kingdoms. This was useful since it meant they could hold off serious discussions until military successes hardened the terms they would offer.

So the spring of 1644 saw the 'win the war' groupings getting on top. But there were snags. Whatever happened at Westminster, commanders were unable, if not downright unwilling, to work together. There was still the blind localism of troops who saw victory in a single battle as the end of a campaign, justifying a return home. Always there grew the problem of supplies and pay. Appeals to the City, as suggested in April by Essex, might bring temporary sustenance, but nothing consistent and permanent could be built on such an uncertain basis. Then in May the first term of the Committee ran out before a re-appointing ordinance could pass the Lords, who true to form, were trying to modify composition and powers in favour of men of peace. By a piece of sharp, very sharp, practice Vane did get the Committee renewed with almost universal powers—on paper (22 May). Essex continued to smoulder and to flout its orders, and it had hardly more luck in its dealings with lesser commanders who, whatever they may have thought of Essex, shared his contempt for civilian interference.

But now in the summer of 1644 military interest had passed from Essex and Waller in the south to the north where Rupert was speeding to the relief of York. If he could bring it off, something might yet be done to hold the north for the King. By the end of May he had taken—and rudely sacked—puritan Bolton, 'the Geneva of England', and Stockport. Lord Derby, whose wife was still incredibly holding out after three months' siege in Lathom House, could still call upon the duties of some of his tenants, who, now that the parliamentary pressure on Lancashire was relaxing, flocked in their thousands to join the King's glamorous nephew. When Rupert reached Wigan on 5 June he was feted, and had a sufficient force for the relief of York. But for once he was taking no chances. Before moving east he turned to seize Liverpool to use as a channel through which Irish forces could come in to reinforce whatever successes he might achieve. It was a sensible move but gave his opponents more time to build up their resources in Yorkshire. Fairfax and the Scots were joined before York by Manchester, flushed with successes in Lincolnshire. However, the news of Rupert's bloody progress had alarmed the Committee of Both Kingdoms and early in June Sir Henry Vane was sent to the leaguer at York to get the commanders to see what could be done to check the prince before he became too strong. (Vane also sounded the generals on the possibility—it was no more than that—of declaring the deposition of the King.) Fairfax and Manchester were both reluctant to weaken the siege, and preferred to deal with Rupert when, as he was bound to do, he turned up at York. Then, they argued, if they beat him all Lancashire and Yorkshire would fall to them. But Rupert's advance was quicker than anyone had dreamed it could be and on 29 June, although Newcastle was clearly almost at the end of his resources, the parliamentary generals decided to leave the siege and march out to meet the relieving forces. They concentrated on the Knaresborough road which surely Rupert must use. By 1 July they were at Marston Moor, half a dozen miles west of York, ready for battle. Rupert, always unpredictable, left them to it, and making a long detour towards Boroughbridge, crossed the Ure and moved along the north bank of the Ouse, well away from the allied armies. There was nothing they could do. At nightfall he was in York.

But not to stay. Rupert was eager to get to grips with the allies, particularly as he had a letter from the King which he read, rightly, as an emphatic order to knock out the Scots. Dawn on 2 July saw the royalists moving up to Marston Moor. The allies had begun to spread

87

out with a view to cutting Rupert's communications, but during the day they came together again. Rupert held off, waiting for reinforcements from Newcastle to join him in an attack on the morrow. But unexpectedly the initiative passed to the allies who at dusk made a full-scale assault. For two hours the fight raged without a clear advantage to either side. Taken by surprise, the royalists fought back so energetically that panic fear took hold of some among the Scots at any rate. But, at the last, victory went to the allies, thanks in part to the stern discipline of Cromwell's cavalry—'the Ironsides', as Rupert ruefully named them.

Marston Moor saw the disintegration of a fine army and the end of the royalists' chances of a real come-back in the north. Apart from their material losses, there was the surge in morale it gave to the enemy. 'Behold, in a moment, when our credit was beginning sensiblie to decay, God has come in',[5] exulted Robert Baillie. Newcastle gave up the struggle and slipped off into voluntary exile. Rupert, more resilient, got together a band of troops and within three weeks was back in Shropshire looking for work. York, left to its fate, capitulated on 20 July. Newcastle garrison was taken and the city sacked by the ungentle Scots early in October. Soon only a few isolated, and mostly purposeless, garrisons were left. Marston Moor was, in fact, a decisive turning point in the war, followed as it was by moves within parliament and army which led on to the formation of the New Model and the temporary eclipse of peace parties.

All this while the complicated and shifting divisions within the parliamentary alignments had survived. Pym had been able to cope with them, even to make use of them in House and committee to effect his positive policies. His death, as we have seen, made them more confused and more dangerous, nowhere more than in the military command. When the war, which no one really wanted and everyone had hoped would be short, began, both sides tried to secure control of the ramshackle militia system, supplementing it with regiments, raised by magnates like Lords Paget or Brooke, who often to start with paid for them out of their own resources. Like the officers who commanded them, the regiments were of very mixed quality, and frequently if not always under full strength. Most of them were rabidly local in outlook. They had little stomach for long marches and thought the problems of even neighbouring areas very trivial when put beside the security of their own 'countries'. When they won they were often more inclined 'to visit their friends' or families than to prepare for the next stage of a campaign. The royalist Hopton found his splendid Cornishmen dragging their heels once across the Tamar, and the City trained bands who did such a fine job at Turnham Green—even that was a close thing—were less enthusiastic when they were ordered to move 'to the fields' outside[6] the home counties. As late as June 1644 it was claimed that if the pressures on the King forced him to march northward, he would hardly be followed by those armies which consisted of Londoners, for it was never heard that any force or inclination could lead them so far from home.

Moreover, command on parliament's side, at least, was grasped by locally-minded authorities. The county committees, even when associated, were every one loth to relax their grip on their own forces and found it easy to turn a blind eye to wider interests. (Impressment of soldiers from 1643 did hardly anything to improve on this situation.)

Unity was not to be looked for at the local level but even in the higher reaches of command clashes were frequent. Essex may have been Commander-in-Chief, but he complained bitterly that he was never sure from whom he was to expect orders and to whom he was to give his own. He found himself competing with a host of lesser commanders and authorities for men, money and equipment. The Scottish alliance and the setting up of the Committee of Both Kingdoms made things worse for a time. Complete agreement between allies on the conduct of a war has been notoriously rare, and in this instance England and Scotland had traditional as well as immediate differences to overcome. There was also the suspicion of strong groups in the parliament, mostly in the Lords, of the aims of the Committee of Both Kingdoms. Civilians distrusted military men, soldiers despised politicians. Agreement was far to seek on how to win the war, or even on whether the war ought to be won at all. Peace parties blocked progress at Westminster, peace parties inhibited forthright action in the field. Marston Moor only tightened the tensions. The great victory won there ought soon to have brought the King to his knees. Instead enthusiasts like Cromwell saw its promises being frittered away in dilatory, if not downright obstructive tactics. The Scots had gone off to grab the port of Newcastle while sections of the victorious English army broke away to sit on their bottoms in garrisons which in the absence of serious royalist threats in the north were redundant. Elsewhere the war was by no means over.

In the south Essex, having (as we have seen) relieved Lyme, went off to do the same for Plymouth. A royalist force began closely to follow him. After Plymouth he wandered into Cornwall, with the apparently laudable object of cutting off that export of tin which was helping Charles to buy arms and supplies from the continent. But Essex had miscalculated. The country rose against him and early in August 1644 he was cut off by forces coming up from the east. The

89

Committee of Both Kingdoms took alarm and ordered Waller to go to his assistance, but Waller, for whatever reasons, was slow off the mark.

Inexorably the royalists closed in on Essex, hemming him in on a narrow neck of land around Lostwithiel. Essex, who had a keen eye for the obvious, made off himself by sea. Some of his cavalry broke through the royalist net, but the infantry surrendered on 2 September. The victors, who could not cope with so many prisoners, allowed them to march away bearing their colours but without arms, and under parole not to fight again until they reached Portsmouth.

It was a great boost for the King, and humiliation for his foes. Essex was to blame and men, even Robert Baillie, were not slow to say so. Was it for this, they asked, that brave and active men had won at Marston Moor? Had they accepted heavy taxation, impressment, free quarter, death itself for this? The King was still out and about. The war had been fought for two years—must they still grope uncertainly after final victory? Fortunately Charles, who might now have risked a rapid march on London, was himself too cautious or dilatory. He let himself get held up before Plymouth and there was time for parliamentary forces under Waller, Manchester and Essex, who had without shame regrouped his army at Portsmouth, to move between him and the old target. Even so, there was little unity among them. Within each army there were squabbles and back-biting, as in Manchester's, where Crawford and Cromwell hit out recklessly at each other. The command of the whole force was vested in a committee made up of the general and two civilian representatives from the Committee of Both Kingdoms. Essex fell ill and the highest-ranking field commander was Manchester, 'a sweet meek man'[7] without much martial enterprise. Under these dubious auspices the second battle of Newbury (27 October) was fought. Victory of a sort went to the parliamentary forces, who had an immense advantage in numbers. Yet once again it was not followed up. Somehow the King got safely back to Oxford and the 1644 campaigning season came to an end, with the royalists still very much in the fight.

Winter brought respite to the soldiers, but did nothing to ease the animosities in the debating-chamber and the committee-room. Soon after Marston Moor, Leven, Fairfax and Manchester sent a letter to the Committee of Both Kingdoms calling for an early settlement of Church government along presbyterian lines and for coming to terms with the King. It is true, they added, that the best way to procure it was to continue their joint efforts, but to men of Cromwell's impatient temper the whole tenor of this appeal was irritating. Cromwell had no heart for the bringing in of presbyterianism merely to please the Scots, whom he suspected of not doing as much fighting as they might. He chafed at inaction and made no effort to disguise his detestation of the bungling and slackness that had wasted the opportunity won in blood at Marston Moor. The moderation of Essex and Manchester seemed to him like a betrayal of the cause itself. He himself was always ready for the foe and was gathering about him and under his command men who shared his initiative—and his religious and political feelings. He worked hard to stir up in Manchester a sense of urgency and a willingness to take risks. But the Earl was unimpressed and those officers—not a few—who despised Independents and sectaries stuck by him. Manchester's army—that of the Eastern Association—was becoming as divided within itself as it was from the other field forces. At Derby House, the Committee of Both Kingdoms could not fail to be aware how these differences were putting the whole cause in jeopardy and some members were inclined to share Cromwell's irritation, especially against the Scots. But the Commons and the Peers would certainly not go all the way with them in condemning the old army command. Indeed, the Houses had reacted to Essex's defeat in the west by thanking him for his conduct, though Sir Arthur Haselrig could not restrain a snort of mocking laughter when the draft was read out.

By September the disputes in the army of the Eastern Association were so violent that Manchester, Cromwell and Crawford came up to Westminster to see if they could get something settled. Cromwell, who had more than a mere back-bencher's political grasp, soon sensed that a majority in the Commons would not go all the way with him. He withdrew a demand for Crawford's dismissal, contenting himself with the promise that the army would be moved west in search of action.

At the same time he managed to get the Houses to issue an order for 'the Committee of Lords and Commons appointed to treat the Commissioners of Scotland and the Committee of the (Westminster) Assembly (to) take into consideration the differences of the opinions of the members of the assembly in point of church-government, and to endeavour an union if it be possible'.[8] If this could not be brought about, then some way should be sought for the relief of tender consciences who could not in all things submit to the common rule. It was a considerable feat to get this 'high and unexpected' 'accommodation order' through the Commons without a division. Presbyterians such as Baillie saw at once the dangers of such a 'high and mightie plot', and prayed for Scottish victories in the north, which alone might bring pressure enough to thwart the claims for toleration. Their anxiety was understandable—presbyterianism had not yet been decided on, let alone implemented. 'This', lamented Baillie, 'this is the fruit of their disservice, to obtaine really ane Act of Parliament for their tolleration, before we have gotte any thing for Presbytrie either in Assemblie or Parliament.'⁹

The campaign that culminated in the second battle of Newbury was partly a distraction and partly the cause of a quickening pace of development. Charles managed to relieve Donnington Castle (9 November) where his baggage lay, and to get back safe to Christ Church College (23 November). At the council of war held after that humiliation Cromwell spoke boldly of the need for a sense of immediacy and determination to attack and keep on attacking. Manchester objected that if they beat the King nine and ninety times, yet he was King still. 'But if the King beat us once, we shall be hanged.' Logic, at least, was on Cromwell's side when he expostulated 'My Lord, if this be so, why did we take arms at first? This is against fighting ever hereafter. If so, let us make peace be it never so base.'¹⁰

The matter could not rest there. The parties to the dispute were mostly members of one House or the other and were bound to air their views at Westminster. On 22 November the Commons asked Waller and Cromwell in their capacities of members of the Committee at Derby House to report on the recent mishaps that had befallen the armies. Cromwell responded with a forthright criticism of the Earl of Manchester as 'most in fault', not from ill luck, but 'through his backwardness to all action', and that not merely from 'dullness' but from 'some principle of unwillingness to have this war prosecuted into a full victory and a design or desire to have it ended by an accommodation . . . to which it might be disadvantageous to bring the King too low'.¹¹ This was not a vague charge irresponsibly flung out but was one backed with a circumstantial account of Manchester's part in the recent campaigns. Apparently it gave great satisfaction to the Commons who made no difficulty about referring it to a committee. Manchester hit back by charging Cromwell with impugning the honour of the House of Peers and straining the bonds between England and the Scots. Already the dispute had gone beyond personalities. A breach between the two Houses seemed imminent. On 2 December in a written statement Manchester accused Cromwell of faction and, curiously, of inertia. He appealed to the corporate sense of the peers by repudiating Cromwell's representation of them as clogs upon the efforts of the lower House, thinking solely of the security of their large estates. Cromwell had also, he asserted, mocked the Assembly of divines. But in the Commons committee Cromwell's own charges, supported by Haselrig and a knot of keen army officers, made more impact. His field reputation contrasted sharply with the implication of inertia, and there was no doubt at all of Manchester's own lack of achievement. The claim by the Earl's supporters that he had been hampered by lack of resources was not widely accepted.

While these recriminations went on at Westminster, commissioners had waited upon the King. He reminded them that in no circumstances would he abandon his Church, his crown and his friends, but otherwise seemed willing enough to talk. So peace-lovers took heart and hinted at proceeding against Cromwell, 'that darling of the Sectaries', as 'an incendiary'.[12] But Sergeant Maynard and Mr Whitelocke, both full of law, reminded them that proof was sadly lacking. Cromwell himself leaped in. He suggested that in the recent troubles many in the army had been at fault. What if they all as members of either House in some positive way denied themselves and their private interests for the public good? Out of the inevitable debate something concrete emerged, proposed by the staunch presbyterian Zouch Tate and supported by the radical Sir Henry Vane—the frame of a 'self-denying ordinance' to the effect that during time of war no member of either House should hold any office or command. On the face of it this meant the removal of Cromwell as well as of Manchester and so could be represented as a conciliatory gesture. Much to the disgust of Baillie, to whom it seemed 'a dream . . . the bottom of which was not understood',[13] it quickly passed the Commons with the mingled support of most groupings. What seems to have happened is that Cromwell and his allies had sensed that no attempt to get rid of Manchester and Essex could succeed in the teeth of the Peers' solidarity in defence of their order and against the dead-weight of the peace parties in the Commons. Yet earlier in the month the Commons had urged on the Committee of Both Kingdoms the need to consider 'a frame or model' for a new organisation of the army. This suggested that a wind of change might blow effectively through the House. If parliament could be induced to go on with the question of a new model while the old commanders resigned, ostensibly of their own free will, the winter might be used to plan an effective, perhaps final, campaign for next year. But the Lords jibbed.

When on 13 December the proposed ordinance was sent up they laid it aside in favour of what they thought really important business— discussing the negotiations which had now opened with agents of the King at Uxbridge, and contemplating the fate of William Laud, former archbishop of Canterbury. This feeble old man had all summer and autumn been defending himself against the accusation, backed by the reports of that tireless nibbler of documents, William Prynne, that he had attempted to subvert the religion and, of course, the fundamental laws of England. In October the Commons had dropped his

93

impeachment and had turned to the same expedient that had got rid of a far more dangerous enemy, Strafford—attainder, this time by ordinance. The Lords wobbled for a time, but on 4 January 1645 finally concurred. On 10 January Laud was executed, his pathetic attempt to gain a respite by producing a royal pardon brusquely rejected. He met death with dignity and courage, emulating the example of his friend Strafford and offering a pattern for his King. The gravamen of the charge against him was that he had made innovations in the Church of England, yet the very day that the Lords condemned him, they accepted ordinances to set up a directory of worship on presbyterian lines and abolishing the prayer book.

The attainder of Laud, then, was quite pointless; he was no threat to anyone and time was already running out for him. His execution was not likely to smooth the way to an agreement with the King. But it served to hold off for a while the problem of what should be done about the proposed self-denying ordinance. On 7 January the Peers put it aside on the ground that 'a new model' army was a more urgent need than blanket changes in the present command. True enough, and the committee at Derby House had been discussing it for weeks. The response to the Lords was to quicken that consideration. On 9 January a 'new model' ordinance was brought into the Commons, passing without a division. On the 13th, the Lords, vaguely aware that they were being managed, threw out the self-denying ordinance, indicating, as Gardiner puts it, 'if there was to be a New Model they wished their own members to be at the head of it'.[14] But the Commons voted on the 21st that Sir Thomas Fairfax—an able and more or less unpolitical officer—should command the new army, with Philip Skippon as his Major-General and 'A.N. Other' as Lieut.-General. Still the Lords did not hurry to co-operate.

XI The War Won

At Uxbridge negotiations continued. Cromwell and his supporters were sure that they must ultimately fail, but were willing for them to go on, in the expectation that Charles's rigidity on the Church question and his slipperiness on the militia would exasperate the Scots and tax the most sanguine of the appeasers in parliament. They were right. On 4 February the Peers did pass the new model ordinance, though with a proviso on the appointment of officers which in effect would have given them a veto. Yet it was a step forward. A mutiny at Leatherhead among soldiers with little but complaints to occupy their time was only one of a number of signs of deterioration in morale and order, sure to worsen unless something effective was done. Since the King offered nothing acceptable, what else could the Lords do now but accept the new model ordinance in its original form?

At last parliament was laying the basis for a national force for general service, free of local ties, uniform and uniformed. War was recognised as a serious business—none too soon, for the spring campaigning season had started. Cromwell and his officer cronies were already out in the field—which they could not have been if the self-denying ordinance had been passed earlier. The situation was not a happy one. In Scotland, Montrose, poacher turned gamekeeper, was setting the Highlands alight in the King's behalf. (It was poor compensation for parliament that he was also binding the covenanters more firmly to the English alliance.) In Ireland the Earl of Glamorgan, whose financial support of the King had been prodigal, was meditating far-reaching schemes involving the Irish Catholic Confederacy and half the catholic powers of Europe, not excluding the Pope himself. That even if the combinations had been likely Glamorgan was not the man to bring them off did not mean they could be ignored. Moreover, tireless Henrietta Maria, 'the she-generalissima', was working on Mazarin, the Prince of Orange, the Duke of Lorraine and who knew whom else for the invasion of England or at least for supplies. There was enough substance in these negotiations to stiffen the resolution of parliament at a time when internal divisions ought to have weakened it. The proposed New Model Army seemed the sole ray of light breaking through clouds heavy with disaster. From being the expression of the machinations of a faction, it had become—for a while—the symbol of a cause, pointing thinly to security.

So Fairfax and Skippon confidently started to form their new army. Early in March a move by a group of lords, among them Essex, to exclude some known Independents nominated as officers was rejected, revealing the new urge to action among even the presbyterians. On 11 March Fairfax was empowered to take any officers and soldiers from the armies of Essex, Manchester and Waller. The direct attack on Manchester and the rest which Cromwell had started could now be dropped. They would no longer have armies to command, and like old soldiers they might have been safely left to fade away.[1]

To meet future troubles a new self-denying ordinance was brought into the Commons and finally emerged from the Lords on 3 April. It required all members of either House at present holding appointments to surrender them within 40 days. In fact Essex, Manchester and Denbigh had laid down their commissions the day before the ordinance was accepted. On 9 April Warwick, the Lord High Admiral, also resigned and his office was put in commission. Both Houses recorded without irony their approval of their high sense of duty. So the 'quarrel' came to an end, and in a way that squared more with the interests of the Independents than did the original draft of the self-denying ordinance, for there was now no legal objection to members being reappointed after once resigning.

Waller had lately complained that his troops for want of pay—they were two years in arrears—were uncommandable and he wished that he were back in parliament giving his aye or nay. By the self-denying ordinance the Conqueror got his well-earned rest. Those of his troops that were ready to continue were absorbed into the New Model, attracted by the promise of regular if not generous pay, secured by fixed taxes upon the counties. No investigations into class or religious outlook were insisted upon, and though officers were expected to take the covenant, the common soldiers were not. Some of the officers, who included a cobbler, a drayman and a ship's chandler, were in fact of 'mean' origins, but the majority were men of substance. In spite of the covenant, it is fair to describe the officers and the army as an Independent force. But in the Houses the Independents were less successful. Their numbers there were reduced in practice by the return of officer M.P.s to their duties in the field, and indirectly by the return to parliament of those of a different inclination who had lost their occupation by the self-denying ordinance. But for the moment they were content to set about winning the war. By and by they could win the peace.

Oliver Cromwell, whom many thought to be the real author of the self-denying ordinance, continued to hold his commission. When Waller resigned he offered to do so too, but the Committee of Both Kingdoms had an immediate task for him in the new campaigns that were opening up. From 20 April he was on active service. He was the obvious candidate for the vacancy of Lieutenant-General (second-in-command) of the New Model and on 10 June the Commons offered him the appointment. A few days later the Lords gave a grudging confirmation, but limited the command to three months. By then Naseby had been fought and won.

The 1645 campaigns began in the west, where the debauched but enterprising Goring interrupted the pleasant routine of a few smug parliamentary garrisons. At Oxford and elsewhere Rupert effervesced, trying to put some sparkle into the gloomy royalist forces. He had some reason for his optimism. The north was gone and the west hung precariously but the forces of parliament and its allies were very uncoordinated, the Scots being mainly around Newcastle and the New Model still in the making. Royalist hearts could leap too at the news of the miraculous achievements of Montrose. The Highlands were now falling to him, and the Lowlands must follow. Certainly the covenanters thought so and sent back the flower of their army to contest with him. As it happened his troops were undisciplined and thought more of plunder than of the King. His strategy, too, was weak. Yet in that brisk spring of 1645 he was an inspiration to the King and his supporters. Moreover, the Committee of Both Kingdoms, prone still to disagreements and distractions, was again interesting itself in military command and was capable of bungling it. Charles's position was, then, by no means desperate. All he needed, he might well feel, was resolution and a little luck.

The plan to march into the west and bring all royalist forces there into a unified command was held up by squabbles between the commanders and the Prince of Wales's council, the King's local agency, and by the rising of the club-men—anti-war activists—in Worcestershire and Herefordshire. Rupert had to waste time by turning aside to deal with them. The scheme was finally frustrated by Cromwell's capture of Bletchington House (24 April), which brought his baggage and artillery trains to a halt, and opened a prospect of bottling the King up in Oxford—if other forces could move up quickly in support. But Fairfax and the nucleus of the New Model had already been directed by the Committee of Both Kingdoms to go to the relief of Taunton. Their absence let Charles slip out to join Rupert at Stow-on-the-Wold for a council of war. He seems at this time to have contemplated a rapid march northward, perhaps to join Montrose, who had spoken of coming into England at the head of a brave army to win back the north. This would certainly have disturbed the balance in the whole of Great Britain. But the council of war, as usual, put contradictory proposals. Rupert was, of course, for the northern project, but Goring and Digby (always inimical to the Prince) spoke up for complete concentration on the west. In the event Charles tried to combine the two suggestions by sending Goring into the west and the rest of the forces northward to pursue Rupert's plan. But early in May, Leven, disturbed by Montrose's success at Auldearn (9 May) plodded into the Lake District to stand between him and the King, while Fairfax forced the royalists to withdraw from Taunton and turned back towards Oxford. On 31 May Rupert took Leicester and incontinently sacked it, alarming the parliamentary high command who saw him poised to leap into East Anglia, hitherto the heart of their military power. Cromwell was sent to put the Eastern Association into a posture of defence, and Fairfax made ready to move northward away from Oxford. It could have been a moment of crisis but Charles let it pass. He neither marched north nor turned east. The country had failed to rise for him and in itself the sack of Leicester did nothing to encourage recruitment. He was worried too about Oxford where supplies were running low. The 'New Noddle' could not be laughed away.

Rupert alone was firm and ready to take risks. He sent for Goring to come up to join him on a dash northwards. Goring's refusal was intercepted by Fairfax, who had now been given his head by the Committee of Both Kingdoms. He raised the siege of Oxford and turned north towards Charles, then sitting down near Daventry, still unclear on his next move and anxious about his long supply line. As Fairfax approached within 20 miles the royal forces fell back on Market Harborough. On 13 June Cromwell, elated by his appointment as Lieutenant-General, joined Fairfax at Kislingbury and was greeted by his men with a mighty shout of welcome.

The royalists were in danger of being caught on the run and so Charles turned—there was really no alternative—to fight at Naseby, a couple of miles from Market Harborough (14 June).

They fought hard on that summer's morning, but numbers told. Charles and Rupert grimly stared defeat in the face and recognised it. As they rode off towards Leicester the last real hope of a come-back went with them. The King's infantry was scattered, his guns destroyed, his treasure and baggage-train taken. Worse, his papers were captured, and soon his enemies were revealing to the world his intrigues with the French, the popish Irish and whatever. Naseby was decisive, too, in that it gave to the New Model Army the boost that it needed to become a confident, disciplined fighting force, one less and less curbed by civilian control. It brought Oliver Cromwell right to the fore as a cavalry commander, a man to be watched, and, perhaps, feared in all his activities. It was in a sense, too, a victory for Independency—for the Scottish army had taken no part in it and the need to pay lip-service to presbyterianism for fear of offending them began to dissipate. (The Scots had not been idle all this time. In fact they took Mansfield and marched south-west as far as Hereford, but they were no longer essential.)

Charles made his way to South Wales, wandering here and there seeking support. The countryside was still peppered with garrisons and strong-points but they were completely defensive. There was a variety of local forces, and under Goring in the west an army of some significance. But the New Model with its new appetite for victory moved to meet it and at Langport, near Bridgwater, on 10 July, tore it to pieces. Cromwell wrote to 'a worthy member of the house of Commons' that 'the Lord hath wrought [it] for us' and, his authentic voice is heard here, 'God will go on.'[2]

Langport was the last pitched battle of a war that dragged tediously on for another year to a now foregone conclusion. Supporter after supporter left the King to try to come to terms with parliament or to flee into exile. Even Rupert advised the King to come to some accommodation 'to preserve his posterity, Kingdom and nobility'. He believed it 'a more prudent way to retain something than to lose all'.[3] But still Charles held out. The west, including Bristol, so important for links with Ireland, fell to Fairfax. Rupert moved north, still hankering after a union with Montrose. But at Rowton Heath (24 September) he suffered a reverse and could do nothing to save Chester, the other great gateway to Ireland. In any case by then Montrose's great run of luck was slowing up to come to a halt at Philiphaugh in September. Cromwell spent the late summer mopping up Dorset and Hampshire, encountering only enfeebled opposition. Only in the west under Hopton did a royalist force of any importance hold out—and that collapsed in March 1646. Charles spent a winter of discontent at Oxford, still hoping for something to turn up, some special kind of King's luck. He began to see possibilities in the dissensions of his enemies, whose ruin he foretold unless they agreed with him. In the apparently simple animosity of presbyterian and Independent there was material in plenty for such a policy and Charles was confident that one of the factions would so address themselves to him that he might without difficulty obtain his just ends. But it was a policy he felt bound to reinforce by other means, and he was all the time still working for a landing of foreign troops—from Ireland, France, anywhere. In February 1646 he was contemplating marching into Kent with 2,000 men to seize a port that would give him direct access to the continent. It was an idle dream. On 23 March a relief force under Sir Jacob Astley from Worcestershire was defeated at Stow-on-the-Wold. 'You ... may [now] go play', said the loyal old man, 'if you will not fall out amongst yourselves'.[4] It was, perhaps, an obvious remark to make. Already Charles, through Sir Edward Nicholas, was working on Sir Henry Vane to detach the Independents from the presbyterians, and to get the King back to London. Nicholas, who knew Vane's interest in foreign affairs, began well:

'Is it not cleare to you (to me it is) that Spaine and France will instantly conclude a peace: and that France makes great preparations to joyne with the Scotts (when the breach betweene you and them shall happen), whilst Spaine labours to be Protector of Ireland, and will undoubtedly carry itt. Consider well, whether the season is not proper for this designe, when the wealth of this nation is already exhausted, and the sufferings of the people soe great, that they are no longer to be supported. This is reason, 'tis not to cast a bone amongst you. The only remedye is (and it is a safe and honourable one for you) that you sett your selfe, the gentleman that was quartered with you, and all his and your friends to prevaile, that the King may come to London upon the termes he hath offered; where, if Presbitery shall be soe strongly insisted upon as that there can be noe peace without itt, you shall certainly have all the power my master cann make to joyne with you in rooting out of this kingdome that tyrannicall Government. .... Loose not this faire opportunity. ...'[5]

But Vane was not to be persuaded, and now that the shooting war was over and the peace was to be won, Charles had to consider other allies. In that new struggle presbyterianism to him was as useful a weapon as Independency. He was already in touch with groups among the Scots, and in April 1646, his hopes keyed up by Montreuil, the French ambassador, he decided to make his way to the Scots army, where he had no doubt he would be received, as a natural sovereign should be, with honour and freedom. This move was directed to make the English 'rebels' and the Scots irreconcilable enemies—an outcome which would for obvious reasons please Mazarin more than any improvement in Charles's prospects. But Charles was in no hurry to commit himself. He clung to his hopes of armed intervention from abroad. He talked of going to Ireland, France, Denmark. But time was running out, taking with it one by one the possibilities open to him. On 27 April he slipped out of Oxford in disguise. On 5 May he gave himself up to the Scots near Newark. A few royalist strongholds held out a little longer, the last, Harlech, giving up as late as March 1647. By then the victors really were falling out among themselves.

The last year of the war had covered up some of the differences between the various groups aligned for parliament, but it had not stifled them. The presbyterians, still fairly well in unison with the Scots, wanted one kind of settlement; the Independents (with strong backing from elated army officers) stood for another. But by now there was another grouping whose emergence no one had foreseen—the Levellers, civilian 'radicals' with some connivance among the rank and file of the army and with some officer support, too. They wanted far-reaching changes in the structure of the State and a very wide degree of religious toleration. Each of these three main groupings was in a fluid state: each had its own ideas and policies to meet the major problems; each was looking for support; each might move against the others; each Charles saw as material to be moulded by a master-hand—a King's hand.

XII A Political Army

What were the problems facing the victors? The first, simplest to state and hardest to resolve, was to convert the victory of war into the triumph of peace; to settle things so that the fruits of conquest might be plucked by the victors. But what were the fruits, who were the victors? To ask these questions—and they were ones that could not be avoided— was straightway to enter the realms of controversy. Of course, the King must be brought to a right understanding of a new relationship between subject and sovereign. But how? And what was this new relationship? Nobody knew—or, rather, everybody knew, but no one agreed. Beyond that, the ramshackle administration that had been sporadically devised in the heat of war, unhistorical, depending more on the quality of men than of institutions had to be converted to more normal uses. Ireland must be pacified, perhaps punished; some new basis of agreement must be reached with the Scots, for whose army the Commons resolved on 19 May they had no further use. Some in the Commons, indeed, had no further use for the New Model Army either. If they got rid of it, they might get rid of the Independents and sectaries together. But could they get rid of it? This was, in fact, the most difficult problem of all, but the presbyterians, who assumed that they held the initiative, were sanguine about it.

Certainly they had a majority in the House of Commons. It is true that the House had since the late summer of 1645 been 'recruited' and that some Independents like Ireton had been elected. But presbyterians —Edward Massey, John Birch and Clement Walker, for example—had found their way in too and the fears of the moderates who had originally resisted the scheme were confounded. The new members were socially and politically much the same as the old. The elections seem to have been fought with as little reference to broad national issues as those of the halcyon pre-war days. In Sir Philip Stapleton the presbyterians had a good parliamentarian with military and administrative experience (he was a member of the Committee of Both Kingdoms); in Denzil Holles, a politician of considerable parliamentary skill and prestige, influential in the north and very, perhaps too, articulate; and in Sir John Clotworthy, an energetic and experienced intriguer. Men of this stamp were not religious fanatics like so many of the Scots or like some of their own supporters. (Some of them would slip with ease into the episcopal Church of England after 1660.) Now they stood for authority and government in the Church and order and stability in the State. They saw these highly desirable qualities in the Directory of Worship set up by the Westminster Assembly, and in the authority of a parliament wisely led by themselves. They opposed religious toleration because they feared the social consequences of the restless 'seeking' of the sectaries, and because they could not fail to observe that religious radicalism lay down happily with revolutionary politics. (Thomas Edwards's *Gangraena* (1646) is almost hysterically alarmist on the dreadful civil consequences of sectarian activities.) The spread of novel notions into an army already in the grip of Independency only made Holles and Stapleton more determined to assert their control of parliament, which, with the King, was the only historically constituted authority in the State. Holles went as far as to accuse the Independents of intending to ruin the King and as many of the nobility and gentry as they could, to alter the government and to have no order in the Church nor any power in the State over them. He can hardly have believed all this, but the suspicion that the Independents were, consciously or not, skirting the edge of anarchy was clearly a genuine one. Fortunately he could console himself with prospects of allies. In the City, Baillie's 'great hope on earth',[1] there was support particularly among the Aldermen for action against the sectaries and for the implementation of the Directory of Worship. It is still impossible to estimate how far the City was genuinely presbyterian in its religious sentiments—there are too many imponderables and it may not be irrelevant that City men were doing well out of speculation in bishops' lands. Holles and his friends could also count on a decided majority, for what it was worth, in the Westminster Assembly, and by their ostentatious loyalty to the covenant they could make a strong bid for Scottish support. (Hence the anxiety of the Independents to get the Scots out of England.) Through the Scots the presbyterians could work upon the King, who was now in honourable captivity at Newcastle. They could not imagine a settlement without him—in fact they saw in an accord with him a guarantee of their kind of England. They might have been right if this King had been someone other than Charles Stuart. Yet he was all they could hope for and they had to try to make something of him. In the meantime the Independents, the Levellers, and above all the army, that 'mere mercenary army',[2] must swing into line behind them and

103

do what they were told. For the presbyterians the war was over—but for Charles and, from a variety of points of view, for their opponents, it had only entered a new phase.

In July 1646 parliament presented the King with a new set of propositions firmly based on those offered at Uxbridge. Religion was to be settled according to the covenant and with the advice of the Westminster Assembly—in other words a form of presbyterianism was aimed at, even if a diluted or Erastian one. The King himself was to subscribe to the covenant. A final solution to the militia question, still as in 1642 the most acute problem, was in effect to be shelved for 20 years during which parliament would control the armed forces. (It was likely that at the end of 20 years a new King brought up on 'the right lines' and uncontaminated with either outworn or new-fangled notions of royal power would be on the throne.) Other clauses would have given to a parliament as at present constituted something like an ascendancy in the State. There was plenty, then, to negotiate about.

Meantime the victory over the royalists was being consolidated. The burden of taxation continued and a start was made in confiscating Church property. (The ordinance of 30 October 1646 for the sale of bishops' lands passed the Lords with difficulty, some peers openly wondering whose lands would go next.) Repentant or realistic royalists were coming in to make composition, trying to salvage what they could of their fortunes and estates. It is remarkable how many of them were able to do something effective. Recent research has shewn that the land upheaval of the Interregnum was not as catastrophic as royalist complaints against the Restoration land settlement suggested. There were many in parliament who saw nothing to be gained from driving ex-enemies, often their own kinsmen or neighbours, to desperation. There was little systematic about all this—the piecemeal methods of the war were continued into the peace and it seems clear that contemporaries were as puzzled by what was going on as are historians. Leniency and harshness were perfectly compatible. A new censorship demonstrated to critics who were ever-ready to circumvent it that new presbyter was but old priest writ large. In corners men were muttering that if tyranny be resistible in a king, so it was in a parliament. All the more need, then, for a quick settlement between King and conservatives.

But Charles himself was in no hurry. He had little liking for any of the propositions, but he was ready to talk about them. Paper-debates were always to his taste and he never grew weary of drawing up the 'handsome denying' answers which would keep things in suspense and help him with his chosen plan of playing one group off against another while he continued to sound out foreign aid. It was clear to him that there were many political forces that for different reasons liked the propositions no better than he did. They might unwittingly prepare a soil out of which some seeds of monarchy might spring. His first answer (1 August 1646) argued that the 'great alterations' proposed needed more time and thought for a positive answer. (Oliver Cromwell said much the same thing ten years later when faced with the attractive yet very speculative Humble Petition and Advice.) Most of all, said Charles, he would like to come to London where 'his personal presence ... might raise up a mutual confidence between him and his people' and clear up doubts on all sides.[3] His motives are plain: he knew, none better, that London was the political heart of his kingdoms. Here, if anywhere, he could make and maintain the contacts that might bring him back to power. Not least in his calculations was the hope of being able more readily to talk with foreign ambassadors and agents.

The parliamentary majority were ready to take the King out of the hands of the Scots but they had no intention yet of bringing him back to his capital. His return might be the signal for smouldering royalism in the country to burst into flame. In any case they wanted to use him, not be used by him. So the game continued. As the factions grew so Charles increased in confidence. Yet it was a very dangerous ploy. His 'remeediless induration' alienated many who had 'comiserated his condition'.[4] Baillie commented as early as May 1646: 'it has been the King's constant unhappiness to give nothing in tyme; all things have been given at last; bot he hes ever lost the thanks, and his gifts have been counted constrained and extorted'.[5] A few days before he had written to Henderson, who was with the commissioners waiting on the King, 'The great God help you to soften that man's heart, lest he ruin himselfe, and us with him. . . . He must either yeeld to reason, and altogether change his principles, or else he will fall in tragicke miseries. . . . If that man now goe to tinckle on Bishops and delinquents, and such foolish toyes, it seems he is mad.'[6] In August Baillie had got to the point of forecasting the self-destruction of the King, 'that madd man', and 'I feare he will downe with him all his posteritie, and monarchie'.[7] Not everyone was so pessimistic, but no one could fail to notice that things were 'in a marvellous ambiguitie'.[8] The royalists were defeated, disarmed, dejected, but other political forces were enterprising, confident, and likely to find some backing in force. Independents were in a minority in parliament and the City, but they could count on some response in the army, both among 'the grandees', as the chief officers were coming to be called, and the rank and file.

Other forces might wish to push beyond the limits set by the Independents, but at least they were pushing in the same direction and might back up any positive demands they made. None of them would sit back while a settlement was forged which in their view robbed them of the due reward of their services to the community—and by that some soldiers did not only mean back pay. (The extent of serious political interest among the rank and file is uncertain—if in fact there was, as is sometimes suggested, hardly any at all then the events of the next few years are surely incomprehensible.)

Parliament pressed its propositions on the King. At the beginning of 1647 agreement was reached with the Scots whereby they were paid over half a million pounds for their services. They returned thankfully to their own country, handing their royal prisoner over as a farewell gift to parliamentary commissioners. To have possession of the King was thought to hold the most vital, indeed, indispensable, piece on the political chess board. Parliament brought him to Holdenby House in Northamptonshire—his passage there was more like that of a conqueror than a defeated prince—where they, Holles and Stapleton among them, might talk with him and give attention, too, to other problems. Confident that the uncommitted members would turn towards them now that the King was in their hands, the presbyterians felt strong enough to deal with the army whose very existence blocked the road back or forward to more normal conditions. Charles in his latest conversations seemed to be moving towards them on religion and the militia. Time was ripe for action.

The scheme hit upon was to disband part of the army and to send the rest to Ireland where it would be too far away and too busy to cope with English politics. The royal Lieutenant there had asked for help against the native Irish as early as September 1646. He would be pleased, and a great source of discord at home would be removed. Independents and other dissidents would have suffered a serious blow and might go into a decline. The burden of taxation could be reduced and the population conciliated. A military settlement in Ireland was desirable on all counts—both as a short-term and a long-term consideration. While it was going on a purely civilian settlement could be surely achieved in England. Yet there were snags, and in their eagerness to rub their opponents' snouts in the dust, the presbyterians overreached themselves. The regiments to be disbanded were to be turned adrift without a promise of payment of their genuine arrears or of an indemnity. The force for Ireland was to be a new one, raised out of volunteers, presumably hand-picked. The Independent officers were to be pushed aside, since, apart from Fairfax, no one above the rank of colonel was to be retained. All officers were to take the covenant. None could be a member of either House of Parliament. The choice was between being exclusively military or being political—a hard one to men like Cromwell who wanted to be and shewed capacity for both. In these circumstances it seemed the Independents and their allies were being ordered to cut their own throats. Some of them, as Cromwell pointed out, would rather have cut the presbyterians' throats. The parliamentary leadership may not have been besotted with malice, but certainly shewed a lack of imagination. Such shabby treatment turned professional discontents into political grievances in an army which was already political, professional, restless and confident. It would be difficult now to keep it inactive.

Here, in short, was what Charles was hoping for—a widening public rift among his enemies, for so he regarded them all, even as he talked with them. But it had not been brought about by him. He was not in control of these forces—they were not puppets for him to play with. Nor were the presbyterians in as dominating a position as they fancied. The resentment of the army meant trouble. There was now a split between the military force which had won the war and a parliament dominated by men some of whom at least could be fairly charged with having done little to bring victory and who might be suspected of working against a fair settlement. The army concluded that it was needed to win the peace as it had won the war.

The danger did not stay there. In the genuine deeply felt hurt to the soldiery there was material for more radical political and social movements going beyond the notions of the grandees. An apparently spontaneous movement flared up in the cavalry regiments, who were in the nature of things more aggressive and self-confident than the more plebeian foot-sloggers. In March and April 1647 ranker delegates, or 'agitators'—men who were to get things done—were chosen in some regiments to put and argue the professional case of the army with the parliamentary commission charged with the disbandment. They went so far as to contemplate presenting parliament itself with a long petition in which they claimed payment of arrears (these ran into many months), pensions for widows and orphans and indemnity for actions undertaken during the war. This activity was condemned by the Commons as seditious and its promoters labelled enemies of the State. Cromwell and Ireton supported the rejection, a step sometimes regarded as inexplicable. But it suited them just then to try to play down differences, and in any case they regarded the appearance of the agitators as a grave threat to military discipline, which was something that Cromwell genuinely believed in. (This explains in part the readiness of a professional soldier like George Monk to serve under him.) Clement Walker had another explanation. It was all part of Cromwell's perfidy

—he encouraged parliament to follow its present course to embroil it with the army, which he was spurring on to harsher demands. In fact parliament, with or without Cromwell, was certainly determined to hold out against the army and there is no reason to believe that the army would have been inert unless Cromwell was prodding it on. The soldiery were by now well accustomed to acting together, whether in the field or in religious services. There were contacts, too, with civilian Levellers skilled in drawing up and promoting petitions. Agitation was bound to continue.

In April a further petition called for the return of the old commanders. A last-minute vote of the Commons to pay six weeks' arrears did nothing to help matters; instead it probably encouraged the view that if enough pressure was applied redress must follow. On 29 April three agitators were bold enough to come to the House to present in person a letter of grievances. They were the redoubtable Edward Sexby, soon to be a Leveller leader and in the 'fifties a royalist terrorist, William Allen, later Adjutant and General in Ireland and Thomas Shepherd. The determination of these 'soldiers three' was an ominous sign of the extent of political restlessness, which now embraced infantry regiments too.

From the start these men, who in some way or other did represent the rank and file, were imbued with principles more radical than those of most of the officers. So, if there was a lack of respect for parliament, there was also a sharp threat to military discipline—a danger all the more serious at a time when the King by his ostentatious willingness for an accommodation was drawing presbyterians closer to him. Parliament was not discouraged from going ahead with its plans for the army. Skippon, Cromwell, Ireton and Fleetwood were ordered to talk over with the officers at headquarters in Saffron Walden the complaints of the army. They reported what was obvious—that the army was under a deep sense of some sufferings and the common soldiers much unsettled—and if they were to do their best to keep the soldiers in order they would have to talk very fully and frankly to the House. They did so, and impressed the House enough for an order for legislation to be drafted to meet the chief professional grievances of the soldiery. But some presbyterians went on working at a plan to send the King to Scotland and, using the Scots army and perhaps, old royalists, to impose a presbyterian system on England. The King, of course, was to take the covenant. This scheme called for the prior disbandment of the army.

On 25 May parliament was persuaded to overlook its earlier promises and to order the demobilisation, troop after troop, of the regiments, each in a separate place. This move to break the unity of the army in fact stiffened it. As Ireton told the House, it was a provocation that would make men think of what they never intended and must quicken the drift from professional discontent to political dissidence. The Levellers saw an opportunity and were not slow to take it. Here surely lies the explanation for a good deal of Cromwell's apparent shiftiness at this time. He had no wish to see presbyterianism with or without a covenanted King riveted on England—but he did not want, either, the political anarchy which he saw forecast in a breakdown of obedience within the army. In this he was by no means alone. Skippon, too, was accused of deliberately trying to please everyone. But Cromwell was always ready to come to a definite decision when he was convinced that it could no longer be put off. So now he chose to go with the army, because he saw that it had the one vital element parliament lacked—physical force—and was ready to use it. He wanted to have some say in how that force was used, and so set himself 'to ride the whirlwind and direct the storm'. It was perilous, but as his career shews Cromwell, though never reckless, had an Elizabethan taste for a calculated risk.

On 2 June, the regiments came together at Newmarket in a general rendezvous, which they had indicated they would have with or without their officers. There they resolved that if it became necessary they would resist parliament. On 3 June Cornet Joyce went to Holdenby House and took the King into his charge. He had, as he put it, authority from the soldiers to prevent Charles from being used by someone or other for some design against the army. Once in control he wrote—it is no surprise—to Lieut.-General Oliver Cromwell in London to know what further to do. This letter is so sharp, curt, and matter of fact that it is difficult to believe that the recipient cannot have been already briefed for what was happening. However, without waiting for a reply Joyce, seemingly on his own initiative, decided that it was safer for Charles to be moved out of reach of the army's enemies and without any resistance offered took Charles, who in fact appeared cheerful at the turn of events, which flattered his sense of his own indispensability, towards Newmarket. Meantime Cromwell quickly got out of London and joined Fairfax, who was visibly upset, at Kentford Heath near Newmarket. There, on 4 June, the army drew up what they called 'an humble representation' in which they demanded to be informed of the names of those members of parliament who had pressed the resolution branding their petitioners enemies of the State. In fact, the Commons had hastily expunged the vote from its records as soon as the news came in of Joyce's exploit. Some of the presbyterians who had been in communication with the Scots, the Queen and the Prince of Wales for an accommodation on the basis of the King's first answer to their propositions backed by an invasion, were obviously terrified. In the City the militia was called out. Meanwhile the army went on to 'engage' not to disband until its grievances were redressed (5 June). Surest indication of the drift of events was the formation in the next few days of demands for an acceptable political settlement, which should include some liberty to tender consciences. This emerged as 'a representation of the Army' which also asked for delinquents' lands to be sold to meet arrears—some part of the army's attitude to parliament was surely the result of the reluctance of many members of the Commons and most of the Peers to take the step the rank and file, less interested in the maintenance of property rights, thought the obvious and just one to meet their needs. The newly-constituted general council of the army, consisting of the general officers and two officers and two privates from each regiment (i.e. an assembly dominated by officers), worked out a programme which included reform of the franchise and the redistribution of seats. The City, which was as anxious as parliament to get rid of the army and thereby reduce the burden of taxation, was assured that the soldiers were pressing just demands *as soldiers* and were not, in spite of appearances, intending to meddle with civil government or to open the doors to religious dissidence and licentiousness. When the authorities did not respond to this appeal to detach them from parliament, the army started a slow march on the capital. The trained bands, command of which was given back by parliament to the City authorities, refused to march out, whether from solidarity with the army or for fear of coming to grips with professionals is uncertain. In any case, the general council indicated that if they were resisted they would regard themselves as free and clear 'from all the ruin that might befall that great and populous city'.

The busy hand and working brain of Oliver Cromwell has been discerned in all this talk and movement. There can be no question he was deeply involved—but it is an open question how far he was controlling events and how far being swept along by them. What is certain is that in such rapidly changing circumstances Cromwell felt he had to be up and doing. He was essentially a man of action and not in any profound sense a thinker. His most recent experience of applying himself to events was in war when circumstances changed with bewildering rapidity and when a man who would stay alive, much less win battles, needed great flexibility and a willingness to trust a little to his intuitions. Here was a political warfare just as sharp, perhaps as unpredictable, as fighting in the field. He had to find some way through and bring his side—which was it?—to victory. Enemies must be confounded, and there was no time, even if he had the will, or capacity, to explain to his own forces the motives of his actions. Safety must be first plucked out of the nettle. Two great threats remained—a presbyterian accommodation with the King, and the loss of all control in the army. His activities were designed to check them both. How successful was he? Who can say? In the event there was a second civil war—but for him might it not have come sooner and been bloodier?

XIII Marching on London

On 15 June 1647 the army, still edging slowly towards London, putting out manifestoes galore, accused 11 members of the Commons, including Denzil Holles, who was not surprised, of treason and plotting new civil wars. This charge was tacked on the end of a declaration drafted by Cromwell's son-in-law, Henry Ireton, now coming to the fore as the best practical thinker among the army officers and a powerful man with a pen. It argued that no settlement was likely until the present House of Commons was dissolved and a new one elected—a song that would be sung again and again between 1647 and 1653. The whole draft of the document is towards something like sovereignty of the people, arguing considerable mobility in the minds of the army leaders.

The Commons, though worried by the deterioration of its own position—it was 'but a cypher', said Holles[1]—would still not consider the army's claims. So, like a great sword, the regiments drew nearer and nearer to London. But not very quickly, as Cromwell and Ireton and their associates were anxious not to shew too naked a use of force, at any rate, not too soon. They had themselves started talks with the King, who was delighted and could see nothing but good for his cause in this impossible situation. Ireton felt compelled to remind him with some asperity that whatever hopes he might have of being an arbiter, the army intended to be one—the only one—between himself and his parliament. Charles was not impressed; his skill for self-deception was always greater than his capacity to deceive others, especially in dark days. The officers' notions, which eventually emerged in a draft known as 'the Heads of the Proposals', bolder and more explicit than the earlier declarations, ran towards checks on future parliaments as well as on the throne. (Cromwell's 'fundamentals' of 1654 are found in embryo here.) They also suggested a number of sensible reforms—legal, parliamentary, financial, religious, including a reconsideration of tithes as a maintenance for ministers and some form of religious toleration. There was to be a redistribution of parliamentary seats according to rates, not population—a proposal which would, curiously, in view

112

of the existent situation, have given London a much increased representation. Altogether the usual description 'statesmanlike' fits them
very well. But they had at least one glaring defect—they were the proposals of the officers alone, and at this point in time something more
was wanted than that: heed to the organised opinion of the rank and
file with its mouthpiece in the agitators on the general council and its
connexions with the civilian Leveller movement. They were both
impatient and suspicious. General Cromwell and the rest were getting
on very well with the King, giving him every sign of respect, letting
their ladies make up to him, but what was happening to the festering
grievances of the army? When was parliament to be brought at last to
see that the army meant it when it called for the impeachment of the
11 suspect, or rather, guilty, but still sitting members? They knew that
anti-army groupings in the City, taking a leaf out of Pym's book, were
petitioning violently for enforced disbandment, for action against the
sectaries and for the King's return. Under pressure a council of war
was held at Reading (16 July) to consider the agitators' demands—at
first without their company. When they were invited in they called
violently, with the support of some of the lesser officers, for marching
straight into the City. 'We cannot have anything unless by the way of
advancing to London',[2] said one. A fierce argument blew up, the
agitators urging speed lest all be lost. Cromwell was ready to agree that
things were tending that way. Yet ... yet, he said in effect, what we
want is a treaty and until we are morally certain we cannot get one we
ought not to use force. 'Whatsoever we get by a treaty ... it will be
firm and durable ... it will be conveyed over to posterity. . . . We
shall avoid that great objection that will lie against us, that we have got
things of the Parliament by force.'[3] (Not a word about the recent war!)
The whole parliament, he ventured to suggest, was not corrupt. There
was a party there that had through thick and thin stood by 'the cause'.
It might be 'the gaining party'.[4] Parliament might in fact be even now
purging itself—a reference to the non-attendance of members either
impugned by the army or fearing they might be.

William Allen, one of the agitators, pertinently interjected that a
march on London might make the gaining party gain quicker, and
Sexby added that the concessions parliament might make would come
in any case 'from fear not love'.[5] Nevertheless Oliver had his way, and
the march into London—which he saw as a crossing of the Rubicon—
was held off, though significantly, never abandoned. Further demands
were made on parliament for disabling the 11 members. Meanwhile
work was done on the Heads of the Proposals, which were offered on
17 July to a committee including a few agitators to perfect them.

In the House of Commons the presbyterian groups continued to dwindle. The 11 named members were now given leave, which they promptly took, to withdraw. Fairfax was named as commander of all land forces. It looked as if events were going the way Cromwell wanted them to. But suddenly there was a rising in the City—in favour of 'King and covenant'. A mob held, as Denzil Holles once had done, the Speaker in his chair while a resolution to call the King back to his capital was passed. Force called out to force. The army marched quickly. A group of about 60 Independent members and eight peers taking with them the Speakers of the Commons, William Lenthall, and ironically, of the Lords, Manchester, fled for refuge to the army. They were a very mixed batch, some well known, some obscure, some future rumpers but of the less radical section. It is as difficult to draw conclusions from the composition of this group as from any other of the Interregnum. The latest historian of the Independents contents himself with the remark that they were 'presumably leading ones',[6] which does not carry us much further. Certainly their defection was decisive, though the remnant at Westminster defied the army to the last.

Meanwhile Charles, charmed by the City demonstrations in his favour, had rejected the army proposals, with the warning, 'You cannot be without me. You will fall to ruin, if I do not sustain you.'[7] It was a profound misreading of his situation—his frail shoulders would not for much longer support the burden even of his own head. What sustained the army was its own unity and sword-power. The City authorities, deserted by considerable sections of the population, shewed a true appreciation of the realities when the army entered London on 6 August. The Lord Mayor, the Aldermen and the Common Council hastened out to greet them and invited the chief officers to a banquet. The apprentices, alarmed at the sight of swords that had actually tasted blood, melted from the streets. The Speakers and the other members went back to Westminster, and now undistracted by the skilful parliamentary tactics of Holles and his cronies—most of whom had fled to the continent—passed resolutions approving the coming up of the Lord General and the army, voted one month's pay to the N.C.O.s and privates, and waited anxiously for the next vicissitude.

XIV Debates and Discussions

The army was not in London to relax. All the problems remained, if in new forms. Cromwell and the grandees had now to work for some concord between King, parliament, and army, while cautiously watching the growing power of a new political force—the Levellers, with their intimate association with the army. John Lilburne, their stentorian leader, was speaking gratefully of his true friends, the agitators, and as early as May the army had been described as 'one Lilburne throughout'. In dealing with King and parliament the grandees could expect to count on army support. But they could hardly approach the Levellers with the same confidence. The agitators might describe themselves as but young statesmen but they had an incalculable influence with those honest blades, the private soldiers, and might capture the regiments for the radical Leveller programmes now pouring from the presses. Their pressure might force the army leaders to modify their propositions to King and parliament in such a way that they could be rejected as tending to anarchy. The army then was a tool—a weapon rather—that might be turned against King, parliament or themselves. It was unpredictable but could not be ignored. It was a sword to put in somebody's hand. What Cromwell and his henchmen wanted was to put that sword back into its scabbard until they needed it themselves. Meanwhile they had to see what they could do outside and inside the army. So they talked interminably with the King, whom they still tended to regard as the legitimate head of the State, more or less indispensable, and with the parliament, which they agreed could not be dissolved without its own consent. There a conservative element—still labelled presbyterian—hung on, in face of a rising demand in the army for a purge. (The Levellers at the same time were attacking not merely the presbyterians but 'the silken Independents, the broken reeds of Egypt', who, in their view, were ready to sell the cause to the highest bidder.) Attendance in the Houses was dropping and by the end of August only seven peers thought it worth while coming to Westminster, and the Commons rarely mustered 150 M.P.s. This underlined the reality of the army's power, but the Cromwellians, mostly themselves members of the Commons, were anxious that this fact should not be too nakedly exposed. So they supported parliament's almost inexplicable offer to the King of a slight variant of the old Newcastle propositions. Charles ironically indicated a preference for the Heads of the Proposals, and carried on scheming for Scottish intervention to put him back on the throne on other and vaguer terms. All the while nothing was done by parliament to deal with the vital issue of the professional claims of the soldiers, and more of the would-be non-political troopers were forced into the ranks of the politicians in the army and their civilian Leveller allies. No doubt there was still a good deal of apathy and some reluctance to follow the lead of the agitators, but vocal opinion was certainly with them. John Lilburne himself was now in the Tower at the order of the Lords. The army leaders were glad to see him there, incapable, as they hoped, of breeding 'new hurley-burleys'.[1] But stone walls never made a prison for 'Honest John' and he was as voluble a martyr as ever. In the Commons, too, by this time there was a small but busy group of what might be called extreme Independents, who were beginning to believe that there was no need to come to terms with Charles simply because there was no need for a King. Henry Marten's proposal in September for a vote of 'no addresses' to the King brought them into the open and alarmed the moderates. To deny the King altogether was to break down yet another screen between security and the Leveller ambitions.

Once again Cromwell was in the thick of things, once again he appeared inconsistent and unfathomable. But the old thread can be seen running though all his actions. He meant to achieve some sort of stability before the radicalism in the army and reaction outside of it had time to destroy the tottering fabric of the State. He knew that the army was a wolf held by the ears which might just as readily turn and rend its legitimate leaders as the King and the right-wing generally. It seems certain that in September and October Cromwell still thought that something could and must bridge the gap between the King's and his own intentions, before the agitators pushed rank and file into even more obviously illegal courses. Major Francis White, who had the bad taste to say at an army council that there was 'now no visible authority in the kingdom, but the power and force of the sword'[2] was expelled after strong pressure by Cromwell. Remarks like that could only upset civilians and might give the agitators inflated ideas of their own importance.

But Oliver's tireless negotiations with, it seemed, almost anybody could not lull suspicion. The respect that the grandees and their ladies shewed for the trappings of monarchy was carefully noted and as one commentator put it 'how the agitators will take these things I know not.'[3] Yet the answer was simple—they took it increasingly badly. In October some regiments elected new agitators even more anxious than the old to shew their mettle. At Guildford they drew up a truly remarkable document, 'The Case of the Army Truly Stated', in which sharpened professional demands lay cheek by jowl with long-term constitutional and social claims—for a wide suffrage, biennial parliaments, the abolition of the excise, of tithes and monopolies of all kinds. There should be serious legal reforms. The common-place assertion that the people is sovereign was reinforced by the unambiguous statement that 'all power is originally and essentially in the whole body of the people',[4] a fundamental law indeed, and a very different interpretation from that peddled in earlier parliamentary propaganda. This was something more than an expression of a political theory—it must be read against the background of Lilburne's avowed intention of appealing to 'Hobnayles and clouted Shooes,'[5] and the fact that John Wildman, a civilian Leveller with legal training and a subtle political sense, had a share in drafting it. This declaration was quickly hammered into a written constitutional platform, neatly entitled 'The Agreement of the People' (28 October), which agitators and civilian Levellers together now put forward as their solution to the problem of sovereignty in general, and their answer, forthright and drastic, to the positions taken up at various times by King, parliament, presbyterians, Independents, army officers and all the other claimants to State power. All of these had accepted a king and a powerful parliament on a restricted franchise. The Agreement assumed the end of monarchy and would erect a totally elective representative assembly, itself explicitly inferior to the sovereign people themselves. No wonder Oliver Cromwell said at the Putney debates held by the army to discuss it, 'truly this paper does contain in it very great alterations of the very government of the kingdom . . . that it hath been under . . . since it was a nation'.[6] It could be a turning point in English history for wise men and godly men to consider well.

These discussions in the little church at Putney (October–November 1647) have rightly attracted the attention of historians. Here are the insistent tones of men, some of them godly, some of them wise, many of them of a type never before called into the magic circle of political life, deliberating urgently about problems of government, testing the ties binding men together in society. All this they did when England, their world, was being turned upside down and needed to be put right side up. Yet what was the right side? They could not agree. The individual answers they offered were coloured by circumstance, by their social position, their religious outlook, their personalities. Any interpretation which neglects the religious basis of attitudes taken up in the House of God must be incorrect. They were all influenced by the doctrine of calling or covenant, some more, some less. They all were looking for a new heaven as well as a new earth. Any interpretation that discounts the practical and material aspirations of these soldiers must also be rejected. Man, they were sure, does not live by bread alone, but without bread he does not live for long. The debate was worked out very much in theological terms, but it is not cynical to discern political grounds of principle and of tactics. Moreover, personality played a big part in the divergence of views. The Levellers and their friends were harsh towards Cromwell, not only because they could not grasp his theology, but because they mistrusted him personally. They were, they believed, in a grim situation and for his own obscure purposes he was frustrating the only sure way out. Cromwell did not only find their theology unpalatable, he suspected their social aims and gravely doubted their political capacity. The heat engendered in these arguments was not solely of the spirit. 'The debate on 29 October had opened on a high religious level', writes Mr Robert Paul in his study of Cromwell as a spiritual force, 'but had degenerated as tempers became more frayed.'[7] To the historian what was said in a temper might well be as interesting and perhaps as significant as remarks made in 'a notable spirit of prayer'.

On the first day the agitator Edward Sexby began to put the point of view of the rank and file. (He made very few religious references.) They were miserable, he said, because they had sought to satisfy all men, including 'a rotten parliament'[8] and a King who could only be pleased when they had all cut their throats. This was an unkind thrust at Cromwell, who had taken the lead in the officers' negotiations. If, Sexby asked, 'you are convinced God will have you to act on',[9] how can you explain the clear failure of your endeavours? Cromwell and Ireton were stung to defend themselves, but the Levellers were unimpressed. When the actual proposals of the Agreement were read out Cromwell was taken aback, or professed to be, by their radical content. Shifting his theological position he urged that faith in the justness of their claims was not enough—reason, too, must come into it. 'What the consequences of such an alteration as this would be . . . wise men and godly men ought to consider.'[10] It was all very well to draw up paper schemes of government; anyone could do that and for all they knew at that very moment some other group of men might be doing just that. Who should prevail? In any case they were not completely free to act. They had certain—it would be more accurate to say 'uncertain'—

118

obligations which were binding on conscience. But the Levellers wanted to know who it was that had made these engagements, and could unjust and unequal engagements be binding anyway? It was an awkward moment, but, assisted by 'Praying' William Goffe, Cromwell managed to get serious debate adjourned overnight. Meanwhile they should each wait upon God. Next day detailed discussion was held up by Goffe's determination to prophesy. (A recent commentator, anxious to emphasise the basically 'theological nature' of these debates, urges us not to dismiss his speech too easily, and then goes on to admit that it had no effect whatever![11]) When Goffe fell silent, the suffrage, clearly regarded as the great point, was quickly taken up. Ireton stated his view bluntly enough and it had very little to do with the spirit of Jesus Christ to which he had appealed earlier. 'No person hath a right to an interest or share in the disposing of the affairs of the kingdom . . that hath not a permanent fixed interest.' A political role was rightly confined to 'those persons in whom all land lies, and those in corporations in whom all trading lies'.[12] (Not a word here about faith or vocation or morals.) 'Liberty cannot be provided for in a general sense, if property be preserved',[13] yet to deny property is to deny society itself. Natural rights meant, if they meant anything, anarchy. ('Men are corrupt and will be so.') Therefore, Ireton concluded, there must be government, strong government, yes, even, if he were pushed, in religion. Colonel Thomas Rainsborough counter-attacked in favour of poor men oppressed by rich men's laws in a world they never made. Cromwell, who had no love for Rainsborough, backed up his son-in-law. Manhood suffrage, there could be no argument, must end in anarchy because 'all bounds and limits' are taken away if men who have 'no interest but the interest of breathing'[14] had a voice in elections. (What of the interest of praying, believing, worshipping, of being God's creatures?) But, as Sexby heatedly pointed out, these men without interest had been in fact 'the means of the preservation of this kingdom'.[15] They had opposed, not welcomed, anarchy. They had fought for their birthrights—and now they were told they had none. 'But . . . in a word,' said Sexby, 'I have as much a birthright . . . as any . . . and whatsoever may come . . . I will give it to none.'[16] Rainsborough concurred, mocking the fainthearts who dreaded great changes. All good laws, he had already claimed, had once been dangerous innovations. There had been 'scufflings' before in England. As for himself, changes would not find him wanting. 'When I leap I shall take so much of God with me, and so much of just and right with me, as I shall jump sure.'[17]

So the debate went on, swinging to and fro, and as usual, even in a crisis, discussion went into side issues and dead ends. One senses something of Cromwell's and Ireton's satisfaction at this. They were waiting —perhaps working—for something to happen. A week went by and found the two main groups—Levellers and Cromwellians—as far apart as ever. Respect due to property was continually emphasised, but as Professor Haller has pointed out, the men in the ascendancy in 1647 owed their position not to their property but to their military power.[18] The supporters of the Agreement remained unconvinced by the arguments about engagements and were more and more certain that they must have nothing to do with the King. On 5 November Rainsborough did manage in the absence of Cromwell to secure a vote for no further addresses to Charles, whereupon Ireton left in a huff. It seems certain that Rainsborough's threatening success made Cromwell and Ireton cast about for some way to bring the discussions to an end before the Leveller element prevailed. Opportunity soon came. Cromwell moved that there should be a rendezvous to sound the general feeling of the army and that meanwhile the agitators should go back to their regiments.[19] This was agreed without any vote being taken on the main issues, the Levellers presuming that decisions would be made at or after the rendezvous. In fact Cromwell's resolution meant that representation of the rank and file by agitators on the general council was broken, though a general council consisting entirely of officers remained and in fact met automatically on the next morning (9 November). Mr Robert Paul, the chaplain of the Cromwell Society, considers that all Cromwell could do now was to wait on Providence.[20] If so, he had weighted the dice in his favour—the Levellers were, after all, eliminated from the army council and effective rank and file participation in the deliberations of the commanders had ceased. This clearing of the air no doubt made it easier for Providence to work with him.

Cromwell claimed that 'the end is to deliver this nation from oppression and slavery, to accomplish that work that God hath carried us on in, to establish our hopes of an end of justice and righteousness in it'.[21] Everyone would agree with that, but some could not forget that the man who uttered such fine sentiments also believed that men who had no interest but that of breathing had no direct part to play in deciding how to realise those ends. Yet such men had fought in the wars and some of them had openly and eloquently put a case for themselves. Would they be ready to sink back into obscurity? Again, no doubt Providence would decide.

It has been suggested that in these meetings exegesis was more important than political definition, and theology than the theory of government.[22] Only a very selective reading of what was actually said could justify this interpretation. Ireton's theory of property would sound out of place at a prayer meeting. Sexby and Wildman—even Cromwell —had their feet firmly planted on the ground in this world. The messianic utterances of Major Goffe and Col. John Jubbes were received 'with respect' and nothing else.[23] The fact is that no more than the law was theology capable in 1647 of providing the practical and immediate answers these men looked for. These political and social issues remained at stake then and in the events that followed. To say this is not to deny the very real impact of religion in all these men's lives, or to accuse Cromwell of hypocrisy. He was waiting for a further extraordinary dispensation of God's will, but was looking for it not like a hermit meditating in a wilderness but actively like a soldier in the crowded world of affairs. He was a seeker who meant to be a finder.

xv A Second War and Regicide

While Charles was in the hands first of parliament and then of the army, he was as we have seen ready to talk with anyone who cared to approach him. A few days before the army council met at Putney he came to a written agreement with the Scots Commissioners for aid in recovering his freedom and authority. Everything hung upon his escape from Hampton Court where the army had lodged him. He had given his captors his royal word not to attempt it, but at a time like this Charles would not be too scrupulous. Even in the remarkably free-and-easy atmosphere in which he was detained it became clear that he was plotting something and his guards were tentatively reinforced. It was reported that all men of estates feared a new war. (It is amazing how loose security could be—Charles seems to have been remarkably well-informed about even the most intimate discussions of the army council.) Charles evidently enjoyed himself discussing with his attendants where he should go, and finally settled on the Isle of Wight, where the new governor was Robert Hammond, a kinsman of John Hampden, but also of the noted royalist divine, Henry Hammond, and believed to be troubled by recent events. Such a man might be pliable in the presence of his King. From the island Charles could continue to bargain with the parliament and army, and, indeed, with the Scots, for the recent agreement need not be the final one. If the worst happened, he could flee to the continent. But this was a last extremity. Charles was so confident of his own abilities that only in rare moments of despair did he seriously contemplate becoming King over the water. Such a King he firmly believed would be no King at all.

On the evening of 11 November he rode off with three companions and the 14th found him being put up at Carisbrooke Castle by the very diffident Hammond. He had left behind a 'declaratory message' in which he appealed 'to all indifferent men to judge, if I have not just cause to free myself from the hands of those who change their principles with their condition'; and claimed that he had cause to fear 'for their intentions to my person'.[1] He had received an anonymous letter that some agitators had resolved 'for the good of the kingdom' to take his life away. But he emphasised that in escaping he was putting the 'public good' above his personal security. The ease with which he got away has suggested that Cromwell may have deliberately provided an opportunity for him. It is true that at this stage he was strongly against any 'horrid design' upon the King, and no doubt felt relief that Charles was out of range of agitators and Levellers, while at the same time an eye could be kept on him at Carisbrooke. When the news of the escape broke, there was an upsurge of royalist feeling in the City and rumours of 'a new war'.[2] Here, perhaps, was one of these dispensations for which Oliver was always waiting. The danger of the situation would justify strong measures in the name of military discipline and security, and, it might follow, an opportunity to detach the soldiers from the Levellers and radicals generally. With this in mind a moderate 'engagement' was drawn up and rendezvous fixed at various places—Windsor, Kingston and at Corkbush field, near Ware— to isolate the more disaffected of the regiments.

But on 15 November the volatile regiment of Robert Lilburne, a brother of the Leveller leader, marched on to Corkbush field in a state of mutiny, with 'papers' stuck in their hats demanding in a neat juxtaposition—'England's Freedom: Soldiers' Rights'.[3] The other regiments were fairly easily persuaded to leave matters to the army council—a few arrests worked wonders. But eyes kept turning to Lilburne's troops—if they were not brought into line the present concord might rapidly break up. Once again Cromwell shewed himself to be 'the man of opportunity'. Slow so often to move, he could sometimes take without a qualm utterly ruthless action to cut across and solve a problem. Sword-drawn, he rode with 'rough brisk temper' into the ranks.[4] The mutineers wavered and, hesitating, were lost. In a few moments the ground was littered with papers pulled from their hats. It was not enough. Military discipline and political stability both required a sacrificial victim. The ringleaders were tried and found guilty by drumhead court-martial. They diced for their lives. Trooper Richard Arnold lost and was shot on the spot. Order was restored.

The defeat of the army radicals pleased the House of Commons, especially as it was followed by the withdrawal of a number of regiments from the City. But though the recent elections had been under army influence and had produced an Independent Lord Mayor, the City authorities were still very reluctant to provide money for the maintenance of troops whom many regarded as a bundle of sectaries. They trusted the officers no more than the rank and file. For their part men like Cromwell and Ireton can have had few illusions about their own safety should the sword be torn from their hands. Charles reinforced suspicions by sending up from the Isle of Wight a new offer to parliament, conceding presbyterianism for three years, limited toleration, and giving up control of the militia for himself if it might revert to his successors. There was also to be some parliamentary reform more or less according to the Heads of the Proposals. A veritable ragbag, it offered at once too much and too little and was therefore dangerous, especially as Charles proposed to come up to London immediately to negotiate a personal treaty. Everyone knew that he could look for some support there, and certainly his presence would be an embarrassment to the Independents. Their group in the Commons was able to defer consideration of Charles's offers pending the formulation of counter-proposals from parliament itself. These merged in a poorly attended House in the shape of four bills—the most critical of which would vest the militia in parliament for 20 years—to which the King must assent before any further negotiations took place (14 December). The bills were to be supplemented by propositions including one for a very limited toleration. During earlier discussion on this, Selden and Marten (both libertarians in religion) urged extending it even to catholics. In reply to the charge that papists were the tools of a foreign potentate, Marten remarked that a tyrant abroad was less a threat than one in every parish—a sharp reminiscent thrust at the presbyterians. Fewer of the latter were now attending the House and others must have been thinking of some more viable means of getting their own way. (It is curious that when they were in a majority in the House they did not vote a dissolution. The answer probably lies in their assessment that by such action the King would be strengthened as much against them as anyone else.)

At about this time the Agreement of the People was presented to parliament and spurned as seditious and contemptuous (9 November 1647). The Levellers were, of course, disgusted and added their quota to the growing fears and suspicions. In this confused situation Cromwell and Ireton, hitherto apparently over-anxious to come to terms with the King, now started working desperately against him. Why did they change? Complicated explanations based on hearsay—e.g. 'saddle letters' from Charles to Paris *via* London and the like—abound. But even without these the most obtuse observer could have seen that Charles was up to something, and that that something would not make things pleasant for the army leaders. They knew he was sounding the Scots. They felt the chill of war-weariness becoming incipient exasperated royalism in the City and elsewhere.[5] They knew that army

discipline teetered on a fine edge. They had every reason to fear a
breakdown of their control and with it the loss of their lives. Men who
are ready to risk their lives in the heat of battle are not always so
prodigal in a political crisis.

Suspicions were clinched when in December Charles and a significant group among the Scots made an accord on the basis of an invasion of England and presbyterianism in both countries for three years.
Cromwell was ready in the new crisis to appear to meet the Levellers
half-way in the interests of army solidarity. 'If we cannot bring the
army to our sense, we must go to theirs', he remarked.[6] But the breach
with the King was not immediately made public. Until on 28 December Charles rejected the four bills, Cromwell and his son-in-law
walked on slippery paths. The King's denial, which no form of words
could make handsome, fused Levellers and Cromwellians together. Once
more Cromwell had recognised that, his eyes dazzled by 'the glories of
the world', he had not been able to 'discern clearly the great works the
Lord was doing'.[7] With army unity on the way parliament by 141–92
at last brought the present series of negotiations to an end with a vote
of 'no addresses' (3 January 1648). At once a parliamentary mission
went off to the United Provinces to work against foreign aid for the
King. The matter was urgent. The Thirty Years war was almost at an
end, and soon there would be plenty of soldiers, some perhaps even
more experienced and certainly more venal than the New Model
Army, wanting employment.

Meanwhile in England a committee of safety, more or less independent of parliament, based on the old Committee of Both Kingdoms,
minus Scots and presbyterians, was given control of the executive.
Charles, whose perfidy in the eyes of Cromwell now exceeded his un-
questionable great parts, was to be kept at Carisbrooke under tighter
guard. On 8 January the army council meeting at Windsor Castle
ostentatiously surrendered its powers to the committee of safety—a
clever move which at once disguised the political role the army was
still likely to play and prevented a revival of agitator representation in
the officers' counsels. On 15 January troops were again posted at Whitehall. It looked like a victory for Oliver.

Yet was it? Nothing positive or permanent had been done. Cromwell
had set his face against the King, but where was there to be found a
substitute for him? There was no sudden general conversion to misty
republicanism. Instead there was a political vacuum. It must be filled.
Cromwell meant to control the process, but was obviously uncertain
what filling he wanted. So we hear of him dining with all sorts—republicans, Independents, citizens and the rest—picking their brains,

testing their opinions. The results were slight, except that he grew more and more antagonistic to the person of the King. His opponents—a wide spectrum—saw him slipping in the direction of personal dictatorship, a fear brought out in the lively ballad *O brave Oliver*.[8] If the royalists, old and new, had kept quiet, a strong reaction against the Lieutenant-General might have come about, but in the spring they made their own inept ploy.

Early in March there was a mutiny among the troops in Pembrokeshire—these were not New Modellers. Later the same month, the twenty-third anniversary of the King's accession was celebrated in open defiance of army and committee of safety. Early in April apprentices rioted in favour of the King. In Ireland the presence of a parliamentary army inspired more hatred than fear, and moves for unity among the factions began again. In Scotland the 'Engagers' were making ready for yet another crossing of the border. In this heavy atmosphere the ties between Levellers and grandees rusted. A meeting of rankers at St Albans in late April called for the immediate acceptance of the Agreement of the People. On the other hand a majority of the Commons (apparently including Cromwell) expressed itself in favour of the maintenance of government by King, Lords and Commons. A council of war met at Windsor to look at the situation and felt called upon to reprimand the St Albans agitators. We know little of their other discussions, except that they seem to have been very earnest about the need to maintain the army on a war footing, for without it the present régime would find itself naked, shivering in a cold wind of enmity or indifference. News that came in on 1 May was a godsend. In Pembrokeshire a high-ranking officer had been killed by neo-royalist rebels. Here was a challenge. No more time to talk, only to act, and a clear sign that until Charles Stuart (for so far had he dwindled), 'that man of blood',[9] was brought to proper punishment there could be no hope of settlement. The work of reconstruction must be put off till the rubble was cleared away. During that time a benign Providence would surely point the way to safety. Meantime they must be up and doing to meet the invaders from Scotland, to crush the rebels in Wales and to nip the risings of royalists old and new which were to break out all over England, but particularly in the heavily-taxed and regimented south-east. This area, with its close City contacts, its wealth, its closeness to the continent and the narrow seas, was a danger, the more so as the Navy could no longer be relied on. (In fact it was to be taken over soon to the royalists.) John Lambert went north, Hardress Waller hurried down to Cornwall, and Cromwell with the largest force pushed into South Wales. Fairfax stayed to deal with trouble in the Home Counties.

A second civil war had begun. To many war was not unwelcome. With a fight on their hands the troops would have little energy left for politics. Discipline and unity could be brought back together. But for a while the situation looked like getting out of hand. All South Wales was in a ferment. In the north royalist groups appearing from nowhere seized Carlisle, Scarborough, Pontefract and (in conjunction with some Scots) Berwick. Kent and Essex rose in fury. All over the country there were signs of discontent, as much economic as political—a reaction against the excise and the excessive burden of taxation, following the bad harvest of 1647. It was not positive royalism but weariness of parliament, the army and the county committees:

> *So long as ravening soldiers on us prey*
> *We must look for peace the clean contrary way.*[10]

The speed with which the army dealt with these scattered areas is a tribute to the restoration of discipline and to its training. Of course, there were advantages in this situation. It might look as if the army were surrounded—in fact the ring around it was not a ring at all but isolated links. Geographically divided, the 'rebels' were also politically incoherent and strategically unco-ordinated. Old royalists with a love of episcopacy feared new presbyterian allies. Both were doubtful of the sentiments of Irish catholics. It would be difficult to implement all the various aspirations concealed under the slogan 'a personal treaty with the king'.[11] Moreover, London, vital in any successful *coup*, though restless, never looked like slipping out of the grandees' control. So the second civil war failed to improve the King's position.

The Scots invasion, which might have proved critical with Cromwell and Fairfax heavily engaged in South Wales and south-east England respectively, flopped badly and was readily contained by Lambert's limited forces. Not all the covenanters were ready even at the start to follow their leaders into new adventures. The long months since the Engagement was taken had given time for rifts to widen. Hamilton found many of the nobility eager to back him, but the clergy, supported by Argyll and then Loudon, dragged their heels. The complications of Scottish politics in this period are endless. It is worth noting here that there were many clan and personal rivalries running athwart the national issues. (Much the same can be said of England, where localism was endemic even at the height of the civil war, and a major impulse in the second.) In the end Hamilton, by some desperate methods including dragonnades, did get on top, but shewed the disunity of the nation in doing so. The army that actually entered England in July 1648 was one half-trained at best, with many raw levies—the well-tried troops who had fought under Leven were not available. Besides, English presbyterians, themselves at loggerheads, did not trust Hamilton, and many suspected that the King, who had not yet taken the covenant, was as much tied to the Irish and Welsh—catholics and prelatists—as to the Scots. They preferred talking with him to fighting for him. The early royalist successes, obtained by the wrong kind of people, hardened the suspicions of men like Robert Baillie, who, as usual, started to lament that if 'his restitution shall come by these hands, and be so ill prepared, . . . the glorious reformation we have suffered so much for shall be much endangered and the most that shall be obtained be but one Erastian weak presbyterie with a tolleration of Poperi and Episcopacie at Court and of diverse sects elsewhere'.[12] But the right-wing were encouraged to hope by parliamentary concessions to the City. At the instance of the Common Council and over the outspoken opposition of republicans, the Commons again took up the possibility of negotiating with Charles. This change was the result of the withdrawal of officer members to the field. The conservative civilians were in charge again and celebrated by passing an ordinance against blasphemy and heresy, with penalties including death, an obvious riposte to an army riddled with dangerous notions of toleration. Yet this, like the terms offered to Charles, old stuff long ago mulled over, was an empty gesture, meaningless once the risings were over.

The royalists might have done better if Charles had escaped to one of the local centres in England, to Scotland or to the continent, anywhere so long as he was free. He certainly intended to get away, and scheme after scheme was worked out. All failed, since while the fighting was going on he was very closely watched. So the war went on without him. At the end of May Kentishmen, too impatient to wait for the Scots invasion, rose and the fleet mutinied in the Downs, allowing royalist squadrons to blockade the Thames and bring trade to a halt. Fairfax got on top in a sharp engagement at Maidstone (1 June), helped by the reluctance of the ordinary folk to join the gentry who were, however, strongly represented. While Kent was being mopped up, Essex made its gesture. The unpopular county committee was taken at Chelmsford. Refugees from the Kentish fiasco joined in an unsuccessful assault on the county magazine. Then the entire force settled down in Colchester, seeking to rally the discontented throughout the whole Eastern Association. But the Suffolk trained bands thought more of keeping their 'country' clear of war than of any royalist cause. So Colchester was besieged, holding out till August, a gallant but lonely effort. Meanwhile, the Earl of Holland, with a commission from the Queen, failed lamentably to stir Surrey. The quarrelsome Irish factions, from whom so much was expected, not surprisingly could not agree on an objective and let opportunity slip by. Shortly after the Scots invaded Pembroke fell to Cromwell (11 July), and he was able to move back to help Lambert. But already Hamilton's slowness—he was hanging around waiting for men and supplies—the wet weather and the inability of the poverty-stricken countryside to provide a fat living for his army had reduced the danger. By the time Hamilton reached Preston and joined a force of English under Sir Marmaduke Langdale, Cromwell caught up with them (17 August). It was a fierce battle, bravely fought. Langdale's troops took the brunt of Cromwell's assault and were cut to pieces. The main Scots army, out foraging, was not brought into the engagement, but Cromwell pressed into them at Winwick and forced the surrender of the remnants at Warrington. Hamilton, who had so feebly handed over the initiative to the New Model, was taken by Lambert at Uttoxeter. It was said, 'he was too much a statesman and too little a soldier',[13] perhaps not an unkind judgment. As for Cromwell he went on to take Berwick and Carlisle, and to enter Scotland unopposed. He contacted Argyll and Wariston and other opponents of the Hamiltonions whom he found only too willing to agree to drive all Engagers out of Scottish government. (Some critics of his policy feel he made a mistake here—he should have dealt with the Scots once and for all and made further dealings with the Stuarts impossible. This argument presupposes that he knew that Charles I would be executed and that his son would be ready to take the covenant.)

With Argyll triumphant over his enemies (7 October) Oliver left a small force behind and turned south to clear out the residue of resistance in Yorkshire. This bogged him down in the siege of Pontefract, during which the Leveller leader, Col. Thomas Rainsborough, was assassinated by terrorists. That was not the only curious feature of these weeks. One wonders why Cromwell let himself be distracted till December from the intense political struggle at Westminster.

Preston had been decisive. Pockets of resistance held out (Pontefract till March 1649), but the royalist cause everywhere was in ruins. The victory was the army's and not the parliament's, though, while the soldiers were fighting, the politicians had enjoyed themselves. The civilian Independents proved no match for the presbyterians, who were reinforced by the return of men like Denzil Holles, Sir William Waller, and Edward Massey who had either been secluded in the purges of late 1647, or like Sir John Clotworthy had been abroad.[14] These men were able parliamentarians and soon dominated the debates, working hard to get something settled before the summer's business in the field was over. But all they could do in fact was to rescind the vote of 'no addresses' (24 August) and to start again the weary round of talks with the King. Commissioners of both Houses including Holles, Vane, Salisbury and Pembroke, waited on him at Newport, I.O.W. (18 September). A proposal to have the 40 days allotted for treating divided up into specific periods for specific proposals was rejected as a means of destroying the fruit of this treaty. A member who argued that any treaty made with the King was likely to be 'utterly unsafe and dangerous', was told that as an office-holder under the present régime he was prejudiced. Someone else nastily demanded that no office-holder or other gainer by the war should be a commissioner. It was also resolved that M.P.s failing to attend the House should be fined since 'in the multitude of counsellors there is safety'.[15] £10,000 was borrowed from the City to meet the expenses of negotiation. It is obvious that in spite of previous disappointments there was an urge for a settlement. Unfortunately the men who thought they could treat with Charles had no idea of how to treat the army. In spite of appeals by Fairfax nothing was done about soldiers' pay—still the greatest professional grievance. Something of the likely attitude of the army had been seen in September when a petition from citizens of London and thereabouts, probably drawn up with the assistance of Henry Marten, was presented against a treaty with the King as something 'cryed up principally by such as have been dis-affected unto you', and demanding a settlement along Leveller lines without King or peers.[16] Foolishly it was rejected more or less out of hand.

The commissioners, Holles and Saye and Sele, in particular, struggled to convince the King that he must accept their terms before it was too late. Otherwise, they stressed, the army would proceed in its own way, depose the King, change the government, and settle a republic by its own rules and invention. But Charles could not resist manœuvering. He persuaded the 'peace group' on the commission that nothing should be set down in writing and held binding until a whole treaty was agreed upon. The Independents, who were not present when this dangerous proposal—'the King's last refuge'—was accepted, protested that it was taken at 'an unseasonable hour'. They were tartly reminded that most votes that had lately been made in favour of the army had been secured by tricks or at late hours.[17] The 'peace group' were enjoying being on top. But they were not as safe as they imagined.

At Newport the talks droned on, Charles asking for more information and arguing in circles over minor details, still thinking that by gaining time he must in the end regain his throne. He was encouraged by the fact which could not be concealed that on many matters, particularly religion, on which he had himself well-reported scruples, there was no real accord among the commissioners, some of whom like Vane, hankered after a toleration close to that adumbrated in the Heads of the Proposals. In the event more than the 40 authorised days were spent in a wilderness of words, until on 24 November Charles made it clear that he was not prepared to sacrifice his Church of England for good and all. Whatever hopes he had held out, in his heart, it seems he had always kept this grand reservation, as he had told his wife in January 1646: 'The difference between me and the rebels about the Church is not bare matter of form or ceremony, which are alterable according to occasion, but so real that if I should give way as is desired, there would be no Church and by no human probability ever to be recovered. . . . My yielding this is a sin of the highest nature.'[18] Against this rock the breakers had rolled in vain. All the 'peace party', in fact, had achieved was to embroil themselves with the army and its allies, 'cavilling' time away 'untill Cromwell had done his worke in the North, and marched up to Towne to make the Treaty ineffectuall'.[19]

While Cromwell sat down at Pontefract and the debate continued at Newport, others had not been idle. Ireton, leaving the siege of Colchester, took up his pen again, offering a remonstrance to Fairfax (1 October) calling for impartial justice on all criminal persons. By implication these included the King. Just before the King's final rejection of all proposals, an army remonstrance, again probably the work of Ireton, demanded the public punishment of the traitor King, 'that grand and capital author of all our woes, . . . in whose behalf and in whose interest only (of will and power) all our wars and troubles have been.'[20] A 'competent number' of his associates must suffer, too. A draft was argued over by army officers at St Alban's (mid-November), and opposed by some, including Fairfax, who thought an agreement between King, parliament and army was still to be had. At the same time Lilburne (lately released from prison by parliament, some thought merely to make things awkward for Cromwell and the grandees), Wildman and some Independents were getting down to other fundamentals at the Nag's Head Tavern. The atmosphere was electric. Lilburne might hold no brief for Charles, but he was acute enough— he had learned quite a lot from his royalist fellow-prisoners in the Tower, Judge David Jenkins and Lewis Dyve—to see that merely to get rid of Charles was not enough. What was wanted was a settlement agreed upon beforehand, one in which the principle of the supremacy of the people was explicitly stated. The need of Leveller support was regarded as so pressing that a scheme rather like that of the Agreement of the People was written up. Later Lilburne denounced Ireton's 'machiavellianism' in these discussions, and indeed it is more than likely that Ireton with his eye to property was all the time banking on the eventual repudiation of the proposals, after they had served his turn. The 'Whitehall debates' which followed in December are of prime importance for the insight they give to the considerable differences between the Levellers and the Independents, particularly over religious toleration.

Cromwell, too, was at last beginning to stir at Pontefract. He wrote to Fairfax that in his heart he concurred with the troops' desire to see impartial justice done upon offenders. The republican Ludlow, later a prodigious opponent of Oliver, stated the question thus: 'Whether the King should govern us as a god by his will, and the nation be governed by force like beasts, or whether the people should be governed by laws made by themselves, and live under a government derived by their own consent.'[21] Less prejudiced observers might not have seen it in quite those terms. Was not the army, in fact, in a far better position than Charles to govern by force? Was it not more likely to do so?

The army remonstrance—'a thing called (by those that use to miscall things) *An humble Remonstrance*'[22]—was ultimately presented to the Commons (20 November) and tactlessly laid aside, confirming the more extreme officers in their view that sooner rather than later the House would have to be shocked into its senses. At the end of November Fairfax, pushed by his officers, agreed to march on London 'for the public interest' and safety of the nation.[23]

On 1 December, the day Holles reluctantly reported Charles's final negative to the Commons, the regiments were back in quarters around Whitehall. At the same time Charles was removed from the Isle of Wight to Hurst Castle. On 4 December parliament recorded that this 'insolency' had been done without its consent. Two days before at the motion of William Prynne, as emphatic in this as in everything, they resolved to continue negotiations with the King, and, indeed, on 5 December after a wordy all-night sitting, declared by 129–83 votes that 'the answers of the King to the propositions of both Houses are a ground for the Houses to proceed upon for the settlement of the peace of the kingdom'.[24] This was a contemptuous repudiation of the army's practical claim to be a fourth estate. Reaction was sharp and perhaps unexpected. On 6 December members making their way into the Commons found troops everywhere around the palace of Westminster and at the entrance to their house a detachment under the plebeian professional Col. Pride, whose regiment was responsible for guarding the Houses. In his hand the Colonel held a list of members whom he was to consider likely to be unfaithful to 'the cause'. Unknown to

Fairfax, the night before a group of officers and Independent M.P.s had discussed the possibility of a dissolution of the entire parliament. Not unnaturally the M.P.s were reluctant to abandon their own occupations, so as a compromise, a purge was agreed upon. The way in which it was carried out emphasised at once the urgency of the situation and the effective grip of the army. Lord Grey of Groby stood by Pride— peer and drayman, a strange partnership—to point out men to be refused entry. Pride, no politician, was presumably unfamiliar with many of them. Some protested, others resisted and of these, or 'the most suspected', some were arrested and taken off one by one to 'Hell'—a nearby inn. Forty-one members proved too much of a strain on the informal hospitality there, and they were soon lodged in more commodious quarters in the Strand. (There is a story that one of them was soon released to give the Commons a quorum.) That night Cromwell, summoned by a bewildered Fairfax—'that cypher'— got back to town.[25] Before he went to bed in Whitehall he had declared his support for what had been done. A purge, after all, was better than a naked expulsion. There was still a little bit of a parliament to do what had to be done, and what he, among others, was now determined to have done.

The renewed expulsion of 'the 11 members'—strangely Holles was not one of those secluded by Pride—was soon voted. The revocation of the 'vote of no addresses' to the King was itself revoked. A few more arrests were ordered, the Conqueror himself, Sir William Waller, and Sir John Clotworthy, among them, accused of connivance in the Scottish invasion. But these were really small fry. The big culprit was Charles, who was brought to Windsor in readiness for an early trial. The same day (23 December) this fag-end of a Commons set up a committee to seek out how to proceed in a way of justice against the King and his leading associates. It was a difficult question to answer, but an answer there must be. A proposal, acceptable to Cromwell, was made whereby Charles was to be assured of his life if he accepted some terms to be put to him confidentially by the Earl of Denbigh, making a bid for a political comeback. But Charles, who had perhaps by now fallen in love with the idea of being a martyr or, perhaps, saw in his enforced presence at a trial a sort of fulfilment of his long, worked-for return to his capital, refused to meet Denbigh. On 1 January 1649 the Commons declared it treason in the King to levy war on the parliament and the kingdom. His trial must follow. The Peers refused to have anything to do with it. Unabashed the Commons, seeing that the people under God were the original of all just power and that they were chosen by the people, assumed the supreme authority of the nation. Henceforth their decrees should be 'acts' of parliament with full force. The first of these acts decreed the appointment of a special high court of justice. One hundred and thirty-five commissioners were nominated, headed by Fairfax and Cromwell, and including both officers and civilians. The charge that all this was the effect of the work of a single perfidious man—Cromwell—is untenable. There were many features about the arrangement with which he disagreed, and at first he shewed a strong objection to the haste with which the Lords were brushed to one side. His power and prestige were considerable but he was hardly a dictator. What was being done was no doubt against the will of the nation and was the work of a very small minority, yet it was a minority, as he said later, that had had 'somewhat to do in the world' [26] and which would not be pushed around by a parliament or a lieutenant-general. In fact Cromwell was rather late in making up his mind that the King really must die. But once Providence by about the middle of January had shewn him the one true course he was impatient for action, brushing aside considerations that would have weighed heavily with him a while before. 'Go and do your duty', was now his theme. He would not hesitate to do his.

PART THREE

The Road Back

XVI New Chains Discovered

The trial of Charles I is one of the great set-pieces of English history. It is also a truly tragic affair, not only because of the superb but unavailing performance of the King, but because it is one of those deeply moving occasions in which right struggles with right, or, if you like, wrong with wrong. Here is no simple case of sharp blacks and whites, but of those diverse shades of grey which make up the colour of English January skies. The theme has appealed to imaginative writers who have ruined rather than heightened the drama by coming heavily down on one side or the other, usually the King's, making buffoons or inhuman monsters of Cromwell and his associates. The true inwardness of this tragedy lies in the fact that both sides were honest in this moment of truth. It is their inability to escape from the implications of their actions that is moving. In a sense the execution itself is an anti-climax. It is the trial itself that engages our sympathies. Charles's own contribution is superb. For a few days he puts on a splendid performance of majesty. Dignity, quickness of wit, eloquence are his, even his stammer seems quieted. But nothing he can do, nothing anybody can do, we feel, will stay his progress to the block.

Fairfax stayed away from the trial, as did many other commissioners, uncertain in their minds and troubled at heart. Lady Fairfax cried out in protest at the trial. But Lady Eleanor Davies, the crazy prophetess whom Charles had long ago slighted, gurgled in delight at one more forecast coming true. Charles refused to plead before those who dared to speak in the name of his subjects. By default he went guilty, silenced when he sought to speak against the sentence. On 30 January 1649 outside Inigo Jones's handsome Banqueting Hall—symbol of his own tastes and temperament—he died, one might say, like a King.

With Charles there died an era. The days of shuffling and procrastination were, for some men at least, over. The chief stumbling block in the way of settlement had been broken up. It was a wonderful moment. Yet it was only a moment. The great prize remained out of reach and sooner or later disenchantment would set in and men now elated would begin to wonder what went wrong, and see in the killing of a King the source of all their woes.

There is, however, this much to be said for the regicides. Charles I was not the first English King to meet a violent end at the hands of some of his subjects. What they did was not 'done in a corner'.[1] He was not privily stabbed or hacked to pieces. He was given an opportunity for a last flawless performance and provided with a perfect setting for it. Most of them felt no shame, and when, after the Restoration, they, too, found themselves condemned they shewed it was not the peculiar prerogative of a King to know how to die. A few, too, spoke with golden tongues.

So began the rule of the Rump, a government regarded from the start as a stop-gap, a mere expedient, never an experiment. 'The Rump was an oligarchy with no positive policy, except that of self-interest'.[2] There was every expectation of a new system soon, and many groups intended to see that hope fulfilled. The Levellers certainly did not regard as final the parliamentary rejection of the proposals put forward at Whitehall the previous December. For them the trial of the King could be but a beginning, the preliminary clearing of the ground for a noble constitutional experiment, the outcome of which must be—they had no doubt—human happiness as never before. They had been hard on the King not merely for revenge, or for simple self-preservation, but because they saw in monarchy, and in the only representative of it most of them had known, a barrier against a new and better world. Now that day had come, and ideas which they regarded as not merely desirable but essential and urgent could be implemented here and now, lest a new 'regal tyranny' get fixed in the King's place.

They were confident that through them God was working out his purpose. As early as 1647 Colonel Rainsborough had cried that he was not afraid to jump into the dark, certain that God and right would jump with him. Rainsborough was gone, mysteriously 'liquidated', but his attitude survived. For such men the royal blood spilled in the snow had expiated the blood of many humbler men who had died in a good cause and whose souls wanted, more than revenge, the peace that would come of knowing they had not died in vain. Such a peace depended upon England being a land fit for free men to live in. Unfortunately for them the Levellers and similar radicals, for all their enthusiasm and dedication, were, however the count is taken, a minority. Support they had in the army but it would be easy to exaggerate their numbers even among the rank and file. At the Putney debates there was Buff Coat, the Bedfordshire men and Sexby and a couple of others, but they were mostly over-shadowed by officers like Rainsborough, gentlemen Levellers like Wildman, on their own side, and the Independent grandees on the other. The ease with which Cromwell restored order on Corkbush Field argues a lack of persistence among the soldiery—and this is confirmed by the utter obedience of the regiments at the other rendezvous. A good deal of the rank and file volubility and volatility in 1647 to 1649 was, of course, for professional grievances—pay, indemnity and whatever. Long-term political notions were beyond the grasp of most of them and could only have an impact within the context of soldierly grouses and weakened discipline. This could be, as we have seen, very effective in the special circumstances of 1646–8, but was an unsure basis for radical political and social movements.

The civilian Levellers were more formidable in argument if not in numbers. They included educated men like William Walwyn, with practised prying minds, eloquence in speech or writing, with courage and some organising capacity. Given the disturbed conditions of the time, their phenomenal growth is not surprising. Their programme of destroying commercial and industrial privilege, of the abolition of the excise, freedom from pressing, bringing in agrarian and legal reforms was attractive to both Londoners and provincials. Attacks on the survival of titles of honour and on the blatant speculation in land in which important politicians were obviously involved give them a wide appeal to a variety of critics of the régime. But they attracted chiefly an unstable element of society—literate groups with tiny stakes in the country, artisans, apprentices, small employers (and these mostly urban), men who could express their discontent, but who, because they were either going up in the world or going down were without much staunchness or consistency. They were, perhaps, the seventeenth-century equivalent of 'the floating voters'. Their hopes and fears could make them momentarily flare into political passion, but it was often too intense a heat to last long. Moreover—this is quite fundamental—they never at any time held actual power. Cromwell nipped in between them and the army in the crises of 1647 and (as we shall see) 1649. They never won real support in the parliament or captured any part of the governing machinery of the City. There is a suggestion of something like party organisation in the speed with which they could get petitions drawn up, circulated and supported, but it was something that did not spill over into the more mundane but also more necessary field of political construction. John Lilburne could appeal to City crowds with a perhaps more immediate impact even than John Pym—but the latter had known far more about the way in which political enthusiasms to be creative must be put into appropriate channels. If

Lilburne was a spate, Pym was a whole irrigation system. There is no doubt which has the greater utility. For all their splendid hopes, proliferating ideas and wide publicity, the Levellers stood very little chance of actually controlling events in 1649. The Independents did. They, too, were men of ideas. Though they cannot be readily identified with any one social class or with any rigid political outlook they had enough in common to give them the initiative in the disruptions of 1648-9. They may not have known exactly what they wanted but they were fairly certain what they hated. It has been shewn that Independency was a rag-bag of political, social, religious and constitutional opinions. What is impressive about these opinions is not only their diversity, but the intelligence and force with which they were pushed. Independents ought to have been quarrelling with themselves all the time. Independency ought to have collapsed from internecine warfare. Disaster was always round the corner but was in fact held off until the debacle that brought on the Restoration. The Independents made up a composite party, always in a state of flux, always shedding someone or something, winnowed by Providence, but somehow managing to survive, even to prosper.

The Rump represented, if it represented anything, the civilian wing of the Independents. About 210 Rumpers have been identified. Of these very few sat at all regularly, and the average attendance at the deliberations of the sovereign House of Commons was about 80. This was a small segment of the whole, but not disproportionately so, when we consider how low attendance had often been during the last few years. Analysis of the membership has shewn that it accorded pretty well with the membership of the Long Parliament itself. There is no obvious social or economic difference between the Rumpers and the 'secluded members'. Certainly the Rumpers were not all lesser or declining or 'mere' gentry. Wales, where most of the gentry were surely 'mere', had a smaller proportion of Rumpers than the rest of the country. Lancashire had none at all. Yet it does seem that the older parliamentary families were being thinned out and some 'who would normally have been too far from the centre of national . . . politics [had] now found the way less crowded and obstructed'.[3] (The same development can be seen in county committees, and in the army itself.) This is not unexpected. Such men had, like Henry Stone, the ex-merchant turned soldier and governor of Stafford, a tendency to be enthusiastic for the cause. But, even so, the way was never easy for them, as Stone was to find when during the Protectorate he tried without success to get into the Commons. In fact, the composition of the Rump certainly did not directly reflect the support there was among 'new men' for the régime. Part of the explanation lies in the fact that during the Rump period there were no elections, and the recruiting elections had been fought earlier on the old franchise, which gave little chance for men without the traditional local political 'pull' to get in.[4] (This difficulty is one reason for the great interest in parliamentary reform during the Interregnum.)

What the Rump represented was, then, that heterogeneous party, the Independents. Baxter described the Rumpers as composed of 'the Vanists, the Independents, and other sects with the democratical party'. These have been identified by Mr George Yule as the republicans ('the democratical party'), the conservative Independents ('the Independents'), the radical Independents ('other sects'). The Vanists are harder to pin down. They may have been as Mr Yule suggests 'the upper gentry', but more likely were merely a loose knot of men who for personal or other reasons might perhaps have adhered more closely to the leadership of Sir Henry Vane, Jnr, than to that of anyone else.[5]

There is room for further investigation of the politics and backgrounds of the Rumpers. The simple contemporary view that they were a crowd of venal men who had flung in their lot with the devil (i.e. Oliver Cromwell) was answered by Sir Henry Marten: 'a whole parliament can have no plot at all; they are so numerous and so mingled in temper and education, age and interest that so great a party would not drive on any project of that bulk, so long abrewing, with secrecy sufficient for such an enterprise'.[6] It is true of course that the Rump parliament, like its predecessors (and protectorate successors) was dominated by a small core of active and able men and that these might have formed an effective working cabal. Among them there may have been crude careerists of the kind so vigorously denounced in Walker's polemical *History of Independency*, but it is difficult to imagine some of the others in this light. Men are rarely all black—or all white—and at times are moved by things outside of self-interest. Haselrig did well out of bishops' lands, but his policy embraced more than a mania for acquiring 'pleasant manors'.[7] Marten and Wallop were in debt later on in the Interregnum but had begun as rich men. They worked most of them hard and in a few cases selflessly. 'The finances were managed with economy and exactness. No private person became rich by public extortion.'[8] Men of the stamp of Sir Arthur Haselrig and Edmund Ludlow, whatever they did in the Rump, suffered by its expulsion, but never would respond to the blandishments of the Protectorate. If they had a price, Cromwell as Lord Protector could not find enough to pay it.

Charles I had been executed on 30 January 1649. On 6 February it was resolved without a division to lay aside the House of Peers for the general good as 'useless and dangerous'. 'It was never commanded that the whole nation should be oppressed to maintain the lust and riot of a few drones' was one comment. (The act was passed on 19 March.[9]) On 17 March monarchy itself was formally abolished, and the kingdom was solemnly transformed into a republic on 19 May. This late date suggests that enthusiastic republican principles were somewhat lacking in the régime. A declaration on the judiciary asserted an intention to maintain the 'fundamental laws', and some judges found it not too much of an effort to take oaths for the new government. All this served notice on the Levellers and doctrinaire republicans that they could not expect much in the way of rapid and far-reaching change from this parliament. Hence the determination of the radicals to press for a new assembly elected on a wider franchise. It has often been assumed that this would at once have led to a royalist majority. That is, however, by no means certain. There is little evidence of support for the 1648 risings among the unfranchised—but, of course, without a secret ballot and new property relationships a new electorate might have been politically timid. In any case the Rump was not ready then—or later—to take chances. The call for deeds it answered in resounding words. A splendid new Great Seal was struck in the name of 'the keepers of the liberties of England by the authority of parliament', and grandiloquently inscribed 'in the first year of freedom by God's blessing restored'. (The engraver was Oliver Simon, who had struck seals for Charles I, the civil war parliaments and would do so for the Protectorate and restored monarchy.) Having taken power as 'the only visible authority in being' (a claim later made by Cromwell when he expelled it), the Rump intended to retain it. Confident that the army grandees associated with its birth would not desert it, the Rump intended to hasten slowly, if at all, in the direction of basic reform. An army must be maintained, but as a disciplined non-political force, led by non-political officers. This happy state was superficially brought about by the failure of the Leveller mutinies of the summer of 1649. Cromwell did not hesitate to suppress them lest the whole cause—what this was was not defined—be lost. The international situation helped too. With the possibility of invasion from the continent and intervention from Ireland and Scotland, where Charles II was proclaimed, the ranks closed. These problems tied up Cromwell, his grandee disciples and the bulk of the army until 1651. Now and then they reminded the government of the need for various reforms, but their main energies were flowing down other channels. Their preoccupation with external matters and readiness to preserve order and national security misled the Rump into overestimating their patience, and contributed directly to the ultimate expulsion. With an appetite for political power growing with possession of it, the Rumpers were unready to bring in reforms that they saw as cutting their own throats. They were safe so long as the armed forces had soldierly work to do. Just as in 1647-8 Cromwell had worked hard to minimise differences between army and civilians, so he did now, at least until early in 1653. It was the Rump itself as much as its critics that finally persuaded him of his folly and urged him to decisive action.

Meantime the Rump governed, and in many ways governed well. The executive was vested in a council of state of whom the first temporary president was Oliver Cromwell, though no specific individual was nominated for that office in the initial instrument of appointment. The sword was soon tactfully replaced by the civilian John Bradshaw, a common lawyer, who had presided rather ineffectively at the trial of the King. The council was empowered to direct the armed forces, to promote trade, to conduct foreign affairs, to make charges upon the inland revenues by warrant and to put into execution orders directed to it from time to time by parliament. Members nominated—not all of them served—included Denbigh, Pembroke, St John, Fairfax, Grey of Groby, Skippon, Pennington, Vane, Haselrig and Ludlow— an indication of a desire to embrace civil and military power and to appeal to men of social and economic standing. Thomas Harrison the religious zealot and Henry Ireton were proposed for membership but were turned down. Ireton, one notes again and again, was a man too 'full of invention and industry',[10] arousing strong antagonisms both from right and left.

This council was the heir to the old royal Privy Council. Something like it would be established under all the régimes until the Restoration, though the powers of these bodies varied widely. The council of state established in 1653 by the Instrument of Government—frankly dominated by the army officers—was perhaps the most powerful reaction against the superiority assumed by parliament during the Commonwealth. It sat while there was no parliament. But the Rump sat during the entire duration of the Commonwealth and jealously guarded its own sovereignty. It refused, for example, to allow the council to control parliamentary executive committees such as that for Compounding. In practice, relations were generally good, since most councillors were also active M.P.s, but the tendency for the military element to increase on the council—its composition was reviewed annually—led to strain as relations between the army and the Commons deteriorated.

From the start the régime was ringed with enemies and critics. There were those active parliamentarians who had been snatched from political life by Pride's Purge. Clement Walker threw himself into lively and spiteful propaganda. His *History of Independency*, as already noted, is a stimulating but doubtful source of information on the Rumpers. William Prynne, who in the critical days of December 1648 had supported with 'iron arguments'[11] continued negotiations with the King and had hoped the parliament might have 'no great need of (the army's) future service', now published a spate of violent (and predictably long-winded) pamphlets against 'the present unparliamentary juncto'.[12] He remained unreconciled to any régime of the sixteen-fifties and was to play a prominent part in the restored Long Parliament on the eve of the Restoration. Prynne and his like detested the Commonwealth not only because it was a regicide republic but because it seemed to be playing into the hands of those working on the left for social reform and toleration (or revolutionary religious anarchy). Lesser Prynnes were to be found among the City authorities and had to be winkled out. (Every change in parliament during the Interregnum was associated with a purge or enforced change in the City.) Similar purges took place in the county committees. Some of those secluded from central or local politics made contact with Charles Stuart, particularly after his reconciliation with the Scots, who had protested at the King's trial and execution and refused to accept the new order in England. Others, however, made their peace with the Commonwealth or at any rate abstained from actually working against it. Their motives were mixed—lack of courage, weariness, apathy, perhaps even genuine change of heart. Moreover, the suppression of the Leveller mutinies and the clear indication that the Rump and the grandees were going to do nothing to implement any major part of the Agreements of the People were very reassuring. (The Protectorate was later to appeal also to men who were ready to take Cromwell, whatever his faults, as a kind of saviour of society.) On the whole, though the right-wing groupings were not openly reconciled to the government, they were not eager to put themselves out to destroy it.

More serious at the start were the Levellers, men with frustrations and a programme. Ardent propagandists, they rammed home their view of the usurpation of the Rump and claimed that under it and its new-fangled council of state there was as much if not more danger of despotism as under the King and his Privy Council. In forceful pamphlets they piled up criticisms and shouted their demands for immediate and long-term remedies. A bitter animosity to Cromwell was revealed. His waiting on Providence was denounced as mere deceit. Ireton, too, was labelled a villain. His critics pressed for the re-establishment of an army council with direct representation of the rank and file. They appreciated the vital part that military force could play in politics and intended to have a share in directing it. They pressed inexorably for the widened franchise, the religious toleration and social amelioration that formed the main planks in their platform.

Civilian agitation was bad enough, but attempts to capture the army appalled government and grandees alike. On the initiative of the officers an act was passed against civilians disaffecting the soldiery. It was not enough to prevent a crisis. In March 1649 some troops (including Richard Rumbold, who nearly 40 years later was to be executed for his part in Argyll's rebellion) attempted to present to the council of officers a remonstrance urging the implementation of a Leveller programme. They were promptly cashiered 'and foure of them sentenced to ride the horse with their faces to the taile [and] swords broke over their heads. . . .'[13] At the court martial one of them, Robert Ward, expressed the disillusionment of Levellers generally when he said that it was as good for him to suffer under the King as under the keepers of the liberties of England, since both in practice maintained one and the same thing. In his view, that thing was not liberty. Next month some troops ordered to Ireland—where certainly the situation needed attention—refused to go unless Leveller demands were accepted. The danger of this call to sedition in the army was underlined by rumours of a projected invasion from the continent covered by Rupert's fleet. Sharp measures were called for. In spite of appeals to the appropriate clause of the Petition of Right, there were more courts martial. Robert Lockyer, a 23-year-old trooper, was shot. His funeral procession, through streets of silent mourners, among them many women wearing the sea-green Leveller favours, was a moving and impressive one. Moreover, the execution of Lockyer failed in its intention. A mutinous spirit seeped into more and more regiments. At a rendezvous in Banbury (May) a group of disaffected soldiers under 'Captain' William Thompson drew up a manifesto—*England's Standard Advanced*—stiff with Leveller notions and calling for a restoration of representation by agitators. Troopers Arnold and Lockyer were spoken of as martyrs. The manifesto confirms recent views of the nature of Levellerism by pointing out that its signatories were not paupers but men who had sold farms or given up trades to fight. The mutineers were seized but Thompson got away towards Salisbury, where there was another Leveller group in arms. Appealing successfully to the need for discipline and loyalty in their own regiments, Cromwell and Fairfax caught the remaining mutineers at Burford and there coldly and cruelly broke the back of the movement. Thompson escaped again, but was finally killed, fighting desperately near Wellingborough.

Thompson's legendary 'last stand' marks the effective end of army Levellerism, though there was a belated outbreak of no real significance as late as September 1649, in Oxford, then as ever the home of lost causes. The destruction of the Levellers was a political campaign, though plausibly disguised as one for military discipline. Cromwell was as firm as William Prynne in condemning soldierly politics where they conflicted with his own desires. Perhaps the security of the infant state did demand the destruction of a movement so intractable as the Levellers', but there is more than a tang of 'the tyrant's plea—necessity' in the evident relish with which the radicals were put down. Had the King been executed solely for security? Were the Levellers wrong to want to see in his removal the fated prelude to better things? Not for the first or the last time something precious may have been lost in the name of the safety of the State.

Taking without shame a leaf out of the presbyterians' book, the Rump had the tainted regiments shipped to Ireland, cutting them off from English civilian contacts, and dissipating their energies in fighting. There would be from time to time talk of a Leveller revival. Like foreign invasion or popery, it was used as a nay-daddy to scare the politically timorous. But even in the breakdown of 1659–60 there seems to have been little chance of it ever again developing into a really dynamic force in the army. Perhaps if Rainsborough had not been assassinated in 1648 there would have been a different story.

Among the civilians unrest continued. Lilburne had refused to accept the compromise Agreement of the People and had actually gone away to the north pursuing private business, to which he brought the same kind of aggressive conviction that marked his public progress. Back in London in February 1649 he asserted that he had given up politics. Not surprisingly it was a brief retirement. On 26 February he was at the bar of the Commons again with another hefty petition (published as *England's New Chains Discovered*—he was never at a loss for an arresting title). In March a fascinating account of Leveller activities since 1647—*The Hunting of the Foxes*—condemned *en passant* the prosecution of the regimental petitioners. Needless to say the foxes were Oliver Cromwell and his *éminence grise*, Henry Ireton. The hunt was reinforced by *The Second Part of England's New Chains Discovered* (April) in which the army officers, who ought to have been the salvation of the people, were accused of betraying them. The Levellers made it their business to open people's eyes so 'as that these men, this Faction of Officers, shall never be able to goe through with their wicked intentions'.[14] For their pains the reputed authors, Lilburne, Walwyn, Overton and Prince, were sent to the Tower by the council of state, charged with treason. Prison could not silence them—pamphlets like the unflattering *Picture of the Councel of State* somehow or other got written and published, while outside their supporters, including the by now inevitable women, volubly called for their release. But support among the respectable—'the saints'—who had stood up for the Levellers in the heyday of presbyterianism was dropping away, seeing that the cause was an unworthy one, man—instead of God—centred, too much burdened with the 'practical Christianity' of that 'wolf in Sheep's clothing',[15] the unfathomable William Walwyn. Undeterred the leaders put out on 1 May—traditional day of the people—yet another Agreement, a detailed platform for a true English Commonwealth. The tone was deliberately low-keyed, designed to persuade 'that we are not such wilde, irrationall, dangerous Creatures as we have been aspersed to be'.[16] The Rump, of course, must go, making way for a new assembly elected on new principles with a wider, but still not universal, franchise. This assembly was to have definite prescribed powers. Freedom of conscience was to be complete and inviolable, 'nothing having caused more distractions, and heart burnings in all ages, then persecution and molestation for matters of Conscience in and about Religion'.[17] The representatives should have no power to amend the agreement or to 'level mens Estates, destroy Propriety or make all things Common'.[18] This moderation was genuine enough, but it had no appeal for the authorities, who with army mutinies on their hands, responded, as we have seen, by making it a new treason to attempt to seduce soldiers from their obedience. Released on bail in June the Leveller leaders kept up their pressure. Indeed from June to September 1649 Lilburne was utterly tireless. Then, escorted by thousands of protesting admirers, he was back in the Tower again. This time the charge of treason was pressed home and in an absorbing public trial that brought out all the mingled charm and exasperation of his prickly personality, he was acquitted by the jury. The commemorative medal struck by the enthusiastic Levellers has often been reproduced. It symbolises triumph, but in fact the fire was beginning to burn out. The army had been purged, the sectaries were drifting away into chiliastic meditations.

Leveller leaders like Wildman had already defected, others would follow and Lilburne himself was to find his personal business increasingly pressing and attractive. Still from time to time he could not forbear to speak out, was exiled and at the time of the Little Parliament had to go through another trial to another stunning acquittal. (Even so he was kept in protective custody.) But even his resilience was weakening, and baulked of what he clearly thought of as something like paradise here on earth, he turned more other-wordly and became a quaker. Walwyn, never in the limelight, faded even more surely into obscurity. The references to him after 1649 are irritatingly brief—a pamphlet on juries, memorials to Cromwell's council of state against monopolistic trading companies, a sojourn in the Tower for an indefinite period on an unknown charge. In 1659, by which time Lilburne was dead, he may have been concerned with Harrington's schemes for a Commonwealth settlement. After the Restoration, still absorbed in things natural to man, he seems to have become a herbalist. Sexby, after a continental education in frondeur intrigue, became a terrorist in the pay of the royalists. It all reads like the last hurried cleaning-up at the end of a Victorian novel with a large cast of characters.

Was it—Levellerism—all a waste and a vanity? Certainly in their own time the Levellers failed, but their ideas were not completely forgotten. Later generations of radicals and democrats on both sides of the Atlantic found them an inspiration and a guide, and it has recently been suggested that their influence worked the other way as well. By putting an ill-defined but sharply asserted natural property right at the centre of their advocacy of the people's cause, they made it easy for Locke to confuse, in the general estimation, the equal right to property with the right to unlimited property, and thus to harness democratic sentiments to the Whig cause. Walwyn, certainly, would have spun in his grave at this knowledge. History has a habit of surprising us. But the Levellers' failure was shared in the long run by the man who more, perhaps, than any other blighted their hope—Oliver Cromwell. He cut them to pieces and in the process cut himself. Each use of the sword argued more for the sword; embarrassed by it, hampered by it, he could never repudiate it. The Levellers had little general support, Oliver little more, perhaps less. What he did do was to take the army from the Levellers and, making it his instrument, made himself its prisoner. That curious relationship was peculiar to his own lifetime, inalienable. With him it died and the flowers of 'the good old cause', their stalks scarred by the sword, finally withered. Cromwell was no closer to the mainstream of English life than the Levellers. After all his efforts it is difficult to say what was his permanent contribution to the modern world. It is easier to point out the Leveller notions that were realised.

At about the time the Leveller mutineers were being given their quietus, another more radical but even less practical group was at work. Under the leadership of an unsuccessful cloth merchant from

Wigan, a band of landless peasants and labourers tried to set up a communistic Utopia in Surrey at the heart of what is now a solidly respectable and conservative area, St George's Hill, Kingston-on-Thames. Driven to the conclusion that all the ills of this world, including individual psychological tensions, were the effect of private property, Gerrard Winstanley sought to restore a pristine English freedom in community of ownership, taking the execution of the King to mean the abolition of the Norman yoke which had robbed Englishmen of their birthrights. It was a little local affair but even in that hectic time it gained a notoriety and a suspicious council of state (pressed by local landlords) sent Fairfax to see what was going on. Eminently unimaginative himself, he adjudged Winstanley and his associates as cranky and harmless and took no further action. The men of substance round about were less sanguine and eventually found the way to break the colony up. What happened has taken the attention of historians in a way that contemporaries would have found incredible, and some nowadays deplore. Certainly it was little more than an episode—but that little more is important. It shews how deep when, as Winstanley himself wrote, the times were 'running up like parchment in the fire',[19] social criticisms could go. For a whole year a group of lumpen labourers, simple, timid folk, defied the pressure, often physical, of authority and power. Something fired them, their own condition or the eloquence of their leader. Winstanley was a man of deep thoughts and feelings, with a vivid style. Even now his voice can call us across the centuries. Whether he looked backward or forward or both, he speaks to us with an intimacy and directness that tugs at our affections.

But the régime had little to fear from the Diggers—'the true Levellers' as they called themselves. More attention was rightly reserved for royalists, old style and new. Monarchy had been rolled into the grave of Charles I, but there was still a claim and a candidate for a throne, one calling for foreign support against a regicide republic in a world of monarchy. There was reason to suppose he might get it. English agents in Holland and Spain were murdered without redress. The English revolution had had from the start an international significance—the role of conflict over foreign policy in producing the revolutionary situation is palpable, and the whole development has been seen as a part of a general European crisis producing at least six contemporaneous revolutions in the 1640s. Awareness of this malaise is shewn in the diplomatic rupture which followed the execution of the King, even distant Russia hastening to express its hardly heeded abhorrence. Some kind of *cordon sanitaire* might perhaps have been drawn around the wicked republic. So far the energies of most of Western Europe had been engaged in the meaningful conflict now known as the Thirty Years War, and fortunately for the Rump, when that struggle was over in the Empire France continued to fight Spain elsewhere. Then, the Frondes, themselves influenced by the English example and by some English agents and propaganda, tied up the French government at home in the crisis years. Similarly Spain was involved with Portuguese and Catalonian risings, while the United Provinces were caught up in one of their periodical demonstrations of internal incompatibilities. The conflicts of the catholic powers ensured ultimately that no holy war of counter-reformation and outraged monarchism should be launched against England. It is an only momentarily curious fact that the first continental conflict of the Commonwealth was not with a catholic monarchy but with the protestant quasi-republican one—the United Provinces and that over commercial and colonial disagreements. True, Cromwell as Protector would later take up arms against the old enemy Spain and appeal to popular anti-papist sentiments to back his vigorous policies—but he fought in alliance with catholic France under a Roman cardinal. Meanwhile the Rump had taken advantage of the dynastic preoccupations of its potential enemies to depress domestic opposition and through the New Model Army to control Scotland and Ireland. These successes were enough to discourage invasion on behalf of that precious exile, the Prince of Wales. In any case moderate royalism, which was always more substantial than enthusiastic, reckless royalism, certainly at home, argued against a King put back on the points of foreign bayonets.

But domestic and foreign dangers, if more potential than real, were used by the 'keepers of the liberties of England' to justify a rule which was quite simply that of an oligarchy—'the fag end' of a parliament, though a 'great parliament which had done great things'—backed by force. Unrepresentative, regarded even by its most vocal supporters as an expedient, a makeshift, it managed for a while to argue with apparent cogency in justification of its unwillingness to take into speedy consideration arrangements for its own retirement. But its very successes were bound to make things more and more difficult. The Leveller movement, civilian and military, was, as we have seen, collapsing. The royalists in England were depressed long before the disaster at Worcester in 1651 was to shatter Prince Charles's own hopes. He might have seen a red light in his failure to get a response from the west and Wales where his father had for so long been able to call up active loyalty. What was happening was not the growth of positive support for the new régime, which can hardly be said to have gone out of its way to encourage it, but rather of apathy, war-weariness and cynicism. Against the advice of Cromwell ruthless executions of prominent royalists like Derby, Holland and Hamilton were carried out as a dire example to lesser men. They may have had their effect. An act of oblivion for all offences before September 1651 was stuffed with so many exceptions as to be meaningless. Such lack of generosity meant that many men kept bitterly quiet, trying to avoid attention and waiting upon some new twist in the vagaries of Providence. Meanwhile lest things got worse many were ready to compound for their estates or to employ agents, like the erstwhile Leveller John Wildman, to buy them back for them. A hard core of royalists remained, but their leaders were mostly well known and were watched, their letters intercepted and their movements proscribed.

A confiscation act of July 1651 saw the estates of some 70 'big' royalists taken over wholesale and sold to pay the expenses of the government—which were huge. Outspoken critics preferred to see this as dividing up the lion's skin among the party for their own advantage, not the easing of people from taxation. Crown lands, and indeed all crown property—including Charles I's magnificent art collection—together with Church lands, were taken over and in various ways disposed of. Some attempt was made to meet the arrears of soldiers' pay by issuing to them debentures for parcels of confiscated land. Needless to say, as in the case of the *assignats* of the French revolution, this led to speculation by men with ready money, many of them officers, who bought up the paper certificates cheaply. In spite of all this the 'forty hogens-mogens'[20] of the council of state and the parliament had to continue the heavy regular assessments of the war period and to introduce new ones for *ad hoc* purposes. The burden was intolerable, all the more so when it could be pointed out, as it was, that some people were doing very well out of it all. 'They give daily to one another for pretended services', lining their pockets through exercising 'their more than regal or parliamentary power'.[21] Cromwell himself was voted land and money galore by a grateful and apprehensive Rump. He was certainly by this time a rich man; whether he was corrupt is more difficult to say. It is an English habit to heap rewards upon successful generals and Cromwell considering his position might well be astonished at his own moderation. Everywhere there were 'jobs for the boys' and it had never been a principle of government that any body of external rules should dictate appointments. Loyalty to the new régime was obviously a prime qualification—how else would it survive? Down to 1652 at least it would have been unthinkable to risk disaster by offering office and favour to open critics. In any case it is possible to overstress the self-help and venality of the administration. Many were efficient and by the standards of the day disinterested. The Venetian ambassador, not usually a friendly observer, said of the council of state that they were skilled and economical in their private affairs and prodigal in their devotion to public affairs, for which each man worked as for his private interest.

The lack of definition and settlement characteristic of the Commonwealth period is nowhere better shewn than in religion. The presbyterian system only partially pushed in 1648 was still loosely maintained, but there was much confusion. Church and State were not rigidly separated, maintenance by tithes was not interfered with. The rights of lay patrons were continued, those in the gift of the crown falling to the individual congregations, those of delinquents being taken over by county committees, who were to appoint in consultation with congregations. The effect was a wobbly State Church with Independents, baptists, presbyterians and other denominations being selected by some authority or other as fit and proper ministers. This meant considerable toleration, certainly too much for the Scots, who were stiffened in their support for Prince Charles by a desire to rescue England from the hands of sectaries. A blasphemy act (1650) was devised to clamp down on the extremer sects, like the Ranters, whose conduct was regarded, perhaps with some justice, as a public scandal. There was a light initial penalty for a first offence, banishment for a second. The acts for going to parish church on Sundays were repealed, but attendance at some place of worship was expected. How far this was enforced is not clear. If the Independents had been a clear-cut and well-organised religious party some definite Church settlement would surely have been worked for, but this was not the case even under Cromwell. In religion as in everything else the Independents were a mixed bunch. The nearest attempt at some kind of organisation was found in the activity of a group of laymen and ministers, including some of the dissenting brethren of the Westminster Assembly, which had last met in February 1649. These men sat as a committee for examining ministers every week until with the dissolution of the parliament in April 1653 they faded away. Before then they had drawn up proposals for the propagation of the gospel, advocating a public maintenance for preachers approved by the county committees. There was to be a commission to travel around examining established incumbents and ejecting those adjudged scandalous. Those who could not accept the loose State Church might meet for worship in public places if notice were given to the magistrates. At such places preachers might not impugn any of some 15 Christian fundamentals. It was a thoughtful and possibly viable scheme, but though it was presented to parliament little was done about it before the dissolution. Only in an act for the propagation of the gospel in Wales, which was considered a singularly unenlightened area, was anything substantial attempted, let alone achieved. The search for a religious settlement had indeed hardly begun.

XVII The Reduction of Ireland and Scotland

The first big military effort of the Commonwealth was against Ireland. Ever since the 1641 rebellion in Ulster there had been schemes for coping with a worsening situation. King and parliament had at least agreed that the first English colony should not be abandoned. Indeed it was only the squabble over who should command the military forces to put Ireland down that prevented a serious effort to obtain a quick solution. The arguments helped to bring on the civil war and, of course, complicated the position further. No one could give complete attention to Ireland, yet no one could ignore it. The King, encouraged by some English catholics, was ready to accept the support of their Irish co-religionaries in arms. So he came to that 'cessation' of 1645, which smacked so much of popish plottery that it told against the royal cause even among moderate men.

When the civil war was won parliament, as we have seen, was keen to get to grips with Ireland, but disaffection in the army and the rest of the political struggles stopped them. So in 1649 the Rump took over a dangerous drifting situation. Protestantism demanded the crushing of rampant catholicism among the native and 'old English' Irish; security called for the destruction of those forces—very diverse ones—which might be willing, if not eager, to back the cause of royalism; economic interests spoke up for the continued exploitation of Ireland by Englishmen. Ireland controlled again by England would rob the royalist fleet of possible harbourage; English merchants might be won over by a forward economic policy for Ireland, reinforcing what was already being aimed at elsewhere, in relation to the Dutch, for instance; lands confiscated from rebels could be used in lieu of pay for soldiers or engage the attention and thereby the loyalty of speculators. The Irish rebellion had forged a sort of unity in Ireland—suppression of it might do the same for England. In particular the civilian Rumpers would be happy to think that ambitious politicians in the army—

Cromwell and Ireton, in particular—would be so busy over there that the government could actually be a little and seem more free from naked military pressures. Fairfax could stay at home—he was no politician and therefore safe. On the other hand Cromwell was willing to go because he sensed the dangers of allowing Ireland to slide away. '. . . [If] our interest is rooted out there they will in a very short time be able to land forces in England, and put us to trouble here. . . . If they shall be able to carry on their work they will make this the most miserable people in the earth for all the world knows their barbarism.'[1] Perhaps he was also genuinely anxious to let the civilians shew what they could do.

The struggle in Ireland was a tense one. The English forces already there, whose commanders included the up-and-coming former royalist, George Monk, had been compelled to come to a truce with O'Neil's catholic army, which was working in conjunction with a royalist group under Ormonde. This piece of bargaining looked curious against the claim of waging something like a protestant crusade. Then Monk had to give in to another group of royalists under Inchiquin and, indeed, many of his troops actually joined the Irish army. All through the summer of 1649 preparations—including money-raising—had gone on in England for a large expedition. Cromwell got his commission on 22 June. Fortunately, just before Cromwell sailed from Bristol at the end of July better news came—Michael Jones's forces had defeated Ormonde at Rathmines. Once in Ireland—he landed in mid-August—Cromwell did not hang about. On 11 September Drogheda fell to him and the garrison, including English royalists, civilians and catholic priests, was given no quarter. This was not merely for revenge but part of a policy of terror warning others of what to expect if they did not submit, and so prevent the 'effusion of blood'[2] for the future. It certainly had its effect. Some garrisons were promptly abandoned. But Wexford held out for terms Cromwell was unwilling to grant. When the final assault came there was no mercy—a bloody massacre followed and Cromwell wrote his name in blood and fire across that unhappy land. Not even the policy outlined above and the English attitude current in Cromwell's circle can justify or condone this appalling work. It is an ineradicable blemish on Cromwell's humanity. A clue perhaps is to be found in a remark he made a little later: 'I have been crazy in my health.'[3]

The terror did not end resistance and when winter clamped down, forcing the break-up of the siege of Waterford and generally inhibiting military movement, there was much still to be done. Fortunately for Cromwell adversity made for quarrels among catholic and protestant royalists, and some of their forts, including Cork, surrendered without a fight. Spring, however, revived native Irish spirits—what after all had they now to lose?—and the English forces did not have things at all their own way. But by the time he left Ireland in May 1650, recalled for action elsewhere, Oliver had ruthlessly swung the balance in favour of what someone with a bitter sense of humour might call 'the mother country'. Ireton could now be left to carry on. The ports, which might have supported an invasion of Wales or England, were in his hands. The main river valleys, the best ways into the interior, were under control. Even so, not until May 1652 did the last garrison give up—at Galway. But Ireton, who had drafted so many settlements, was not to write one for or impose one on Ireland. He died in November 1651 and was succeeded by Edmund Ludlow, the republican, later one of Cromwell's most outspoken critics, and then by the seemingly more amenable John Fleetwood, who married Ireton's widow. There is, however, nothing to choose between in the attitudes of any of them, and the harsh settlement imposed on Ireland in the sixteen-fifties and largely continued after the Restoration, has been fairly called Cromwellian. In this, at least, the Interregnum was decisive.

One other thing Cromwell had done in Ireland, and that was to prevent the possibility of a joint Irish-Scots effort to put young Charles Stuart on an English throne. The danger had been real. Relations between England and Scotland had been strained ever since 1645. The settlement of the second civil war had not helped. Scots who welcomed the defeat of the Engagers and were ready for talks with the victors yet could not applaud the execution, done without consulting them, of a man who was King of Scotland as well as of England and was a scion of a Scottish line. They had no wish to leap blindly into a republic at the mere call of the prevailing group in England. As noted above, Scottish commissioners failed to get the trial and sentence postponed, but the Prince of Wales was proclaimed King Charles II at Edinburgh in February 1649, with the proviso

> 'that before he be admitted to the exercise of his royal power, he shall give satisfaction to the Kingdom in those things that concern the security of religion, the union betwixt the Kingdoms, and the good and peace of this Kingdom according to the national covenant and the solemn league and covenant, for which we are resolved with all possible expedition to make our humble and earnest address to His Majesty'.[4]

This address was made at The Hague, where Charles had found a temporary home with his brother-in-law, the Prince of Orange. The commissioners, a peer, three commoners and two ministers, dealt very earnestly with the King, but were initially unsuccessful. Though they confidently told him that God's blessing would be withheld if he joined with Irish papists, Charles still thought he might come into his own with the help of Irish and foreign forces, who did not seem to want to impose on him the irksome conditions entrusted to the Scots commission. But his optimism waned when Cromwell brought Ireland to heel. Charles's fortunes were now very low.

'He hes not bread bothe for himselfe and his servands, and betuixt him and his brother (James, Duke of York) not ane Inglish shilling. . . . France is neither able nor willing to helpe him: The Prince of Orange hes suffered not a little for his Father and himselfe, till he is forced to alienate the most considerable thing of his ancient patrimony: Scotland is neir exhausted; soe that his case is very deplorable, being in prisone where he is living in penurre, sorounded be his enemeis, not able to liue any where ells in the world, wnles he would come to Scotland, by giuing them satisfactione to their just demndis; yet his pernitious and deuillish Counsell will suffer him to starue before they will suffer him to take the League and Covenant. . . . If he could once be extricate frome his wicked Counsell their might be hope.'[5]

So wrote one of the Scots commissioners. It was true. Charles would be persuaded to put his hand to a covenant that could be used to salvage something or other from the shattered wreck of his fortunes. With Scots support he might rally English presbyterian and royalist loyalties and win England. Afterwards he would make his own arrangements. In the spring of 1650 he met the commissioners at his poverty-stricken court at Breda. (He had had to leave The Hague.) There in the words of Alexander Jaffray, covenanter who later turned quaker,

'we did sinfully both entangle and engage the nation and ourselves, and that poor young prince . . . making him sign and swear a covenant, which we knew, from clear and demonstrable reasons, that he hated in his heart. Yet, finding that upon these terms only, he could be admitted to rule over us . . . *he* sinfully complied with what *we* most sinfully pressed upon him. . . . In this he was not so constant to his principles as his father.'[6]

Why were the covenanters so keen to come to an accord with Charles? Jaffray gives us the answer. England was failing to impose a presbyterian system on the British Isles and there was 'likely to be set up a lawless liberty, and toleration of all religions. . . . To prevent this deluge and overflowing scourge, . . . the prevailing of the Sectarian [English] army . . . no means was thought to be so fit, as to bring home our King; otherwise, it was conceived inevitably to follow, both Monarchy and Presbytery would be ruined.'[7] 'No monarchy, no kirk' then was the argument. What would James I have made of that?

'Repenting ever of being born', Charles arrived in Scotland on 23 June 1650. From the start he had a hard time of it, being forced by the inexorable covenanters to sign a declaration in which he acknowledged in abject terms the sins of his father and had, as he put it, to spit in the face of his Roman catholic mother. He was harassed in public and private, and it is easy to understand why later, half-bitter, half-rueful, he remarked that presbyterianism was not a religion for a gentleman. But he stuck it for a while, wanting Scotland as a stepping-stone to England. The Rump, who had no doubt about his aspirations, were ready for him. Indeed they had determined on a preventive invasion. One difficulty beset them. Fairfax, who was to command with Cromwell (flushed and bloody with Irish victories), hung back, claiming that there was insufficient evidence of Scottish intentions to satisfy his conscience. A parliamentary commission, including Cromwell, who could find no such scruples, argued the point with him. 'That there will be a war between us, I fear is unavoidable', asserted Oliver.[8] For him the choice was whether to have it in the bowels—a favourite word—of England or of Scotland. Fairfax, who had long been unhappy about the trend of English politics and who welcomed this opportunity to extricate himself without embarrassment, refused to be convinced. In the event Cromwell took sole command and at the end of June 1650 an invading force was moving northwards.

Unlike in Ireland, Cromwell was ready to negotiate with the Scots so long as he lost no military disadvantage. But the Scots, elated at having a covenanting King among them, were not ready to treat. Yet their military position was uneasy. Leslie, the general in chief, stolid and experienced, was hampered by the interference of a commission of laymen and ministers—including the egregious Archibald Johnston of Wariston, whose diary provides a disturbing insight into the tortured psychology of some of the covenanters. They wished that the mind of the Kirk—which was so obviously the mind of God—should be brought to bear upon everything. They gave unsought advice 'with great freedom' to the King, the general, indeed to anyone who could not avoid listening to it. Most damaging, they insisted on the dismissal of able soldiers who in some way or other shewed themselves to be ungodly, 'the rag and tag of engagers'.[9] For Leslie this was a military campaign, for the Kirk a crusade.

Time was frittered away while the two armies manœuvred for position around Dunbar, Leith and Musselburgh. Cromwell could see no advantage as yet, so he treated and used his ready pen. A plea for a settlement on a basis of mutual toleration—'I beseech you in the bowels of Christ, think it possible you may be mistaken'[10]—was rebuffed. By the end of August, what with sickness and lack of provisions—the Scots forces had already 'eaten up' the thin, desolate country thereabouts—Cromwell was getting worried. Leslie refused to come out into the open for a pitched battle. There seemed nothing to do but to retreat for the winter. His 'poor, shattered, hungry, discouraged army'[11] settled down at Dunbar. Leslie followed him and on 2 September 1650, outnumbering the English two to one, cut off his line of withdrawal towards England. Things looked grim.

But all was not well with Leslie. His troops were unsettled by repeated purges, harassed by the Kirkmen. Wariston's diary paints a vivid picture of the tensions in the Scottish ranks, at one moment buoyed up with 'deplorable carnal confidence' at another defeatist, and always bickering. 'All in confusion; no counsel amongst us. . . . Continual complaints. . . . Confusion in our great-committee, jealousy at our sub-committee: no meeting amongst the officers, no stopping enemies in all parts spoiling the country. . . .'[12] Leslie, who, in spite of all distractions, had certainly out-manœuvred Cromwell, might well have been able to bottle him up in Dunbar for weeks, leaving the way to England open to the Scots. But the men of the Kirk accused Leslie of being too cold in a time of opportunity. Cromwell, 'that proud piece of clay',[13] could now be destroyed, they argued, and insisted on attack. So the Scots moved down from their splendid controlling position, were caught at a disadvantage, and routed. Three thousand Scots died and ten thousand were taken prisoner for negligible English losses. Cromwell may be forgiven for seeing in the turn of fortune that gave such a startling victory the very hand of God, which also pointed the right way for the Rump—to reform for His glory and that of the Commonwealth.

From Dunbar Cromwell went on to take Edinburgh and the entire lowlands south of the Forth. His treatment of the defeated was far more humane than in Ireland and shews his capacity for using conciliation as a political weapon. Though the Kirkmen had 'done their do' and lost, they would not recognise defeat. But Charles, as Cromwell had prophesied, now 'set up upon his own score'[14] in the rest of Scotland with support that was more royalist than presbyterian. Argyll dwindled from being the proud leader of a nation to a common courtier, one of many, a role in which he was soon outstripped by more subtle and congenial men. Charles was still willing to keep on terms with the Kirk, even to listen to three-hour sermons and tasteless advice, but a more general support for him seemed to be growing. This was too much for Wariston, who slipped away to the English camp after the fall of Edinburgh. At Scone on New Year's Day 1651 Charles was crowned King by Argyll. Already, although only twenty, he was old and experienced. A new army was levied with no periodical purgings and no awkward questions asked. Pretty rapidly an alliance was thrown together which reflected almost every kind of Scottish opinion—a tribute to Charles's tact and to Scottish patriotism. But it was also helped by the foul winter weather and Cromwell's serious illness—the occasion of hopeful rumours of his death—in the spring of 1651. By the time he was about again June was almost over and the military position drifting in favour of the royalists. He tried to get the Scots into a pitched battle, but their line was to delay the war while they built up a large mobile force to march into England, where they had no doubt of ready assistance. The failure of a royalist plot in January 1651 was no deterrent. The formation of a militia in the north of England during 1651 indicates something of the fears of the authorities, but perhaps also suggests a certain amount of positive support for the régime. It may additionally represent an expression of Scotophobia on the border.

Cromwell took the risk of getting behind the Scots, and with Lambert's victory at Inverkeithing on 20 July gained control of the Firth. Against his own inclination, Leslie, who found Charles's new advisers as meddlesome as ever the Kirk had been, crossed the English border on 5 August. The hope was that Cromwell would be held up in Scotland while they cut through the green militia men of the north and rallied English royalist support. Cromwell saw the danger. He accepted the surrender of Perth on 3 August and left the conquest of Scotland—now practically empty of seasoned defenders—to a small force under the highly professional George Monk, as it happened, a decision which helped to determine the ultimate restoration of Charles II. On 6 August Monk took Stirling, on 1 September Dundee. A few days earlier an English force 'miserably surprised' and captured the Scottish 'committee of estates' at Alyth, 'a sad disaster and blow', which robbed the country of the only central authority left behind.[15] Monk's policy was not merely to win military victories but to convince the Scots there was more to gain from submission than continued intransigence. He punished severely soldiers caught plundering the countrymen 'to whom we endeavour to show as much favour as may be (especially to the poorer sort) to convince them, if possible, of the slavery they have been under and the freedom they may now enjoy under the English'.[16]

Monk's illness that winter slowed up the pace of English consolidation but did nothing to help resistance, for by then Cromwell had pulled off the 'crowning mercy' of Worcester, and the Scottish forces had been squandered in England.

While the main Scots army pushed southwards, no one in England was idle. Harrison joined Lambert at Newcastle; Fairfax, his scruples now satisfied, came out of retirement and raised Yorkshire. In the midlands Fleetwood was busily collecting a force. The Scots zeal evaporated as they got further from home. Loudon and Argyll slunk off in the Lake District, no great military loss in themselves, but considerable numbers of soldiers deserted at the same time. A detachment from the Isle of Man, the Stanley stronghold, was not an adequate compensation, especially as Lancashire failed to throw up the expected enthusiastic partisans. Then Charles found that the way to London was barred by Harrison and Lambert at Knutsford. So he hurried down the Severn towards Wales and the west where his father had so often drummed up recruits. September found his army tired and dejected at Worcester. There Cromwell, after a remarkable march down the east and across the midlands, caught up with them. The battle (3 September) was as stiff a one as he had ever engaged in, but he won. The royalist forces scattered.

Charles after some romantic adventures, involving an oak tree, priests' holes and disguise as a countryman, eventually got away to France—a miraculous escape, it may be, but one certainly well organised by the Western Association of royalists and a group of midlands recusants. England was at the feet of the army. Soon the Isle of Man was taken, the Channel Islands and the Scillies cleared of royalist shipping—which was chased and engaged as far as the Mediterranean. For Cromwell Worcester was the climax of his military career, leaving him at the real end of the civil wars the unchallenged power in the army, and indeed in the State, a fact recognised not only by Englishmen but by the practical statesmen of Europe who courted him. The Rumpers, though relieved at the Scots defeat, were more suspicious of Cromwell and even less willing than before to undertake drastic reform which they saw as extinguishing their own *raison d'être*. Obviously jealousy played some part in their attitude, but it must be remembered that many of these men were convinced republicans and for sincere political reasons deplored anything that looked like putting power into the hands of a single person—especially when these hands already held a sword. Defiantly they took up rash policies, domestic and foreign, which they knew were approved by hardly anyone.

Scotland, apart from moss-troopers in the farthest reaches, gave up for a while the struggle with England. Future relationships between the two countries were a problem. Some in England favoured outright annexation and a bill to that effect was read in parliament on 30 September 1651. But a scheme of union was ultimately decided upon as more politic. In January 1652 Commissioners went to Scotland to put it into effect. They were charged to annul all vestiges of royal authority, to arrange the administration of justice and replace military rule. Representatives of 'integrity and good affection' were to be elected to a convention 'with full powers' to assent to a union.[17] By the spring it was being reported that most of Scotland had assented. The Commissioners, working with great efficiency and impartiality, went on to make arrangements for the national finances on a regular assessment basis. Most of the money went to pay for the military occupation, but, in fact, the bulk of the cost was found by England herself. Regular pay reinforced a stern discipline imposed within the occupation forces. The resultant order certainly helped to reconcile some of the Scots to the English ascendancy, especially as it was associated with a deliberate policy of detaching the lower and middle classes from the tutelage of clergy and aristocracy. A special amnesty was granted to repentant tenants and 'vassals' who had let themselves be led astray by 'Noble-men and Gentry (the chief Actors in these invasions and wars against England)'.[18] Unfortunately some who might have been won over in this way were put off by the religious settlement which granted what seemed 'a vast and boundles'[19] toleration, letting in 'manie grosse errores contrarie to sound doctrine and the power of Godlienes'.[20] The English Commissioners and military commanders confessed themselves astonished at the hold the Kirk had even on 'the less precise' sort of people. Moreover, although taxes were, by English standards, rather light and were fairly distributed, they were regarded not unnaturally as burdensome. Though there was 'a strange kind of hush'[21] in 1652, 1653 brought serious royalist risings and at no time in the next few years could a withdrawal of military occupation be seriously considered. Work on the scheme of union went on and Scottish deputies in London, arguing tirelessly, managed to secure some recognition of their points of view. Yet when Cromwell expelled the Rump in April 1653, no formal acceptance had yet been secured. But by then attention had anyway veered towards English domestic politics.

XVIII The Nominated Assembly

The army which had all this time been fighting the republic's battles grew restless. Success in the field and the collapse of armed resistance only increased its malaise. 'In this time of their idleness'[1] the army brooded over grievances and there was a danger, as Whitelocke noted, in 'our proness to destroy ourselves when our enemies could not do it'.[2] Apart from political and constitutional issues there were matters of sheer self-interest. Officers noted how the Rump, an essentially civilian body, gave neither profit nor preferment nor places in government to military men. The rank and file brooded over pay and conditions. Officers and men, though their interests might not coincide at any deep level, could at least agree that the Rump must reform or go. In August 1652 the council of officers presented a petition for the 'outing' of scandalous preachers, the abolition of tithes, legal reforms and a reduction of the civilian establishment. The House gave them formal thanks, but 'many (members) were unsatisfied with this Petition . . . as improper if not arrogant . . . to their Masters'. Cromwell was advised to 'stop this way of petitioning by the officers of the Army with their swords in their hands'.[3] Nothing was done to implement any of the demands.

By the end of 1652 Cromwell's own patience was wearing thin. In conversation with Whitelocke he remarked on the army's 'strange distaste' for the parliament, and wished there were not so much cause for it.

'Really their Pride, and Ambition, and Self-seeking, ingrossing all Places of Honour and Profit to themselves and their Friends, and their daily breaking forth into new and violent . . . Factions, their Delays of Business, and Designs to perpetuate themselves . . . do give too much Ground for People to open their Mouths against them. . . . So that, unless there be some Authority and Power so full and so high as to restrain and keep Things in better Order . . . it will be impossible . . . to prevent our Ruin.'

Whitelocke protested that they were not all bad, but Cromwell said he saw little hope that a good settlement could be made with them. They must be curbed. But how, seeing they have been 'acknowledged the supreme power'? Thinking as he must often have done on the utility of a government 'with somewhat of monarchical in it', Cromwell asked, 'what if a Man should take it upon him to be King?' Whitelocke was properly shocked and proposed that Cromwell should work for a private treaty with Charles Stuart on the basis of limited royal authority, and at the same time 'secure yourself, and your Friends, and their Fortunes'.[4] Cromwell wanted more time to consider that—as well he might.

Now and again the Rump responded enough to pressure to discuss in a desultory fashion arrangements for future parliaments and its own demise. In March 1653 a newsletter reported that the soldiers had resolved to have speedily a new representative and parliament had resolved the contrary. Every Wednesday in the intervals of amending proposals for the propagation of the gospel, they did contemplate a new franchise based on £200 real or personal property (too narrow for Levellers obsessed with the Agreements of the People, but at least uniform). None of the discussions indicated a willingness of the Rump to fade out completely in anticipation of a new assembly. Rather the reverse. 'Do you intend to sit here till doomsday come?' went a ballad of the day. By now Cromwell was one of those who thought it must be helped to go, though the prospect made his 'hair stand on end'.[5] In April a committee headed by the younger Vane proposed that existing M.P.s should automatically sit in any new assembly and should judge the qualifications of elected members. There is evidence of a proposal to dismiss Oliver and to adjourn to November. Cromwell's mind was made up. On 20 April he appeared in the Commons and after listening to the debate for a while, rose to his feet and announced his intention of putting an end to their prating. Troops were called in and the members bundled out as Cromwell complained that it was all their fault, 'for I have fought the Lord night and day that he would rather slay me than put me upon the doing of this work'.[6] The same afternoon he turned the council of state adrift: 'this is no place for you'.[7] Later that day some wag put a notice up in Westminster: 'This House to be Let, now unfurnished'.[8] There was no overt opposition. 'Scarce a dog barked',[9] Cromwell said later, but, in fact there was a fair amount of comment at home and abroad. 'The time was, when that the challenging of five members of parliament was cried out upon for an unheard of breach of privilege of parliament; but afterwards the impeaching of 11 members was a greater, and made a mighty noise amongst the presbyterians. What think you now of turning them out of doors?'[10] It certainly was a startling course that had been followed but the Cromwellians were quick to defend it. They argued that they were led by necessity and Providence to avoid 'new troubles at a time when our enemies abroad are watching all advantages against us'.[11] The same argument had been used for abolishing monarchy and the House of Lords. It might convince some, such as the 'Churches of Christ' who declared in favour of the expulsion and tritely compared Oliver to Moses. But for others the argument was threadbare—what they wanted to see was what sort of settlement Cromwell would offer.

One thing was certain. So naked a military sword was indecent, even to soldiers, and haste must be made to sheath it in a civilian scabbard. There seemed to be plenty of courses open:

> Some like this change and some like it not
>   For they say they are sure it's done in due season;
> Some say it was jesuits' plot
>   Because it resembled the gun-powder treason.
>
> Some think that Cromwell with Charles is agreed,
>   And some say 'twere policy if it were so,
> Least the Hollander, French, the Dane and the Swede
>   Do bring him in whether he will or no.
>
> And now I would gladly conclude my song
>   With a prayer as ballads are wont to do;
> But I'll forbear, for I think ere't be long.
>   We may have a king and a parliament too.[12]

The Venetian ambassador thought too that Cromwell might restore the Stuarts, but he did not consider enough the likely attitude of the army, who opposed monarchy anyway and saw Charles as bloodstained as his father. This view was reinforced by the officers in Scotland as soon as they heard what had happened. They hoped they would not 'be led back again to stoop to any Aegyptian Yoke of Bondage, either in Spiritual or Temporal Kingly powers'.[13] Cromwell is reported to have approached Selden and St John to help him to draw up 'some instrument of government that might put the power out of his hands',[14] but even before the dissolution the plausible courses of action had been reduced to two. One (advocated by John Lambert, who had taken Ireton's place as the man with the pen close to Cromwell) was for supreme power to be vested in a small council of state which would eventually share authority with a parliament elected on new principles, and in a relationship set down in a written, inviolable constitution. The second scheme was peddled by Major-General Thomas Harrison, who had sat next to Oliver when the Rump was put out. Harrison, an enthusiastic fifth monarchist (the epithet is hardly necessary) had seen in recent events God's warning that Christ's second coming was imminent. In these circumstances power in the land must go to a body of 70 men, or, rather, 'saints' (equivalent to the Sanhedrin of the Israelites), chosen for their capacity to lead the nation along the paths of righteousness. This seemed a perfectly natural expansion of congregational government, with which the saints were accustomed to entrust able men, fearing God, honouring truth and hating covetousness.

Each proposal had powerful support, each had its attractions to Cromwell, each was seriously discussed. Behind the scenes there was 'hard labour' and the Lord-General was said to be 'at a nonplus'.[15] On 29 April a new council of state of ten members, seven of them military, was appointed to deal with current business. It looked as if Lambert had won. But Cromwell—it was clear that the major decision must be his—had plumped for a variant of Harrison's proposal. Letters were sent to various congregations to submit names. Others— the bulk—were simply nominated by the officers themselves. Cromwell and the council went carefully through the list. On 6 June writs went out to 121 men in England (seven for London); six for Wales; five for Scotland and six for Ireland. Five of the last were in fact Englishmen. It may be noted that by a simple gesture Cromwell had united the three kingdoms and produced the first imperial parliament, though perhaps the title of parliament ought not to be given to this assembly at all.

The nickname 'Barebones' bestowed on it later by royalists, after Praise-God Barebone, a leatherseller, who played a none-too prominent part in its proceedings, suggests it was through-and-through fanatical and hysterical. Clarendon saw the nominees as 'mainly inferior persons of no quality or name . . . known only by their gifts of preaching and praying . . . a pack of weak senseless fellows'. 'This ridiculous assembly' or 'little daft parliament', made up of 'old bottles', of men of 'mean and ignote extraction' who had made their way up in the world by serving on country committees, irritated contemporaries, and has amused historians and partisans ever since.[16] But the charge of the Venetian ambassador that it consisted mostly of 'ignoramuses in government' was quite wrong.[17] Some members, like Anthony Ashley Cooper and Francis Rous, would certainly have found their way to any seventeenth-century parliament. Rous, prominent in politics and puritan circles for half a century, became a learned and very articulate Speaker. There were few if any lawyers, it is true, but no shortage of men of 'honest minds and sincere intentions'.[18] The estates of many were not 'bulky' but none were of 'broken fortunes'. Fairfax refused to sit[19] but other officers, well experienced like Robert Blake, Charles Fleetwood, John Lambert and John Hewson were not ashamed to join in. There were merchants like Samuel Moyes and John Ireton, Henry's brother. Though the assembly may perhaps be fairly accused of having more private virtues than political capacity, that charge does not automatically carry with it proof that the Nominated Assembly was ludicrous. Perhaps some practical men, too, in those difficult times might see a value in a parliament 'owning God, and being owned by Him'.

Certainly Cromwell did. At the first meeting[20] (4 July 1653) he reviewed in one of his long rambling discourses the astonishing history of the last decade, justifying on many grounds, especially religious, the recent expulsion. By it these men had now received a call from God to settle His people—a noble enterprise. He formally handed his power and that of the army officers over to them. They listened soberly and took him at his word. An enlarged council of state was entrusted with the executive, while the House itself got down to the job of reform. The two most striking characteristics of it were energy and seriousness. During the six months sitting the saints went into a vast range of problems, including many raised in the Heads of the Proposals and the various Agreements of the People. These were difficult and controversial issues upon which divergences—'trouble in paradise'—soon revealed themselves. It was noted that 'they brake palpably into factions'[21] in the assembly as a whole and in its various committees. The radicals were in a minority, but in one or two committees did get on top, notably in that for the reform of the law. In this committee there were no lawyers, a disadvantage that meant, however, that professional prejudice and vested interests were absent. Some hard things were said about the law—it was 'a Mystery of Wickedness' and 'a standing cheat'.[22] Somebody remarked that 'no Ship almost that sailed on the Sea of the Law, but first or last put into that Port (of Chancery); and, if they made any considerable Stay there, they suffered so much Loss that the Remedy was a bad as the Disease'.[23] Without a division the committee concluded that Chancery with its 'faculty of bleeding the People in the Purse-vein',[24] its delays, esoteric procedures, fees and officials, should simply be abolished. The law should be codified and made 'easy, plain and short',[25] especially the debtors' law, which 'pays no debts, but defrauds the creditor, feeds the lawyers and jailers and murders the debtors'.[26] The laws relating to lunacy and marriage should be reformed, but a proposal to allow divorce for adultery was voted down.[27] A small group of bold extremists, stimulated by the frenetic sermons of Christopher Feake, who called Oliver Cromwell 'the old Dragon',[28] wanted all law abrogated in favour of the Mosaic code, but to reduce the whole 'war with the lawyers' to this level would be quite unjust to a seriously-conducted examination of what many men who were not necessarily saints and did not think themselves inspired saw as a crying social abuse. Other committees soberly discussed treasury reform, the reorganisation of national revenues, the advancement of learning, the review of the poor law and the commissions of the peace. Proposals were put forward for economies in the number of offices. Many useful and practical acts were passed as a result of the committee's findings. Some of these were continued under the Protectorate, such as those for revenue reform, civil marriage and union with Scotland.

But while an impressive agreement was possible between moderates and radicals on many issues, in the committee on tithes a breakdown occurred. There membership was finely balanced, and the problem was one which had caused violent discord for decades. The attempts of Archbishops Bancroft and Laud to make tithes bear some relation to the real wealth of the country had helped to break the peace of Church and State. The whole thing was complicated by the fact that so many tithes had become impropriated into the hands of laymen and were a form of lay property. The holders were not unnaturally opposed to any measures which might, like ship money in another sphere, 'alter' that property. During the Interregnum the sects spoke out against tithes as ungodly and unnecessary. Some urged that as Christ was a carpenter and his disciples fishermen, ministers must support themselves by manual labour, a suggestion that prompted William Prynne, that gentleman-born, to write at his usual inordinate length to prove that Christ had never worked with hands. Still the arguments flew about. The Levellers had taken up the demand for abolition and even the Heads of Proposals had suggested the provision of some less contentious form of clerical maintenance. Petitions for root and branch abolition of tithes, which led to the 'undoing' of men by 'crafty lawyers' and 'musty statutes', had poured into the Long Parliament. So they did, with perhaps more hopes, into this assembly.[29] In its final report the committee by a very small majority favoured tithe retention and argued that impropriators had a legal tithe. But on 10 December by 56 votes to 52 the assembly rejected the report and the way lay open for a general attack upon tithes and lay patronage. The majority it seems clear was not aiming at mere abolition but at seeking out some more equitable and less litigious maintenance. But the moderates, who feared that such action would disquiet so articulate an interest as the ministers and lawyers, were not ready to go so far. Cromwell himself was getting worried. He had left the assembly to its own devices, evidently thinking that the kind of settlement he wanted would automatically emerge. But there were growing disorders in the City, where really messianic lecturers, including, alarmingly, women, were letting themselves go and urging the assembly on to more and more radical courses. There were hints of a Leveller revival with Lilburne, armed with 'his old buckler, Magna Carta'[30] back in England and in action. Charged with sedition, he was again triumphantly acquitted, confounding predictions that he would 'speedily be hanged'.[31] (It should be noted that it was this radical parliament that had had him put in prison.) The royalists were taking heart from the signs of confusion. Even the sensible taxation reforms had an unwelcome side—they would make it more difficult to pay the troops and thus maintain discipline within the army and security in the country. No wonder Cromwell murmured that he was 'now more troubled with the fool than the knave'.

The moderates, however, were not without resource. In November they had secured the erection of a special high court of justice, unacceptable to the radicals, by the pretty expedient of voting it in while the others were at a prayer meeting. On 12 December they repeated the exploit. A great group of them got to the House very early—a clear premeditated plan—and with the connivance of the Speaker, as ever a zealous supporter of a preaching ministry maintained by tithes, voted a resignation of their authority on the grounds that they were unable to check the prevailing 'confusion and despoliation of the nation'.[32] They then trooped off to Whitehall and handed power back to Cromwell. Some of the radicals shewed a determination to carry on in the House, but after a 'sweet argument' with soldiers, sent apparently by Lambert, they were cleared out. The colonel in charge is reported to have asked them what they were doing there. 'We are seeking the Lord.' 'Then', he said, 'you may go elsewhere, for to my certain knowledge he has not been here these 12 years.'[33]

XIX The Establishment of
the Protectorate

So fizzled out an experiment which most historians seem to agree deserved to fail, for in excess of zeal 'the members tried to give the nation not what the people wanted, but what they thought was good for them'.[1] No doubt this is true, but much the same might be said of every administration since 1641. Perhaps 'this thing called a new parliament'[2] was bound to fail, too, but unlike the Rump it had the distinction of being too active. So now experience, shot through with prejuduce, had taught that even saints might not answer the people's expectations and that what was wanted now was 'somewhat' (to use a favourite Cromwellian vagueness) that would do enough and no more, and do it in the right way and at the right time. A large demand, but luckily that somewhat seemed to be at hand, in the form of a constitution drawn from the original proposals of John Lambert and embodied in the 42 articles of The Instrument of Government.

On 12 December 1653 Cromwell accepted the constitution and his own place in it as 'the single person', and was installed as my Lord Protector. A shuffled pace back towards monarchy had been taken, some would say forward, to the Restoration of 1660.

'Resignation' of the Nominated Assembly had left Cromwell's power once again boundless and shockingly military. Swiftly the Instrument plunged his dripping blade into an elaborate civilian scabbard, a studied gesture of restraint. Faced by the need to 'create a little world out of chaos and to bring form out of confusion',[3] a small group of men, chiefly military but with some civilian associates—the exact membership is unknown—produced under the certain guidance of John Lambert, that subtle and working brain, the first practical written constitution in English history. The object was to give stability and at the same time to perpetuate the predominance of the army. 'It was high time some power should pass upon the wavering humours of the people and say to the nation as the Almighty himself said once to the unruly sea, 'Here shall be thy bounds, hitherto shalt thou come and no further.'[4] But it was also high time Oliver Cromwell's personal ascendancy was checked, too. Cromwell was later to claim that a first draft of the Instrument offered him kingship—if it did it was unlikely to have been absolute monarchy. In the final version he was 'the single person', sharing power with a legislative single-chamber parliament and a heavily military executive, the council of state. In relation to the one he was strong, to the other weak. Charles I had not been bound to take the advice of his Privy Council, but in most things the Protector had to consult his council and act by its advice. It could and did meet in the Protector's absence and he was not always involved in or even aware of its deliberations. The council in fact was the keystone of the newly-flung-up arch of government.

Ostensibly the Instrument offered an ideal 'mixed government', reflecting Cromwell's reported dream of a constitution with 'somewhat of monarchical in it'. 'If war there be'—wrote Marchamont Needham, the ex-royalist turned able Cromwellian apologist—'if war there be, here is the unitive virtue (but nothing else) of monarchy to encounter it; and here is the admirable counsel of aristocracy to manage it; if peace there be, here is the industry and courage of democracy to improve it.'[5] Propagandists played the Instrument up as a seasonable mean between tyranny and anarchy, and confidently forecast a durable settlement. But they were assuming that the elements in the mixture would cheerfully mingle in the stated proportions and that those proportions were just right to enable a controlled fusion to come off. Time would shew that no parliament, however elected, however winnowed, would tamely accept the minor role allotted. The old tussle with an hereditary King would slide into another with an imposed Protector and an armed junto. The conflict might be even fiercer because in answer to critics the paper constitution was unilaterally declared by its framers to be sacred, fixed, inviolable. They were inexperienced or optimistic or wily enough to set up no machinery for amendment or interpretation, an omission or miscalculation avoided by most later 'founding fathers'. In effect, under the Instrument, legislature and executive faced one another not through a glass darkly but without a screen of any kind, and each deplored what it saw. Every clause of the Instrument was big with suspicion and distrust, distrust of the people, of parliament, and even of the Protector. The franchise, a new one, discussed in more detail below, was limited and there were some tight restrictions upon both electors and candidates. Nine months were to elapse before the new self-constituted régime would have to cope with a parliament and during this pregnant period the executive could legislate and raise money by simple ordinance. It did so, copiously.

Few were persuaded by this blunt instrument. Some of its notions were taken over from the titular Agreements of the People, but were so distorted that Levellers and radicals generally took no comfort from them. Fifth monarchists and saints, smarting from the abrupt rejection of God's golden opportunity, saw here only carnal machinations and flayed Cromwell as 'the dissemblingest perjured villain in the world'.[6] Major-General Thomas Harrison, losing his councillorship and his army commission, went home to mope in Staffordshire. To republicans the inflated single person, the expanded executive and deformed parliament were treachery to their 'good old cause'. Col. Edmund Ludlow thought it—or so he says—'in substance a re-establishment of that which we all engaged against, and had with a great expense of blood and treasure abolished'.[7] Royalists, old and new, preferred a real monarchy of Stuarts to the uncrowned quasi-kingship of the bumpkin House of Cromwell. Some conservatives and moderates—it is hard and perhaps would be misleading to be more precise—were prepared to wait and see what the man who, with all his faults, seemed on his record to stand firm against social revolution and anarchy, might do. As soon as the régime shewed viability a few were ready to give it support, initially of a passive sort.

The inauguration of the Protectorate was a rather fussy affair. Wearing civilian garb of black velvet and surrounded by officials and officers, cheek by jowl, the new Protector symbolically accepted a civilian sword, handed him apparently without a smile by John Lambert. The Venetian Ambassador noted that Cromwell sat amid deep cushions on something like a royal throne, itself set on opulent carpets. Men pressed forward to do him homage, bare-headed 'in the obsequious and respectful form observed to the late kings'.[8] But this critical observer also sensed an apathy among the ordinary citizens, and set down his own opinion that for all the show very little inroad was being made into the realities of the political situation.

At bottom it was an army that propped Oliver up, and unless that army turned in on him or broke up in internal squabbling, there would be no fundamental alteration in circumstances. Foreign powers generally took this line. On a cue from their industrious envoys in London they concluded that Cromwell was securely placed and likely to stay that way for a good while. So they sped congratulations and formal recognition, depressing the exiles who deplored yet another wasted chance: 'Good God! What dam'd lick-arses are here!'[9] It was even put about that the Spanish ambassador, zealous to out-bid France, was urging the Protector to make just one more little jump and assume the crown, confident Spain would stick by him. For his part Cromwell valued diplomatic recognition by any power and the new government fostered the dissemination of appropriate propaganda on the continent. Thus Frenchmen could read an enthusiastic account in good French of the magnificent banquet given to the Protector in the City, at which the Lord Mayor assured him of the steady affections of London, 'the heart of the nation'.[10] Another heady address labelled Oliver the man of God's right hand, 'whom He has made strong for Himself'.[11] Well-publicised flattery of this sort made him—a man who could be King if he would—appear impregnable to all Europe. The writer of an intercepted letter from Paris assumed that Cromwell would take 'the old title' as 'better known' and 'better esteemed abroad and at home' after that 'wild government by Parliaments'.[12]

The exiles' gloom was deepened by Cromwell's dynamic foreign policy. Within a few months he had ended the expensive and generally unpopular war with the Dutch, more or less 'on such conditions as he thought to give them',[13] as Clarendon put it, and so robbed Charles Stuart of a possible base and backing for invasion. This retrenchment placated substantial groups in the City, whom Cromwell would continue to woo with some success. The relations of the Protectorate (not only of the Protector himself, but of his court, his administration and the various military groups) with the City have yet to be searchingly examined, but it seems clear that Cromwell was able to establish fairly friendly relations, reinforced by mutual self-interest, with the Lord Mayor and Aldermanry, whose financial stake in his régime was akin to that of their predecessors under Charles I during 'the personal government'. On the other hand among the common councillors, a wider group, less traditionally intimate with government and uneasy on other grounds, little headway was made, as is revealed in the elections for the two Protectorate parliaments. Among the populace, the anabaptists, who, like the Nominated Assembly, had supported the Rump's war with the United Provinces, lamented the wilful failure to push through the campaign which they saw, rather perversely, as a necessary prelude to the building on earth of the new Jerusalem.

With France serious feelers for an accord if not an alliance were put out, and although the penny-pinching Charles Stuart stayed on in Paris, harassed by his relatives and advisers, Mazarin did little to supply him with peaceable comforts, let alone encourage him with arms and men to mount an invasion from French soil. Portugal and the Danes were soon reported to be making amiable gestures. Fortified by such auspicious omens, all through 1654, 'our new Protector' went on swimmingly in his high office. 'All things hear are in a calme, expecting what his highness will settle, and what lawes he will make. All stand bare to him.' [14]

The new government did not waste the vital nine months it had allowed itself before meeting a parliament. The fresh councillors of state, more than half of them officers, most in some way resonant to the multitudinous views of the army, had lively notions of 'reformation', and soon proved vigorous and thorough. Perhaps on their own initiative, or more likely on that of Cromwell himself, much was done, more attempted towards that 'healing and settling' that was the theme of so many protectorial speeches to come. 'Cromwell proceeds with strange dexterity towards the reconciling all kinds of persons, and chooses those of all parties whose abilities are most eminent.' [15] There was a certain truth in the comment, as Bulstrode Whitelocke, one of the Commissioners of the Great Seal, would complacently have agreed. Something of what was in the forefront of the mind of the new government can be grasped by an examination of its early legislation.

The Instrument had given the executive the right to issue 'ordinances' for 'the peace and welfare of these nations . . . which shall be binding . . . until order shall be taken in parliament' (Clause XXX). [16] (This last vague phrase would cause difficulties later, when the first Protectorate parliament was sent home before it had passed the anticipated confirmatory measures.) Presumably this new type of ordinance was an equivalent of the old royal proclamation, but with more teeth. Forty years before Lord Chief Justice Coke in a famous decision had established that proclamations could not create new law, but these newfangled ones certainly claimed to do just that, going far beyond being merely explanatory and concerned with routine matters. Some were constructive, others even adventurous. Altogether over 80 were issued covering a very wide area.

Social and economic problems were energetically tackled. Thus duelling was forbidden. Like Richelieu and Hobbes, Cromwell looked at it through unromantic spectacles, making it out a form of private warfare—a mocking contempt of the right of the organised State to settle by the forms of law disputes between subject and subject—and the occasion of public disorder. Cock-fighting and horse-racing too were impugned, less an expression of a pharisaical jealousy of the simpler pleasures than of a will towards security and social discipline. Cockfighting led to wagers, wagers to disputes, disputes to fighting and riots. Besides, like horse-racing, it brought people together, where under the comfortable guise of sport or gambling political information could be exchanged, flagging spirits revived, royalist or terrorist plots hatched, nurtured and set on the wing.

Measures to regulate fen-draining hark back to Cromwell's early concern for the way of life of the fenmen, but hint again at the quest for order by prevention. (Much of the social policy of the first '11 years tyranny', that of 1629-40, had similar mixed motivations. Even less than Cromwell could Charles I afford to have folk in the localities rioting and rising.) Some tentative legal reforms—matters dear to radicals and even to some more conventional men—were set in motion, notably a regulation of Chancery, making it easier of access, a disappointment to those, like some members of the Little Parliament, dedicated to its abolition. Even so, the milk-and-water ordinance was unwelcome to legal vested interests, typified by Bulstrode Whitelocke, close to the government itself. The Interregnum ought, one feels, to have been a great turning point in the history of the legal system—its institutions, procedures, purposes and principles. Breakdown in traditional government against a background of fervent ideas, some very cogently and clearly expressed, provided opportunity. From time to time there was an intention among men in power to do something, but somehow the priorities were never properly worked out and the inertia of centuries, in which was embedded some profit and, perhaps, even some virtue, prevailed. But the Protectorate must be given credit, if credit is due, for a few gestures of change. There might have been more if conditions had really settled.

Union with Scotland was achieved without fuss by incorporating Scotland into 'one free State and Commonweath with England', with 30 representatives in an imperial parliament.[17] (Another ordinance arranged for elections there, as did one of the same date for Ireland. The significance of these arrangements is discussed further below.) Union might have proved a turning or fresh starting point in the histories of both kingdoms, but it did not survive the Restoration. The dark period that followed 1660, darker surely than the years of military occupation, was an ironical comment on the deficiencies of national independence, while the union eventually achieved, the result, it has been well said, of one of the most blatant pieces of political jobbery of the eighteenth century, was a mixed blessing. It may be that had a modified unitary relationship been worked out from 1660 more would have been gained for Scots as well as Englishmen than would have been lost. But the history of the unions of England and Wales, England and Ireland discourages an optimistic appraisal of Scotland.

Inescapably, finance called for detailed attention. Ordinances continued the excise and monthly assessments, made a few minor treasury reforms and reinforced aspects of the work of the old parliamentary central executive committees, which, like the county committees, seemed indispensable. The Protectorate was not notable for financial or administrative innovation at the centre. If anything there was a strong suggestion of conservatism, fostered by officials who, ready to support the powers that were, wanted in general to make them as near as might be to the powers that ought to be.

The most spectacular of the ordinances were those which dealt with matters of treason and those which were pointed at religious settlement. It was declared treason to compass or imagine (i.e. to plot) the death of my Lord Protector, whose life friend and foe alike judged the surest warranty of the survival of the régime. There would be a number of attempts or intended attempts to assassinate Cromwell, often elaborately schemed, usually inept in execution. Absurd and desperate essays like these, the progeny of unrestrained private enterprise, gave ample excuse for repressive 'police' actions, which harassed more responsible royalists, active or passive. Treason was also stretched to take in the denial of the supreme authority of the Lord Protector and parliament. (Curiously, nothing was said about the council of state.) To stir up mutiny in the army, not unexpectedly, was also deemed treasonable and subject to harsh penalties. The treason code of a government is generally a pointer to its self-confidence and stability. On that count the Protectorate was lacking in both.

Oliver Cromwell had long since felt himself charged with the divine responsibility of framing a peaceable religious settlement for God's distracted Englishmen. No less than Laud he saw much of the worship of God performed in the unity of men, but unlike Laud he did not worship uniformity. Ordinances which smack of his personal intervention provided a tolerant and flexible Church 'system', within the terms of the Instrument of Government, to smooth the troubled waters, long enchafed by the abolition of episcopacy and uniformity. The arrangements follow in part the proposals of John Owen, Philip Nye and a group of other leading Independent ministers submitted to the Rump in February 1652, and other suggestions put forward in the Nominated Assembly. There was little, if anything, new in the Protectorate.

A general commission ('the triers') based on London, was set up in March 1654 for the approbation of 'public ministers', with power of ultimate confirmation of appointments to benefices. The rights of lay patrons were expressly retained—many livings had come into the Protector's gift—and it was not until they had received a patron's blessing that candidates appeared before the commission. Its 33 members were mostly Independents, but with some presbyterian and anabaptist colleagues. Ten were laymen. To receive approbation and to go on to take over a living with rights to tithes, glebe and so on, the hopeful applicant had to satisfy the triers that he was religious, moral and capable, qualities perhaps more difficult to prove than to deny. Relief to candidates living remote from the capital was given by allowing them to be examined by local incumbents who would report direct to the board. In August 1654 a second ordinance set up county commissions ('the ejectors'), each of 15–30 laymen, with 8–10 divines as assessors, with authority to expel ministers and schoolmasters 'scandalous in their lives and conversations',[18] or who were guilty of the blasphemous and atheistical opinions punishable under the blasphemy act of 1651; or were swearers, perjurers, papists, adulterers, gamblers, drunkards, users of the prayer book, scoffers at the godly, defenders of maypoles and stage-plays, or disaffected to the government in print or pulpit, non-resident, or otherwise neglectful. Anyone adjudged guilty of anything on this formidable list could be expelled and replaced by a better man, subject to confirmation by the triers. In the matter of expulsion, it should be noted, the arrangements were emphatically local, allowing no doubt play to prejudice, but assuring detailed knowledge of the past and present carriage of incumbents.

The family of an expelled minister might claim one-fifth of the income of his replacement provided the former left his living without making a nuisance of himself—a humane if not indulgent provision. But it was not always possible to force the newcomer to live up to his commitments, especially where, as was too often the case, the full stipend was exiguous. The sufferings of some, perhaps many, clergy and of their dependents must have been real enough, but it would be a mistake to see their successors triumphantly gorging on the fat of the land. Thus the work of triers and ejectors was supplemented by trustees (endowed by ordinance in September 1654) for the better maintenance and encouragement of preaching ministers, that much-felt want, which had exercised puritans, lay and clerical, for decades. As managers for the state of alienated ecclesiastical lands they were to do what they could to raise low stipends and to support directly lecturers where they might be of spiritual benefit. How far they managed to improve matters is an open question. What is important is that there was an unequivocal recognition that there was a problem and some readiness to solve it.

Beyond the commissioners, central and local, there was no specific Church organisation, no detailed code of internal discipline, no canons of uniformity, no creed or confession of faith to be sworn to. Yet it was

177

not anarchy. The parish survived, favoured by many gentry of an Independent inclination, who, true to their class, were unwilling to let every vestige of system and discipline be wiped out, particularly where their own property rights as patrons or rectors were involved. Tithes, again, were not, in spite of earlier pledges and continuing agitation, abolished. Without them incumbents might find themselves in financial difficulties. To lean on the charity of the faithful was laudable but foolhardy. No doubt the arrangements generally suited Independents and sectaries best, but enough of a hint of a State Church was left to appeal to those presbyterians who took livings under it, notably in the City and suburbs. Certainly many of the presbyterians who were ejected after the Restoration had come into livings under Cromwell. Richard Baxter commented that if 'some over-busy and over-rigid Independents' got preferment, 'they did abundance of good to the Church. They saved many a congregation from that sort of man that intended no more in the ministry than to say a sermon, as readers say their common prayers, and so patch up a few good words together to talk the people asleep with on Sunday, and all the rest of the week to go with them to the ale-house and harden them in their sin.' 'Many thousands of souls', he went on, 'blessed God for the faithful ministers whom they let in, and grieved when the prelatists afterwards cast them out again.'[19]

In practice, there was a good deal of leniency, too much for the preciser sort and both Protectorate parliaments saw attempts to tighten the discipline within the system and sap the toleration outside of it. Episcopalians may not have suffered as much as might be inferred from the literal text of the ordinances, and the triumph of Laudian Anglicanism at the Restoration may owe something to the fact that no sharply consistent campaign was waged to destroy it. Many of the high-flying Anglicans of the Cavalier and other Caroline parliaments were young men brought up in their exuberant faith under Cromwell. The prayer book was certainly used, if mostly privately and discreetly, and the government knew it. At St Benet's, Paul's Wharf, it was read within shooting distance of Whitehall. The friendly contacts of Cromwell and Archbishop Ussher are well known. When that temperate divine died he was buried honourably in Westminster Abbey according to the forms laid down in the Book of Common Prayer. The royalist Thomas Fuller continued to preach through the good offices of John Howe, the Protector's Chaplain, who was touched as well as amused by his typically 'quaint' appeal: 'You observe, sir, that I am a somewhat corpulent man and am to go through a passage that is very strait. I beg you would . . . give me a shove and help me through.'[20] As only about 3,000 ministers lost their livings by the 1662 Act of Uniformity there is a suggestion that several thousand parishes—there were about 9,500 altogether—were served earlier by men episcopally ordained and yet willing and able to stay on during the Protectorate.

Catholic laymen, too, may have found some relief under this régime in spite of the loud identification of popery with anti-Christ. The penal laws and Church courts were taken off and so long as individuals avoided contamination by political dissidence they might have found religious conduct less perilous. Exigencies of foreign policy—the French alliance—may have been the most telling argument here, but Cromwell was probably sincere when he assured a sceptical Mazarin that under his rule many papists were 'plucked out' of 'the raging fire of persecution'.[21] Even the Jews had experience of a genuine toleration. It was chiefly Cromwell's own efforts in 'many disputations'[22] over the reluctance of his more hide-bound councillors that allowed the re-admission of 1656. (This episode is important not only for the light it shed on Cromwell's tolerance but as a revelation of the practical re-strictions on his free action as head of the executive.) More typical than the Protector of the common attitudes was William Prynne. That indefatigable pen-pusher immediately put out a remonstrance accusing the government of a criminal leniency, materialistic and an affront to the Son of God, a bargain comparable only with the execrable pro-posal made by Simon Magus to the apostles.[23] Anti-semitism had deep roots, deeper, perhaps, than those of anti-popery.

Walker's *Sufferings of the Clergy* is eloquent about what happened to certain ministers under the Protectorate, but tells us little about how the upheavals affected churchwardens and other Church officials and, most important, congregations. Little that has been written since has been helpful. Perhaps the disruption has been exaggerated. Obviously, in religion as in everything else, local conditions varied, and the activities of the local-based ejectors encouraged diversity. In some areas, in Hull and Newcastle, for example, Independents and presby-terians agreed to share churches. In spirit and practice religious dis-cipline under the Protectorate, even as stepped up in the last years, was looser than in any other period in the seventeenth century, apart, perhaps, from the brief spells of 'prerogative indulgence' under Charles II and James II. The celebrated Toleration Act of 1689 was grudging and circumscribed. Of course, this is not to say that no one could feel he suffered for his faith under the Protectorate. But perhaps some of them met difficulties more because they seemed, like the quakers, 'the scum of all', 'as infectious as the plague', railers, stirrers-up of sedition,[24] contemptuous of authority and their neighbours' peace.

Such men could fall under the terms of a variety of existent acts and ordinances, sometimes and in some places laxly administered, but otherwise and elsewhere harshly implemented by bigoted local authorities, whose zeal could outrun not only the intentions of the Protector and his council, but even the letter of the law. Exasperation with the unconforming and the awkward is not the prerogative of governments. Indeed in the matter of toleration the Protector seems to have been well ahead of his time, even of many of his closest associates, as the Commons debates in 1656 on 'the case of James Nayler' suggests. In religion, as in so much else, Oliver saw himself as a constable to keep the peace of the parish. To do this should not have called for eavesdropping on his neighbours' private devotions, though of course it might mean keeping a wary eye on their public behaviour.

Other ordinances reflect in their condemnation of drunkenness, swearing and sabbath-breaking, the puritan concern for morals and godly conversation that has been charged with completing 'the decline of merry England'. How far these measures were really implemented it is hard to say, but the major-generals instituted in 1655 were definitely charged to stiffen the resolve of other local authorities to work a moral reformation. Some seem to have been active in it, too active, their zeal outstripping discretion and contributing to their downfall in the second Protectorate parliament. Yet too much can be made of roundhead censoriousness. Cromwell had a lively though rather adolescent sense of humour, and was not devoid of appreciation of art, music and literature. He drank wine and allowed dancing at his daughter's wedding. The puritan conscience in this period was generally set itching by more fundamental matters than some of those plaguing latter-day nonconformists. Its positive vitality was shewn to advantage in protectoral patronage of education and scholarship, conspicuous in the attempt to found a new university in Durham, and in the employment in government of John Milton and Andrew Marvell. Less publicised was the consideration shewn to an Anglican scholar, a man of repute for learning throughout the world, Edward Pocock the orientalist. The contribution of puritanism to science and intellectual adventure, providing the essential foundations of, for instance, the Royal Society, is receiving at last its meed of understanding and credit. Nor was the education of the young forgotten. It has been said that the Protectorate was a golden age for the grammar school. Perhaps in reality it was a golden age for nothing and no one, but it was not simply leaden.

xx A Single Person and a Parliament

The Instrument of Government arranged for regular single-chamber parliaments, elected triennially for a minimum sitting of five months, and vested in conjunction with his Highness with legislative authority (Clauses, I, VI, VII, VIII). Failure of the appropriate central authorities to send out the writs could be met by spontaneous action by local officials (Clauses XIX, XX). There might also be interim parliament summoned for *ad hoc* purposes (Clause XXIII). The 400 seats for England and Wales were distributed roughly according to the arrangements laid down in the abortive 'compromise' Agreement of the People drawn up on the eve of the trial of Charles I, and some other proposals made in the Rump. (The Instrument of Government was quite eclectic in its source-material.) Membership was thus allocated in proportion to the rating obligations of the various areas—a serious attempt to put representation on a more rational and equitable base. Ireland and Scotland were each to have 30 members in the new parliament. In May 1654 Fleetwood objected from Ireland that 'that desolate country'[1] was in no condition to consider parliamentary elections, but, even so, ordinances in June established constituencies there and in Scotland. It has been asserted rather than demonstrated that Scots and Irish seats were 'safe pocket boroughs' for direct government nominees. Elections were certainly held for both Protectorate parliaments and not all of the members returned were Englishmen or patently connected with the military ascendancy. But in the nature of things some army officers were returned, not all of them actually sitting, since they could hardly be spared from their commands.

Attention must focus on the vastly predominant membership of England and Wales. The effect of redistribution there was to increase the number of county seats, to be filled by 'knights with swords girt' elected on a franchise of £200 real or personal property. The boroughs were drastically reduced, though a few populous places not represented before, such as Manchester and Durham, were added. The old two-member constituencies mostly gave way to single-seaters. Cornwall which used to send 44 members, 42 of whom sat for tiny boroughs, was to have 12 now, eight of them for the county itself. In a brilliant but not entirely convincing paper Professor H. R. Trevor-Roper has argued that stress on counties was laid because Independent 'honest country gentlemen' without borough patronage aimed at securing a more equitable representation of themselves.[2] But the Instrument of Government as we have seen was not of their devising. It was the product of a group chiefly of army officers upon whom the label 'Independent country gentlemen' will not readily stick. Some of them were and perhaps some of them would have liked to have been, and perhaps Oliver Cromwell was typical of them. Perhaps not. True, they wanted to be sure that the kind of people they expected to support them were well set up in parliament. These included Independent country gentry, but stretched to take in other segments of the community. The destruction of really rotten boroughs smacks as much of the reforming notions of the sixteen-forties as of calculated political jobbery. The ghost of Cromwell's son-in-law Henry Ireton broods over the whole Instrument.

Just how the new arrangements could have been confidently expected to favour the new government is something of a mystery. It is an irony that it was the despised boroughs which turned out to provide the more loyal members. The point is, of course, that boroughs, even though the list was purged, were small and readily susceptible to outside pressures. This was the lesson of the elections for the first parliament (1654). How well it was learned was shown by consequent revision of borough charters, chiefly narrowing the franchise, tightening a governmental grip on the officials, and by probing of the major-generals in the elections for the second parliament. Charles II and James II learned a lot about the possibilities of increasing royal influence over the towns from the example of the Protectorate. When the seventeenth century is viewed as a whole the sixteen-fifties fit fairly neatly into a pattern of local and central governmental relations.

It has been said that the Instrument of Government was 'an expression of the ideals' of the men who made the Protectorate.[3] So it was. But it was also the practical scheme of men looking for what was actually possible at a particular point in time. Lambert and company were too realistic to forget that, in spite of their own military power and the bleak situation of 'the opposition', they could not hope to impose their principles just like that. They knew that completely free elections, allowing who would to stand, would, even with revised and restricted franchises, most likely produce a hostile assembly. So safeguards were written into the constitution. They were of two kinds, pre-electoral and post-electoral. The first excluded from voting or standing those who had acted against parliament in any way since January 1641 (Clause XIV). 'Parliament' here meant any régime supported by the army up to the present. A rider excused those who had 'since been in the service of the Parliament, and given signal testimony of their good affection thereunto'.[4] This allowed in turncoats like George Monk, now Cromwell's best trained agent in Scotland. All abettors of the Irish rebellion—still a nayword of horror—were disfranchised for ever more. So were professed catholics. Penalties of forfeiture for illicit giving of voices were laid down, but since there was no formal registration of votes, it seems certain that some men plainly disqualified under these terms did in fact vote, and some candidates—predictably, losers—claimed that sheriffs were allowing men unseized of £200 property to attend the hustings. These insolent intruders no doubt included many old 40-shilling freeholders, former electors, who turned up out of habit or loyalty to the local magnates whom they were used to supporting. It was up to the sheriff or mayor whether they actually gave their voices. Since the Protectorate had to rely often on men of somewhat uncertain loyalties in these offices it was more than likely they did. Moreover local authorities had a long tradition of private enterprise and were not easily impressed by central government regulations. Even the presence of the major-generals, regular forces and the militia during the 1656 election could not enforce an impeccable implementation of the rules. The two Cromwell elections, like every other of the seventeenth century, were rough-and-ready affairs, reflecting the actual social conditions and values of the age. These did not change overnight just because there was a civil war, a new constitution or a 'popish plot'.

More effective might be other clauses condemning false and fraudulent returns and allowing the council of state oversight of the actual indentures. Persons chosen were to be 'such . . . as are of . . . known integrity, fearing God and of good conversation, and being of the age of twenty-one years' (Clause XVII).[5] This vague but comprehensive formula could be applied by the executive for the first three parliaments, i.e., for nine years, at the end of which it was expected or hoped the régime would be firmly based in the hearts of the political nation, realism tinged with the optimism typical of the founding fathers. A further guarantee was given in the proviso that those elected should have no power 'to alter the government as it is hereby settled in one single person and a Parliament' (Clause XII).[6]

The elections of the summer of 1654 were keenly contested, even in Scotland and Ireland. In spite of changes in seat-distribution and franchise most of the men returned were of a moderate and conservative inclination. The usefully vague epithet 'presbyterian' fits most of them. In many areas the only national issue raised was: should the radical reforming schemes uttered in the Nominated Assembly be confirmed and continued? The reply of the new electorate was an emphatic 'No'. Only four identifiable radical saints got back to Westminster, but moderate members like Francis Rous and Anthony Ashley Cooper were luckier. Sir George Booth, the future leader of a neo-royalist rising in 1659, was returned by Cheshire. But no doubt his success came more because he was a Booth than because he was a presbyterian. Over a hundred members had sat in the Long Parliament, not only republicans and Rumpers like the inevitable Scot, Haselrig and Bradshaw, but others excluded at Pride's Purge or earlier. From the west country came a few who were certainly crypto-royalists. All these potentially unmanageable victors were allowed initially to sit. Only a few Levellers and kindred 'dangerous spirits'—they included John Wildman, Lord Grey of Groby and the outspoken Samuel Highland—were kept out by a council committee charged in August with identifying men not of known integrity and likely to be disturbers of law and peace. It might have been better if the committee had been less reticent and clamped down on the more respectable republicans, skilled parliamentarians of the negative sort, hot for destruction. But the nucleus of government support, army or civilian, Lambert and Whitelocke, Desborough and Fiennes, no doubt bred over-confidence. Col. Edmund Ludlow, a congenital grouser, complained that it was 'undue methods'[7] that brought them in, but normal procedures would have been sufficient in many cases. That a few men who would not have got to Westminster a decade earlier were returned—many more suffered ignominious defeat—should not hide the fact that in this election, as in that of 1656, the usual local influences, prejudices and *parti-pris* passions outweighed all other pressures. Thus 'the first parliament returned under the Instrument, like the first parliament after 1832, showed no significant change in social composition or outlook'.[8]

The new House—or rather about 300 of the members, seventeenth-century Commons being slow to get together—assembled on 3 September 1654, the fourth anniversary of Cromwell's great victory at Dunbar and the third of Worcester—a date no doubt seen, as Hobbes put it, as 'lucky to him'.[9] But it was also a Sunday and some of 'the preciser sort' were offended. Resilient Stephen Marshall, famed for his 'taking' and 'zealous' delivery[10] preached on *Hosea xii, 3, 4,* stressing Ephraim's exhortations to repentance. At four in the after-noon, the Protector standing on a pedestal in the Painted Chamber briefly welcomed the members. Next day there was a service at the Abbey attended by the Protector in quasi-royal state. This time Thomas Goodwin preached. Back then to the Painted Chamber for a fervent discourse from his Highness on what he thought must be 'the greatest occasion ... England ever saw, having upon your shoulders the interest of three nations, and truly ... the interest of all Christian people in the World'.[11] He went on to enumerate the difficulties, domestic and external, that faced and split the nation, pointed out with some pride what had already been done in remedy, and called upon them to join him in the truly godly task of 'healing and settling'. He did not ask for their opinion of the Instrument itself. He assumed that it was of force, since they had met under its terms. Now they must put its individual clauses into operation, notably, providing the executive with money, sinews of both war and peace. Reforms there might be but they must be compatible with the Instrument. This cheerful (or coolly calculated) assessment was soon proved mistaken.

For many an M.P. the nullification of the Instrument was the *alpha* and *omega* of their attendance. Haselrig's bitter republicans were out to restore parliamentary sovereignty and had no shame about exploiting the simple prejudices of their more conventional colleagues. So as a sop to rigid presbyterians they proposed limitations on the religious toleration guaranteed by the constitution and envisaged in the recent ordinances. Experts at the parliamentary game, swift with points of order, adept with snap motions and sudden divisions, they could also work on moderate or uncommitted newcomers, who might not of themselves have grasped the true inwardness of the Instrument, but could be informed of its deficiencies, actual or invented.

The committee of privilege, with Haselrig as its energetic chairman—a choice surely organised—reasserted the Commons' claim to judge its own election returns and promptly allowed two members, previously rejected by the council, to come in. On 7 September the Instrument was forthrightly impugned by a proposition that the government should be in a single person, perhaps, but one limited and restrained as the Commons should think fit. In the debate that sprang up, kept on heat by the republicans, a member declared bluntly that the Protector's right to rule could 'be measured out no otherwise than by the length of his sword'.[12] The court party frantically prevented an immediate resolution but the matter went by a small majority to committee. Parliament was already shewing its distaste for the lowly place assigned it in the new constitution. The old hands were winning over the tyros.

Outside the House opinion was inflamed by blaring sermons. Though no crowds milled round Westminster as in the early days of the Long Parliament, their absence was less a symptom of passive acceptance of the régime than of the fear awakened by the army.

Cromwell was often slow, even dilatory, in reaching a decision. This time he moved fast. On 12 September at his summons the members trooped again into the Painted Chamber to meet a flushed Protector who harangued them in defence of the Instrument, claiming in an over-long review of his own career, that he was no self-appointed authority but one called to his place. As for them they were a free parliament and would be so long as they acknowledged the sanction under which they sat. That sanction was a proper constitution—the Instrument. He was ready to see it altered if need be, but not in some things which were so basic they must be preserved to be handed over intact to posterity. Liberty of conscience, parliaments of limited duration, joint protectoral and parliamentary control of the militia, and government vested in a single person and a parliament—these were not circumstantial but fundamental, bedrock things. So much so that only those who could solemnly—one thinks of Coke's phrase 'by a record and in particulars'—accept them might be allowed to sit on in the House. He then referred them to 'a paper', the Recognition, to be signed. Curiously enough after all this elaborate build-up the Recognition mentioned only one 'fundamental', that of the single person and a parliament, and that was one to which members were presumably bound already by the election indentures.

This dramatic intervention forced the withdrawal of about 100 members, chiefly of a republican turn of mind. Haselrig and his cohorts had clearly embarrassed the government but had characteristically over-played their hand. To withdraw was a striking gesture, but to have continued to sit and to have used their grasp of parliamentary procedure to keep up the pressure while denying the government justification for strong measures would have been more sensible. But it would have been beyond their political imagination. As it was other critics did take the Recognition, determined to probe the Instrument as deep as may be. Under the leadership of the 'political presbyterians' Arthur Onslow and Colonel John Birch, with astute mediatory interventions by Anthony Ashley Cooper, they started sifting matters to the uttermost. Persistence might pay.

Cromwell was desperately anxious not to break the Instrument himself by a forced dissolution before the five months' minimum sitting was up. Wanting both money and legislation, he agreed that the fundamentals were not utterly impregnable, but could be altered, though only with great difficulty. So clause by clause the Instrument was dismembered; piece by piece, a new constitution, emphatically a parliamentary one, was put together. Each alteration cried up the Commons, and the council was prised from its key place in the frame of government. Thus councillors were to seek confirmation of their places from successive parliaments and might therefore have even in the intervals to act in a way calculated to buy the Commons' approval. Military men were unlikely to be able to pay the price demanded. Protectoral succession, obviously a vital thing, was to be resolved by parliament if in session—a direct thrust at John Lambert, the most probable successor under the existent arrangements. The single person's veto was whittled away. Toleration was mutilated. Lest a future Commons should be 'a mere Jack-a-Lent'[13] parliamentary control of the armed forces was demanded. Meanwhile the standing army, first charge on revenue, was to be reduced and a return made to the traditional militia, cheap and safe, based on the localities and controlled by amateur country gentlemen as deputy-lieutenants and officers. Cromwell was ready to consider some demobilisation, if only for economy's sake, but it had to be consistent with security and, like James II 30 years later, he was rightly doubtful of the ability or desire of truly local forces to provide effective national protection.

The upshot of all these searching proposals and the lively debates upon them was renewed unease and tension—between Protector and parliament, parliament and the army, possibly Protector and the army, certainly within the army between those who stood by the Instrument root and branch and those—chiefly among the lesser officers—who would cheerfully throw it over in favour of something more radical and enterprising, say, yet another Agreement of the People.

Cromwell has been charged that, though he had more official supporters in the Commons than any Stuart king, he failed dismally to manage parliament.[14] This is certainly true, but it is hard to see how in fact he could have controlled parliament without abandoning the Instrument entirely and probably the army as well. Obviously in the circumstances of 1654–5 he could do neither. Moreover he had to contend not only with debates at Westminster but an inflamed rather than informed public opinion. Dangerous petitions were circulating, some like that of the Three Colonels,[15] within the army itself. Vicious pamphlets and broadsheets defied censorship. The pulpit thundered. Rumours thickened of mutiny in the navy, Leveller coups in the regiments. Royalist invasion was confidently predicted. From November 1654 onwards there were plausible expectations—hopeful or alarmed— of an abrupt dismissal. But still Oliver persevered, still seeking in parliament the chance that the grip of his fellow-generals, whose insensitivity and tactlessness must often have irritated him and his 'court', might yet be relaxed.

But the Commons could not see that in Oliver himself they had their best means of checking the Lamberts, Desboroughs and other over-mighty subjects. They could not see that Protector and parliament had as much to win in common as in conflict. Blindly they pressed the facile claims and awkward motions that exacerbated the grandees without encouraging the civilian Cromwellians. They proposed a re-duction in revenue, certain to lead to free-quarter and civilian-military recriminations of no help to their cause. Exclusive parliamentary control of religion pointed to renewed intolerance, unthinkable to Oliver. Not a single piece of legislation had been passed in all these months. In January 1655, the civilian courtiers, glimpsing the shadow of impending dissolution, struggled gamely for a compromise. But a vote that 'the militia ought not to be raised . . . or made use of, but by common consent of the people assembled in parliament' marked the parting of the ways.16 Dismissal followed soon enough, on 22 January, after a sitting of exactly five lunar months, or as Carlyle, mindful of the generals' impatience and the rankers' obsession with their four-weekly pay, called them, 'soldier's months'.17 The Instrument was still intact, and carried out to the letter, perhaps to the spirit, too.

Besides their ejection the members had to submit to another 'long and domineering discourse' from the Protector. Harshly he accused them of fertilising weeds—Leveller terrorists and royalist invaders—to grow in their dank shadow. Dangers to public peace had risen by their care-free attitude. 'If it be my liberty to walk abroad in the fields . . . yet it is not my wisdom to do so when my house is on fire.'18 Quite. Parlia-ment had failed him and thereby the nation. Yet so had the Instrument, and in his heart no doubt he knew it. All those nicely constructed checks and balances between branches of government were irrelevant. The real issue remained what it had been all along—between civilian and military interests, or what men thought those interests were. They were if anything even more incompatible.

Parliament, on a reformed or the old franchise, simply would not accept a permanently inferior place in the constitution, and certainly would not accept a perpetual military ascendancy within the executive. This position was inevitable and understandable. What is less excusable was the blind will to throw away the advantage of continuing to sit and to drive wedges into the none-too monolithic military party. Parlia-mentary management can come from outside or within. Cromwell may have been more or less adept with the Commons than Charles I:

in 1654-5 he had no John Pym to contend with. It might have been better for both Protector and parliament if he had. As it was by their perversity the members had flung him back into the jealous embrace of his generals. Ranks were closed and the Venetian Ambassador did not have to be a political genius to observe that so long as the Protector and the power of the army remained united and the troops were content, he would retain his authority. Oliver's arm might be tiring, but he must still keep the sword erect.

XXI Satraps and Bashaws

In the 21 months before another parliament sat at Westminster, an interim not a triennial one, the sword was really out of the scabbard. A few gestures of conciliation, chiefly after the decision to call a new parliament was taken, were lost among the generally threatening attitudes. The pattern was set by an abortive royalist rising within weeks of the dismissal of January 1655, seemingly confirming the Protector's bitter complaints of flourishing weeds and thereby justifying brutal executive action.

'The insurrection of March 1655 was the one occasion between the end of the first civil war and the Restoration in which the Royalists attempted a rebellion by themselves.'[1] Its arrant failure was a cruel comment on their inadequacy. A concerted effort had long been the aim of a select group of intelligent cavaliers calling themselves hopefully 'the Sealed Knot'. All through 1654 they had been gathering information, granting commissions, caching arms for a blow that would take in most English regions and even stir Scotland and Ireland. The Sealed Knot were, however, a cautious lot, prepared to wait for that 'division and faction in the army'[2] which for reasonable men like Edward Hyde, the King-in-exile's most balanced adviser, saw as the *sine qua non* of success. But there were hot-heads among the royalists, some childishly indiscreet, a few of doubtful loyalty. The council of state in England, through its secretary John Thurloe, a very dextrous man at getting intelligence, generally knew pretty well what was going on and took appropriate counter-measures.

Though the abrupt dissolution of parliament delighted the enthusiasts as an irrevocable opportunity, the Sealed Knot were less sanguine. They condemned 'the madness of those people that are resolved to begin' and by 'precipitations' frustrated the effects of 'a fitter conjuncture'. In their turn they were charged with 'a continued coldness and backwardness to action', 'an improper reservedness'.[3] The result was that real division and faction prevailed among the royalists, at home and in exile, at a time when the army was drawing together and the government was embarking on a policy of prevention. Support planned for or wishfully hoped for was struck off by the arrest of John Wildman, 'the noisiest man in England', and other suspects 'that they may not be made use of by the cavaliers and vile levelling party'.[4]

Thus though there were rumblings all over the country it was only in Wiltshire that anything noteworthy happened. There in March 1655 a few hundred men—mostly minor gentry and their tenants, called out as by a sort of feudal levy—appeared under the command of John Penruddock of Compton Chamberlayne, 'a country gentleman of moderate estate'.[5] Their gallant efforts struck no response in a county which, whatever private thoughts may have been, understandably preferred quietness to further bloodshed. The little revolt was soon snuffed out by regular forces under Desborough and Boteler, helped, significantly, by a local militia. The dejected rebels were treated with somewhat contemptuous moderation—the obvious contrast with Jeffreys' 'bloody assize' in the same area 30 years later has often been made. But local leniency was accompanied by a national campaign to magnify the extent of the danger and the worthy role of the State and army as a shield against yet another bloody civil war. Thus a large declaration asserted that 'the [royalist] party generally' and not just 'a few inconsiderable persons' were involved in a nasty business 'that fell out not by chance'.[6] The decision was taken to treat known or suspected cavaliers as incorrigible malignants, men of blood, to be harried out of public life, to be watched, chivvied and chased, and to have to pay for the very machinery devised to keep them under.

In fact, it is very doubtful if the royalists in England in themselves represented more than a negligible threat to the régime, but there were plenty of other enemies, some of them well organised and quite ruthless 'imaginers' of assassination and mutiny, 'a sly and secret generation' who might do Charles Stuart's fell work for him.[7] However many arrests were made there was no warranty that some totally unexpected *coup* was being plotted. Moreover, though government informants were helpful, it was in the nature of their profession to exaggerate too. Repression at times of crisis may have been as much the child of sincere, if uncritical, fears as of a coldly calculated policy.

'Bold and dangerous' in itself 'the insurrection in the west' was not the only upset of 1655.[8] The government found itself facing ugly legal difficulties. Though Cromwell had 'modestly denied to assume the legislative power' since the dissolution, financial and security necessity forced him to issue a spate of proclamations in the spring and summer of 1655. Most were unpopular, all had an even less legal validity than the unconfirmed ordinances of 1654. Both kinds were called in question in

1655. In June 'an eminent Fanatick',[9] George Cony, a London merchant, refused point-blank to pay a tax on Spanish wine. Brought before the Upper Bench (formerly the King's Bench), this latter-day Richard Chambers urgently attacked the validity of the ordinances for customs and excise. His counsel—they included Sergeant Maynard—were put in the Tower to prevent not only the financial but the whole constitutional foundations of the Protectorate from being impugned, since if those ordinances were void, then presumably the rest of the Instrument must be, too. Their gesture over, they soon gave in, but the Chief Justice, upon whom they made an indelible impression, felt compelled to resign.

Then Sir Peter Wentworth claimed that no taxes could be raised but by common consent in parliament. He lacked, however, the bold tenacity of his great namesake, the bane of Elizabeth I, and ignominiously capitulated at 'a message from Caesar'.[10] But the government's victory was a tribute to force not to legality. Meanwhile in Yorkshire two judges had uttered doubts about the treason ordinances and had been dismissed. It was in answer to these spiky legal problems that earlier suggestions that Oliver should be made King would soon be pushed with fresh vigour, calling in the agreed more or less known constitution to redress the balance of the new. But before then the military men had seized a chance to settle things in their own way.

Lack of money ran through all the Protectorate's difficulties. Civil government was costly enough, as Charles I had found even in the period of retrenchment that was his personal government. But Cromwell had a huge military burden to lug, not only in England and Wales, but in still unsettled Ireland and Scotland. Large fleets were kept afloat for policing but also to back the forward imperial and foreign policies that Cromwell felt compelled to pursue. Diplomacy on a European scale was expensive, too. Parliament had done nothing to help. Government credit was uncertain. In the City fifth monarchist and some presbyterian interests opposed government policies and though the régime in its civilian aspects did court the Lord Mayor and Aldermanry, the raising of large sums of ready money was always a strain. The City needed the State to prosper, but the State needed the City more if it were itself to survive a financial crisis. But there was always another impending crisis—the death of Oliver Cromwell. Too much was tied up in his unique personality and prestige for it to be contemplated with equanimity. He was visibly ageing; he was also the target of assassins. Major-General Berry wondered 'if any of them should take . . . what will come of our preferments?'[11] A pertinent question, echoed by investors and creditors.

So far the plots had been laughable failures. Most, like Miles Sindercombe', called for too much time, too many assistants and too many accidents or lucky chances, but who knew when a stray bullet might not yet find a mark. Anarchy would follow, or a new order probably repudiating the debts of its predecessor. Even now the great windfalls of crown, Church and confiscated royalist lands had been used up. There was nothing to follow. In spite of the generous experimentation of the past decade no really satisfactory means of anticipating revenue had been furnished, and none looked likely now that the government was in finance as in everything else turning back to the procedures of the past. In any case neither restoration nor experimentation in financial machinery could expect to do much to reduce outlay. Only a savage pruning of commitments could do that. The obvious area for economy was in military costs, either by demobilisation or by pay cuts. Either policy had its dangers. Each would disgust officers and men and whether directly or indirectly weaken the executive's grip on the country.

Yet something had to be done and by May 1655 most officers had been educated to accept a reduction of both bodies and pay. The anticipated weakening of security was to be met by raising a supplementary militia in the localities, one more centrally and professionally controlled than the old misnamed trained bands. This national scheme followed a regional try-out in the south-west by Desborough earlier in 1655. In August England and Wales were divided into 10 (later 11) military districts, each under a major-general supplied with some very explicit instructions. Not only were they to command the forces— regular or part-time—in their areas, or 'cantons'[12] as someone aptly called them, but they were to help in the general administration of the country, supplementing the existing local authorities, the traditional J.P.s, mayors, churchwardens and constables, and also the newfangled county committees. They were to assist but also to chase up. There was an urgent need, from the point of view of Whitehall at least, for energy here, since there was a disturbing lack of able men willing to undertake office, particularly that of constable, always unattractive even under more normal régimes. The generals were also to disarm enemies of the State, not only obvious royalists, and to report regularly on their doings to a central registry. Riots and unlawful assemblies, horse-races, stage-plays were to be put down. Superfluous ale-houses, haunts of the disaffected and anti-social, were to be suppressed; laws against enclosures, depopulation and neglect of tillage enforced and the poor law code implemented. To achieve this formidable programme, which embraced the routine ambition of any seventeenth-century

193

government as well as the peculiar necessities of the present one, the major-generals were established as at once soldiers, administrators, censors and police, seeing to 'the security of the nation, the suppressing of vice, and encouragement of virtue, the very end of magistracy'.[13] It was an end in which most of them conscientiously believed. They claimed to have made it their business to promote the public interest generally.

That was the trouble. They had vast powers and broad responsibilities. They neglected neither. Disliked as an unwarrantable encroachment of central authority on local autonomies, parallel to that of the 'thorough' government of 1629–40, they were detested because they intruded with swords in their hard hands. Resistance to them was to be found from local officials who had been formerly apathetic, keen or refractory—again, as under Charles I. They were despised because they were men of inferior quality, 'silly mean fellows',[14] scum flung up by the boiling wars, associating with them in their iron rule local parvenus like themselves. It was noted, for example, that none of the larger gentry of Nottinghamshire were to be found among Whalley's commissioners. They were accused as the civil war county committees had been, probably with equal justice, of enabling some groups of men to lord it over others. Seemingly purged of their own provincial patriotisms, they shewed short patience with and feeble grasp of local ways. Worse, they set themselves up as moral inquisitors, of whom in ministers and lecturers there were enough already, pruriently prying into private lives, 'doing what was good in their own eyes',[15] but reluctant to let anyone else make up his own mind how to behave. (Lambert has been credited with 'the little, poor invention'[16] of this system of satrapies, but the grave emphasis put on godliness and virtue probably owes more to Oliver, who saw here one means of working towards that 'reformation' that lay so close to his heart.)

The major-generals look like Richelieu's *intendants* anglicised and armoured. They were ambulatory star chambers, personal councils of the north, lay ecclesiastical courts. They were also efficient. 'You may ride all over Nottingham and not see a beggar or a wandering rogue', wrote Whalley.[17] 'There is hardly a meeting of three cavaliers together upon any account, but I am suddenly acquainted with it', was the plausible claim of Worsley.[18] It is not surprising that after the Restoration the county authorities, having in the collapse of military rule come back into what they regarded as their own, resisted all renewed attempts to control them. Charles II was more or less content to leave it at that. James II, stolidly conscientous in this as in so much else, was not. It was the drastic interference with local immunities that accompanied his policy of indulgence that helped to bring on the revolution. In 1688 he was faced by a strike of local government as total as that which in 1640 brought Charles I to his knees to a parliament. His claim for a standing army to breach the local monopoly of enthusiastically amateur gentry officers must have reminded many a J.P. as much of the not so distant days of the Protectorate sword-rule as of the dragonnades of Louis XIV.

The system of the major-generals was not cheap. Apart from running local administration, they were responsible for the militia. The heavy costs of this, at least, were met by the royalists, for, as Oliver was to put it to the 1656 parliament, 'if there were need of greater forces to carry on the work, it was a most righteous thing to put the charge on that party that was the cause of it'.[19] Estates of men caught in arms were confiscated. Those who appeared to adhere to Charles II—a conveniently vague formula—were subject to a ten per cent charge on their income, 'the decimation tax'. (It is possible that Lambert or one of the other generals had read Sir Robert Dudley's *A Proposition for his Majesty's Service to Bridle the Impertinences of Parliament*, written in 1614 under James I and published in curious circumstances in 1629 under the title *A Project How a Prince may make Himself an Absolute Tyrant*. This advocated a military despotism supported by 'a decimation, being so termed in Italy, where in some parts it is in use, taxing a tenth of every man's estate, to be paid yearly to the Crown as rent'.[20] Dudley suggested that the catholics should be singled out for this tax. Other parts of the 'project' come pretty close to advocating what the major-generals actually did in the sixteen-fifties.)

The decimation tax was directed against men of some substance. A proposal to extend liability to smaller men was resisted by Whalley with the interesting argument that people of that sort were either 'all for the parliament or neuter', and that in any case it would 'discontent many, and ruinate some'.[21] This points straight at the dilemma before the government. To be too lenient might encourage the irreconcilables to make the final shove that would bring the whole wobbly edifice of the Protectorate tumbling down: to be too harsh was to make actual enemies of those who might otherwise be formally content and obedient. In time the major-generals, getting to know their respective areas and beginning to appreciate their peculiar needs, might have found they could afford to be a little indulgent. But they were born of an emergency, however inflated it may have been, and their system was swept away while most of them still felt they had to be heavy-handed. Moreover, for all their effectiveness and capacity, there is a suggestion of despair about their creation. Accompanied by repression in other spheres—packing of juries, press censorship, arbitrary arrests and tampering with municipal charters—they were a negation of that spirit of healing which Oliver always so eloquently adumbrated. The decimation tax with its effect of political excommunication gave permanence to the divisions of the civil war, widening the old and opening new ones. It was a case not of divide and rule but of divide and fall. In the second parliament there were few to stand up for the system and the Lord Protector, shrewdly judging the mood of the political nation, quietly left them to their fate.

Discriminatory taxes might support a militia, but they could make little impression on the growing financial stress of a government active at home and aggressive abroad. The autumn of 1655, following the apparent failure of a grandiose onslaught on the Spanish West Indies, brought an all-out war with Spain. From the start there was a shortage of revenue to pay for it. Everybody in the government knew the problem: everybody had a solution. Unfortunately they conflicted. Suggestions, redolent of their origins, included a doubling of ordinary taxation and a sort of capital levy. Someone proposed that the Protector should imitate Charles I and send out letters under his privy seal demanding loans or gifts in proportion to the value of estates. Such inept expedients had been no help to Charles I. It was unlikely they would pay a ruler whom many regarded as a brutal tyrant and more as an usurper. Charles I had found in 1640 that wriggle as he might he could not escape meeting a parliament. Realistic men about Cromwell had no doubt that an extraordinary parliament, the routine triennial one not being due till the autumn of 1657, must be summoned, and, if suitable precautions were taken, might actually be welcomed. Cromwell himself was genuinely anxious as ever to clothe his rule in constitutional garments, partly because, in spite of his unparalleled career, he had in many ways a conventional view of government, and because, as has been already indicated, he was keen to extricate himself from the enervating grasp of his military partners. He had failed with one parliament, he might yet succeed with another. The inevitability of the collapse of the Protectorate which so many historians blandly take for granted was not so obvious to him or to many other of his contemporaries.

After great striving at Whitehall, by June 1656 the great decision was taken—a parliament there should be. But of what kind? There seems to have been a proposal for another 'nominated assembly', this time less restricted to saints. But common sense prevailed, helped no doubt by the hopeful forecasts of some of the major-generals and officials that there was scope for deploying governmental influence in the elections. Besides there was the cheering reflection that, the amend-ments of the proposed parliamentary constitution having died at the dismissal of 1655, the council were still empowered under the Instru-ment of Government to examine election returns and to exclude the unqualified. In short, the elections could be 'rigged', a possibility soon put to the test.

Writs went out in July. Soon keenly-fought elections were under way. The major-generals mostly worked hard to get a choice of good men, including, naturally enough, themselves. But their influence was patchy, stronger in the boroughs, especially in those whose charters had been revised. In the counties the traditional influence of the sub-stantial landed gentry could not be side-tracked. Major-General Whalley could say confidently of Nottingham that the corporation would not choose any without his advice, but he could not stop the return of his royalist kinsman, Penington Whalley, for the shire itself. From the west country Desborough reported 'great contendings and struggling, in all parts. 'I have consulted', he went on, 'with the honest people of every county, as I came along, and with them agreed upon names, and have sett them at worke. . . . I must confess in every county I yet came in, I heare of their making parties; and undoubtedly their designs are to overthrow all. Therefore my busines is . . . to prevent and break all such contrivances.' [22] Well said: ill done. News came into London that 'the ill-affected are so bold and ungrateful as, at elections, to cry out: No soldiers, no courtiers!'—this last phrase ominously echoing popular slogans of 1640. Sir Harry Vane, it was said, was busy persuading 'the people from electing swordsmen, Major Generals and Decimators'.[23]

In these circumstances some of the major-generals understandably showed a want of patience and tact. Major-General Haynes prepared to put his troops 'into a condition of service' but unfortunately left it too late.[24] 'Where our honest Soldiers can appeare,' a newswriter reported, 'a reasonable good Choyce is made, but the farther off from London the worse.'[25] Thus Captain Henry Stone, active in Staffordshire for the cause from the start of the wars and 'a busy man in sequestrations', stood for knight of the shire, 'but was put back with disgrace'.[26] He was a man of 'mean extraction' and his débâcle was probably as much the effect of his social effrontery as of the unattractiveness of his poli-tical image. It would be wrong to see in all the opposition to those favoured by the government sentiments deeply stirred by concepts of national interest and genuine constitutional criticism. Much the same may be said of this election as of that of 1654, that the contests were chiefly between the usual local influences, distorted but not subdued by the intervention of the major-generals. They represented the sort of central interference attempted in any election—but in an intensified, because armed, form. But it seems unlikely that Cromwell was enthusiastic for too blatant a show of force at the hustings. Maximum support for the Spanish war and for another essay in settlement called for conciliation. He knew of the unpopularity of the major-generals, and it may well be that his keenest wish was for a stronger representation of the civilian Cromwellians.

The results of the elections are fairly hard to assess. Major-General Goffe's summary expresses the common judgment on the government's side: 'not so good as we could have wished them . . . and not so bad as our enemies would have had them'.[27] Certainly many men who could be in no obvious way held favourable to the régime were returned, crypto-royalists 'of the utmost malignity' as well as open republicans. But there was a nucleus of government support, civil and military. About 100 officers, high and low ranking, and officials were chosen, aside from those sent in from Scotland and Ireland. (Elections were held there, too, and though the members elected were not unexpectedly government supporters, more searching investigation of the actual contests is called for before the blanket assertion that they were 'chosen by the sword'[28] can be confidently accepted.) Among civilian officials were President of the Council Henry Lawrence, its secretary John Thurloe, Sir Gilbert Pickering, the court chamberlain, Lord-keeper Nathaniel Fiennes and the clever Irish opportunist, Lord Broghill. Lambert, Fleetwood, Desborough, Goffe and Skippon led the military contingent.

But analysis of the actual sitting membership is made difficult by the enforced exclusion by the council of many members after the returns came in and by voluntary absentees and withdrawals. Some officers and officials were too necessary to be released from their posts, even for a parliament. But most of the missing faces were those of critics of the régime. Among those refused admission at the start—some of whom managed to sneak quietly in later and to vote for Cromwell to become King—were republicans (Haselrig, Scott, Bradshaw, the inevitable trio), presbyterians (Harbottle Grimstone, Walter Moyle, John Birch and Sergeant John Maynard), royalists and prelatists (Richard Browne of the City of London and Challenor Chute of Middlesex) and individualists like Anthony Ashley Cooper, who had sat in the council of state till January 1655 and had supported a proposal in the first parliament that the Protector should assume kingship. Some of the exclusions were easily predictable but some of those who failed to please the council, whom Oliver claimed later to have left completely free in the matter, were nonentities. On the other hand the four City members, including a former Lord Mayor, Theophilus Biddulph, were certainly men of substance. The unpopularity of the Spanish war in some mercantile circles was no doubt reflected in the reluctance of the City electorate to return men amenable to the current Lord Mayor and the Aldermanry, who, as indicated earlier, had their own convincing reasons for backing the Protector. Among the surprises was Samuel Highland, excluded in 1654, now chosen by the same constituency, Southwark, and allowed to sit. It should be noted that members did not have to make a specific 'recognition' in order to take their places, but obtained a 'ticket' from the council. Those without it were 'kept out by soldiers'.[29] Thus exclusion was not a once-and-for-all event, and at various times after the first meeting of parliament stray individuals made applications for leave to sit and received it.

About 180 members were new to Westminster. Of the rest 230 had sat in the 1654 parliament and eight in the Nominated Assembly. Even allowing for exclusions and absences there was a richness of parliamentary experience to draw upon. There was also a sense of the privilege of parliament and the exclusions did not pass without protest. Soon after parliament assembled the Speaker, Sir Thomas Widdington, a commissioner of the Great Seal and recently Lord Mayor of York, received a letter of complaint from a large group of excludees. A sharp debate followed in which the council was charged with an illegality 'as gross as a mountain, open, palpable'.[30] The government *bloc*, who often enough failed to use their potential influence impressively, on this occasion worked well. The matter was let drop, 'a great providence of God', thought John Thurloe. It 'hath wholly discouraged the other partie, many whereof are withdrawne from the house, because they could not have their will in this voet; but the house proceedes on very cheerefully in their buissines'.[31] About 50 members stayed away in disgust at the Commons' voluntary relaxation of its privilege, though some of them were unable to resist the lure of congenial society and political discussion for long. But a group among the excluded, bitter at their betrayal, published a slashing remonstrance in which they condemned the assembly then sitting at Westminster for meekly submitting to 'daily awe and terror of the Lord Protector's armed men', denying itself any claim to be 'the representative body of England'.[32]

The Lord Protector saw this 'emergency' parliament as primarily a means of raising war taxation with the minimum of offence to legally tender consciences. But he still had in mind his great objective of healing and settling. Thus his opening speech, while setting out the immediate dangers at home and abroad, dealt warmly with his ideals. The Levellers were castigated. They were conniving with Spain, England's natural enemy, and the exiles to put 'a poor nation' wallowing in its own blood again. Foul designs had justified 'a little inspection upon the people', 'much regretted'—the system of the major-generals, which had in fact not only preserved the Commonwealth but had 'been more effectual towards the discountenancing of vice and settling religion than anything done these fifty years'. For his part he would 'abide by it, notwithstanding the envy and slander of foolish men'.[33] These seemingly unequivocal words must have reassured the grandees, and depressed the county members who saw a fight on their hands. But Oliver, whose speeches shew little evidence of detailed preparation, rather of a turbid 'stream of consciousness', was off again in pursuit of his favourite topics: religion, manners, law and finance. Much had been done on all of them; support was demanded for more. Avoiding disputes in unnecessary and unprofitable things, M.P.s should join the man who was 'by the voice of the people the supreme magistrate', and God himself in bringing 'mercy and truth' together, 'righteousness and peace' to kiss one another. It was a copious programme.[34]

Most of the exuberant harangue must have passed the audience by, but the moral earnestness here did strike a spark or two, fanned by courtiers and officials into a little warmth for discussion of social and legal reform. By mid-November the Protector was congratulating them that 'though you have sat but a little time . . . you have made many good laws', a sharp contrast with the first parliament.[35] Measures included sumptuary regulations touching on dress and cosmetics, taking in a denunciation of artificial beauty-spots that might have dripped from the vitriolic pen of William Prynne himself. Over the resistance of 'the long robe' bills were brought in to carry 'the administration of the law . . . into provinces',[36] and John Lambert startled the lawyers by proposing the creation of a branch court of equity in Yorkshire, where the loss of the facilities of the council of the north was still regretted. Some of this legislation received support less for what it was than for the hope that it would help hack away the arbitrary authority of the major-generals, though obviously this was far from Lambert's intentions. Moreover, fears that this parliament, as an 'interim' one, might by the terms of the Instrument be blessed with only three months' guaranteed sitting, may have given urgency to those members who wanted to have something positive to report when they got back to their 'countries', while ready agreement on these 'circumstantials' might encourage the Protector to keep them by him for matters of more substance. Yet all this while, too, they busied themselves with bills of naturalisation and similar apparent trivialities. 'It is private business jostles all out',[37] complained a bored official. But this was a good sign—a hint of normality. Few Stuart parliaments lived all the while in the hot-house atmosphere of constitutional controversy. Much of their work was placid routine, things indifferent to the whole nation, but perhaps of the essence to the local or private interests concerned.

But behind this easy-going co-operation lurked a feverish question: what should be done about the major-generals? Few were unaware of it, few, remembering the Protector's ostensibly uncritical panegyric, had the nerve to coax it into the parliamentary arena. Unexpectedly it was the major-generals themselves, following that doubtful soldierly precept that offence is better than defence, who forced the question. They did not like the answer.

On Christmas Day 1656 Major-General John Desborough asked leave of a thin House—attendance had been dropping 'owing to the shortness of the days', and perhaps because the less precise members had gone home to enjoy Christmas in the hearty fashion deplored by puritans—to bring in 'a short bill for the continuance of a tax upon some people, for the maintenance of the militia'.[38] It was, of course, the decimation tax. A brisk debate sprang up. Col. Hewitson spoke warmly, for the bill arguing that 'you are not laying a tax upon the people, but upon your enemies, whose estates are at the devotion of your enemies. They are active people, whom they will employ to your destruction.' Others accepted that there was a problem, but 'no necessity, at present' for haste. Mr Puller wanted the reading deferred 'till the house be full, that all men may speak their conscience'.[39] Ultimately by a tiny majority leave was given to go on with the bill, but the outlook was bleak for its sponsors when it was noted that the minority included civilian officials and some of Cromwell's kin. In a full House they would surely make an unmistakable majority.

Cromwell could see he had a choice between preserving the major-generals, a drag upon his kind of settlement, and continuing his courtship of a House with which he was on terms. It had voted in favour of war with Spain and had not taken amiss a hint that Spain could not be taken 'with a bare vote'. Even now, though 'loath, exceeding loath' to turn to the only really effective taxation, on property, they were seriously investigating ways and means of prosecuting vigorous war.[40] It was Oliver's need for money rather than petty jealousy of Lambert's influence and capacity, that spurred him against an Instrument that had served its turn and was now turning in upon him.

So when the bill was given a first reading in January 1657 a better attended House was startled, then delighted, to hear Cromwell's son-in-law, John Claypole, moving its rejection as a provocation. At this invitation the courtiers edged into the open. Sir John Trevor claimed the measure would 'divide this Commonwealth into provinces ... (under) a power too great to be bound within any law'.[41] Someone else bluntly described the bill as 'the usher to an arbitrary power'.[42] Lambert, part-author of the system and (by proxy) major-general for the five northern counties, replied mildly that this was not the time for squabbling over legal niceties. 'Good words will not do with the cavaliers.... The quarrel is ... whether we shall live, or be preserved, or no.'[43] His comrades, whose personal interests—prestige, honour, rewards—as well as principles were deeply embedded in the system, leaped in now and later to reinforce this plausible case, not without a momentary effect. A newsletter writer saw the debates of 'so even a cast' on 24 January that he would not risk a forecast of the outcome.[44] But resentments of the past and fears of the future harsh administration of the 'satraps' told. The Protector's nephew, Col. Henry Cromwell, went so far as to accuse the major-generals of acting 'unjustly and against law' and pugnaciously offered to prove it.[45] On 28 January, by 124–88, after a staunch rearguard struggle by the bill's supporters, who were 'very loath to surrender',[46] to have a decision deferred, the bill was rejected. The major-generals had not mustered a single vote more than on Christmas Day. Smarting from a defeat that looked like helping the Protector to worm his way out of military tutelage, they prophesied that this parliament, crazed with victory, would hare off now after more matters of discord. The wish, no doubt, was father to the thought.

XXII The Case of James Nayler

The grandees were confounded. The very day after the decimation tax was rejected the House voted £400,000 for a 'just and necessary' war with Spain. It was a vote in which some supporters of the militia bill were 'exceeding cold'.[1] Lambert was certainly no favourer of the war and had in council spoken hard against the Penn–Venables expedition to the West Indies as improbable of success. It was not mere pique or obstructionism. Lambert was in many ways a very realistic politician and his views on this matter were the result of sober calculations. But the line he was taking in this and other issues was straining his relationship with the Protector. His influence on Oliver, hitherto considerable but never overweening, was weakening. A coolness began that ended with an open breach. It is not known whose notion it had been to raise the decimation issue so early in the parliament. Desborough, an inept parliamentarian, may well have acted on impulse without Lambert's connivance. But once the matter was brought on the floor of the House, Lambert was bound to join in. So when Cromwell was criticised for his own seeming change of front on kingship, he could justly mock Lambert: 'Who bid you go to the House with a bill and there receive a foil?'[2] he demanded of the army officers' deputation that waited on him on 27 February 1657. By then the offer of the crown had been made, a tempting reward stemming directly from his abandonment of the 'satraps' and 'bashaws'.

The anxiety of the Commons to snap the authority of the grandees did not distract them from the pleasant effort to add to their own. Religiously, they were generally right-wing puritan ('presbyterian'), contemptuous of toleration, fearful of sectaries and papists, eager to tighten the bonds of discipline. So far the Protector had been in practice more kindly disposed to religious dissidents, even to catholics, than any government since the Long Parliament had first sat. But war with Spain, an evil land traditionally seen as the spiritual home of English recusancy and treachery, encouraged the urge to persecute that lay latent in many English protestants. Cromwell's own epithet for papists

—'spaniolised'[3]—and some passing remarks he had made in his opening address stimulated a demand for the re-imposition of old penal laws and the introduction of new, equally if not more nasty, measures.

A bill bristling with unkind clauses was brought in during November 1656 and passed after some staunch opposition. Prominent among the minority was Lambert, who was ostentatiously more tolerant, possibly indifferent, than many of his fellow commanders and who was, perhaps, showing here an author's resentment of trenchant criticism of the religious terms of 'his' Instrument of Government. The new and unblushingly retrograde legislation was in no sense the work of the Protector himself, as he placatingly pointed out to his ally, Cardinal Mazarin, who felt he ought not to appear unmoved by the fate of his co-religionaries in England. Though Cromwell promised Mazarin to 'remove [these] impediments' and 'to make a farther progress',[4] he did not veto the measure because he wanted to keep on terms with this mainly congenial House. But it is to his credit that he took no action towards having the thing effectively operated.

Not only papists, easy prey, but radical protestant sects found themselves unloved by Parliament. Under the Instrument liberty was allowed in effect to all except the licentious and peacebreakers.[5] Such generosity was widely regarded as extravagant if not lunatic. The opinions and practice of some of those adjudged 'safe' were deeply disturbing to conventional men for whom decency and reverence were synonymous. They had taken the Protector's earlier proclamation against disturbance of ministers and congregations in their formal acts of worship as a hint that he had come to recognise the need of the magistrate to maintain discipline. Some of his remarks about sectaries since then suggested he was putting them in the same category as papists, that is, as potential if not immediate threats to national security, restless abusers of liberty.

Religious freedom had obviously been a fecund and feckless mother of sects. Every week seemed to spawn another variety, bizarre, insolent, confident, delinquent. One group in particular had lately been attracting alarmed attention. The so-called Society of Friends—or 'quakers in the sight of the Lord'—'founded' (if that is the word) by that puzzling blend of the mundane and the mystical, the humble and the arrogant, George Fox. Under the spell of his blunt eloquence and pressing personality Friends grew as the garden of the Lord—weeds, some would have said. Quaker ideas, centring on the concept of the unerring guidance of 'the inner light', were as yet in the framing. They seemed, and indeed they were, a far more radical, even revolutionary group than their later history of respectable moderation might suggest. 'Waiting on the Lord' with them did not preclude action—as, of course, it never had with Oliver Cromwell himself. The quakers did not withdraw from the world, they wanted to change it. Devoid of clear-cut, matter-of-fact political concepts, they affected to despise constituted authority, lay or clerical. As a result of widely reported, probably inflated, instances of awesome insolence to priests and justices, they broke out like a raw blister on the left flank of the English Reformation. ('They' is perhaps to suggest more uniformity than there actually was among the earliest Friends. They were not without internecine rifts and Fox was not able to impose a fixed pattern on those who trembled to spiritual awareness at his touch.)

In a stratified age, the notion of an inner light burning or flickering in all human beings appealed more to emotion than to reason, more to the unlettered than to the erudite, and to women as much if not more than to men. It quickened a female excitement that seemed unhealthy, if not downright indecent. It should not be forgotten that earlier the more obviously political radicalism of the sixteen-forties had awakened many women, and the fact that some of the leaders of these movements, John Lilburne certainly and possibly Gerrard Winstanley, had moved on to quakerism enlivened uneasiness in a man's world. The threat that quakers uttered, then, was one felt at all levels of society and experience. Its impact, which amounted to shock, was vividly brought out in 'the case of James Nayler' which took up a great part of the business of the autumn sittings of the 1656 parliament.

James Nayler was an ex-Independent, ex-soldier (in fact John Lambert's quartermaster on the Dunbar campaign), and now an elated follower of George Fox, or, more accurately, of his own flickering 'inner light', an eloquent preacher, vigorous, unhandsome but with a curious, almost mesmeric power over women. In October 1656, then aged 36, he re-enacted at Bristol Christ's entry into Jerusalem, seated on an ass, accompanied by hysterical women singing and casting their garments in the muddy ruts before him. (Such was the state of the main road from Glastonbury to Bristol!) The extraordinary, somewhat comical, strangely pathetic incident might have been just a local sensation had not an M.P., confessing himself shattered to the soul, directed the attention of the House to this 'blasphemy'. As a connexion with the matter of toleration was at once established, a committee was named to look into the whole affair, questioning persons, including Nayler and his gaggle of women, who had been sent up in custody to London. The committee painstakingly reported on 5 December that James Nayler had attempted to assume the attributes of

Christ, using them as a cloak for immorality. Debates revealed an outraged compulsion to punish him and through him to strike at all abusers of liberty. One angry swordsman hit a resonant note when he confessed he had 'often been troubled in my thoughts to think of this toleration'.[6]

But how could this wretch, however deserving of condign punishment, be legally convicted and his sentence made exemplary? After inconclusive talk of appointing a special high court of justice—the sort of thing for which good parliament-men were expected to show a professional aversion—and an act of attainder, Nayler was brought to the bar of the House and closely questioned. He freely admitted the facts, but denied that he had taken part in or condoned immorality. What he had done had an allegorical significance, nothing more. He had not set up to be Christ, but to be a symbol of Christ.

The distinction was too fine to be grasped by many members, but Nayler had made contrasting impressions. For the next few weeks almost daily the House searched into the matter. Many though not all government supporters, including John Lambert, were for caution and moderation in these strange circumstances, arguing the difficulty, if not sheer impossibility, of defining blasphemy so as to leave intact a basic toleration. Other members worked themselves up into savage, indeed hysterical denunciations of quakers generally and of this typically obscene example. One of them, ironically echoing a proposal of 1641 for dealing with Strafford, wanted Nayler taken out and incontinently knocked on the head. Eventually he was voted, hardly adjudged, guilty of a vague but alarming something called 'horrid blasphemy' and thereby meet for an appalling punishment. But still the aching question nagged: could he be legally sentenced and could that sentence be implemented? 'The merciful men' pointed out that by the terms of the Instrument then in being he could not. Such pusillanimous pedantry was spurned out of hand. 'If this be liberty, God deliver me from such liberty!',[7] cried the grizzled swordsman Philip Skippon, hero of Turnham Green. To leave this monster to the ordinary courts of law was too gentle and milksop an expedient, unless, as someone unblushingly suggested, they could be assured that the statute *de heretico de comburendo* of that cold bigot Henry V was still of force. They could not be sure of that and so fell back upon a judicial power deemed to have devolved automatically upon the Commons at the abolition of the House of Lords, which had definitely had, as in impeachment, authority to act as a court.

Nayler's case was broadening out in significance. Religious intolerance was slipping into constitutional controversy. If the Commons could act as investigators, as the committee had done;—accusers, as individual members had done; judge and jury, as the House was now doing, where was the limit of their sovereignty?

Debates opened up the widest spectrum of constitutional understanding, from considerable sophistication to the feeblest of naiveté. There is a danger in assuming that politicians in the thick of things really know what they are doing and that lawyers fully grasp the implications of what they say. In these heated exchanges muddled thinking and genuine puzzlement—not the same things—met head on. Prejudice and detachment, intelligence and stupidity all expressed themselves. The results, laconically reported in Burton's *Parliamentary Diary*, are illuminating. Nothing shows up more vividly the astonishing diversities and contradictions of opinion and temperament that made up 'the court party', 'the country party', 'the major-generals', 'the Independents', 'the presbyterians' and the other groups which contemporaries dimly discerned or historians have invented to bring perspective into their investigations. Nayler's case raised religious, legal, constitutional, humanitarian and intellectual issues that blasted all artificial categories. This vain, rash, sincere, deluded man brought unwittingly to a focus the ideals and realities of the whole Interregnum. If there was one moment when the whole mingle-mangle of the English revolution might have been glimpsed as in a lightning flash it was when James Nayler appeared before the House of Commons to hear his sentence and was, over the protests of some members, not suffered to speak. All that was good and all that was bad in the Great Rebellion seemed to turn in on him—from the poles of liberty and authority, law and necessity, convention and experiment, imagination and obtuseness, interest and impartiality—as he stood there, a little bewildered but unrepentant, in the sight of his persecutors and defenders.

Nayler's sentence was a brutal one, not, it is true, of death, but of humiliation, branding, tongue-boring and flogging, not once but twice, an affront to the spirit, a contempt of the body. 'The merciful men' worked hard to have the punishment mitigated, particularly the mutilation, since his tongue 'may afterwards praise the Lord'.[8] But the zeal which some men have to break other men's bodies to save yet other men's souls would not be thwarted. On 18 December the first instalment of the ordeal was performed in London. Nayler behaved with reproachful dignity. A week later the Protector celebrated the anniversary of the birth of his Saviour, in whose face Nayler had been judged to have spat, by sending to the Speaker to ask 'the grounds and reasons'[9] upon which the Commons had proceeded. It was a cruelly pertinent and awkward question.

What simple answer could the Commons give? As William Sydenham put it, if they replied 'by our judicial power',[10] they must surely satisfy his Highness by some definition of that power, for as had been said by some all along, the case might become a general precedent and parliament be in the way of turning into a court of will and power.[11] How could the major-generals, still undefeated, remember, be deplored then? That deeply-experienced deviser of written constitutions John Lambert was quick to seize the point. 'We cannot tell what kind of parliaments other ages may produce. We ought to take care to leave things certain.'[12] (The case of James Nayler might be the case of John Lambert.) The debate petered out in embarrassment. The second grim part of Nayler's sentence was carried out. Tactfully, or weakly, Cromwell did not press for an answer to his enquiry. Obviously he was unwilling, in spite of what must have been a genuine human sympathy for Nayler, to risk a brush with the parliament which though friendly had yet to vote him money for war.

Yet the case could not be so lightly brushed aside. The constitutional issues were too sharp. By claiming the right to sentence their victim parliament had in effect impugned the validity of the Instrument of Government, which assigned it neither by letter nor implication any such authority. If in spite of that glaring defect, judicial authority was successfully asserted, who could set its limits? 'No judge upon earth!', bewailed Lambert Godfrey, a member for Kent.[13] But prudence, if nothing else, demanded an arbiter. Here was a cogent argument for the proposal, long played with, now gaining serious consideration from other sources, namely, that the present Lord Protector should become King, stepping upwards from a position alien to English traditions to an office and title known to the laws of the land, defined by them and in its own certainties pointing to the definition of that parliament of which the crown was itself in some measure an integral part. Here was a pleasing notion, apparently a full answer to all contemporary constitutional problems. But it was an optimistic if not an illusory one, since anyone who had given even the most cursory of glances back over the constitutional conflicts of the last half-century must have been made aware that in great part they had arisen precisely because the known laws did not in fact set agreed immutable limits to the spheres of the various agents of government. It is a puzzle how a lawyer like Bulstrode Whitelocke, obviously well versed in the realities which had produced the civil war that had culminated in the abolition of monarchy, could make himself believe that a return to kingship in the House of Cromwell would take off for ever the incubus of constitutional discord. But such was the fact, making for the ideal consumers' response to an 'advertisement' for monarchy.

Other men were less credulous but saw the makings of a *prima facie* case for constitutional reform. Late in February 1657 Cromwell told a critical deputation of army officers that the Commons 'by their judicial authority . . . fall upon life and limb, and doth the Instrument in being enable me to control it? . . . The case of James Nayler might happen to be your own case. . . . '[14] There was the rub. His seeds of doubt did not fall on entirely stony ground. But, by then, the offer of a crown had already been made and a new phase in the relations of parliament and Protector, the legislative and the executive, had already opened.

XXIII The Offer of a Crown

A Protector, what's that? 'Tis a stately thing,
That confesseth itself but the ape of a king;
A tragicall Caesar acted by a Clowne;
Or a brass farthing stamp'd with a kind of a crown;
A bubble that shines; a loud cry without woole;
No Perillus *nor* Phalaris; *but the Bull.*
The eccho of monarchy till it come;
The but end of a barrell in the shape of a drum;
A counterfeit piece that woodenly shews
A golden effigy with a copper nose.
The fantastick shadow of a sovereign head,
The arms royal revers'd, and disloyal instead.
In fine, he is one we may Protector call,
From whom the King of Kings protect us all.[1]

The survival of the Protectorate depended on military might. It dangled also on the life-line of a single person, Oliver Cromwell, in his day a vigorous, strong man, but now often ill, prematurely worn by a too active life in field and council chamber in middle age, followed without a break by the cares of government in an atmosphere of crisis. Tirelessly he had uttered his ringing pleas for reciprocity and recognition but disappointment, distrust, exasperation and uncertainty kept court with him. Now there was a tang of mortality in the air. Friends feared his sudden death by exhausted nature or by some subtle anticipatory hand. A pungent pamphlet, *Killing No Murder*,[2] had nastily suggested the Protector ought to die for the good of the country. There were many men ready to turn witty words into desperate action. It was to meet this pendent threat that the treason legislation described earlier had been drafted.

If a plot came off—and the shooting of President Kennedy in 1963 underlines how impossible it is to be sure one will not—the assassins felt they had a moral certainty that the present régime would founder and the House of Stuart would be sucked into some kind of political vacuum. Possibly Charles II, to stay, would have to offer terms which would seek to match the political complexions of the exuberant conspirators, of whom there were already mutant varieties. On the other hand, searching observers among the government's own supporters could see at best bloodless but upsetting competitions among swordsmen for Oliver's warm place. More likely there would be another bitter civil war, followed by yet another arbitrary military despotism or, worse, by mere anarchy. No one else had established Oliver's special relationship with the army. If he sat on a throne of pikes, he sat there more comfortably than any of the likely successors could ever hope to do.

An open succession had been for the Tudors at once a well of strength and of trouble, encouraging on the one hand bids for the throne, justifying on the other the maintenance of a powerful executive authority. It was much the same with Oliver. Hopes of the irreconcilable opposition were fed by the precariousness of his position. His supporters and the broad mass of those who, while never enthusiastic, saw in changing abruptly from him the threat of something worse, were spurred by fear to preserve him, either immaculate or, preferably, remodelled. Brooding perils argued for keeping him going and, while he still breathed, to provide in some way an assurance that 'perturbations and interreigns' should not come to pass. In the spring of 1657 kingship looked like the favoured panacea.

Cromwell once claimed that the original draft of the Instrument of Government had offered him a crown, but that he had spurned it. (A question arises: if Lambert were for kingship in 1654, why had he changed his mind by 1657? There are many likely answers, the best, perhaps, that by now Oliver was a disappointment to him, less amenable to soldierly advice, hankering after older kingly ways and less reliant on or pliant to John Lambert himself.) In the first Protectorate parliament tentative motions for a proffer of the crown had gone almost unheeded. In the summer of 1655 a revival of monarchy was reputedly canvassed in the council of state, but could not be agreed upon. Opposition then and there came both from military and civilian councillors, the former regarding kingship, any kingship, Stuart or Oliverian, as anathema, the latter, already playing with the notion, scared that taking so long a step backward without consultation with a parliament might hinder rather than help stability. Yet, significantly, from about October 1655 the council of state is often referred to as 'the Privy Council', a hint of the direction in which the drift towards security was making.

211

The most formidable barrier was the continued existence of the Instrument of Government. We have seen the first parliament repudiate it, but the army officers, with John Lambert standing *in loco parentis*, were all the more wedded or glued to it. Yet who but they really liked it? The Protector must have long felt that chafing of which he was to complain in 1657. Civilian officials found the permanent and tactless military ascendancy written into this unprecedented piece of paper galling. Such men came mostly from the traditional political classes— unlike a good many officers. Some were lawyers and hankered after the pleasing intricacies of old legal ways. Some, like Lord Broghill, a slick politician and expert 'manager', were probably royalists still under their veneer of 'commonwealthsmanship'. Others, though not Johnnies-come-lately to 'the cause', were equally tuned in to the resentments felt by provincial officials and of the private gentry at the rise to unnatural authority of upstart soldiers, sown in the localities like dragons' teeth. Some, merchants and financiers, engrossed in getting and spending for the State and themselves, jibbing at the deadweight of the vast military machine, dreamed of a genuine civilian recognition of the régime as the only reliable safeguard of their investment. For them all kingship was an enchanting lure.

The way things were going was shewn early in the new parliament. Col. William Jephson, an Irish member, not unknown to Broghill, offered on 28 October 1656 a resolution for an hereditary Protectorate. 'Some debates were concerning itt as to the safety of itt; butt there was noe conclusion made.'[3] (Shortly afterwards Jephson was sent to Sweden as Ambassador, possibly a reward for his initiative.) During November the matter was mentioned several times and the suggestion that some headway was being made is reinforced by reactions outside the House. A meeting of 30-odd higher officers went on record against any alteration in the constitution, especially in that great point, the succession. At about the same time Col. Bridges, 'a very honest sober man',[4] drafted a 'paper' in which it was advised that kingship should not be sought after, but that the present Protector might name his own successor to offset a likely disorderly transition, through 'the impendent danger by a competicion . . .'.[5]

Bridge's proposals evoked little enthusiasm. At this stage a gesture, however tentative, towards kingship would disgruntle the army, officers and rankers alike, convinced as many of them were that the destruction of monarchy had been an inexorable dispensation of Providence. To revive it would be to spurn the inscrutable will of God. Republicans yearned after a full sovereignty for parliament, not a check on it. Fifth monarchists and other sectaries saw in secular kingship merely the inordinate ambition of a proud Lucifer, Oliver Cromwell, to usurp the golden throne which awaited Christ the only, the risen King. Levellers, whether they had flung in their lot with royalism or not, glimpsed another barricade flung up against real social change. Royalists, of course, had their own candidate for coronation, a right-down, regular royal King, not a country bumpkin with bloody hands. (Of course, some royalists were ready to foster any scheme for backing towards the old order: 'King' Oliver could smooth the way for King Charles II.)

The gentlemen of the long robe and the officials pressed on with backstairs discussions, fussing over Cromwell's health, and scaring themselves with the reminder that as things stood the most likely second Protector was John Lambert, who apart from his blatantly military outlook, was a young man, only 38, in full vigour of mind and body, probably with decades of action ahead of him. But they found comfort in the conviction that Oliver was coming of his own accord to grasp the necessity of constitutional change. Nayler's case obviously made a deep impression on him and Sindercombe's plot, exposed by Thurloe in January 1657, seemed to clinch things. Though inept in conception and ludicrous in its execution, this attempt at assassination brought home the dangers circling like wolves around Whitehall. When an address of felicitation on the Protector's lucky escape was mooted in the Commons, John Ashe, a 'presbyterian', proposed that he be begged to take up 'the government according to the ancient constitution',[6] and to preserve peace and liberties by setting them upon a tested foundation.

The major-generals, still not put down on the militia issue, smarting under the verbal whips of Ashe, who had earlier flaunted his contempt for them, were up in a flash to head off his motion. It was, indeed, laid aside for the time being as an inappropriate rider to a formal congratulation, but it was patent there was support for it, and more would be heard of its intention. Soon bets were being taken in the City that parliament would offer the Protector a crown. Excitement quickened at rumours of imminent Spanish and royalist landings and that a *rapprochement* between Dutch and Spaniards was likely for a joint effort against England. All this uncertainty spoke urgently for a new approach to constitutional modification.

Open and serious discussion became unavoidable when on 23 February City Alderman Christopher Packe asked leave to read 'a paper ... somewhat come to his hand' and 'tending to the settlement of the nation, and of liberty, and property' (note the juxtaposition).[7] Packe, lately Lord Mayor, heavily involved in State finances (as he would be after the Restoration of 1660), influential in the City and right-wing puritan circles, a good speaker, in every way a safe man, was obviously not playing a lone hand. This was no sudden spontaneous gesture, but the first move in a carefully planned campaign. Writing to General Monk in Scotland, Thurloe summarised the new remonstrance as asking his Highness to assume kingly power and, a further stride backward, to summon bi-cameral parliaments, from which none should be excluded 'but by Judgment of the house whereof they are members'.[8] Of course, the Secretary hastened to assure the general, his Highness had known nothing in advance of these propositions and for all Thurloe knew would spurn them even if they should pass parliament, certainly if he thought them unapt for the public interest. Thurloe's own views can be glimpsed in his fears that 'unquiet spirits' might react to the scheme by seeking to 'put the Armye into discontent'.[9]

He was a true prophet. Newsletters were soon referring to the angry mutterings of the major-generals at their failure to check the reading of the paper and that most of the officers 'now in towne talke openly of their dislike of it'.[10] Lambert started 'a distemper' in the army by telling yet another meeting of officers that, though he and other grandees might be for the moment members of parliament, they were always 'fellow members of the army'[11] and would join their comrades in a united front against the intended alteration in *their* constitution. Meantime they pleaded for 'moderation and patience', waiting upon a wink from 'the eye of providence'.[12] The French ambassador reported that Lambert argued that he was quite indifferent whether Richard (Cromwell) or John (Lambert) should succeed, but he was concerned whether the army should retrace their steps or go forward. But everybody knew that if kingship came Lambert would dwindle from being heir presumptive to a mere subject. Whatever Packe's motives he had precipitated a crisis.

Just who framed the remonstrance remains a mystery. Fiennes, Glynn, Broghill and other civilian leaders must have had a fair idea of what was going on, and Packe was hardly the man to whip up a controversy unless he were confident of substantial backing in the Protector's entourage. They would not have let the matter be raised at all had they not suspected that their chief was getting ready for it. Oliver may have been unaware of the manner and timing of the initiative but he must have suspected some plan 'made for him' was in the offing.

When on 27 February 1657 a group of about 100 officers including a few 'grandees', though not Lambert, waited upon him to express opposition to Packe's proposals, he sharply upbraided them for blind enmity to necessary changes. In the past they had 'made him their drudge upon all occasions'. They would no longer. The title was but 'a feather in his cap' but 'the paper' was stuffed full of good things.[13] This parliament had done well so far and he meant to encourage them. But the Commons, as Nayler's case had shewn, needed a check upon their judicial authority, and that the Instrument did not provide. It was a telling point, all the more effective perhaps because the reference to Nayler echoed some of Lambert's own observations on the significance of his 'trial'. Some officers were said to have been stunned and silent and soon it got about that many were 'fallen from the rest'.[14] Cromwell had scored if not a triumph, at any rate, an advance. From now on there would be some army acceptance of the need for constitutional reform, stopping short of kingship, but reaching out to a review of the succession and to a second Chamber to balance the Commons. Some high-ranking officers might agree with Thurloe that another House might be 'a great security and bulwark to the honest interest', particularly if they themselves were taken into it.[15] The lasting appeal of the notion is seen in the way in which army schemes in the year of troubles—1659—extended the 1657 proposition by providing for 'a select senate' with a direct 'negative voice'.

So far, so good. But the actual remonstrants had put kingship as the essence of their offer and the Commons followed them by voting that the remonstrance must be accepted *in toto*. Before the Protector should utter his yea or nay, the original draft had to be worked up into something systematic and detailed, another Instrument of Government, in fact. To ease its passage Sir Richard Onslow (an experienced parliamentarian who had been secluded by Pride in 1648) suggested that discussion of the title should be left to the last, in hopes that the other clauses would shew themselves so attractive that it would become unthinkable to sacrifice them even for that great point of contention. Good parliamentarians appreciated that a wedge is best inserted at its thin end. So March went by in long sittings debating each separate item. There was also a good deal of extra-mural activity, both by 'kinglings'[16] and their opponents. 'The other House' (as it was tactfully called), its members to be selected by his Highness, was welcomed without a division. The council lost its power over election returns. A revenue was voted which even at its maximum would entail a reduction of the standing army. Significantly, no part of this revenue was to be raised by a land-tax, and all variations in its imposition were to be approved by King and parliament. Changes were to be made in the composition of 'the Privy Council' and in the tenure of councillors. Religion proved a tough problem. As they finally emerged the provisions stiffened the State Church, sapped at toleration and left a route for further restrictions 'much more to satisfaction generally then as in the Instrument' [17]—another unwilling legacy of James Nayler.

Not until New Year's Day (old style, 25 March) 1657 was 'the title' introduced. Onslow's cheerful expectations of an easy passage were dashed when Lambert and Fleetwood, weeping profusely, struck out at the retrograde proffer. But their bitter eloquence failed to move the majority. Next day the revised and expanded remonstrance became the Humble Petition and Advice.

On 31 March this new written constitution—for in spite of all the mincing steps back to the old order it was novel—was presented by a solemn committee of 60 to the Lord Protector. It was impressed upon him that he could not pick and choose among its many provisions but must take it whole or leave it. When it was noticed that Lambert, who on these occasions carried the sword of state, was missing, an immediate acceptance was prophesied. But Oliver, thanking them, begged time to 'ask counsel of God and of my own heart',[18] the usual procedure of this man of opportunity. His hesitation is explicable. Kingship might put him in the way of winning what he longed for—a parliamentary settlement—and he must have seen that if he did not get it from this strangely amiable House he would hardly get it from another. But he sensed that in the army, which he understood far more than any other man, even Lambert, flowed a strong contrary current, pulling in not only the big men of ambition and envy but the broad rank and file. Monk's army in Scotland might be 'very well satisfied'[19] with whatever he should decide, but that was a purged and docile force, isolated from the more volatile and 'political' regiments in England. For nearly a decade the latter had associated their 'good old cause' with the elimination of earthly monarchy. It has been said that to take the crown would mean Oliver 'exchanging the experience of Christian friendship learned in the only real Church fellowship he had experienced [Independency] for the dubious loyalty of the lawyers and sycophants'.[20] There may be something in this, yet if that fellowship could be offered to a military despot why could it not be given to a man who took it upon himself, or let others press it upon him, to be a King?

The fact is that no one argument weighed fully with him. He was of the army and yet for a long time he had been half outside it, a soldier but also a civilian. Most of all he was a man charged—whether by himself or by God is irrelevant—with the responsibility for the peace and stability of nations. His decision must be one that reconciled duty and his own inclinations, his ideals with practical possibilities, immediate needs with future prospects. Nearing the end of his days, he wanted to be sure to leave things at least a little better than he had found them. Yet the past haunted him, too. To see in his tergiversations about kingship merely the posturings of a hypocritically ambitious parvenu is not only ungenerous but stupid. Always when you peel one layer off Cromwell you find another, more tender, underneath. Risen by the sword, he was not a simple military adventurer. Even if he knew better what he would not than what he would, he was a genuine man of religion. More than a politician, he had longings for statesmanship. In 1657 this complicated man was much more sophisticated and imaginative than Professor Trevor-Roper's 'natural back-bencher'. Each crisis, each opportunity he had struck had demanded of him sensitivity and skill. None called in vain. The present conflict of interests and aspirations tried him hard. It did not find him wanting.

There might have been quicker and shorter cuts to action. Why not have cashiered a few grandees as examples to the rest and have exploited his unique reputation to assuage the lower ranks? The question answers itself. Petulant and bickering though they might be on so many smaller issues, on this the generals would cohere. They already had a platform in the council of officers and they would hardly hesitate to use it to bring the army to their way of thinking. A few commanders detached by threats or promises would mean very little in the long run. Moreover, these men knew, and Oliver knew that they knew, that he himself had genuine qualms about the providential nature of monarchy and was far too conscientious and introspective to forget about them. It is a tribute to his integrity that though subjected for many weeks when his health was poor to the most insistent of pressures, compared by Hewson without a hint of blasphemy to Christ's temptations by the devil, he wrestled and did not yield.[21] (Charles II tempted similarly by the Scots a few years before had soon capitulated.) The notorious 'dark' speeches, each more 'promiscous' than the one before,[22] are witnesses to the internal fight as well as the political play to keep all things in train.

While the conflict went on, changes were in fact occurring in the political alignments in and out of parliament. More swordsmen came to see something attractive in the Humble Petition and Advice. Soon some were ready to swallow it whole, apart from kingship. Either that stuck in the narrow throat of their consciences or they had more mundane reasons, not necessarily corrupt or unenlightened, for regurgitating it. These shifts only made the kinglings more set in their view that Cromwell must take all or nothing, pointing out that though the Protector by virtue of his office was already obliged to the law, until he was a legitimate monarch, grounded in a general and universal consent of the people, he could not have the advantage of the law.

A crisis blew up early in May when it leaked out that a group of Independent ministers and officers was circulating a joint petition to be presented to parliament urging the abandonment of the kingship campaign. There was loose talk, too, of a revival of the army councils of the late sixteen-forties, complete with rank-and-file agitators. Religion, army loyalty, army discipline combined together to bring Cromwell to that firm and final decision to which he had been working and from which he had been hanging back. Even though it might mean losing the parliamentary stability he yearned for, he knew at the last that he could not break with the army and its religious allies. It is surely no accident that the conclusive rejection of the title came on the same day that there was an attempt to get the matter of the new petition raised in the Commons. On 8 May at the Banqueting House, from which the last King of England had stepped to his doom, the parliamentary committee confronted a sober Protector, who stressed his desire to meet them in all things possible, but confessed that as an honest man he was persuaded that he could not 'undertake this government with that title of King'.23 A definite answer at last, firm, precise and negative. The discussions were over, Cromwell had 'come out of the clouds'.24 The kinglings had failed.

Did denial come because Cromwell was afraid of Lambert, Desborough and a few other generals? It is doubtful. Cromwell knew now what he was uncertain of in February, that the great matter of kingship drew together all threads in the army. To accept the crown would be to test whether those threads of solidarity would be cast around his neck to throttle him. Cromwell could take a calculated risk but this time the gamble was too desperate. If it failed, all that had been gained would be lost. (It might be claimed that so far nothing had in fact been gained since the death of Charles I or even earlier, but Cromwell— and others, too—would hardly have agreed.) Faced with a naked choice between unarmed civilians and soldiers with swords drawn, Cromwell was bound to choose the latter—out of comradeship and political realism equally.

At the blunt denying answer the kinglings crumbled, some to fall back on the rest of the petition, hoping that kingship could be eased in again at some later opportunity, others to abandon all interest in reform. Many of the latter, especially the country gentlemen, cared little for Cromwell. They had seen him as a lever to lift power from the swordsmen. He and the Petition had broken in their hands. Attendance in the House dropped sharply and the final recension of the Humble

Petition and Advice,[25] which the Protector accepted on 25 May 1657, passed with a majority which included many of the most savage critics of the original. In June some minor improvements, many in response to suggestions by the Protector, were embodied in an Additional Petition, also welcomed.[26] On 26 June Cromwell was installed for a second time. It was an elaborate affair, variously compared to a coronation or a state-funeral, with trumpets, heralds, oaths of fealty, commendation to the Almighty, and a jostling crowd of gawping sightseers. This time Cromwell received from the Speaker a purple robe, a bible, a sceptre and a sword, everything symbolic, in fact, of royal power and authority except a crown. A second written constitution was about to be implemented, this time the work, not of a taut congeries of generals, but of civilians, though distorted to suit at least some of the army.

The new Protectorate began with at least an apparent accretion of strength. Most historians agree that it was merely a stop-gap and that restoration of the Stuarts drew perceptibly nearer when monarchy in a new line was spurned before it had begun. Yet few contemporaries saw it like that and perhaps we are too ready to listen to the after-comment of events. The royalists, those not already engulfed in despair, continued to look to Spanish invasion supplemented by risings rather than to an irresistible march through constitutional and political disarray to an inevitable return of Charles II. Republicans dreamed on about sovereign single-chamber parliaments. More radical men still believed in more radical projects. They were all short-sighted, of course, but there was still a long way to go yet across uncharted regions. What lay on the other side was quite unknown. Meantime there was much to be done and the newly refurbished government set seriously about it.

XXIV The End of Oliver

With the acceptance of the new constitution the session of parliament ended. Relieved for a while of constitutional argument and political criticism, the government hoped to turn now to a vigorous pursuit of a bold foreign policy, leading to such a triumph over Spain that English hearts would beat as one, as they were reputed to have done at the time of the Armada, a legend of deep appeal to these latter-day Elizabethans. But there were domestic problems enough without a parliament and in any case the effecting of the new constitution called for some difficult decisions. Foremost among these were the selection of men to sit in 'the other House' and the prescribed modification of the membership of the Privy Council. There could now be a maximum of 21 councillors, all to be approved restrospectively by parliament and, once approved, to be removable only by parliamentary consent. Every councillor had to take an oath of fidelity to the person and authority of the Lord Protector. It was not unlike that required in Clause XLII of the Instrument of Government, itself similar to the Engagement of 1649.[1] Loyalty to the constitution as now modified was implicit.

Early in July 1657 at a series of meetings the oaths, including that of the Protector, were formally taken. Of the old council only Lambert held aloof and in effect refused. For once Cromwell did not deliberate long about what was to be done with his former 'demi-colleague' turned apparent adversary, whom he must by now have known very well indeed. He judged that Lambert had little personal following outside the army, and as many enemies as friends within it. Thurloe thought that there was 'noe such thing as a formed knott . . . to remande H.H. back to his former station'.[2] At any rate the Protector took the risk of ordering 'the great man' to hand in his commissions (13 July). Lambert took three days to consider and then quietly obeyed. Nothing else happened. No one protested. The earth did not stand still. 'Never was any man less pitied or lamented after', commented a pamphleteer two years later. Why was this? The same writer gives a cogent answer. 'He was all for himself; he hoped to be the next protector'.[3] Lambert was regarded, rightly or wrongly, as too much the self-appointed understudy of Cromwell to stir the sympathy of rival candidates or reluctant subjects who, like Mrs Lucy Hutchinson, concluded from his past career he was likely to be a worse tyrant.[4] But now that Cromwell had obtained the right to name his own successor there can have been few who could imagine he would have chosen Lambert. The long deliberations on 'the title' had shewn that Oliver, like many another usurper, was somewhat taken with the hereditary principle. The continuance of the House of Cromwell was more likely than the emergence of the House of Lambert. Realistically Lambert appreciated the situation and retired to Wimbledon House to grow tulips, to paint and to watch events at home and abroad. (He made a short trip to Holland but appeared briefly in the Commons in the second session of parliament.) The dismissal meant considerable financial loss, but he continued to draw a pension of £2,000 p.a. Still in the full vigour of brain and body, he must have regarded this turn in the wheel of fortune as a temporary set-back. His time would come. In the meantime his isolation was underlined by army officers meeting to put on record their undying loyalty to the Protectorate as at present established. On the very day Lambert received his *congé* Thurloe became a voting councillor as well as Secretary. Soon all the old councillors had regularised their position. Otherwise no change was made until on the last day of the year Oliver's eldest son, Richard, who had also acquired command of a regiment of horse, was sworn in. It seems that Cromwell, sensing his life trickling away, had already decided he would nominate Richard to succeed him and was now seeking to bring the somewhat diffident but by no means negligible young man closer to affairs of State. This view would be reinforced if it could be shewn that Richard took a particularly active part in the work of the council. Unfortunately it cannot.

Lambert's fall, then, like Harrison's before him, passed off quietly, but there were standing dangers. *Killing No Murder* continued to circulate, a nudging reminder of death's unremitting grasp. Its part-author, Edward Sexby, by now a fearsome combination of radical, royalist and terrorist, was arrested in July. (He died, insane, six months later.) Autumn and winter 1657 rocked to rumours of revolts and invasions and certainly action groups among the royalists were working for a general rising to come off in the spring of 1658. Once again the government was well primed with what was going on. All this was worrying and consumed ministerial time and energy, but plenty of both was left to apply to the nice problem of settling the composition of the other House. What was required was for it to be so constituted that, whatever the intentions of the mixed groups that had voted for it, the Protector's own purposes prevailed. His view of its function we have noted already, expressed in that brief but pregnant speech to the officers on 27 February—a screen or a balance between himself and the Commons. To make it this demanded some skill. As Thurloe put it, 'a mistake here will be like that of warre and marriage, it admits noe repentance'.[5] There were many 'parties' to conciliate. The army must not be ignored, nor the civilian officials and courtiers. Members must be reliably dedicated to the Protector, but must have the weight and standing to be able to resist the pressure and changeability of the Commons. They must be apt to work with the council, too. In some rough and ready way at least they must represent three nations, four, if you include Wales. In the original draft the initial members nominated—for life—by the Protector were to have the approval of the Commons, but, over the protests of some critics who saw the new Chamber as 'of necessity' adhering to the single person, Oliver was given a free hand to choose whom he might. He did not decide in haste. Not until 10 December 1657 was the final choice made and writs, closely modelled on those of the old House of Lords (another instance of the return to normality), issued. There were 63 names on the list. Seven 'old' peers were summoned of whom Fauconberg and Eure—two former rivals of the great Strafford—were prepared to sit. Warwick, it seems, was disinclined to rub his elegant shoulders with shoemakers and draymen, and feared that acceptance of a new-fangled writ would be tantamount to abandoning the hereditary rights of the ancient English peerage—so much for the abolition of the House of Lords![6] The solitary Irish peer, Broghill, appeared delighted to serve, but the Scots Cassilis uttered a vigorous nay. Some peers' sons and four baronets were called upon but only a handful actually sat. Eighteen members were connected with Cromwell in some way or other of blood, kinship or marriage. The army was there in force, among them Pride, Hewson, Goffe and about a dozen others in active commands. Among officials and lawyers Whitelocke, Glynn and Steele stand out. All the councillors—apart from Mr Secretary Thurloe—received a writ. If Charles I had his great officers of State in the upper Chamber, so would his demi-royal successor. It is possible that some of the supporters of the about-turn towards the old order saw in the other House a knot around which a new Court might form to take over the functions of its legitimate predecessor.

Thirty members of the Commons, including a few knights of the shire, and, in rather pathetic optimism, Sir Arthur Haselrig, were invited to climb a step up. Among them were a goodly number of landed gentry, an element essential if this mongrel assembly were to have any appeal outside the narrow circle of Cromwellian clientage. In the event, out of the 64 nominated—William Lenthall, Speaker of the Long Parliament, was a late addition—about three dozen actually sat at one time or another in the brief session of 1658. But rather more may be assumed to have been willing to assist. Forty-two accepted writs, but William Lockhart in France, Henry Cromwell in Ireland and George Monk in Scotland were prevented from attending by other duties.

The list, naturally enough, met with criticism. Any list would have done. Some thought it far too slight to perform the tasks assigned to it— tried in the balance with the Commons and the council it must prove wanting. These were friends, but many enemies of the Protectorate agreed and mocked 'their lordships of 17-pound-land a year, their farmer lordships, dairyman lordships, cobbler lordships'.[7] Ludlow wrote off 'the principal part of them' as 'such as had procured their present possessions by their wits and were resolved to enlarge them by selling their consciences'.[8] Another report spoke of the House as scorned by the nobility and gentry and generally of the people. John Maidstone, a friend of the Protector, summed up common feeling by quoting *1 Cor. i, 26*: 'Ye see your calling, not many wise nor noble.'[9]

Parliament reassembled on 20 January 1658. The Commons were summoned by Black Rod to the Chamber of the other House to submit to a rather tepid speech by the Lord Protector. He addressed his remarks to 'my lords and gentlemen' but made no direct reference to the functions of the new Chamber.[10] There is a tiredness about the speech that might suggest a lack of interest, but equally tact and an urge to mystify could be inferred. It may be that Oliver was deliberately copying Charles I in leaving the main burden of the unveiling of his government's intentions to the Lord Keeper. At any rate Nathaniel Fiennes in a lengthy discourse—the pompous phrase is entirely appropriate—made copious reference to the new dispensation. 'Some years since', he began, 'we have not thought to have seen a Chief Magistrate again among us; and lo! God hath shewn us a Chief Magistrate in his two Houses of Parliament!' (A chief magistrate, maybe, but not a King!) In a clumsy metaphor he likened the appearance of the second Chamber to the raising of dry land out of the deep at the Creation. It was all done with a purpose and this was for the other House to act as a medium to reconcile, when the need arose, extremes of opinion and to check overhasty legislation.[11]

'Whilst the Representative of the Commons provideth and strengtheneth the Sinews of War to preserve the Commonwealth from Destruction in Gross, by public Force and Violence, the other House will preserve it from the Destruction by Retail, through the due Administration of Justice, suppressing private Wrongs and Oppressions which would soon break out into open Flames and public Rapines, if they were not prevented by the Courts of Judicature, *whereof the highest and last Resort is there.*'[12]

So much, then, for the Commons' claims in the matter of James Nayler! So much for the republicans' claim of representative sovereignty!

The Lord Keeper also made it abundantly clear that the Protector and the new House each had a veto. This assertion was unlikely to appeal to the Commons, particularly as it was now a very different assembly from that which had framed and offered the new constitution. About 30 useful, if not brilliant, government spokesmen had been whisked into the other House. So far they had not been replaced by right-minded recruits. On the other hand about 100 members formerly excluded, mostly of a republican turn of mind and all in a critical mood, slipped back in, making no difficulty about taking the new oath to the government. Haselrig—'the great Sir Arthur'[13]—spoke for many when he said, 'I shall heartily take the oath. I will be faithful to my Lord Protector's person. I will murder no man.'[14] No great sacrifice was being made here. The tactics of these enthusiastic debaters, delighted to be back in the old familiar surroundings,[15] had already been decided upon: by niggling criticism and major votes to provoke Cromwell into yet another abrupt dissolution which would ruin his credit with constitutionally-minded groups. Forgetting nothing, learning nothing, they were still utterly negative.

Not much is known of the doings of the other House. It spent most of its sittings deliberating about the appointment of divines to serve the Protector. The Commons were not palliated by such seemingly innocuous procedures and, although they did in fact during the session discuss some constructive measures, from the very first day they succumbed gladly to the temptation to query the role and authority of the rival establishment. The discussions centred on what style should be adopted in addressing it.[16] Here, surely, was a matter of substance. If it were called, as the Protector and Lord Keeper obviously intended it to be, 'the House of Lords' it might well be argued that it had thereby inherited all the rights, privileges, powers and co-ordinate authority of the old Peers, except where these had been expressly lopped off by the Humble Petition and Advice. If the title 'the other House' were to be retained, then presumably it could have only those powers expressly allotted in the new constitution. Though vague, these certainly attenuated the claims of the old House of Lords.

The republicans, harking back to 1649, would have nothing to do with a House of Lords. They painted in lurid colours the sins of the old Peers, and hinted darkly at a worse future for the new model. How could the Commons do the good work that they alone could do if there were a negative upon them? These views were shared at least in part among other groups. William Packer, Cromwell's own major, who had served him staunchly for 14 years, 'thought it was not a Lords' House but another House'.[17] (He soon lost his command.) The wayward Ashley Cooper considered that once to admit Lords was to admit all. 'There is nothing but a compliment to call a man Lord; but if he call himself Lord of my manor, I shall be loth to give him the title, lest he claim the manor.'[18] It was a pertinent point. There were others to whom the notion of a House of Lords appealed more or less strongly, but they could find little to say in favour of recognising this one. It was too insubstantial. 'They have not the reason of the quality of Lords.' Above all, 'they have not interest, nor the forty-thousandth part of England'.[19] We can hear a faint echo of Cromwell's own voice a decade before denying at the Putney Debates a share in politics to those who had but the interest of breathing. A sword will insist on turning in the hand.

Yet the new Chamber did not go undefended. It was said that to call it the Lords was to define it, and in definition lay safety, not danger. (The argument for kingship is being put to fresh uses here.) 'We know what the House of Lords could do.'[20] Besides in this 'crazy time'[21] there was plenty to be done. For example, some oversight was necessary on hasty legislation. 'This Parliament did pass more in one month than the best student in England can read in a year, and well if he can understand it then. . . . A check is necessary upon us.'[22] As for the much-deplored insubstantiality, it was felt that there were other weights than wealth and land. What of religion, State service, loyalty, honesty and courage?[23] 'The sword is there. Is not that a good balance? He that has a regiment of foot to command . . . is as good a balance as any . . . and can do more than— . . .'[24] Precisely. 'More than' what? This well-meant reminder of political realities blew like a chill wind across the trivialities of a sometimes merely academic debate. The Commons was being inched once more towards the brink. Sir Arthur Haselrig spoke of 'living long in a little time',[25] but one senses here more an elation from a challenge than despair.

On 25 January the Lord Protector came to Westminster and spoke urgently to both Houses, lecturing them on the necessity to resist the temptation to fritter time away on inessentials while the facts of the times, simmering threats at home and abroad, called for drastic and immediate measures. All that stood between them and 'another flood of blood and war' was his government and a 'poor unpaid army'.[26] This strong hint that priority should go to a money grant was ignored. In phraseology reminiscent of that of early parliaments of Charles I, the members claimed that in no circumstances might the grievances of the people be put aside pending a supply vote. Nor were all the rebuffs in parliament. A petition was going round in the City, almost certainly with the connivance of republican M.P.s, and supported by mal-contents in the army, sectaries and fifth monarchists, demanding the abolition of the Protectorate, the immediate restoration of a single-chamber parliament, presumably the Rump, with complete sovereignty and unencumbered by the dubious facilities of a written constitution. There should also be a complete freedom of conscience. This was a broad and superficially enchanting programme—with something, if only something negative, for almost everybody. Few of those who signed it and urged others to join them can have really given deep considera-tion to what they were committing themselves. One interesting clause required that no officers should be dismissed without a trial by court martial. This meant that a *military* offence had to be proven against individuals. At a glance this would seem a fair provision. But was it? Army officers had been playing a political role. To have security of tenure they must stop dabbling in politics and settle down to be soldiers *tout court*. Past experience, present circumstances and immediate expectations suggested this was unlikely. What were the military men who supported this petition or other similar activities doing but being politicians? But this was no time, many felt, for niceties. The maximum support, no matter if once its turn had been served it disintegrated, was needed. A good deal was forthcoming—thousands signed, the move-ment grew 'like a snowball'.[27] Another crisis was at hand.

The intention of the anonymous framers of the petition—by this time through experience some men had become almost professional drafters—was to present it on 4 February 1658 to the House of Com-mons, to whom alone, significantly, it was addressed. The night of 3 February was a disturbed one, heavy with rumours of plots, mutinies and risings. At 10 a.m. on the following day Cromwell, who as usual had been struggling to come to a decision, made up his mind, so sud-denly that Thurloe knew nothing about it. According to Ludlow, once determined, Cromwell rushed out, too impatient to stay for his own state-coach, and taking the first carriage that he saw, with a scratch guard, sped down to the other House. His appearance spoke brutally of his intention. Fleetwood weakly intervened to dissuade him. The Protector brushed him aside with the vow that 'by the living God'[28] he would dissolve this parliament. The Commons, thinly attended, was in the midst of debate when Black Rod made his summons. Not all the 'Lords' were present either. But Cromwell hurried on. In uncompromising phrases he defended the government and his own peculiar place in it, stressing his constant hunt for 'a just reciprocation between the government and the governed'.[29] If there had been any earnest of a desire for settlement among the members he would have moved far to match it. But it was palpable that many in the Commons were simply bent on destruction. It followed that there was unrest and anxiety throughout the whole country, fed by uncertainty and enheartening the malignant royalist interest at home and abroad. The bitter tirade ended on a categorical dismissal. 'And let God be judge between you and me!'[30] It was Cromwell's last speech to his last parliament, not golden in the sense of the great set-piece of 1601 of Elizabeth I, that lady of 'famous memory' whom he admired so much, but certainly not base metal. This Protector had a sword in his tongue as well as in his hand.

The threat of commotions was possibly a genuine one. The royalists, of course, were always—factions among them, anyway—getting poised for action of some sort, fuddled though their plans might be. In 1658 they were at something of an impasse. 'The Spaniards . . . demanded a Royalist rising as a precondition of invasion; the conspirators were . . . laying down exactly the contrary requirement.'[31] A more immediate danger—and a graver one—lay in the restlessness of the army, always snatching at the Protector's attention. His enemies were excited by the dissolution, as if it were a positive gain for them, a thing good in itself. Yet it is doubtful if they got anything at all from this stark demonstration that the régime could only support itself by force and arbitrary motions. The point is that it *could* support itself. Soon, it was noted, 'the truth is he did the best for himself [by dissolution], for things began to look strangely and to turn against him in the army and town by reason of the parliament sitting'.[32] Before long he had regained effective control. A few sackings, some rather more tactful discussions, and a month's pay with a promise of more very quickly, appeased the bulk of the soldiery. 'His Highness's great care of the army doth much indulge both officers and soldiers.'[33] Those whose 'dissatisfactions did still remain with them were isolated'. The rest, including Monk and his Scottish cadre, confirmed their resolve to 'stand and fall, live and die with my Lord Protector'.[34] Robert Baillie noted how Scotland in 1658 was 'exceeding quiet: A great armie, in a multitude of garrisons, bydes above our head, and deep povertie keeps all estates exceeding at under; the taxes of all sorts are so great, the trade so little . . .'[35] No trouble need be expected from there. By April the City authorities had indicated approval. Once again it was Cromwell's personal initiative which had cleared the air. As so often it meant tremendous demands upon his constitution. Observers had noted earlier how his devastating interventions left him supine and temporarily exhausted. Now his reserves of strength were attenuated. He was not likely to survive another strain of this magnitude.

While Oliver's grip on the State was relaxing, his agents had been forthright in repression, seeking relief from pent-up fears in bustling activity. The late parliament had approved an act to set up a special high court of justice to try offenders against the security of the Lord Protector's person and government and against the maintenance of the peace of the nations. Such a court was nominated at the end of April 1658 to deal with a clutch of royalist suspects rounded up in recent drives to uncover attempts and conspiracies. A hundred and fifty persons were named as commissioners, but of these only 40 actually sat when the court began hearings towards the end of May. At no time did any professional judge take part. Apart from a group of small fry, the chief accused were Dr John Hewett, John, Lord Mordaunt, and Sir Henry Slingsby, all of whom were definitely deeply involved in optimistic manœuvrings mostly well known to Thurloe. Slingsby, indeed, had been carefully led by government agents to commit himself to treason. Hewett refused to plead, and, although Elizabeth Claypole begged her father to intervene to save him, was condemned and executed. So was Slingsby. Mordaunt, who had boldly demanded trial by jury, appealing rather unfashionably to Magna Carta and the Petition of Right, was acquitted by the casting vote of the President of the Court. He was lucky that Col. Pride was unable to attend through illness. There can be no doubt that the gruff old campaigner would have leaned to the severer side. This was an accident with important consequences. Mordaunt was released and went on to play a significant part in the events leading to the Restoration of 1660. But meantime the executions of Slingsby and Hewett, followed by a few others, had cast the royalist ginger groups into confusion and despair.

All this while the house-searchings continued. Private papers were seized and read for seven or eight types of ambiguity. Fifth monarchists, some of whom were suspected of gearing themselves to welcome a stop-gap fourth monarchy of Charles Stuart, were scooped up into preventive custody. Catholics and known royalists hanging about London were ordered to their homes. Landlords were bullied to give particulars of their tenants and lodgers. The régime seemed teetering on the bank of panic. Yet there was as much method as madness in it. In any case the prospect of foreign invasion continued to languish in the glare of spectacular military victory and diplomatic initiatives in continental Europe.

But these striking hallucinations of strength had only deferred a day of reckoning within England itself. No one but a political innocent could have thought the government had broken with all its difficulties. In the surface of achievement the cracks that spoke of subsidence in depth continued to grow. Need for money was at the root of all evil. Thurloe saw it as putting the government to the wall in all its enterprises. In July 'particular aldermen' were being 'begged' for a few hundred pounds to send post haste to the troops at Dunkirk.[36] Petty sums like this could not cope with the piling deficits. Prospects of larger amounts were bleak. Yet without them the stability of government could hardly be preserved much longer. Want of pay remained the primrose path to indiscipline in the regiments. It was indeed an almost inextricable business. Soon a bruit of disaffection was running once more through the newsletters. Cromwell's own regiment, even after Packer's departure, was said to be the most vocally discontented of the lot. It is not surprising, then, that almost from the day of dissolution of the last parliament there was talk of another and of modifying the brand-new constitution in such a way as to make it easier to raise a large and, equally important, constant revenue.[37]

On these matters the council was at odds. Some, led by Desborough and Fleetwood, of whom there is evidence that they were at this time in touch with the brooding Lambert, wanted to wring a few more pounds out of royalist and others that 'love . . . to live in troubled waters'.[38] Secretary Thurloe and the civilians generally were still prepared to dabble in ostentatious conciliation. To them a new parliament was bound to be a telling gesture. But what sort of parliament? Advice was plentiful, if not always helpful. Someone had noted that even compliant and unanimous parliaments moved forward slowly. When divided, 'which cannot but be expected upon a promiscuous election',[39] they would bring forth nothing of value. Obviously a lesser body, a kind of 'council' of like-minded men, was a desirable substitute—a cheerful suggestion presumably ignorant of the fate of Charles I's Great Council summoned to York in the summer of 1640. If, however, a parliament seemed inescapable, then it ought to be called quickly and only for particular purposes. No meddling in any other business should be allowed. Elections should be searchingly overseen and 'if any get in unfit, the council may put him out by the words of the government' (i.e. clause IV of the constitution).[40] All this was tempting history to repeat itself, whether as tragedy or farce.

As early as March men spoke of the writs being got ready. The council certainly was looking into the matter, but nothing happened, largely because the Protector, sinking into the torpor which was the natural consequence of his recent sally, failed to give a positive lead. In April, Thomas, Lord Fauconberg was writing to Henry Cromwell, his brother-in-law, about the possibility of a further proffer, this time to be accepted, of the crown of three nations. This scheme, if it were ever anything so definite, petered out in uncertainty and dispute. The trouble was two-pronged. The ultimate survival of the present system lay in a fairly broad base of consent. Its immediate stability hung on the fast-fraying threads of the life of the present Protector. In spite of the Humble Petition and Advice's succession clauses few men could imagine anything but discordance when Cromwell died. His successor, whoever he might be, would have to steer a tricky course between the rock of consent by the political nation and the whirlpool of acceptance by the army. There seemed no fully-equipped helmsman. The nagging certitude that all Cromwell had worked for and all he had achieved were still in jeopardy must have depressed him in what were to be the last fading months of his life. The decision to choose Richard to take up his burden cannot have been an easy one. Richard was no fool; indeed, he was like his father intelligent, thoughtful and conscientious. His defect was that with all that he was simply not his father. Henry, the younger son, able and openly ambitious, was not brought forward because he was unpopular with the army, at best the darling of a faction. Richard was not disliked but was without a positive personal impact either. To have nothing known to his discredit was an asset, but to be unknown was not. Now there was to be an effort to sell the private country gentleman to the men with the power. It came too late. The father had been in and of the army since hostilities had begun. He had moulded it and been moulded by it. He knew, by now as it were by instinct, its moods and aspirations. He could hear it muttering a hundred leagues away. He might hand over his office to Richard, but at that point his legacy would run out. Richard would soon grasp the situation and sensibly resign. The officers drew together at first in September 1658 to install him because just then they could see no viable alternative. The death of Oliver was not unexpected, yet it found them quite unready to meet the challenge of the times—a searching comment on their collective and individual incapacity. Richard seemed a godsend. He filled a gap—or at least narrowed one for a while. When the grandees, predictably, failed to rise above their personal and political rivalries, they made his position, first, precarious and, then, utterly intolerable. With him went the last vestiges of unity in the Protectorate. Collapse was probable, because if Richard was no Oliver, neither Fleetwood nor Desborough, nor even Lambert, who had by then insinuated himself back into politics and military command, could leap, or slide, into his place. Anarchy could. Anarchy did.

So the last days of Oliver's Protectorate were grey, indeed, without prospects. Illness dragged at his energy and dampened his customary zeal for business. His listlessness was reinforced by private griefs. His son-in-law, Robert Rich, died, apparently of 'the king's evil', a disease which the quasi-royal ruler was unready to claim to cure by the customary 'touch'. In August the loss of his favourite daughter, the vivacious, tender-hearted Elizabeth Claypole, staggered him. Exultant royalists devised circumstantial reports that he was going crazy, weeping like a Bedlam woman, howling like a dog, consoling his flayed conscience with drugs. There is no need to swallow these wishful legends, but it is patent that from the spring of 1658 the iron man was buckling under the strains of his unending burdens. Events of 1658 must be read in the light of the condition of a man eking out the last tiny reserves of physical and emotional stamina, his nerves, always taut, stretched to the sticking point by sorrow, spiritual tussles, political failures and perhaps by portents. (The last were remembered after rather than spotlighted before his death.) Now and then a spark of the old Oliver blazed in the gloom, but by the end of August his quittance was obviously close at hand. After a formal nomination of Richard on the morning of 3 September as his legitimate successor, he sank into a coma. That afternoon, anniversary of the superb victories of Dunbar and Worcester, he met death as it were a sleep, peacefully, without fuss, far from the smoke of match and push of pike. Quietly his house of clay crumbled away. Argument about his aims and character was no longer politics, but history.

xxv The Fall of the Protectorate

The new Protector was proclaimed without incident. Hopes of royalists that the death of Oliver would be the signal for a general rising were soon dissipated, and as Clarendon put it 'the King's condition never appeared so hopeless, so desperate'.[1] The Anabaptists loudly denounced the new régime but 'that party' wanted 'a head in the Army'[2] and could therefore do nothing effective. A newsletter writer commented wonderingly on the seeming unity in the land and noted that 'all thinges are att quiett in the Citty'.[3] Foreign powers soon added their recognition, prudently concealing whatever aspirations or qualms they may have had.

Royalists were inclined to write off Richard as 'a clown', a 'country bumpkin'.[4] Charles II himself issued a declaration describing his usurpation as that of 'a meane person whose pretence is only founded on iniustice and tyranny'. It is true that Richard had lived obscurely as a mere country gentleman, and would do so again, but there was more to him than that. He had a good presence. There was, in fact, nothing of the 'ape on horseback'[5] about him. He was affable, a competent speaker with a clear mind. It was not his fault that he had not been trained up to his office. Certainly he performed as well as anyone could be expected to do who had greatness rather suddenly thrust upon him. He took everything seriously, and was determined to be no pseudo-Protector. So from the start he tried to ingratiate himself with all those whose support seemed likely or necessary. His lack of previous commitments might be a decided help, leaving him room to manœuvre.

Within a short time congratulatory addresses had poured in from the various armies and the fleet, assuring him they would live and die with my Lord Protector. Even so, a sour note was struck. It was made clear that Richard should not expect to occupy quite the unique position of his father. It was suggested that there were men close about him whose loyalty to the good old cause might be faltering. Turbulent spirits like these should be discountenanced, and trust reposed in faithful members of the Commonwealth. These, standing modestly in the wings, were army officers, who intended to pursue a political role and who regarded the sword as representing a fourth estate in the realm. A petition for Fleetwood to be Commander-in-Chief (an office Oliver had combined with the Protectorship) was circulated. Army officers met frequently for prayer meetings and political discussions, which readily ran into one another.

Richard saw at once he needed to be careful with the army, not to drive it into open enmity, yet at the same time to avoid becoming its prisoner or creature by getting backing elsewhere. From Scotland where he controlled with iron discipline a completely a-political force, General George Monk sent a cogent letter of advice. Citizens and soldiers should be denied any meetings 'to interpose in public affairs'.[6] Richard should narrow religious toleration, thereby winning the support of 'the godly ministry' ('presbyterians'), and 'what influence they have upon the people it is not hard to deduce'. A parliament should be called, as was in any event customary at the beginning of a new reign, and to the other House the 'most prudent' of the old peers and some of the leading gentry—Monk named a few, including Sir George Booth of Cheshire, who within a year would be leading a 'royalist' rising—should be summoned, to counter the swordsmen there. (At the same time Henry Cromwell was writing to Fleetwood that the army should be so governed that the world may never hear of them unless there be occasion to fight—sentiments with which Monk would have heartily concurred.)[7] The army forces should be reduced to get rid of 'some insolent spirits that may not be very safe to be continued'. Richard should not think this rash advice because 'there is not an officer in the army, upon any discontent, that has interest enough to draw two men after him, if he be out of place, as his Highness may remember by a late example'.[8] (The late example was, of course, John Lambert—but Lambert, though still out of sight, was by no means out of mind. A few days before Oliver's death the Venetian Ambassador was forecasting that he might 'come to life again'[9] and strike some unexpected, telling blow.)

Monk may have been giving good advice, but he was in Scotland. Things looked very different to Richard in London. It is true that Monk would in 1660 work with consummate skill to master England, but by then the army had disintegrated. Richard in 1658 can hardly be blamed for seeing it as more monolithic than it was. So he took part of the advice only—notably that for calling parliament, a decision taken at the end of November.

Meanwhile there were reports that at the meetings of army officers 'the language flew high'[10] in grumbling that good men were put out of office and worse put in. 'The army is monstrous high', groaned Thurloe.[11] The name of Lambert was hopefully mentioned. In October a petition went around that no officers might be dismissed without court martial, the old demand that had worried the late Protector. The lead in this was taken by inferior officers, many of them upset by their arrears of pay, and Richard's tactful handling of the situation was at this stage helped by the attitude of the grandees like Desborough and Fleetwood who frowned on an initiative from beneath. The Protector addressed a number of meetings, stressing his wish for 'a good correspondency'[12] with the army, asking for advice and support from a quarter from which he made it clear he felt he had a right to expect it. He was ready to name Fleetwood as Lord General, under his own ultimate authority, and indicated that normally there would be no dismissals without court martial. He was not without effect in all this and by the end of the year army restlessness had moderated, on the surface at least. But no acute observers, and Richard must have been one, could have thought that more than a temporary respite had been bought.

There were other problems. The Privy Council was divided between competing military and civilian groups, neither at ease with itself, and consequently was inefficient. Thurloe, its Secretary, was a great filer of correspondence and amasser of miscellaneous information, but at this time had little idea of what to do with it. (Historians may have made better use of his State Papers than he did.) Sir Charles Wolseley, Sir Gilbert Pickering and the rest were hardly strong-minded men, and were much suspected by the military for their support of the kingship proposals of 1657. The cleavages were revealed in arguments over proposals for remodelling and recruiting to the council, which included the suggestion, resisted by jealous fellow-generals, that Henry Cromwell might be brought home from Ireland. They also objected to the speedy calling of parliament and some, at least, seem to have been ready to have money raised without legal authority. But by the end of November the decision was taken and the writs prepared.[13] The civilians were elated at the check to the high flying of the army officers who had nothing but force to offer as a solution to the government's problems. Oliver's Lords only were to be summoned to the other House, while the Commons were to be elected 'according to the ancient rights of the nation in the late King's time', except for the disqualification of overt royalists and papists. This return to the old arrangements was possible because the Humble Petition and Advice had been silent on electoral provisions and the special act intended to follow it had not been completed when the second Protectorate parliament had been abruptly dissolved. The change in franchise considerably altered representation. Cornwall had had 14 seats in 1656, now 44; Essex's 16 was reduced to 8. The suggestion, of course, is that experience had shewn that the old boroughs were more readily influenced, or corrupted, than the counties.[14] Scotland and Ireland were to be represented as under Oliver but their seats were to be filled by nomination. Those chosen were, however, not to sit until the House of Commons had itself decided to admit them.

The elections have not been studied in detail. But there is evidence of 'great striveings' for seats.[15] At Hythe, a Cinque Port, where government influence might be felt, the Governor of Sandgate Castle and the Mayor supported rival candidates. After an active campaign, heavy with localism, a compromise was reached, whereby one of the Mayor's and one of the Governor's protégés were each returned. (The unsuccessful Governor's candidate was Henry Oxinden of Barham, a Kentish gentleman, reputed to support the abolition of tithes.) Elsewhere government pressure, organised but, in fact, hardly systematically, by Thurloe, had some successes, grossly over-estimated by a contemporary at 80 seats.[16] The political complexion of the House as a whole was and is difficult to assess. There were many new men unknown to parliaments, certainly royalists encouraged to stand by the Court in exile. But no clear directions seem to have been given them, once elected, and they failed to form a coherent *bloc*. The presbyterians who were close to them on many points were hostile on others, especially religion. There were, of course, some commonwealthsmen, inevitably Scott, Haselrig, Weaver and Ludlow, who had set themselves to destroy the Humble Petition and Advice. Against this divergent opposition was ranged the government grouping—or rather groupings, for the divisions already indicated in the council were reflected in the Commons. In between the activist minority lay the bulk of the private members, moderates, if not 'neuters' who could be swayed one way or the other. After scrutinising the returns Thurloe ruefully concluded there was 'so great a mixture no one knows which way the major part will incline'.[17] Yet there was perhaps one thing on which all members, apart from the few swordsmen, were agreed—the independence and recalcitrance of the army must be reduced. Any proposal that would blunt the sword was sure of an attentive hearing.

The session began with a neat speech by Richard (27 January 1659) delivered in the Lords' Chamber, where only a few of the Commons attended, the rest not wishing by their presence to commit themselves to recognition of the other House. Like his father before him, but more briefly, Richard urged the need for unity and settlement at home and a forward policy abroad, stressing dangers which were certainly real enough. Apart from the perennial problem of royalist intrigues, English interests were at stake in the Baltic where tension between Denmark and Sweden, threatened the peaceful passage of the Sound. Relations with the Dutch, too, were disturbed by England's tariff policy. Lord Keeper Fiennes 'closed up' with another of his tedious addresses.[18]

Richard's sober appeal made little impression. Few members were really interested in strengthening the government. Early discussions on minor matters soon revealed the basic clash of outlook between civilians and soldiers. It would soon be a crime to be an army man, complained one indignant colonel. As a change from baiting the army, the republicans tore into measures which a sanguine council had regarded as mere routine. Thus a bill for the recognition of Richard's right and title was held up to win time, as Ludlow put it, to teach the new members 'good principles'.[19] Though the commonwealthsmen were in a minority—as they had been in every parliament since 1653— they had an influence out of proportion with their numbers. Their leaders were practised time-wasters and carpers, they knew the parliamentary ropes and how to tie complicated knots in them. They were good talkers, always ready with a speech or a point of order. Haselrig, as wily a tactician as ever stood up on the floor of the House, treated the numerous 'young men' present to a tendentious lecture on English history from Anglo-Saxon times, concluding with the assertion that though he saw Richard as a man without gall or guile, he could not recognise him until the liberties of the people of England were settled.[20] By this he meant the re-establishment of 'an absolute Commonwealth within the walls of the House of Commons, exclusive of all others'.

The debate that ensued roamed far afield into 'a wood, a wilderness, a labyrinth'.[21] The Speaker seems to have done little to control the debate, and at no time did the government group give a lead. Indeed, they lost all coherence and at one point Thurloe found himself in a minority of one.[22] An exasperated outsider complained that the politicians were as active as ever in words,[23] while concluding nothing; however, they sometimes sat till midnight. Harringtonian views were put by Captain Adam Baynes and Henry Neville. 'The people were too hard for the King in property, and then in arms too hard for him. We must either lay the foundation in property or else it will not stand. Property, generally, is now with the people; the government, therefore, must be there'.[24] On the other hand, a member boasted, 'I shall not go back to time past, nor look forward to *Oceana's* Platonical commonwealth; things that are not and never shall be.'[25] The Rump was praised by Scott, but impugned by Colonel Birch, who had been secluded by Pride. At length, Richard was recognised, but in such a manner that the way was left clear to further constitutional discussion and reform—a rather hollow victory.

More heat than light was raised, too, by the question of the Irish and Scots members, regarded as blatant government clients. Scott and his associates argued that the other two kingdoms should have parliaments of their own as of old. If Argyll wanted to sit in a parliament, let him do so in his own—a foreign—country. Another member saw in the acceptance of nomination a dangerous precedent—'Admit 60 now, 300 tomorrow'.[26] Eventually they were allowed to sit on the understanding that the decision was not a final one.

Though a recognition of sorts was accorded to the other House there was a tussle over its powers and composition reminiscent of the second session of the last parliament. Its members were said to be as much government clients as Irish and Scottish nominees for the Commons. They included officials—men who should be servants not hopeful masters. There were too many swords there, too many men of little estate or of personal obscurity, men who could not have 'the same naturall interest in making of lawes that the old Lords had'.[27] The conflict in the House was reinforced by pamphlets flung about outside. Many called for the return of the old Lords, denying the arguments which in 1649 had justified their abolition. The points made were reiterated in the Commons' debates. The peers had produced Magna Carta. The petition of 12 of them in 1640 had tipped the scales in favour of summoning parliament. 'They always fought battles for our liberties.' As for the other House it was 'an oleo, an equivocal generation betwixt his late highness and the dregs of the Commons'.[28] When recognition was finally granted (28 March) for the duration of the present parliament, there was a proviso which delighted 'the cavalierish party' that it was not intended to exclude 'faithful' members of the old Lords. They felt, as was pointed out in the debate, that to admit the old peers was 'to make a pair of stairs for Charles Stuart to run up to the top into the room of the single person.'[29] While all this excitement was agitating the Commons, the other House was calmly devising amendments to the acts against swearing, drunkenness and profanation of the Sabbath.

By now the army was losing patience. Hard things had been said about it and nothing was being done, surely deliberately, to settle its arrears and secure its financial future. So much wasted time, so many insults were dissipating the spirit of conciliation that Richard had striven to preserve. The officers began to meet again in March and in looking up their old grievances revealed themselves as faction-ridden.

Some, including Praying Goffe, veered towards 'the young gentle-man,'[30] Richard, who could also count on the support of his brother Henry in Ireland and of Monk in Scotland. Another group much tainted by republicanism, objected to the kingly nature of the régime established under the Humble Petition and Advice, while the Wallingford House group—so-called after the town residence of Fleetwood—resented civilian encroachments in the government generally and stood for the full maintenance of the power and influence of the grandees. Discussions in March between the commonwealthsmen and the Fleetwood party came to nothing because the former, though hopelessly indefinite about what they really wanted, could not compromise. (Their inability to differentiate between what was possible and what was desirable was at the heart of their ignominious collapse in 1660.) On the other hand the Wallingford House group had a clear aim—to maintain their ascendancy—and their overtures were only cynical expedients. On 2 April, with the innocent approval of Richard, a council of officers met to frame a petition demanding tough measures against royalists, who were becoming bolder with their libels and affronts to 'honest blades',[31] payment of arrears, security for future actions and indemnity for the past. This last was a sore point newly rubbed raw by a parliamentary attack on Major-General Boteler for some activities in Rutland. If he were penalised, who among them could feel safe?

Richard received this petition politely enough and passed it on to parliament which laid it aside. Meanwhile drafts of the petition were sent to Ireland and Scotland as resentment grew among the English army at the insulting inaction of parliament. About 16 April some civilian supporters of Richard laid before him a wildcat scheme for kidnapping the Wallingford House leaders, but Richard, who saw that even if successful this move could only encourage more violence, was too prudent to fall for it. Instead he volunteered to order the council of officers to be dissolved. By then parliament had turned to the financial problem. Early in April it voted to take into consideration the continuance of the excise, 'which will breed a great debate, for it must either cutt short the army, or prolong the Parliament very longe'.[32] On 18 April the matter of army pay was given consideration, but two other vital votes challenging the army's political pretensions produced a crisis. (Curiously enough, the republicans opposed the resolutions, no doubt, still thinking something might come of their parleys with the grandees.)

The first vote was that no officers' council meeting might take place without the approval of parliament and Protector. The second, that all military and naval commanders must pledge themselves never to interrupt the proceedings of parliament. In short, the soldiers were to accept a subordinate role as the servants of the State, and to give up the right they claimed 'as Englishmen' to meet together from time to time to consult about what they regarded as their own affairs. In the present posture of the army the votes in themselves were highly provocative, a possible explanation for the republican opposition to them. Moreover, Richard, either on his own initiative or at the instance of conservatives like Broghill, had already ordered the officers' council to dissolve and the commanders to repair to their regiments. When Col. Ashfield objected that it would be inconvenient for him to go, Richard sharply reminded him that it was two years since he had last been with his men. But the officers were unrepentant, and, according to the Venetian Ambassador, who was closely watching events, met later that day and resolved to meet again when they pleased. There was blunt talk of forcing the dissolution of a parliament that was the plaything of courtiers and royalists. The City authorities declared they would stand by the Protector, but the trained bands more realistically flung in their lot with the army. On 21 April Fleetwood, whose arrest Richard was contemplating, called a general rendezvous of the army at St James's, no doubt to consider the rumours that a general demobilisation of the army and its replacement by a civil-controlled militia were in the offing. Richard countered this defiance with an order for a rendezvous at Whitehall, where, in fact, only a few companies appeared. Here perhaps was Richard's opportunity to emulate his father's feat at Corkbush Field a dozen years before. He should have gone to St James's and taken the wolf by the ears. But he was 'fearful and unresolved'.[33] That night Desborough bluntly put before him the army's determination not to be brushed aside. Next day parliament was dismissed. The military had triumphed again, though 'all this was done without seizing any man's person, shedding a droppe of bloud, or making the least confusion in the citty and suburbes'.[34] After a decade of swordmanship, the mere threat was enough.

The dissolution of Richard's parliament marked the practical collapse of the Protectorate. He was doomed, unless he was ready to be an obvious tool, 'rather watched then attended', standing in 'a manner insignificent, haveing not lost onely the harts, But the name of an Armie'.[35] The declaration explaining the abrupt ending of parliament refers to 'divers weighty reasons', but fails to comment on the heaviest of them, military rumbles. Fleetwood wrote a face-saving letter to Monk explaining that the army in England had had to draw together in fear of a general design by royalists. Reports that they had 'forced the

239

Parliament' was malicious and false.[36] Richard had acted of his own volition, and the army had loyally stood by him. (Everybody, it seemed, was anxious to keep Monk informed of what was going on in England or of what they wanted him to think was happening—already there must have been an inkling of his unique potentialities.) Endeavours were made by the council of officers to consider all appropriate ways and means 'to pece and mende up that crakt Government'.[37] Among these was the purging of 'Sicophants, and Parasits' of the Lord Protector, and redistributing their commands among the 'faithful', including Col. William Packer, whom Oliver had dismissed.[38]

By now John Lambert was conspicuously back, in spite of opposition to his re-entry by Fleetwood, who suspected 'Lambert's ambition would quickly supplant him, if he got power'.[39] He was right. Lambert's vigorous personality and deep experience soon brought him back 'in vogue'. It was, perhaps, his influence which induced the grandees to shew some willingness for the continuance of a Protector, provided he was shorn of a veto and denied effective control over the army. But the lower officers, rediscovering republican sentiments, pressed for the return of a commonwealth. Haselrig, Vane, Scott and other civilian republicans were pulled into the haggling. 'Wallingford Howse is the seane for action. There . . . the greatest officers seeke God for councell and act theire owne way.'[40] In the event it was decided that the Rump should be recalled and a council of 'select senate' established, which 'should have a negative on the Remnant parliament when it should be restored, but after much debate that was thought fitter for the debate of parliament than them'.[41] There was even less certainty on the relation of Commons and senate with the Protector. It was clear that Lambert and company were suspicious of the republicans, but divided among themselves. Faced with the recalcitrance of the lower officers, who if not checked might 'supplant them',[42] the grandees could only play for time. Yet time was not on their side. Their failure lay in a lack of unity and mundane political skill, not in a lack of ideas. The air was heavy with these. Pamphlets, papers, proposals streamed forth, stuffed with competing views. Strong among them were Harringtonians, semi-Levellers and frank Utopians, pushing detailed social and legal innovations, besides remodelling the basic features of government. There were signs of stirring even among the rank and file. 'The meanest Redcott catches att the reynes of Goverment; they agitate againe, and fault theire leaders.'[43] Though many people were probably indifferent to the forms of government so long as they themselves were left in peace—'the citty beast is as tame as a tyred jade',[44] it was said on 29 April—men of resolution might in a time of tension direct this apathetic mass along dangerous paths—even those leading towards a restoration of monarchy in the old line. The return of the Rump was certainly preferable to that.

So, on 7 May, William Lenthall, Speaker of the Long Parliament, bewildered by the startling turn in events, was presented with an invitation for the members of the Rump, who were described as eminent asserters of the good old cause, 'to return to the exercise and discharge of their trust',[45] in the assurance that the army would assist them to sit in safety settling and securing the freedom and peace of the Commonwealth. The next day about 40 members came together in the Painted Chamber, and drew up for immediate publication a declaration of their intention to reinstate a commonwealth without a single person, kingship or a House of Lords, and setting up a stop-gap committee of safety. When they met again the next day, several secluded members including Monk's protegé, Sir George Booth, and William Prynne, turned up, claiming an inalienable right to sit. Prynne did actually manage to slip in, whereupon the House adjourned to the afternoon and then had him kept out by soldiers. He continued to protest loudly outside.

During the time the Rump was revived, about 120 members turned up at one time or another. They were very energetic. Committees were set up to deal with public revenues and the army was put under the orders of a commission of seven—Vane, Ludlow and Haselrig, with Lambert, Fleetwood, Berry and Desborough. Henry Cromwell was ordered back from Ireland and his command given to a committee of five. His elder brother had meanwhile seen himself become 'a cipher, and a cipher is nothing'.[46] On 25 May he handed in his resignation 'to this new fabric',[47] asking only for an indemnity and a satisfaction for his father's and his own debts in the service of the State. So died the house of Cromwell. 'Richard ye fourth hath deserted himselfe.' 'Tumble downe Dick hath kissed the tayle.'[48]

xxvi The Failure of the Grandees

The Rumpers were delighted and 'fortified apace'.[1] Yet all was not well below the surface. The problems which had beaten Richard remained. The army—'the men in buffe that gave them their second birthe'[2]—remained on foot, still growling for pay and redress of grievances. 'Though the army have baptised it, I cannot see that they care much to advance the groweth of it',[3] was one comment. The grandees had recalled the Rump as a smokescreen for their own rule, for their own scufflings to come to an accord among themselves.

The Rump ignored the obvious signs. The rough treatment of parliament since 1653 only argued for it to act toughly itself. It intended to control the army. Fleetwood might be called the Commander-in-Chief, but his powers were very limited. He could make no appointments. Even the committee of seven, though it could nominate, required parliamentary confirmation. Officers' commissions were to be signed by the Speaker, who was in a sense the formal head of the State, and so far as possible were to be delivered in the presence of the members of Parliament. Even Ludlow and Vane thought this insistence provocative, but they were overruled by Scott and Haselrig. Some officers were dismissed. The new council of state, emerging from the stop-gap committee of safety, was firmly civilian and closely integrated with parliament, the bulk of the councillors being M.P.s. From the start it was a conscientious, hard-working body, obviously setting itself to emulate and exceed the efficiency of the old council of state of the Commonwealth, which many men had thought to be its greatest glory. The grandees were depressed by all this but for the moment could do nothing. They knew there was no civilian opinion which could be stirred in their favour, and the inferior officers seemed to have wholehearted faith in the new régime. Their acquiescence gave the Rump a false sense of values. They saw themselves as indispensable, the saviours of society. It did not occur to them that they were merely a convenience to be discarded when they had served a purpose. They failed to consider as the French ambassador did that England was perhaps as likely to 'fall into the King's power as to form a perfect republic.[4] If Haselrig had had more imagination he would not have baited Lambert, nor would the Commons have ordered army purges, not only in England but in Scotland and Ireland, with such confident hauteur. Monk was sent a list of unreliables for removal and told that 'peradventure such things are known to parliament that are not known to yourself'.[5] The General was bitterly offended, though he complied, since 'obedience is my great principle'.[6] It was foolish to irritate him.

Eventually an act of indemnity was passed but it was full of crannies and failed to please anyone in the army. Lambert bluntly told Haselrig so. 'You are only at the mercy of the Parliament', was the smug reply. 'I know not why they (parliament) should not be at our mercy',[7] said Lambert. For a moment the sword jumped in its scabbard. 'The howse hath not yet recovered the reputation of a parliament, a word that formerly caryed armyes in it.'[8] But the army, anyway, wanted more than words—it wanted money to stay or to go. The Rump was not providing it, and, indeed, could only have done so by imposing crippling taxation, which would have destroyed any prospects of national support. That must involve its own disappearance. For it they showed no inclination, thereby dissipating support they might otherwise have gained. As early as June bets were being laid that the Rump would not last another fortnight. Cautious and experienced royalist activists appreciated this and were ready to wait and see what would happen then. But more impatient men could only see the fact that revolutionaries, some of them regicides and proud of it, were in power and ought to be toppled out of it. Such an enthusiast was John, Lord Mordaunt, son of an old parliamentarian, with an entrée to presbyterian circles. He wanted to forge an alliance between them and the old royalists, knowing that they had political backing, financial resources and territorial influence, with the great advantage of being Englishmen. Mordaunt, though willing if need be for Turkey to reimpose monarchy, knew in his heart that an attempt to restore Charles Stuart by foreign arms alone would be a blessing to the *de facto* power, giving it an aura of patriotism. So he set himself to reorganise the royalists, bringing in former neutrals and parliamentarians, who were disturbed by a recrudescence of social and religious idealism, seemingly the effect of unstable political conditions. Elaborate plans were devised for combined risings under local commanders all over the country, to be supported, if possible, by landings from abroad. Poor communications, divided counsels, strong localisms were to prove as in the past destructive to a sudden effective stroke. In any case the neo-royalists were still thinking of imposing conditions on the King, conditions very

243

like those of Newport peddled a decade before. Charles, who had by experience concluded that presbyterianism was not for him, shewed no eagerness for restoration on those terms, while many old royalists who had lost their Church, and sometimes their lands, had little meeting of minds with men who had destroyed the one and held the other. Most of the outstanding men whom Mordaunt and his friends hopefully approached—they included Monk, Edward Montague (in charge of the Navy), Lockhart (Ambassador in France)—were unwilling to co-operate at this stage however much some of them would have welcomed a restoration when a real opportunity beckoned. They had too much to lose to venture out prematurely to restore monarchy 'by tumult',[9] yet (as events were to shew) when some of them did make a gesture, it proved decisive. While this manœuvring, much of it mere bickering, was going on, the government was getting information in plenty about what was intended. Failure to reach agreement meant postponements, and by the time the rising was actually to come off, effective counter-precautions had been taken. In some parts of the country nothing happened at all, though much had been intended. Only in Cheshire was there anything that looked as if it might be serious. There Sir George Booth, whom Monk, as we have seen, had recommended not so long ago as 'a prudent country gentleman', raised about 4,000 men, ostensibly for a free parliament, liberty and property and tax re-duction,[10] and occupied Chester, with the enthusiastic support of local presbyterian clergy, who were obsessed with terrified visions of ana-baptists and quakers, incited by the lax toleration of the Rump, which violently put out the light of the gospel and the ministry. The country folk seem to have been less disturbed about this than their pastors and betters, and the rising, isolated by the collapse of the conspiracy else-where in England and the non-appearance of foreign invasion, failed after an initial wild-fire success to keep in motion. The rebels were melting away even before Lambert, a talented soldier with troops who, though tired after 'long and dirty marches' in typical English August weather, fought superbly well, cut the main body of 'the Boothians'[11] to pieces at Winnington Bridge (19 August). (It was said that Lambert had taken on the job of suppressing Booth at the urgent insistence of Fleetwood, who would otherwise have had to go himself and who was unwilling to leave Lambert with the rest of the army at London, lest working on the officers, he might play his game so as to supplant himself. Such were the true relations among the grandees.)

The demoralised rebels were treated with some leniency, but the Rump took up a proposal to sequester the property of any who might be suspected to be concerned in the late general conspiracy. It was still working on nominating commissioners for this task, and finding many nominees unwilling to act, less from scruples about injustice than from realistic appraisals of the government's mortality, when in October it was yet once more displaced, once again by the army—a depressing thought for the royalists, who had themselves achieved nothing but the demonstration of their own divisions, weaknesses and continuing ineptitude, and a temporary closing of the ranks against themselves. As for the army, it could justly claim that the defeat of the great royalist conspiracy was largely its own work. Discontented before, it now claimed an immediate reward in the shape of pay and reform. The Rump seemed unwilling or incapable of giving either. Instead it began to drift into internecine conflicts with Haselrig and 'the giddy heade of the confused sectaries',[12] Vane, who could be together when against something, but were at each other's throats now they had to be constructive.

The moves that ended in ejection began at Derby where officers in the force which had dispersed the rebels drew up, apparently without Lambert's connivance, a petition of grievances and demands. They wanted Fleetwood, whose commission was on the point of expiry, to be permanent Commander-in-Chief, with Lambert as his deputy: that both State and army should be purged of malignants and neuters and 'good men ... looked upon as friends, encouraged, satisfied their arrears, protected from injuries, and countenanced' by the parliament.[13] They also wanted corporations to be purged to make them more amenable to the Commonwealth, and condign punishment to be meted out to all concerned in the late risings. The petition was circulated among the other forces, except in Scotland where Monk, piously emphasising his detachment from politics, refused to allow his officers to sign or have anything to do with it.[14] His attitude emboldened Haselrig to make a slashing assault in parliament on Lambert as the only begetter of an illegal and insolent pressure. On 23 September the Rump ordered the petition suppressed. Whether or not he was concerned in the framing of the original petition, Lambert was bound to react unfavourably to this provocation. As Mordaunt said, 'Lambert is so put to it' by Haselrig and his cronies 'that he is either lost or must loose them'.[15] The immediate answer to the Rump's confident denial was a new petition—'more high'[16]—asserting that the utter innocence of the Derby one had been flagrantly misrepresented. It went on to demand freedom to petition parliament so that they would incline their hearts to the tasks of making 'these Nations happy by such a Settlement as may not be liable at every Change of Governors, to have the Peace thereof disturbed, by introducing new Governments'.[17]

(That the army had done its own share of that was prudently for-gotten!) Most critical was the reiterated claim for no dismissals with-out court martials. On this demand Monk, still refusing to have any-thing to do with the English political agitation, commented: 'If a general or a supreme authority should be understood to be restrained therein, it might encourage the more inferior officers and soldiers to affront the superior, and would in time make the army a kind of separate corporation from the parliament.'

On 10 October 1659 the Commons 'considered' the petition, but actually passed a bill declaring illegal all patents, grants, acts and ordinances made since the Cromwellian dissolution of April 1653. This was a sharp and, perhaps, reckless counter-attack. Why it was done is difficult to explain, unless it was that M.P.s felt that a forced interruption of their proceedings was coming anyway, and they wanted before it happened to make their position plain. Perhaps a few optimists really did think they could rally active support by indicating that they and the army had very different ends. They learned that Lambert and some other officers were busily circulating letters in aid of the petition and now chose to regard this as a flagrant defiance of the civil sovereign. They revoked the officers' commissions, expelled Lambert from the House and ordered his arrest. Fleetwood's personal command was put into a commission of seven—including himself, Ludlow, Haslerig and (a significant gesture) Monk. A protective barrier of troops was flung around Westminster. It was another crisis.

The question now was, what would Lambert do? He surrounded the troops around the parliament House and by a mixture of persuasion and peremptory orders secured their adhesion to himself. Moved, as John Barwick thought, by 'an itch of having all',[18] he destroyed the Rump by simply refusing to allow Speaker and members to enter the House. The newsletters were soon full of expectations and speculations. What comes next? asked one. 'That which they will break again ere long', was the pertinent answer.[19]

In the new dispensation Fleetwood became personal Commander-in-Chief again, but no one doubted that Lambert was the real power. He left it to Fleetwood to write the inevitable explanatory epistle to Monk, suggesting that what had happened lay in a necessity of Provi-dence, and freely admitting that no decision had yet been taken on what should follow. Soon a committee of safety of 23 members was named to undertake a temporary government. They were a curious bunch—Lambert, Fleetwood, and Desborough in effect nominated themselves. Others included were Sydenham, Whitelocke, Steele, Strickland, Vane, Wariston, Aldermen Ireton and Tichbourne, and

Major-Generals Hewson and Berry—names which suggest a desire to give at any rate an appearance of desire for official and legal support, for a broad religious backing, for the connivance of the City and a general representation of the sword. Ludlow, too, was nominated and seems to have made an effort to bring about a reconciliation between the grandees and the Rumpers. One name was significantly missing—that of Monk, yet it is clear that his attitude could be crucial. He had refused the petitions that had precipitated this crisis, and to acquiesce while a derisively-concealed sword was imposed by Lambert was surely against his professed principles. At length, he announced his intention to stand by the Rump. The eagerness with which his views, and the views of people who thought they knew his views, were canvassed underlined the significance of his position. As early as September 1658, the royalist Culpepper had said that Monk was the person 'his eye was chiefly on' to restore the King, and in July 1659 Charles had written to Monk that if he once resolved to put the royal interest in his bosom, he would leave the way of declaring it entirely to the general's judgment. Now in October 1659 army officers wished that he had not a worse design than restoring the parliament. Monk had first served in the Dutch armies where, as he put it, soldiers received and obeyed orders, but gave none. His whole career can be interpreted as displaying a respect for civil authority. He knew that men like Lambert did not share his expressed principles and had already before October 1659 asserted that Lambert would not let the Rump sit till Christmas.[20] Now he had decided to move but just what he would do remained, even to close observers and apparent intimates, a mystery. Everybody remarked on his 'reservedness', his 'darkness'.[21] The capacity to leave his motives and aims to guesswork was Monk's masterpiece. If he had intended from the start to restore the King, then certainly he went a—if not the—right way about it, leaving his antagonists like tyros at the game of politics to entangle themselves. Yet it remains impossible to prove that at this stage he did in fact intend to restore the Stuarts. He said in October 1659 he was moving to restore civil authority and to take power away from 'Lord' Lambert, who was behaving like some great feudal magnate in faction. This civil authority in the autumn of 1659 was the Rump; by the spring of 1660 it was monarchy in the old line. Just where the transition really took place and how and why are ultimately unanswerable questions.

A day-by-day narrative of the next few months is not called for here. One has already been provided, with somewhat soporific effect, in a solid volume by Godfrey Davies, the coping stone to the great series begun by S. R. Gardiner a century ago.[22] Monk, having declared for the Rump, seemed in no hurry to move, thereby encouraging Mordaunt to urge the King to invade England at once, while confusion prevailed, and by this intervention to secure his reputation and his crown. (Charles was too canny to risk it; besides it was getting into winter, no time for campaigning.) Monk himself sent agents to indulge in complicated negotiations at York with Lambert and Fleetwood, obviously to gain or waste time. Lambert for his part appealed to him 'upon the accompt of old friendship' to note'those dangers and mischeifes [that] must fall uppon this Common wealth [if] that the armies thereof. . . come to blowes amongst themselves'.[23] Saying nothing, Monk continued to purge his well-knit forces, and extracted from a convention of the Scottish estates a promise of a peaceable deportment during his coming absence in England. He needed this because he had no absolute certainty that his passage into and through England would be easy and he feared that a Scottish rising, whether for the King or some other deep purpose, might as so often in the past bring the English armies, larger than his own force, into unity again.[24] (This precaution was a fact suppressed by his earlier biographers, who felt it their duty to clinch his early royalism.) He knew that if that unity did come about the English people, however much they detested the generals, would not dare to move a finger in his support. Their apathy could be dangerous, and it is noteworthy that he tried to break it in his own favour, for example, by sending letters to the Lord Mayor of London, assuring the wavering City that he intended nothing more than the restoration of freedom and authority of the parliament to whom he meant to leave all considerations. At the same time while he was ready to receive representations from all quarters, he did nothing to commit himself, as, for instance, when he ignored an appeal from a group of the old council of state to accept a commission as Commander-in-Chief. This delay and careful mystery tried the nerves of his antagonists, and encouraged divisions among them, since none could be sure the others were not in secret accord with him behind their backs. Among the plain English soldiery loose talk about pay and arrears, and from the presses poison in print, added their quota to the prevailing confusion.

In the midst of this the committee of safety—or 'unsafety'[25]—struggled to produce a plan of settlement to lay before a council of officers. One such scheme envisaged a written constitution with unalterable fundamentals (notably the unacceptability of a king or single person). There should be religious toleration, a bi-cameral parliament (both Houses elective), and a body of 'conservators of liberty' to see that the fundamentals were scrupulously observed. An intention to frustrate notions of total parliamentary sovereignty is apparent. But the whole thing is of academic interest only. Even as it was in the framing, the situation it was designed to meet was changing.

Monk's fabian tactics were paying dividends. Apathy was quickening into positive resentment. Apprentices rioted, and 'the army men are almost watched off theire legs'.[26] Some, it was said, openly cried their shame at their situation. 'Many . . . wish themselves with my Lord Generall Monck, for they say they will bee sure to bee paid and have theire arreares; but now they fight for they doe not know what nor who, and are esteemed rogues and traters.'[27] Some even asserted that as their predecessors had helped to drive out the father, so they were resolved to bring home the son.[28] Lambert's men were rumoured to have said that they would not fight again themselves but would be very happy to make 'a ring' in which their officers could set about each other.[29] But the rot had not yet gone far enough for 'our great and rich ones'—City and landed magnates—whose ultimate resolutions would be vital, not to 'balk all appeasing'.[30] Monk after all was still in Scotland, still to proclaim his objective.

Meanwhile a group of active members of the old Rump Council of State, including an energetic Anthony Ashley Cooper, zealously acquiring intense political experience, had managed to get the Portsmouth garrison to declare for a parliament (early December)—the first overt defection from the grandees. Ominously the troops sent down by the army council to suppress them joined them instead. At the end of the month, Sir Thomas Fairfax, after a characteristic hesitance, declared his support for whatever—more or less—Monk might do, raised the Yorkshire gentry, and, by taking York, helped to frustrate Lambert's plans to close the border. By then the fleet in the Downs, at first leaning towards Lambert, had turned to Monk and sailed into the Thames, where it could impress the City. There a new Common Council was being elected, one purged of 'rotten members' (i.e. buyers of crown, Church and royalist lands) and stuffed with 'uninterested persons' (i.e. royalists). All this made Fleetwood, never a man of steel, panic. All in a daze, he talked of summoning a new parliament to meet, after rushed elections, on 24 January. Though writs were drawn up, nothing came of them, for, as Monk put it, the grandees had no power to summon one, or if they had, it could not be expected that the members would be permitted to assemble and sit in freedom. Someone approached Fleetwood (through Bulstrode Whitelocke) to thwart Monk, whose closeness was still puzzling, and whose army in spite of its much-remarked lack of politics was thought by some 'most uncerteyn fickle' and 'not to be fixed by anything except the citty money', by restoring Charles himself.[31] Fleetwood boggled at the thought, and instead, wantonly leaving Lambert and the rest in the lurch, sent Mr Speaker Lenthall the keys of parliament as a sort of Christmas gift and retired from politics (24 December). The guards around Westminster were called off, and on Boxing Day, the Rump re-assembled yet once more, and the commission of seven verbally asserted its command of the army. Its position ostensibly was stronger than it had been a few months before. The army was visibly disintegrating. The grandees had withered everything they had touched. All parts were 'up for a parliament'.[32] But by 'a parliament' was meant 'a free parliament' and few took the Rump to be that. At the least, it was expected, it must call back its secluded members to join in arranging for a 'free and full' assembly. Worse, hardly had it sat down again when 'George and his boys' crossed the Northern Border, ignoring a cheerful assurance by the Speaker that all was well and that their journey no longer necessary.

> Still *George was wary; his cause did require*
> *A pillar of cloud as well as fire.*[33]

XXVII Restoration

Monk had at last got everything in Scotland set to his satisfaction. Delay had made him even more master of the situation. The Scots would be quiet. His own army was secure in his grasp, his officers '*post-nati* to the spoil of Church and crown'[1] and the rank and file, confident of pay, unswervingly obedient. In England he knew that conservative political opinion—and the swing towards conservatism was quickening—was backing him. He appeared a bulwark against military despotism, administrative chaos, social anarchy. Observers complained, it is true, of the difficulty of getting into his mind. 'Monk no flesh understands, all fear.' 'Monk is so dark a man no perspective can look through him.' 'Never was more said, and less known.'[2] These are all typical royalist comments. Presbyterians felt happier— they thought he would fall into their plans of restoring the King on the old Newport propositions. (Some royalists felt they might be right, and one hoped that Lambert might be persuaded to declare the King restored to prevent this.)

While London and the rest of the country seethed with speculation Monk crossed into England on 30 December, unresisted, as Lambert's forces, desolated by every item of news and rumour that came through to them, slipped away. By slow stages—partly enforced by the thick snow through which they plodded—his army neared London. At every hand there were addresses of welcome and support, and, more valuable, the presence and active adhesion of gentry and magnates. Monk was cautious in his acceptances. All the way he reiterated that he was on the move to protect parliament and not to restore the King. But the Rump feared the worst and were depressed by his triumphant progress towards London. They had frittered away a whole month, holding off the admission of secluded members and even expelling some of their own number, such as Vane, for alleged hobnobbing with the army. Here and there troops were mutinying for want of pay. The contempt of the citizens for their sovereign parliament was undisguised. Monk had refused to issue *en route* a specific declaration of his loyalty to them. A broad hint of things to come was given when Haselrig failed to get a majority for a bill to exact from every present and future M.P. an oath categorically abjuring Charles Stuart.

Arrived in the City (3 February 1660), Monk let himself be lavishly entertained, waited on by all sorts of parties, listening hard, saying little. In a formal address to parliament he urged them to enlarge themselves by bringing in 'sober gentry' but excluding cavaliers.[3] (Not so long ago he had recommended Sir George Booth as a sober gentleman.) The Rump paid no heed, and instead ordered him to reduce the City's defences. At first he obeyed, elating Haselrig, who exclaimed, 'All is our own, he will be honest.'[4] But suddenly Monk broke off, claiming that to go on would only exasperate the people: a clever move, since it blackened the Rump, while exonerating himself. He backed it by a call for the issue of writs to make up numbers. The Rump ignored this, peremptorily ordered him to carry out their instructions, and declared the Common Council dissolved. Monk's reply was to intensify his interviews and discussions with leading politicians and citizens. The mask of obedience was beginning to slip. By letter he upbraided parliament for their lukewarm concern for the liberties of their country, instancing the fact that though Lambert and Vane had been proclaimed against, no step to secure them had been taken, and they were cynically winking at their authority. In any case the House must quickly make itself more truly representative. Defiantly the Rump ordered the forces to be put into yet another commission, with a quorum of three, of whom Monk need not be one. It seems that men like Haselrig and Scott, who pressed this measure, were possessed of a demon of self-destruction. Their lack of political sense after all the vicissitudes is almost incredible. Things were indeed 'at a strange pass and in a very odd posture'. Monk widened the breach by informing the City authorities that he was soliciting the return of the secluded members and the early summoning of a new 'free' parliament. Excitement mounted. On 21 February, without waiting for a formal invitation, the secluded members confidently took their places. Monk had already got them to promise to arrange for the issue of writs for a Convention parliament at the end of April. He indicated to them that he expected a 'moderate Presbyterian government with a sufficient liberty for tender consciences [would] be the most acceptable way to the settlement of the Church'.[5] He believed—or at any rate said he did —that the temper of the nation was against a restoration of bishops, whose lands had in any case been dispersed and sold. He felt the Convention would arrange to confirm sales of land and provide for the maintenance of all necessary forces.

The returning of the secluded members automatically ended Rump rule. The old guard were swamped; many simply stopped coming. Among the old faces to be seen at Westminster were those of Holles, Waller, Grimstone, Fairfax and Prynne. The new council of state, with Thurloe as joint secretary, was dominated by presbyterians, some of whom were certainly 'well affected to kingly government'.[6] They included Sir William Waller, who had forecast a year before that a full parliament would restore the King to his prerogatives. Monk himself was not so open. Either he still had not made up his mind or he had a very strict timetable and would allow no one else any initiative. For instance, as late as 21 February he ordered his officers to suppress any rising on behalf of Charles II. This was not inconsistent with a scheme of restoration—at a delicate time premature and undisciplined action might be disastrous. Restoration without bloodshed would then be impossible.

The readmission of the old members was greeted with enthusiasm, not so much for itself as for seeming a prelude to something greater. Monk's earliest biographer, Thomas Skinner, described the members as men of good estate and quality, who 'now saw clearly there was no way left to settle the nation but by restoring the monarchy'. Even so, they were cautious enough to assure the sitting members that they would follow 'such counsels as might lay a better foundation to the commonwealth'.[7] Monk intended these counsels to be his own and to that end reinforced his grip by extending a continuous purge of all forces in London, dismembering the regiments and dismissing suspected officers. When a group of officers waited on him, praying for an engagement against the return of the King, he blankly refused. He would obey whatever parliament decreed—and so, indeed, would they. They went perforce back to their commands and the whole army subscribed to a resolution to stand by the civilian authorities. With them Monk was on the best of terms—he had particularly ingratiated himself with the City, 'the master wheel', as John Mordaunt put it, 'by whose motions the successive rotations of all the less must follow'.[8] Yet for all his advantages he must have had qualms. They are revealed in his anxiety that the secluded members should sit no longer than necessary to arrange for new elections. Hence he opposed a suggestion that the House of Lords should be restored. 'The one great argument for the admission of the secluded members was their consent to a speedy dissolution; which could not be if the Lords should sit for they would think themselves invested in that perpetuity which some fancy is of right in this parliament still.'[9] Rump major in fact would replace Rump minor—and smell as rank. 'But that which was most convincing was that the army was not yet in a temper for it.' Until it was Monk would 'go his own pace'.

At length (16 March) the Long Parliament dissolved itself, its presbyterian majority having ordered the adoption of the Westminster Confession, the annual reading of the Solemn League and Covenant, the abolition of the Triers and their replacement by central commissioners on a presbyterian basis. This attempt to 'jump the gun' was a foolish move, lacking in reality, and allowing the presbyterians to be charged with an intended domination. Many suspected that they at length only inclined to prepare the way to bring in the King 'lest he should have come in without them'. An interim government was provided by the council of state—and by Monk, who by now was in close touch with the King, sure now that, as it had turned out or as he had intended all along, the coming Convention was bound to bring about a restoration. Through an agent Monk begged the King to forgive him for all that was past, since whatever the appearances, he was ever faithful in his heart 'but . . . was never in a condition to do him Service till this present time'.[10] Charles might be forgiven a cynical smile, but he knew that his future lay in Monk's hands. To forgive was easy. So was it to take advice, which would, he knew, be sound. It soon came. Go, Monk wrote, to Breda, leaving Brussels. (Englishmen still distrusted Spain and it would not be tactful to come direct from Spanish territories.) From Breda he should issue a formal declaration offering a general pardon and indemnity, liberty to tender consciences, a parliamentary land settlement. It was good advice, reinforced by Edward Hyde, who was appalled by the 'unskilful passion and unreasonable warmth' of many royalists. Hyde wrote a masterly draft of a declaration which Charles accepted, aware that its promises were vague enough to leave a wide scope for manœuvre.[11] For example, 'parliament' might or might not mean the coming Convention.

The elections for that ordered on writs issued in the name of the keepers of the liberties of England were fought with some excitement, further whipped up by the escape of Lambert from the Tower. However, he was soon back in residence, having done little but underline the atomising of the republican and swordsmen movements, and providing a welcome excuse for police measures against suspected commonwealthsmen. (Yet Lambert himself, in some ways one of the more attractive men flung up by the revolution, seems to have had a personal if not political following. As late as 12 June 1660 an officer in Scotland was referring to him as 'my Lord' and hoping the King would be kind to him.) At the hustings Independents and presbyterians revived old animosities and by their differences helped to ensure the eventual triumph of the Laudian anglicans, who appeared openly and enthusiastically for the King. Puritans lamented that 'the cavalier spirit breaks out very high and is like to overturn us all'. In Middlesex it was reported that crowds shouted 'no Rumpers, no presbyterians that will put bad conditions on the King'. No Rumper or obvious Independent got a county seat. Sixteen of the Rumpers who had sat in 1659 were returned by boroughs, and of them some had already ostentatiously come over to Monk. Haselrig failed to get in. Regicides, republicans, sectaries, anyone associated with military rule (other than Monk's)—almost all were swept aside. The presbyterian groups who hoped to impose Newport terms on Charles met with similar fate—though there were plenty of presbyterian M.P.s, they were not among the most austere. Yet as late as 23 April, two days before the new parliament was due to assemble, keen royalists were still expressing their doubts. 'It is yet standing water with us', wrote Brian Duppa.[12]

When the House of Commons met so did the House of Lords, initially made up of those peers who had been 'parliamentarian' since 1642. Monk, still hastening slowly, held off others until 27 April when 'the young Lords'[13] (heirs of peers who had died during the Interregnum) came in. Before long the House was meeting as of old, except for bishops, who could not legally make an appearance until the Bishops' Exclusion Act of 1642 was repealed, as it duly was on 30 July 1661. The failure of the presbyterians to secure the exclusion of cavaliers from Lords and Commons led to some despondency in right-wing puritan circles. At last they realised that Monk was on the side of those wanting the King back on the lightest of terms. When the old presbyterians sponsored limiting acts to be presented to the King, Monk pointed out to them that such activity could only lead to delay and that frankly he could not answer for what the army might do if the crisis went on much longer. Divided between 'strict' (irreconcilable) and 'moderate' (or 'reconcilers'), the presbyterians faltered and were ultimately shattered.

On 1 May the conciliatory Declaration of Breda was presented to the House and that same day saw the passage of the famous resolution that according to the fundamental laws—yet again—'the government was and ought to be by King, Lords and Commons'.[14] Restoration was all but a fact. On 8 May Charles Stuart was proclaimed King Charles II. On 25 he landed at Dover amid popular enthusiasm. Making leisurely progress towards London on 26 May he had talks at Canterbury with Edward Hyde and Gilbert Sheldon, anglican State and

Church personified. On 29 May he made his triumphant entry into his capital. Interregnum was over. The wheel had come almost, but not quite, full circle. Not quite, because in history there are no full restorations. The revolution had failed but there were results which no failure, however drastic, could expunge. The civil wars, the Commonwealth, the Protectorate, the anarchy, had all happened. They could not be simply forgotten. The Great Rebellion and its aftermath marked a turning point in English history.

xxviii The Restoration Settlement

After two decades of violence and bold experiment, of expediency and frustrated principles, the old order was back with monarchy in the true line, with a House of Lords soon with its bench of bishops, and a House of Commons of accustomed shape. Almost everything that had been brought in in the 1640s and 1650s seemed likely to blow away in the stiff royalist breeze to which George Monk had opened a window. The reality was, perhaps, rather different. The Great Rebellion willy-nilly had permanent consequences. Like some kind of many-lived Cheshire cat it left a persistent grin behind.

When the elated Charles II had his shabby bags unpacked in Whitehall very little for the future had been decided upon, let alone put into effect. Before a viable settlement could be reached, the King and his immediate advisers, old and new royalists, the Convention parliament, churchmen, indeed the whole political nation needed to take stock. Charles had made fair promises in his Declaration of Breda, but there was no disposition to regard this as much more than a basis for discussion of some of the more urgent problems. Its significance may easily be exaggerated. Monk had prompted it, but how far he or anyone else regarded its principles as binding is an open question. Charles would no doubt have offered more if he had felt it necessary, but now back in England, would have been quite light-hearted about such commitments. Certainly his own position once he was actually at home in residence was far stronger than it had been while he had been impatiently waiting the call to return. It was unthinkable that the nation would acquiesce in the imposition upon him of such heavy conditions that he would think of going away again. The appeal of monarchy had already had a startling demonstration. Charles was aware of it and ready to exploit it. The settlement actually achieved must be seen against the background of it. Thirty years later in the Convention parliament of 1689 members recalled 'the great joy of the king's return' when there was 'nothing settled', and they lamented the consequences.[1]

Many of the positive enactments of the Restoration Settlement were the work of the illicit king-making parliament, the Convention, which lasted until Christmas Eve 1660. The date of dismissal stresses repudiation of the puritan notion of Christmas Day as just another working day. In June the Convention legitimatised itself by an act of the King-in-parliament, but enough doubt remained for the Cavalier parliament (8 May 1661–24 January 1679) to feel the need to re-enact some, though not all of its measures, a nudging reminder of the unsystematic nature of the whole settlement. This very long parliament produced also over the years a mass of quite different legislation, reflecting the notions of its own members, elected after a lively campaign in which puritans of all varieties were trounced by exuberant anglican-royalists, many of them 'lewd young men' with no recollections of Charles I and his government but with a keen sense of recent constraint. By the time their parliament, after many prorogations and bye-elections was given its *congé*, newer political and constitutional issues had arisen, though all of them in some way or other had a connexion with what had happened during the Interregnum and its immediate aftermath. The politics of the whole reign of Charles II (1660–85), often turbid, were stirred by men left over from the revolutionary period, unable, even when willing, quite to shake off the burden of that experience. In a sense the whole period down to the Revolution at least is concerned with a search for a settlement of the difficulties raised by the Great Rebellion.

The Convention, conscious of a rather unattractive public image, worked hard to justify itself to King and nation. Its Speaker, dour Harbottle Grimstone, set the trend by fawning on the young King as 'the glory of England'.[2] Fifty-odd acts were accepted, a few of great importance. If the debates on them seemed flat after the 'ingenious and smart'[3] discourses and open ballotings of the Rota Club at the Turk's Head in New Palace Yard, at least they led to positive action, some of it permanent. The chief failure of the Convention lay in its inability to resolve the intractable problem of religion on the tolerant basis indicated in the Breda declaration. It was left to the Cavalier parliament, its members intimate with confident and well-organised Laudians among the clergy, to create over the years a religious code which exuberantly proscribed puritanism.

But there were other omissions of the Convention that were not seized upon by its successor nor given a twist against the hateful past. Much that might have seemed integral to a genuine balanced settlement was barely glanced at or if taken up dropped without a decision, because at the time it seemed to be in no one's particular interest to press it. In everything the Restoration settlement was expedient, *ad hoc*, mundane, practical.

Like every other Stuart parliament the 1660 Convention found it had time, even in the thick of calling back a king and pacifying a kingdom, to turn aside from the big issues. Routine and minor measures, some of them really trivial, demanded attention and could even quicken excitement. Private acts arranged for the return of confiscated estates of great royalist magnates like Ormonde. Minor acts restored commissions of sewers and confirmed the 1652 Rump ordinance against growing tobacco in England. This latter measure is illuminating of the desire to enhance the economic viability of the colonies. It shews, too, there was no objection to continuity with rebellious activity when continuity paid.

To all this miscellaneous legislation the royal assent was given at odd intervals, thus clinching an earlier advance in parliament's status. Before the Long Parliament the assent was uttered to batches of measures and was taken to mark the end of a session. The newer arrangement suggested that parliament would not much longer be an occasional engine of government called for specific and limited purposes, quickly 'kicked out'[4] (the phrase is a contemporary one) when it had served its turn. Changes of substance lie concealed in modifications of procedure.

The major achievements of the Convention took in a new Navigation Act, akin to that of 1651, pursuing the same end of national self-sufficiency and throwing off the same side-effect—war with the Dutch, who courted, so far with more response, the same coy mistress, trade. Variously modified and extended the new act tightened the English grip on the plantations and gave a more permanent shape to a colonial policy rough-hewn in the 1650s. It would encourage a diversification of the home economy and spur a commercial enterprise that would within a century set off the first tottering steps of 'the Industrial Revolution'. But there was little concern for the remote future. There were too many problems in the immediate present. Notable among these was 'the general pardon and oblivion' already promised to bring the age of rebellion to a definite close. The act was passed on 29 August 1660, on the eve of the summer recess, letting the exhausted members go home to their 'countries' conscious of having been at once generous and exemplary in their treatment of a few of the chief instruments of the destruction of the monarchy. Most offences committed in 'the late unnatural and intestine wars' could now be formally forgiven, if not forgotten. Some named persons, chiefly regicides, were shut off from grace, to be taken up where found and tried for the highest of treasons. Some other less egregious incendiaries were to be excluded from office for life.[5] There was only the roughest of logic, one might say, of justice, in it at all. The Convention itself, ostentatious in its newborn loyalty, was rather more eager to spill blood than Monk, who had sensibly proposed to the King in May that only about a half-dozen really spectacular exceptions should be made from the parliamentary indemnity offered at Breda. He had grasped that a good part of the failure of the 1650s had lain in the reluctance of the various régimes to offer a genuine and all-embracing amnesty. Revenge is sweet but risky. Charles saw the point. Ten years before in Scotland he had been ready to favour men who had spat in his parents' faces. It had seemed inescapable then. It seemed policy now. It was not that Charles was a warmly forgiving or forgetful man. In fact, when circumstances allowed it, he could be cold and vengeful, as his treatment of Sir Henry Vane, Jnr, would soon show.[6]

Some of the hunted victims—including Ludlow, Hewson, Whalley and Goffe—got clean away to the continent or the plantations. A few gave themselves up. Others were captured. In October 1660 those in custody were brought before a grand jury which did not hesitate to find true bills against them. Then and at the later trials at the Old Bailey a few cringed, but others put on dignity and courage, scorning to admit to mere malice in what they had done a dozen years before. Some were even disposed to argue difficult constitutional points. Adrian Scroop tactlessly recognised on the Bench 'a great many faces that were misled as well as' himself.[7] One of the judges was rebuked by Thomas Carew for the impropriety of offering evidence himself.[8] Denied counsel, as was customary in treason cases, they struggled to explain the meaning of their acts, claiming justification by the law of the land, the law of nature and the dispensation of God. From the Bench, Col. John Birch, a former Long-parliament man, dryly commented that in nomine domini was 'an old saying . . . in which all mischiefs have been done'. He had no inkling, presumably, of his own future in active 'opposition' when he would claim that, after all, in the civil war he may have been on 'the right side'.[9]

Hugh Peters, no regicide, but 'a principal actor' in Charles I's martyrdom, 'a trumpeter of war, of treason and sedition',[10] defended himself with characteristic loquacity, strenuously affirming that in all he had done he had had a care for 'sound religion, learning, the laws and the poor'.[11] On the first three he was regarded as hypocritical; the last seemed irrelevant. Sure, then, of his doom, he ended with a ringing appeal to that patriotic tradition, never more gladly honoured than in the Great Rebellion, of the unique role of an elect English nation. 'God', he asserted, 'God, hath a regard to the people of England.'[12] For him as for Thomas Scott, the republican, the cause engaged in 'with God's blessing' was still one 'not to be repented of'.[13] This superb confidence would carry them through the appalling destruction that lay concealed in the flat syllables 'to be hanged, drawn and quartered'. Long after the revolutionary era had ended, something of that spirit survived, sometimes mere chauvinism, but often an urge to do great things while wearing a special badge of favour.

These trials and executions of 1660 did not quite exhaust the vengeance of the Restoration. Sir Henry Vane and John Lambert were neither of them actual regicides, but they had been too conspicuous to slip through the net. In 1662, in a sort of irrelevant post-script, they were tried, separately but simultaneously. Both Houses of parliament asked the King that whatever the verdict their lives might be spared. Charles agreed. Lambert showed a supineness that suggests his entire constitution had been shattered by the *débâcle* of 1659–1660 and the bewildering triumph of men whom he must have estimated as of inferior genius. He was sentenced to perpetual exile in faraway Guernsey. There he died in 1683, a feeble ghost of the dynamic personality of the 1650s, almost, but perhaps never quite, forgotten by men who had frightened themselves from sleep at the prospect of having him as 'single person'.

In contrast Vane was incisive, speaking up with copious learning for a clear-cut parliamentary sovereignty. His range of reference to history, law and political theory was astonishing. But it was deployed to no purpose. Like Lilburne he was to learn that Magna Carta was a broken reed, really decrepit. Charles then revealed his was a word no man might rely on. By acknowledging 'no power in England but a parliament' Vane had shewn he was 'too dangerous to let live'.[14] His last defiant words on Tower Hill in June 1662 were drowned in a roll of drums. With all his faults, Vane, who had exasperated equally Charles I, Cromwell and Charles II, was a man who had fumbled at the lock of greatness. He lived and died aware not only of his own interests and of those 'that are in their graves already but of posterity in time to come . . .'.[15] Long before he went to his death some graves had been rifled and the pitiful relics of Cromwell and Bradshaw, even those of Pym and Blake, had been dragged out and obscenely exhibited. There was only a smear of blood at the Restoration, but a whole streak of meanness.

For many former rebels parading their support of the new monarchy there were smiles and favours, even for one, Richard Ingoldsby, who, though spattered by royal blood, won forgiveness by his capture of

Lambert in April 1660, thereby scotching the only likely leader of a counter-*coup*. Whatever their past misdeeds such men could in their new guise help to consolidate the nascent order, smoothing the way to normality. So the prime mover of the Restoration, General George Monk, became Duke of Albemarle, Captain-General of the Forces, later on, an admiral, Master of the Horse, and, briefly, an absentee Lord Lieutenant of Ireland—resounding triumphs for Mrs Monk, that real-life Mrs Proudie. Strangely the subtle political intuition that Monk had attentively acted on over 20 years, and never more effectively than in the last months in which he wafted a king back to his kingdom, was rarely called into service afterwards. He showed skill, though hardly brilliance, as a commander and naval tactician in the Dutch war, and was expert in maintaining public order in what might have been an ugly situation after the Great Fire of London. But after 1660 he was never really close to the makers of policy. This lack of drive may point to a deterioration, but looks more like good sense. After all in 1660 he had by 'the best stratagem that is extant in History' made a king[16]—to have attempted more, especially after Charles had flashed a warning light by rejecting much of his advice almost as soon as he got back, might have led the great man to overshoot himself. He had provided a model of how to set about restoring a king. It was up to Charles II himself to take it from there. George Monk died in 1670, at home, upright and soldierly in his straight chair. Charles gave him a spanking State funeral. It was Clarendon, the man who welcomed political power in the years just after the Restoration, a politician *par excellence*, who died in exile, unwanted, unsung.

Edward Montague was another who had served the Protector faithfully. But in 1659, turned clandestine royalist, he got on with purging the fleet and found that he had brought it into line with Monk's requirements. In May 1660 he used it with perfect confidence to bring Charles Stuart to Dover. Payment was the Earldom of Sandwich and continued office. Another Montagu, Edward, Earl of Manchester, in spite of calling in the last hours of the Long parliament for terms similar to those of the Uxbridge or Newport 'treaties', became Chamberlain of the Household. Anthony Ashley Cooper had a barony and in 1661 the Chancellorship of the Exchequer. The Restoration marks only one more turn in his extraordinarily devious career. From it, as the first Earl of Shaftesbury, he went on to able government service and ultimately the bold opposition that brought England to the brink of another civil war and himself to flight and death in ignominy. His course, though flecked with strange accidents, seems to bear ineradicable traces of the hectic political apprenticeship he had served in the

1650s. The ruthless old man embraced the brilliant, sneering young one. Less imaginative, combining irascibility with a sure instinct for self-preservation, George Downing, on the basis of what passed for diplomatic skill acquired under the Protectorate, became Ambassador to the United Provinces. His impact upon affairs derived from his confident administrative ability and a grasp of economic realities that helped to bring on the Second Dutch War. (Bulstrode Whitelocke, who had negotiated Cromwell's *rapprochement* with Sweden, in many ways a much more worthy man, but lacking Downing's drive, failed to make the grade with Charles II, though he tried desperately hard.) Sir George Booth and Denzil Holles, who had changed coats long before Downing, each won a barony in the Coronation honours list (a fascinating one). But neither was ever much caught up with the Court and in the 1670s both were involved in some very dark political manœuvres with 'presbyterians' and others ominously labelled 'commonwealthsmen'.

Favour, however brief, to men of this sort reveals the uncavalierlike nature of 1660. Staunch royalists might glory in 'the miraculous manner ... past all human policy' in which their Charles came in again. But they knew that 'the Lord's doing' had as its instruments 'that very army which had rebelled' against the crown.[17] No doubt 'the vast majority'[18] of Englishmen wanted *a* restoration to happen. But *the* Restoration had come from a shift in the position of a comparatively few men. It was a kind of revolution and revolutions are not made by mere revulsion. What was wanted was leadership coupled with the initiative to exploit the inabilities of successive brief régimes to cope after 'the vital incident'[19] of the demise of Oliver Cromwell. Monk and the associates he attracted provided most of what was necessary. The part played by royalists of the old school was more negative. But, even so, it called for a reward. Charles was intelligent, and perhaps grateful, enough to see that he must do something substantial for men like Edward Hyde and Edward Nicholas, who had worked tirelessly for him in exile and helped keep alive a faltering cause. Moreover, by it he could divide his favours and avoid putting himself completely into the hands of any one party. This policy was repeated 30 years later by his nephew William of Orange when another Convention made him King of England.

So Hyde became Chancellor and Earl of Clarendon, a fitting reward for his loyal past and possibly capable future. But he began to bore Charles even more than when in exile and later, becoming expendable, went, unable to emulate his sovereign, travelling again. (We owe his illuminating *History of the Great Rebellion* to this reluctant retirement.)

Nicholas, older and more circumspect, became with Edward Morrice, an influential kinsman of Monk, a secretary of state. Ormonde, the Lord Steward, soon took over and transformed Monk's titular Irish Lieutenancy. Buckingham, bounding up again after his distasteful tergiversations in the sixteen-fifties, became gentleman of the bed-chamber and went on with that headlong career that gave him and a few others a lot of fun, but little solid profit. It has been dryly said that 'even Restoration England was not educated up to his standards of excess and indecency'.[20] Employment was found for other outstanding royalists, both of the respectable and the erratic sort, but for many, equally worthy, at least in their own eyes, of compensation, the Restoration was a bitter disappointment. Charles had more friends than jobs. Royalist distress did not press too heavily on the King's conscience, though if it were not otherwise inconvenient he was ready to throw out a sinecure here, a title there. So Sir Sackville Crowe, his father's Ambassador to Turkey and much else beside, who had spent a good part of the Interregnum in the Tower, more on his own account than for any extravagance in his loyalty, got the management of the revived tapestry works at Mortlake. His gratitude was not unbounded and he asked for more, joining the ranks of aggrieved men who, shocked to find themselves more royalist than their King, continued to petition for redress and advancement. Those who got themselves returned as parliament-men or chosen as J.P.s could express their disappointment by passing and executing laws against dissenters, hitting out through them at old enemies apparently stuck now securely in the bosom of the King. In national politics a period of disenchantment set in when the honeymoon atmosphere of 1660 was dispelled and the more difficult job of living together began. New problems, new situations, new personalities, but also old ones left over from the Interregnum, would make the reign of Charles II one of lively, soon tense and bitter, political strife between King and shifting segments of the political nation.

The monarchy of 1660 was not that of 1603 or 1640 or 1642, though legally it was more the last than any other. All the remedial legislation of the Long parliament down to the spring of 1642 had received Charles I's formal if grudging assent. It was therefore of force. Some of if would be modified and some of the illegal ordinances of the various governments since 1642 would be re-enacted in whole or in part. But superficially the crown might be held to take off from the months just before the overheated political situation had exploded into civil war. Certain royal losses are patent—ship money, industrial monopolies, Star Chamber, high commission, the council of the North. But much remained intact or in potential. War had started in dispute over control of the armed forces. 1660 settled it in favour of the crown. The Militia Ordinance of 1642 was buried. Permanent forces, such as they were, and few wanted them bigger, were in the hands of the crown, so long as it could pay for them.[21] The swollen protectoral regiments were quickly demobilised, with their arrears, about which there had been so much fuss, settled at last by a series of urgent monthly assessments, significantly on Commonwealth models. Slipping into civilian obscurity was eased by allowing the veterans to take up trades without normal apprenticeship. (This turned out to be another step in the long process of bringing industrial regulation into desuetude.) But some soldiers had no homes to go to or had acquired a taste for London life and political excitement. The Poor Law Amendment Act of 1662, amplifying and stiffening the loose Elizabethan code, without in the event much practical effect, was in part designed to harry wandering discharged Ironsides. In an imperfectly-policed society rogues and vagabonds with a military background looked fearsome and sometimes acted that way. A radical tradition survived the Restoration; old soldiers, reluctantly fading away, were part of it.

A few regiments, notably General Monk's Coldstream Guards, formed a regular cadre, a new departure. They had already been 'brainwashed'. But hostility to a standing army in the hands of a junto passed naturally to one employed by a King. Army discipline was allowed to stagger along an uncertain legal track until the Revolution established it by statute, and then only on an initial niggardly emergency basis. Apart from putting liberties and protestanism in peril—James II's regiments were considered to be tainted with popery—an army cost too much. The crown could hardly afford one out of ordinary revenues—the taxpayers would not if they could help it provide more. Things were different with the navy. It could never be the same threat as a land-based force. Defender of the island in peace and war, it could also contribute to economic advancement at the expense of trading rivals. So from 1661 naval discipline had a statutory footing. The post-Restoration period became creative in naval administration. The improvement is symbolised in the career of that superb civil servant, Samuel Pepys. More specialisation, more and better ships, even sometimes superior commanders, all hinted at a future when England really would rule the waves. Yet these were gains rooted in the Interregnum. Pepys had served with Edward Montague before 1660.

Sole command of the local militia was conceded to the crown by an act of 1661 specifically denying parliament's competence to intervene. But in fact within a couple of years these unimpressive forces were reorganised by act of parliament and thereby at least an indirect parliamentary participation in their exercise was assured. If the men were called out for any length of time the King would need parliamentary supply to keep them in the field. Their stultifying local patriotism was impugned but hardly disturbed by the legal requirement to serve any-where in the kingdom in time of rebellion. Their traditional incompe-tence was to be overcome by regular drilling and discipline. So it was hoped. But the militia remained little more than a local tool of the magnates and from a military point of view James II was indisputably right to prefer (after the experience of Monmouth's invasion) a regular force. The trained bands were valued because they could be an elec-toral force, often used for private and 'opposition' political ends—a point tacitly recognised by James II in his purging of the ranks of the Lords-Lieutenant and their deputies as part of his campaign for a pliant parliament.

Obviously the major limitations on the effective independence of royal control of armed force grew out of financial weakness. The same drawback pulled in varying strengths at other aspects of government. The King was sole head of the executive, no question of that, with power to conduct foreign policy in all its detail—appointment of ambassadors, negotiation and ratification of treaties or whatever. Charles II claimed as much as Charles I, James I or even Elizabeth I. But in practice there were clogs upon his actions, while sometimes he found it convenient to repudiate his own responsibility, preferring heaven-sent scapegoats like Clarendon. What was most significant about the Secret Treaty of Dover (1670) was not the King's capacity to negotiate upon those terms—he never implemented them, anyway—but the fact that the treaty was, and had to be, kept a secret from his subjects. It has been suggested, often with warmth, that Charles II was the ablest of the Stuarts. Perhaps he was. It is hardly high praise. If the implication is that he was very astute, his foreign policy would scarcely support it. There is little evidence that he had a concept of an independent English policy designed to further genuine national in-terests, much less the capacity to realise it. Even if he were meanly treated in the matter of revenue—the point is arguable—little can be put forward to prove that want of money was at the heart of his lack of motivation. The last four years of his reign, ostensibly the years of triumph after the years of peril, did not produce a reasoned approach to the European situation. Taking the reign as a whole it may be said that Charles II was hamstrung as much by his own deficiencies as by the recklessness of English politicians in opposition.

Domestic administration was once again, by tradition, the crown's monopoly. Appointments to the Privy Council and the Household, to

State offices, the Church, the bench and a whole host of others were for the King to fill. True, some offices had acquired in practice the nature of freeholds, not readily withdrawable, and often sold profitably on reversion by their possessors. (The 'system' was justified by the lowness of official salaries and nominal fees.) The Interregnum, it was soon seen, had done little to check this—a hint that the permanent social revolutionary aspects of the period can be exaggerated. Clearly there was, at best, a blurred regard for disinterested public service. But all this points, too, to a limitation on the freedom of royal choice, even if a vast area of patronage remained. Moreover, as we have seen, at the beginning of the reign Charles had to allocate offices, whatever his personal inclinations may have been, to men of substance—political or whatever—among old and new royalists. There were those whom it would be reckless to offend, others whose skill or experience he must tap. Ministers had to have some capacity for their offices—a desideratum that would harden to necessity as government and services such as the navy, army and diplomatic corps became more specialised. The reign would also see the emergence of men who might be called professional politicians, who by their parliamentary skill thrust themselves into office, or made themselves nuisances, even dangers, by their obstructionism. The Rebellion had been an expensive, rough but very effective political education. It had ripped the veil from mysteries of State. Men out of office might know as much as the King and his ministers about how to devise a policy and much more about how to thwart one. Impeachment was revived again. It was still the bluntest of weapons, but bludgeons could wound as surely as daggers, especially when, as in the case of Clarendon, the King himself connived at their use. The royal pardon blocked the destruction of Danby (1678-9) but only at the cost of raising questions which would be answered negatively for the crown and for the prerogative in the Revolution settlement. Fused with that of the Rebellion era, the experience of this reign would argue for some more positive form of ministerial responsibility, though it would be a long time coming.

The traditional control by the crown of the executive was facilitated by 'influence'. Royal pressure, applied or relaxed, could in those areas where the state was an employer of labour or consumer of goods and services, as for instance in dockyard towns, be very formative of the right kind of opinion. Sometimes it might be offset or supplemented by the concurrent influence of magnates, depending upon whether they were 'in' or 'out'. At all times it would benefit from deployment with tact or imagination. The unsinkable Earl of Sunderland survived all vicissitudes by his sensitive talents in this field. He provided an alarmingly amenable first parliament for James II and might, if let alone, have done the same for his second—the parliament that never was. Grants of honour could help, too, but, again, needed skilled handling lest the hopeful but denied were mortally offended and those already possessed of dignities felt slighted by their dilution. Besides some men lacked proper gratitude. Shaftesbury and Delamere are examples.

In legislation the King was a *sine qua non*. Apart from an unlimited right and large opportunity to initiate bills, he could accept or reject whatever passed the two Houses of parliament—his veto was intact and, unlike the Protector's, absolute. But it was a somewhat awkward weapon, best held in reserve. Ultimate deterrents are as dangerous to the user as to the victim. If both Houses were really set on a bill, simple rejection might provoke rather than avert a crisis. Charles was quick to see this. By timely interventions, direct or managed, he might head off an unwelcome measure. On two occasions at least bills ready for the royal assent went mysteriously astray. Like his father and the late Protector, Charles II resorted to abrupt prorogations and, ultimately, dissolutions. These could be effective, especially if the difficulties that demanded them could quickly be dispersed by other than parliamentary means. But this was not always possible and new sessions, even new parliaments, could have uncomfortably long memories. To be able to go without parliament long called for a nice relationship of capacity and luck. Charles had as much of the latter as of the former when between 1681 and 1685 he enjoyed 'a personal rule'. Customs duties combined with Tory fervour were a joyous combination that could not be counted upon for ever.

There remained two vaguely-recognised prerogative powers that were caught up in legislation: the power to dispense with laws and the power to suspend them. Distinction between the two was not always clear. Broadly, dispensation allows a relaxation of a particular legal penalty in the case of a particular individual or group, the law remaining otherwise of force. Suspension involves the relaxation for a period of the entire implementation of a law or laws. Obviously in each claim there is something akin to law-making since relaxation is in effect to say that the law is now such-and-such. Over the validity of the claims there was room for dispute, though the dispensing power had been used with general approval in a variety of fields, chiefly economic, in the last couple of centuries. Suspension, inevitably of wider implication, was more contentious. The occasional practice under the first two Stuarts of not pressing the recusancy laws did not provide a sure precedent. Charles II's speedy withdrawal of his Declaration of Indulgence (1672) suspending formally the penal religious laws—a very

268

different thing—did the claim substantial damage. This surrender doomed James II's attempts to impose toleration by prerogative. It is ironical that it was grants of freedom that flung these prerogative powers into the grip of parliament. The Revolution did not destroy them, for such emergency valves are necessary to any serious government, but ensured their use in a parliamentary way. A lesson had been learned from the destructive period of the Interregnum. Slowly it came to be seen by the severest critics that the powers of the executive were not things evil through and through, but potential benefits to the political community—if lodged securely in the right hands. Effective transfer was better than destruction. This was perhaps the prime lesson of all the constitutional warfare of the Stuart era.

The restored monarchy had no need to force recognition of legal freedom to expend its revenues as it thought fit. But resources were inelastic, and apart from the fixed income laid down in the ramshackle Restoration financial share-out, supplemented now and then by special grants and a few new taxes, such as the imaginative Hearth Money, the King found himself, like the Interregnum rulers, scrabbling for windfalls. There were some. Dunkirk, the expensive dividend of Cromwell's abandoned continental imperialism, was sold to Louis XIV in 1662 for five million *livres*. It was useful capital, but was soon spent on subsidies to Portugal, regrettably, perhaps, an express part of the agreement, and on non-recurrent charges for the navy and the royal household. Dunkirk could only be sold once. Louis would be good for a subsidy from time to time, but he was never a lavish provider and unkindly expected a return on his outlay. Routine regular gifts irrespective of results were never his way. Besides, Charles glimpsed that courting the smiles of the Sun King might be as tedious as dependence on parliament.

' Clumsiness and wastefulness'[22] were certainly among the characteristics of Restoration financial administration, as they had been of Interregnum government. It was bound to be so. No really reliable methods had been hit upon to meet the ever-expanding requirements of the State. Yet something had been attempted in the decades of rebellion and a few salutary lessons well learned. In 1643 farming of the Customs had been ended. It was unwisely revived in 1662 but abandoned for good in 1671, the new experience of drawbacks confirming the old. The excise was retained at the Restoration, in *lieu* of fiscal feudalism and contentious charges like ship money. It has remained basic to British finances and John Pym's most enduring monument. After 1683 collection was taken from the farmers and given to State officials, incidentally widening the scope of royal patronage, but also reaching out towards a national financial system.

Much more might be said of incomings and outgoings under Charles II. What is important here is to stress that the Interregnum had just about clinched the inability of the crown as executive to live of its own. Moreover, there were no further attempts to revive obsolescent claims of the type that had incensed the Long Parliament. Charles made one disastrous experiment—if it could be called that—in the Stop of the Exchequer (1671) but otherwise relied upon his fully recognised grants. Benevolences, malevolences, forced loans and free gifts were matters of fading memory. There were no Bates or Vassals or Conys.

The ecclesiastical supremacy, that had brought the crown episcopal support and puritan criticism of it, remained royal. In practice it was largely exercised with parliament. The relation of the Church of England to the monarchy, though close, was now somewhat novel and ambivalent. The Church settlement, worked out in the Cavalier parliament, was not all that the King desired, as his Indulgences indicated. Churchmen, many happily restored to old livings or translated to better ones, preached up divine hereditary right and non-resistance, the trite shibboleths of an age that thanked the Lord for a new young King again. At such a time to reiterate that it cannot be lawful on any account whatever to resist the established power of kings was the easiest thing in the world. Yet limits would be found to patience and loyalty when two successive anointed monarchs, clandestine or open catholics, sought to break the monopoly of the Church by law established in favour of 'phanaticks' and papists. Charles I cast his cloak around the bishops impeached in 1641; James II charged seven bishops, one of them an exceptionally timorous Archbishop of Canterbury, with seditious libel upon his government, sounding thereby, he claimed, the trumpet, raising the standard of rebellion. Was it for this that Charles I had died a martyr for the Church of England? Well might *A New Test of the Church of England's Loyalty*, put out by Daniel Defoe in 1702, when interpretations of the Rebellion were part of contemporary political party propaganda, mock that 'when the Trial came, proving Stubborn, Refractory, *Liberty-Mongers*, even as bad as the worst Whig or Phanatick of them all', rising above principles, they asserted '*Nemo me impune lacessit*', like 'the men of Forty-one'. 'King *Charles* (I) lost his Life, because he did not run away; and his Son, King *James*, sav'd his Life, because he did run away.'[23] There were non-jurings, and heart-searchings, and breast-beatings, but the argument is irrefutable. Tories and high-flying anglicans might openly regret the Revolution of 1688 and violently abuse the Great Rebellion, but in the final analysis they knew they were beneficiaries of both.

Part of the kaleidoscopic pattern made up of the strengths and weaknesses of the restored monarchy is to be found in the difficult personality of the King himself, which has puzzled and misled contemporaries and historians. At 30 Charles was an old young man, stained by unfortunate experiences beyond the common lot of princes. His hard life had bred in him a cynicism that fused readily with the natural coldness of his Stuart temperament. He had schooled himself to hide his true feeling, thinking fast behind a careless smile. His affability was a veneer which could crack and offer momentary revelations of the man within, as in his treatment of Vane and Russell. In 1660 he sensed the hunger for a glamorous but human-like monarchy and responded with calculated alacrity. It is doubtful if he were very intelligent, but he was certainly acute enough to work at putting over the rather obvious lines he wrote for himself. He was a nimble showman and the performance with slight variations, and allowing for off days, was good for a long run. But to win continuing applause called for more than mannered gestures. Charles II kept his throne by making concessions and withdrawals. Outward obstinacy was not among his few principles, if he had any at all. It all worked well, up to a point. After the *débâcle* of Shaftesbury's knavish tricks, Charles handed on to his rigid brother what seemed to be a monarchy stronger than he had got himself in 1660. For a moment the illusion was completely convincing. In fact the short headlong reign of James II made it certain that some of the things Charles had done with general acceptance would not be possible again, nor would some doubtful precedents be decided in favour of prerogative. Significantly the Bill of Rights of the Glorious Revolution commented on Charles II as well as James II. In the debates on it in the Convention Parliament there were some nostalgic references to 'the good old cause'.[24] Perhaps it was a mistake for loyal anglicans to want a special service and sermons on 30 January of every year. The memories and prejudices that significant date awoke were very mixed indeed.

Monarchy did not ride back in 1660 unaccompanied. The famous resolution of 1 May plumping for traditional forms of government asserted flatly that by 'the ancient and fundamental laws'[25] government was by Lords and Commons as well as by a King. Parliament, indeed, was restored before the King was and it was the two Houses, not the god of battles, that called him in. Very quickly they had taken on their old form, the Lords without exclusions (apart from bishops till 1661), the Commons with the old constituencies and jumbled franchises, without representation of Scotland and Ireland. The reforms of the Rebellion perished like premature spring. But the old forms concealed some changes of substance. Parliament ostentatiously abandoned the executive and administrative functions grasped under John Pym. No more Committees met at Goldsmiths' Hall or in the counties. But post-war parliaments, in which sat many of the civil war generation, did not drop their interest in these matters. Moreover, the institution had such prestige that the personal government of 1681–5 looked unnatural almost at once. Nothing quite like it would ever happen again. When men in 1688 called for a free parliament to untie the knot of James II's reign they felt themselves in tune with the inevitable.

The House of Lords in this period calls for investigation. Eleven years before it had been abolished as found 'by experience' useless and —the addition is significant—dangerous. Within a few years something like it was adumbrated as helpful. There had been a new experience. As we have seen the old peers boycotted Oliver's 'other House'. Many preferred to lie low in wait, confident that their order had a future. Some were active royalist leaders, earning prestige; others had a direct impact on Protectorate government. Peers played a big part in the Restoration and the healing and settling by the Convention and its successor. The settlement is signed with their interests. They were active in land questions and peers on the whole did better out of the final arrangements than any other grouping, not excluding the King, who by the 1670s had run through most of his restored estates. Individual peers, blessed again, if they had ever lost it, with provincial influence and drawing on financial credits denied to lesser though perhaps worthier men, were able (as Newcastle did) to get special acts of parliament to bring back their estates. Some went on to become energetic and sharply improving landlords. So far from dissipating their holdings such men were more often able to co-ordinate and extend them. With their acres went the wealth and social, political and religious influence that marked a society based still on land-ownership. Throughout the new reign King and Commons were aware of the weight of a dynamic upper House which vindicated some of its privileges and even, as in the case of *Skinner* v. *The East India Company*, tried to extend them. Though the Peers made losses in the financial sphere to the broadly representative lower Chamber they refused to be ignored. It was a segment of the Lords which ushered in the Revolution of 1688, most aristocratic of *coups d'état*, striking witness to a revival after the disasters of an Interregnum which ought to have been a shattering blow to both House and order. Thereafter they had a long run. If the eighteenth century was the age of the nobility in Europe, so to a great extent was it in England. Only in the mid-twentieth century has it become *de rigueur* for a prime minister to sit in the Commons. In the early nineteen-sixties, at a time of great international strain, a foreign minister managed to hold on to office, if not to restore the tottering globe, from the upper chamber.

Apart from their loosely co-ordinate legislative and judicial authority, the peers had vast electoral influence as land-owners and Lords-Lieutenant—a sought-after office still exclusive in normal times to the greater magnates. Many members of the Commons were in effect clients of individual peers, a fact which facilitated agreement between the two Houses and sweetened the atmosphere of free conferences between them. If the mixed government that emerged from the rough and tumble of seventeenth-century constitutional conflict was one of a balance between King, Lords and Commons, the Lords were perhaps the pivot. Yet when that is said, the fact remains that in politics the Commons had seized the initiative and, however relaxed their grip, would not let it go. A bitter royal quarrel with the Lords would hardly provoke a crisis unbreakable except by dissolution. One with the Commons would. Purging corporations to assure the return of well-affected burgesses reflected the reality that a policy was half-way home when commanding a majority in the lower House. Clarendon went into the political wilderness for refusing to recognise, old parliament-man that he had been, the strength of the Commons. Danby's achievement lay in his own acceptance of it and his capacity—temporary but intense—to do something about it. (Unlike Clarendon he had served in a post-restoration House of Commons.) The activity, already referred to, of Sunderland under James II is the sharpest confirmation of all of the need to manage the lower House. The bitter experiences of Charles I and Cromwell were plangent warnings to their successors.

The Restoration perforce accepted the legislative sovereignty of the King-in-parliament. The crown *solus* would still put out its proclamations but they would have to take their chances of enforcement in the law courts. Common law judges, venal or genuinely royalist in sentiment, might not always be relied upon to do the right thing—and within half a century they were to hold on the practically independent tenure of *quam diu se bene gesserint*. Parliamentary initiative in major public legislation was more common than in 1640—as the Clarendon Code, the Test Acts and Habeas Corpus Act show. The veto, as we have seen, was subject to a law of diminishing returns. Royal dispensation and suspending had marvellous possibilities but boldness in their use was to beckon disaster. From the Interregnum certainly statute had no fellow, and before long even the laws of God and Nature were not worth a mention in relation to it. Whatever happened to statute in the reign of Henry VIII, by the end of the Stuart era its ascendancy was assured. James II brought in toleration by prerogative, but what he really wanted was to make it stick by statute. Ironically, perhaps it was law-making by ordinance during the Great Rebellion that was the final argument for the ascendancy of statute.

Taxation was also firmly set in the parliamentary domain. The financial settlement of the Restoration was a statutory one. The financial claims of 'thorough', some of which had a very respectable pedigree, had perished. Other ancient rights—such as the feudal tenures—were not revived. Their passing, lamented chiefly by the middlemen who had quietly shared proceeds with the crown, was underlined by the permanence of much of the financial experimentation of the Rebellion. The last old style subsidy was collected in 1663. Taxation was directed more at 'the meaner sort of people' through the excise. The bulk of royal income was derived from indirect taxation, voted by a landed parliament. Indirectly parliament would reach out to the control of expenditure, a gradual process to which the Inter-regnum, like the Restoration and Revolution, made its own peculiar contribution. Parliament through its committees had handled enormous sums of money with considerable success. The awareness of capacity here mingled with the urge to comment on other people's handling to produce the kind of approach which would ensure a proper public accountability, and ultimately its own indispensability.

The year 1660 saw the triumph of the common law, as suggested earlier, perhaps, not all gain. Prerogative justice, twisted by fiscal needs and strained by a vague absolutism, had still had a few possibilities of social justice and its simpler processes, better rules of evidence and so on, might in different circumstances have appealed to thoughtful men. But the eclipse of the Court of Star Chamber and other 'bright rays' was a final one. The independence of the traditional courts of law should not be exaggerated. Judges were still royal nominees holding under pleasure, liable to be raised or ruined for political or even frivolous reasons. Yet anxiety not to offend a bountiful sovereign could be accompanied by a genuine belief that the law as it then stood favoured prerogative. There was nothing amiss, they felt, indeed, the opposite, in having some 'consideration' for the government. For men of this stamp—they seem to have included the much-maligned but still odious George Jeffreys—the lesson of the Great Rebellion was the necessity of maintaining independent royal authority backed by a law sensitive to the rights as well as the responsibilities of paternal monarchy. This possibly objective concept, though, could be misunderstood and the reign of Charles II like that of his father heard loud cries for putting judicial appointments on a more permanent independent and presumably more impartial basis. At last by the Act of Settlement of 1701 judges held during good behaviour and were given substantial salaries to head off some not uncommon temptations. The avowed intention and partial practice of the Commonwealth period was thereby attained. Moreover, in the later seventeenth century a few of the legal reforms of the Rebellion were re-enacted and it is the considered judgment of the historian of Charles II that 'the legislation of Charles II owes a substantial debt to the preceding age'.[26] Though surviving Cromwellian judges were formally dismissed, half of them, including the universally revered Sir Matthew Hale, were reinstated at once. Judicial processes already under way were continued and no verdicts delivered since 1642 were voided, apart from those of the much deplored special high courts. Right of appeal was, however, preserved except, significantly, in the matter of land sales, a limitation essential if that hard question were to be finally buried. The Restoration legal settlement was a pragmatic one, then. The footing established in 1660 gave scope for argument and rapid development. It allowed both for the Popish Plot trials of the 1670s and those of the royalist reaction from 1681 to 1688.

It has been hinted already that of all the problems of 1660 that of the land was the most difficult to contemplate, let alone resolve. Men felt strongly about property; for most of it was their strongest interest, the thing which breathed life into all the rest. Invasion of it, actual or threatened, by kings, parliaments, military caucuses, religious and social radicals, had helped to produce the changing alignments of the revolutionary period. During those decades estates had been taken over, dispersed, resold, re-allocated. Whatever was done about them now was bound to upset someone. Many of those with grasping hands sat in the Convention or had contacts there. Alarmed by revived Leveller notions, angered by assaults that made special property rights like tithes 'issues of blood', disturbed by uncertainty about their own and their tenants' titles, they were ready to bring in the King again as a bulwark of general order, but they intended to salvage what they could of their own gains. Any proposal that meant a blanket return to the *status quo ante bellum* was likely to meet resistance. Realistic royalist agents had long seen the estates question as 'the only remora' to the return of monarchy. But the old royalists were very vocal, understandably reluctant to accept an appraisal of the situation that would play down the sacrifices they had made, or fancied they had made. Outnumbered in the Convention, they could expect to do better in any succeeding 'free' and normal parliament. If the settlement went too much out of line with them, they might try to revise it. This would

275

be a disaster and might re-open every wound before healing had advanced. This anxiety explains the emphasis given to legalising the Convention and the prominence given to the land question in the Declaration of Breda. Everything must be done soon in a parliamentary way so that 'the men concerned' might feel 'a just satisfaction'.[27] Yet as it happened even this most ticklish of issues was not tackled in a single well-thought out, co-ordinated measure. The Convention did bring in a bill but it seems to have been a little too tender of existing holders and perished in committee. Two clauses of acts primarily designed for other matters did do something positive. The Act of Indemnity and the act confirming judicial proceedings robbed purchasers of crown and ecclesiastical lands of any title, but they were evasive about other royalist properties. Estates directly confiscated were to be restored, but those sold privately—the bulk, that is—to pay composition fines, or to pay punitive taxation or to raise funds for the crown, were not covered unless the original owners could establish clear legal irregularities in the transfers. In practice, even some of those whose lands had been confiscated might only get them back by appeal to the courts or to the Lords, and they were not always successful in obtaining everything. Lesser men made a great fuss about the unfairness of their treatment. The State Papers are strewn with petitions for redress from discontented 'King's friends'. In many instances the moans had some justification, but, in fact, by no means all the royalists had been permanently replaced by new men. Many were quietly enjoying their old estates even before the Restoration, and some of the 'mean men' who emerge briefly as buyers of and speculators in royalist lands in the 1650s were actually agents fee'd by former owners.

The Irish land problem was resolved by direct royal action; a telling comment on the status of that unhappy land. In the 1650s clever operators like Lord Broghill had amassed huge estates which they intended to keep. A proclamation in the spring of 1660 shewed how things were going in their favour by allowing current holders of lands formerly owned by native Irish involved in the 1641 rising to retain them pending a final decision. Exception was made only of the holdings of regicides, which devolved on the crown. A declaration of November 1660, confirmed later by the Acts of Settlement of 1661 and of Explanation 1665, confirmed soldiers and adventurers (there were more of the latter) in possession of lands held in November 1659. More than half the best land in Ireland was thereby lodged in the hands of protestants, often absentee, marking the indestructibility of the Cromwellian settlement. 'The native Irish were condemned to be hewers of wood and drawers of water on land they regarded as rightfully their own.

The ascendancy class which dominated Ireland for more than two centuries was being created.'[28]

In England the land upheaval was obviously nowhere near so spectacular. Yet even here it was a major episode in the history of land-ownership and management whose long-term effects have never been adequately investigated. Some new landed families were founded, not many it is true; others were made more substantial. Not all were mushroom growths blighted in a night. What happened to the land between 1640 and 1660 brought new energies, new capital, new notions. It was a shock treatment, killing in some cases, stimulating in others, making it helpful to seek 'improvement', concerned in a half-scientific way to increase the yield at once of rents and produce. It had political implications, too. 'Whiggery may have begun when lay preachers acquired real estate.'[29]

The emotions of royalists, who failed to get all they felt they deserved out of the land settlement and who let themselves be irritated by the appearance of old foes in places of profit and trust, had to find an outlet. It was given by other aspects of the settlement. The so-called Clarendon Code reflects more than mordant religious prejudice. The occasion for it was provided by the ineptitude of the presbyterians in the Convention and their associates, lay and divine, outside. By protracted discussions on what were really 'things indifferent' they put themselves into the hands of eager Laudians and threw away the chance to implement Breda themselves. Indeed by the act for confirming and restoring ministers they failed to give any protection to 'intruders'—often men of their own religious persuasion—and opened the way for wholesale evictions. Nothing more was done before the dissolution. The high anglicans sabotaged the Savoy Conference and held off further action till the bishops were back in the Lords and the Restoration irreversible fact. There was no more need for major concessions to the presbyterians; comprehension or broad toleration went by the board. The slow thinking presbyterians were bewildered by the bold tactics of men with closer contacts at court and easy influence with the young bloods of the Cavalier parliament, brought up by private chaplains of Laudian inclinations. The result was an emphatically anglican church settlement—Laudianism with the social conscience and content left out—in which the Church of England was by law established into a monopoly. Those who would not accept this position could be accused of schism, and, it followed, rebellion, hankerers after the tyranny and confusion of the Interregnum. Like the papists, dissenting protestants must be subject to penal restrictions. The Corporation Act put the boroughs under anglican dominance; the Act of

Uniformity with a revised prayer book enforced episcopal ordination, clerical subscription to the articles, censorship of religious writings, licensing of preachers and teachers. 'Unconformable men' (a fifth of the whole body of the clergy) were thrust out of their livings, a spiteful vengeance for the sufferings of those ejected during the Great Rebellion, who may or may not have been worthy men. Other acts—there was one particularly directed at the quakers, as disturbing now as in the sixteen-fifties—amounted to a campaign which by political and social as well as religious disabilities thinned out the ranks of puritanism more effectively than ever William Laud had done. Dissent slid lower down the social ladder as many puritans rejected separatism in their desire, which perhaps ought not to be deplored, to play a political role at the centre or in their localities. They stayed in the Church. The low Church tradition was the fruit of the victory of the high.

All this was the work less of the crown than of the bishop, the squire and the parson. Both Charles II and James II would for their own reasons take up positions in religion, particularly in relation to 'phanaticks', that would seem at a glance wildly out of key with their father's. Yet curiously each had a notion of religion, which, when stripped bare, was really very akin to that of the martyr King, who for all his devotion to the ritual and doctrine of the Church of England, seems at heart to have taken the same essentially political view of its functions. His sons were faced with different political situations, that was all. They found the exercise of the sole royal supremacy over the Church impossible. Charles II's parliaments assumed an initiative in religion that would have enraged Elizabeth I and the early Stuarts, but seemed natural to men who had experienced—often as parliament-men—the Interregnum. Parsons preached loyalty and non-resistance to the crown, but looked more and more to the squire—or M.P.—for protection. He would give it by changing the succession, ensuring that no papist would ever again sit on the English throne, and that the sovereign should in fact be a communicant of the Church of England. These were giant steps to take, and too huge for some of the clergy to be able to keep up with, though within the compass of the great majority, ignoring rumbles about divine hereditary right and non-resistance. To make these strides meant, as has already been suggested, going a long way towards acting upon the principles, practices 'and all that' of the men of forty-one,[30] slowly abandoning the pretence to more loyalty than they actually had.

The Great Rebellion, then, had repercussions that were powerful in depth and extent. However much it might be desirable to expunge from public memory what was performed and what was attempted in those 20 turbulent years, it was not possible quite to reject 'the true experience' of such great events.[31] What has been stressed in this rapid survey of the Restoration settlement, that carping, but not entirely negative, comment on the Interregnum, is only a part of the story, seizing upon the more patent political, constitutional and religious manifestations. Intellectually, morally, culturally and in countless other ways, the Great Rebellion had woven itself inextricably into the fabric of English history. From any angle some piece of the whole stiff complicated pattern emerges. Shift an inch and another rich design dazzles the eye. After three centuries these king-killing, constitution-crumpling decades, of whose doings all Europe rang from side to side, are as strange, elusive but compelling as ever. It was an iron age, an age of destruction, of the squabbles of kites and crows, of petty schisms, meanness and ignorance. It was also a golden age, an age of construction, of the large wars of truth, of unity, generosity and knowledge. To the effects, good or ill, of that 'search and expectation of greatest and exactest things',[32] which the enterprise of the Rebellion set off, we can never be indifferent. All our history is one of change and these years, which, though in the event they failed to turn the world upside down, evidently put England askew, are among the most dynamic in that whole long revolution.

References

CHAPTER I, Pages 9-13

1 W. Notestein and F. H. Relf, *Commons Debates for 1629*, University of Minnesota Press, 1921, p. 104.
2 Rushworth, i, p. 662.
3 Gardiner, *Documents*, p. 97.
4 Rushworth, i, p. 610. The speaker was Sir Edward Coke.
5 Hulme, pp. 137-8.
6 Gardiner, *Documents*, p. 58.
7 Gardiner, *History*, vi, p. 274.
8 Gardiner, *Documents*, p. 70.
9 Hulme, p. 215. On 28 April 1628 Sir Benjamin Rudyard spoke of his delight at seeing 'that old decrepit law of *Magna Carta*, which hath so long kept in and lain as it were, bedrid, . . . walk abroad again with new vigour and lustre.' Rushworth, i, p. 549. See also M. Ashley, *Magna Carta in the Seventeenth Century*, Charlottesville, Va., 1965.

CHAPTER II, Pages 14-21

1 Tanner Mss, lxxii, 300, printed in *The Academy*, June 1875.
2 Judson, p. 19.
3 Judson, p. 221. Speaking in behalf of the King in the 1628 parliament a courtier warned members 'to move not his Majesty with trenching upon his prerogatives, lest you bring him out of love with parliaments. . . . In all Christian kingdoms you know that parliaments were in use anciently, until the monarchs began to know their own strength; and seeing the turbulent spirits of their parliaments, at length, they, by little and little, began to stand upon their prerogatives and at last overthrew the parliaments throughout Christendom, except only here with us. . . .' Rushworth, i, pp. 359-60.
4 Judson, p. 18.
5 In June 1654 the writer of an intercepted letter remarked that he looked back 'without any remorse . . . to the halcion days of the middle of the last king's raigne, when wee had peace with all the world, and soe free and plentifull a trade with all countryes.' T.S.P., ii, p. 270.

CHAPTER III, Pages 22–31

1 Spalding, i, p. 48.
2 Baillie, i, p. 72.
3 Gardiner, *Documents*, pp. 124–34.
4 Spalding, i, pp. 53–5, 61, 81, 87.
5 Dalrymple, pp. 27, 28, 35.
6 Laud, *Works*, viii, p. 512.
7 '. . . and souldiers levite in Fyfe to dreill: a forerunner of warr' (April 1638). Spalding, i, p. 55. See also Baillie, i, pp. 192, 195. For a detailed statement of the royal view of these events see *A Large Declaration concerning the late Tumults in Scotland*, 1639, issued by the King's Printer.
8 Baillie, i, p. 188.
9 Gardiner, *History*, ix, p. 76. Heylyn, pp. 369–70.
10 Knowler, ii, p. 393.
11 T. May, *A Breviary of the History of the Parliament of England*, 1680, p. 13.
12 C. Davies, *The Early Stuarts*, Oxford, 1934, p. 93.
13 T. G. Barnes, *Somerset 1625–40*, Oxford, 1961, p. 233.
14 Baillie, ii, p. 384.

CHAPTER IV, Pages 32–42

1 C.S.P.V., 1640–42, p. 93.
2 J. L. Sanford, *Studies and Illustrations of the Great Rebellion*, 1856, pp. 326–9.
3 Gardiner, *History*, ix, pp. 340–1.
4 L.J., iv, p. 97.
5 Rushworth, viii, p. 9.
6 Rushworth, viii, p. 660.
7 Gardiner, *History*, ix, p. 327.
8 *The Earl of Strafford Characterised*, 1641, in *Somers Tracts* (1748 edn.), iv, p. 231.
9 Gardiner, *History*, ix, p. 330.
10 Knowler, ii, p. 416.
11 Gardiner, *Documents*, pp. 155–6.
12 Gardiner, *Documents*, pp. 158–9, 'The Earle of Dorset (who was faythfull as any man to the Crowne) . . . took leave of the Kinge the night after the Bill for perpetuatinge the Parliament (for soe in truth it did) passed, and sayd, "Sir, I must leave you. Good night, sir; I may live to doe you kindnes, but you cann doe me none."' Bramston, *Autobiography*, p. 83.
13 *The Last Speeches of Thomas Wentworth . . . May the twelfth, 1641*, 1641, p. 8.
14 Gardiner, *Documents*, pp. 144–5. The original draft was for annual parliaments—another respectful glance at an apparent medieval precedent.

15 Bramston, *Autobiography*, p. 74.
16 Sir Benjamin Rudyard aptly described monpolies as 'but leaking conduit pipes.' *The Speeches of Sir Benjamin Rudyer in the High Court of Parliament*, 1641, p. 9.

CHAPTER V, Pages 43–55

1   Heylyn, p. 417.
2   *The Third Speech of the Lord George Digby to the House of Commons concerning Bishops*, 1641, p. 7.
3   C.S.P.V., 1640–42, p. 122.
4   *The Third Speech . . .* , pp. 15, 17.
5   *The Speeches of Sir Benjamin Rudyer in the High Court of Parliament*, 1641, p. 19.
6   *A Speech Made by Master Waller Esquire in the Honourable House of Commons*, 1641, quoted in T. Aston (ed.), *Crisis in Europe*, 1965, p. 267.
7   L.J., iv, p. 265.
8   S. W. Singer (ed.), *Table Talk of John Selden* (revised W. S. W. Anson), n.d., p. 93. See also a speech by Viscount Newark in Nalson, *Impartial Collection*, ii, pp. 253–4.
9   D. Gardiner (ed.), *The Oxinden and Peyton Letters, 1642–70*, 1937, pp. 36–7.
10 M. Coate, *Cornwall in the Great Civil War*, Oxford, 1933, p. 28.
11 C.J., ii, p. 257.
12 Clarendon, *History*, Book iv.
13 Bray, *Evelyn*, p. 765.
14 Clotworthy's estate 'lay in the North parts of Ireland.' Coates, *D'Ewes*, p. 119.
15 Coates, *D'Ewes*, p. 104. D'Ewes's phrasing differs from that of the actual Instruction. Gardiner, *Documents*, pp. 199–201.
16 Coates, *D'Ewes*, pp. 100–1.
17 Bray, *Evelyn*, p. 778.
18 Bray, *Evelyn*, p. 786.
19 Nalson, *Impartial Collection*, ii, p. 668.
20 Nalson, *Impartial Collection*, ii, p. 668.
21 Coates, *D'Ewes*, p. 184.
22 Coates, *D'Ewes*, p. 187.
23 Coates, *D'Ewes*, p. 187.
24 Coates, *D'Ewes*, p. 187.
25 V. Pearl, *London and the Outbreak of the Puritan Revolution*, Oxford, 1961, p. 123. Bray, *Evelyn*, p. 759.
26 Bray, *Evelyn*, p. 791.
27 Gardiner, *Documents*, p. 201.

CHAPTER VI, Pages 56–61

1 Coates, *D'Ewes*, p. xxxiv.
2 Coates, *D'Ewes*, p. xxxiv.
3 O.P.H., x, p. 353.
4 Gardiner, *History*, x, p. 180.
5 Gardiner, *Documents*, p. 257.
6 O.P.H., xi, p. 355.
7 Anon., *The History of the House of Stanley*, Preston, 1793, pp. 189, 193–4.

CHAPTER VII, Pages 62–66

1 Sir William Waller to 'his Noble frend Sir Ralphe Hopton', 16 June 1643, quoted in M. Coate, *Cornwall in the Great Civil War*, Oxford, 1933, p. 77.
2 Burton, i, pp. 155–6. '*Mr Highland*: Those that come out of the North, are the greatest pests of the Nations. The diggers came thence.... *Mr Bampfield*: [James Nayler] came from the North. It verifies the proverb *ab aquilone nil boni.* . . .'

CHAPTER VIII, Pages 69–72

1 C.S.P.V., 1643–7, p. 53.

CHAPTER IX, Pages 73–83

1 Burne and Young, *Great Civil War*, pp. 22–32.
2 Pennington and Roots, *Committee at Stafford*, p. lxi.
3 Spalding, ii, pp. 142–4.
4 Gardiner, *Documents*, p. 268.
5 Baillie, ii, p. 485.
6 Baillie, ii, p. 362.
7 Baillie, ii, p. 165. V. Pearl, *London and the Outbreak of the Puritan Revolution*, Oxford, 1961, p. 261.
8 Abbott, i, p. 278.

CHAPTER X, Pages 83–94

1 Spalding, ii, p. 153.
2 Spalding, ii, p. 156.
3 Spalding, ii, p. 182.
4 Burne and Young, *Great Civil War*, p. 272. Ireland was, of course, the third kingdom.
5 Baillie, ii, p. 201.

6 Baillie, ii, p. 126.
7 Baillie, ii, p. 229. At the same time—September 1644—Baillie described Cromwell as 'a very wise and active head, universallie well
   beloved, as religious and stout, being a known Independent, the most
   of the sojours who loved new ways put themselves under his command . . . .'
8 W. Hetherington, *History of the Westminster Assembly*, 4th ed., Edinburgh,
   1878, pp. 209–10.
9 Baillie, ii, pp. 229–30, 246.
10 J. Bruce (ed.), *The Quarrel between the Earl of Manchester and Oliver
   Cromwell*, Camden Series, 1875, p. 93.
11 J. Bruce (ed.), *The Quarrel*, pp. lxx, 78–9.
12 Baillie, ii, p. 245.
13 Baillie, ii, p. 247.
14 Gardiner, *Civil War*, ii, p. 118.

CHAPTER XI, Pages 95–101

1 Another indication of the new spirit could be glimpsed in the commissions issued to officers. There was no longer reference to their duty
   of defending 'the King's person'. The vote authorising this omission
   passed the Lords by a single vote.
2 Abbott, i, p. 365.
3 E. Warburton, *Memoirs of Prince Rupert*, 1849, iii, p. 149. See also p. 151
   for a letter to Col. William Legge where Rupert mentions having
   written to the Duke of Richmond 'to be plain with the King, and to
   desire him to consider some way which might lead to a treaty, rather
   than undo his posterity'. Charles was angered by Rupert's advice. He
   asserted that 'there is little question that a composition with them at
   this time is nothing less than a submission which . . . I am resolved
   against, whatever it cost me. . . . Low as I am, I will not go less than
   what was offered in my name at Uxbridge.' Rushworth, vi, p. 132.
4 Rushworth, vi, p. 140.
5 Bray, *Evelyn*, p. 811.

CHAPTER XII, Pages 102–111

1 Baillie, ii, p. 362.
2 *Memoirs of Denzil, Lord Holles, 1641–1648*, 1699, p. 149.
3 Gardiner, *Documents*, pp. 306–8. The King's second (20 December 1646)
   and third (12 May 1647) answers are also printed by Gardiner, pp.
   308–9, 311–16. He also prints 'a suggested answer to the propositions,
   drawn up for the King by the leading Presbyterians and a small number
   of Independents and forwarded by the French ambassador to Cardinal
   Mazarin to be laid before Queen Henrietta Maria' (29 January 1647).

Gardiner suggests (p. xlv) that the 'historical importance' of this curious document, taken with the actual third answer, can hardly be over-rated. 'In them the alliance was struck between the King and the Presbyterian party which led to the second civil war and ultimately to the Restoration in 1660.' That the second civil war is connected with them is certain. The connexion with the Restoration is very remote, indeed, dubious.

4 Baillie, ii, p. 371.
5 Baillie, ii, p. 373.
6 Baillie, ii, pp. 371–2.
7 Baillie, ii, p. 386.
8 Baillie, ii, p. 402.

CHAPTER XIII, Pages 112–114

1 Maseres, *Tracts*, i, p. 272.
2 Woodhouse, p. 418.
3 Woodhouse, p. 413.
4 Woodhouse, p. 415.
5 Woodhouse, pp. 415, 419.
6 Yule, *Independents*, p. 69.
7 Maseres, *Tracts*, ii, p. 360.

CHAPTER XIV, Pages 115–121

1 Gregg, *Freeborn John*, p. 194.
2 Brailsford, *Levellers*, p. 59.
3 Walker, *History of Independency*, pt. ii, p. 24.
4 Haller and Davies, *Leveller Tracts*, p. 78.
5 Gregg, *Freeborn John*, pp. 186, 195.
6 Woodhouse, p. 7.
7 Paul, *Lord Protector*, p. 144.
8 Woodhouse, p. 2.
9 Woodhouse, p. 2.
10 Woodhouse, p. 7.
11 Paul, *Lord Protector*, pp. 141–2.
12 Woodhouse, p. 54.
13 Woodhouse, pp. 62, 69–77.
14 Woodhouse, p. 59.
15 Woodhouse, p. 70.
16 Woodhouse, p. 69.
17 Woodhouse, pp. 52–3. 'I do think the poorest man in England is not at all bound in a strict sense to that government that he hath not had a voice to put himself under. . . .'

18 W. Haller, *Liberty and Reformation in the Puritan Revolution*, New York, 1955, p. 310.
19 There were in fact to be several rendezvous, not a single general one. Rushworth, vi, p. 686. Woodhouse, p. 453.
20 Paul, *Lord Protector*, pp. 146–50.
21 Abbott, ii, p. 544.
22 Paul, *Lord Protector*, p. 149.
23 Paul, *Lord Protector*, pp. 145, 149.

CHAPTER XV, Pages 122–134

1 Brailsford, *Levellers*, p. 305.
2 *Clarke Papers*, i, p. 418.
3 Gregg, *Freeborn John*, p. 223.
4 Brailsford, *Levellers*, p. 306.
5 The 1647 harvest was poor and the winter of 1647–8 severe. Haller and Davies, *Leveller Tracts*, pp. 126–9; Gregg, *Freeborn John*, pp. 226–9; Brailsford, *Levellers*, pp. 307–25.
6 Maseres, *Tracts*, i, p. 364.
7 Abbott, i, p. 570.
8 'For Oliver is all in all,
      For Oliver is all in all,
            And Oliver is here,
            And Oliver is there,
      And Oliver is at Whitehall,
            And Oliver notes all,
            And Oliver votes all,
      And claps his hand upon his bilbo . . .'
9 William Allen, *A Faithful Memorial*, 1659, in *Somers Tracts* (1748 edn.), vi, pp. 500–1.
10 *A Choak-Peare for Parliament*, Colchester, 1648.
11 O.P.H., xvii, p. 273.
12 Baillie, ii, p. 512.
13 Walker, *History of Independency*, pt. ii, p. 10.
14 The Commons had dropped the impeachment of 'the eleven members' on 3 June 1648.
15 O.P.H., xxii, pp. 435, 446.
16 Haller and Davies, *Leveller Tracts*, pp. 148–55.
17 O.P.H., xvii, p. 479.
18 J. Bruce (ed.), *Charles I in 1646*, Camden Series, 1856, p. 6.
19 Walker, *History of Independency*, pt. ii, p. 18.
20 Woodhouse, pp. 456ff. Gardiner, *Civil War*, iv, pp. 233ff.
21 Ludlow, *Memoirs*, i, pp. 206–7.
22 Walker, *History of Independency*, pt. ii, p. 19.
23 O.P.H., xviii, pp. 266–272.

24   O.P.H., xviii, p. 446. Walker, *History of Independency*, pt. ii, p. 29, claims
     that the Independents hoped 'to tire out and fright away the moderate
     men.' William Prynne had been elected for Newport, Cornwall, in
     November 1648. His attitude towards the Newport (I.O.W.) treaty
     and, later, to Pride's Purge is discussed in W. Lamont, *Marginal
     Prynne*, 1964, pp. 181–6.
25   Walker, *History of Independency*, pt. ii, p. 32.
26   Abbott, iii, p. 456.

CHAPTER XVI, Pages 137–153

1   Abbott, i, p. 754.
2   Yule, *Independents*, p. 74.
3   Brunton and Pennington, *Members*, p. 52.
4   Three peers (Pembroke, Howard of Escrick and Salisbury) were
     elected in the spring of 1649 as members for Berkshire, Carlisle and
     King's Lynn respectively. O.P.H., xix, p. 107.
5   Yule, *Independents*, p. 64.
6   Yule, *Independents*, p. 64, quoting H.M.C., 13th Report, Appx. iv,
     p. 400.
7   Yule, *Independents*, pp. 61–2.
8   *A History of England in a series of Letters from a Nobleman to his Son*, 1772,
     ii, p. 53. The finances of individual Rumpers have yet to be investi-
     gated.
9   Gardiner, *Documents*, pp. 387–8. 'This act was not a mere by-product
     of the dynamics of war; it was the culmination of a crisis of confidence
     which had been maturing for well over half a century.' L. Stone,
     Crisis of the Aristocracy, 1965, p. 753. It should be noted that hereditary
     peerages were not abolished.
10   R. W. Ramsey, *Henry Ireton*, 1949, p. 156.
11   O.P.H., xviii, p. 378.
12   O.P.H., xviii, p. 377.
13   *Clarke Papers*, ii, p. 194.
14   Haller and Davies, *Leveller Tracts*, p. 187.
15   Haller and Davies, *Leveller Tracts*, p. 292.
16   Haller and Davies, *Leveller Tracts*, p. 319.
17   Haller and Davies, *Leveller Tracts*, p. 324.
18   Haller and Davies, *Leveller Tracts*, p. 327. In *Legall Fundamental Liberties*,
     Lilburne specifically repudiated 'all the erroneous tenents' of the com-
     munism of the Diggers. Suspicions of Walwyn's leanings towards
     communism may have rather more justification.
19   G. Sabine (ed.), *Works af Gerrard Winstanley*, Ithaca, N.Y., 1941, p.
     252.
20   Walker, *History of Independency*, pt. ii, p. 128.
21   Haller and Davies, *Leveller Tracts*, p. 207.

CHAPTER XVII, Pages 154–162

1 Abbott, ii, p. 38.
2 Abbott, ii, p. 118.
3 Abbott, ii, p. 160.
4 O.P.H., xix, p. 9.
5 Baillie, iii, pp. 522–3.
6 J. Barclay (ed.), *Diary of Alexander Jaffray*, Aberdeen, 1856, p. 55.
7 Barclay, *Jaffray*, p. 56.
8 Abbott, ii, p. 270.
9 D. H. Fleming (ed.), *Diary of Sir Archibald Johnston of Wariston*, Edinburgh, 1919, ii, p. 14.
10 Abbott, ii, p. 303.
11 Abbott, ii, p. 313.
12 Fleming, *Wariston*, ii, pp. 8–9.
13 Fleming, *Wariston*, ii, p. 10.
14 Abbott, ii, p. 327.
15 C. H. Firth (ed.), *Scotland and the Commonwealth*, Edinburgh, 1895, p. 247.
16 See Firth, *Scotland and the Commonwealth*, p. 325, for Monk's proclamation against plundering.
17 C. S. Terry (ed.), *Cromwellian Union 1651–2*, Edinburgh, 1902, pp. 11–12.
18 Terry, *Cromwellian Union*, p. xxiii.
19 Terry, *Cromwellian Union*, p. 35.
20 Terry, *Cromwellian Union*, pp. xxv–xxvi, 75.
21 Firth, *Scotland and the Commonwealth*, p. 369.

CHAPTER XVIII, Pages 163–169

1 O.P.H., xix, p. 106.
2 Whitelocke, *Memorials*, 549.
3 Whitelocke, *Memorials*, p. 541.
4 Whitelocke, *Memorials*, pp. 549–51.
5 Abbott, ii, p. 615.
6 Abbott, iii, p. 643.
7 O.P.H., xx, p. 137.
8 O.P.H., xx, p. 137.
9 Abbott, iii, p. 453. 'The parliament was dissolved with as little noyse as can bee imagined.' *Clarke Papers*, iii, p. 2.
10 T.S.P., i, p. 250. See T.S.P., i, p. 361, for a Dutch squib upon the dissolution.
11 Gardiner, *Documents*, p. 403.
12 *The Rump*, or *An Exact Collection of the Choycest Poems and Songs*, 1874, (reprint of edn. of 1662), i, p. 306.

13   O.P.H., xx, pp. 145-7.
14   Ludlow, *Memoirs*, i, p. 358.
15   T.S.P., i, pp. 249, 255.
16   Clarendon, *History*, Book xiv; T.S.P., i, pp. 289, 312, 323, 386; *Harleian Miscellany* (1745 edn.), iii, p. 456.
17   C.S.P.V., 1653-4, p. 160.
18   Ludlow, *Memoirs*, i, pp. 359, 368. Arthur Squibb, one of the radicals, was a lawyer.
19   Sir Henry Vane the Younger was reputedly invited to sit, but 'he answered by a letter extracted out of that part of the Apocalypse, wherein the reign of the Saints is mentioned, which he saith he believes will not begin; but for his part he is willing to defer his share in it till he come to heaven.' T.S.P., i, p. 265.
20   Abbott, iii, p. 64.
21   T.S.P., i, pp. 368, 369 ('great tugging and division of opinions'), p. 385 ('men see the difference of the government of one, and the management of affairs by a multitude, who are still divided and fall into factions'), p. 386 ('they cannot be long in one house, that are so furiously divided'), pp. 393, 501.
22   O.P.H., xx, p. 199.
23   O.P.H., xx, p. 199.
24   O.P.H., xx, p. 198.
25   O.P.H., xx, p. 233.
26   O.P.H., xx, p. 212.
27   O.P.H., xx, pp. 214-18. It read 'that if any Person then married, or to be married according to this Act, should make Proof by one or more credible Witness upon Oath, that either the Husband or Wife had committed the detestable Sin of Adultery during such marriage, then the said parties might be divorced by the sentence of three Justices of the Peace'. We may agree with the mid-eighteenth-century compilers of *The Old Parliamentary History* that this was 'a very remarkable clause.'
28   T.S.P., i, p. 621.
29   O.P.H., xx, pp. 196-7.
30   T.S.P., i, p. 367.
31   T.S.P., i, p. 320.
32   Abbott, iii, p. 133; T.S.P., i, pp. 360, 632, 637.
33   J. Buchan, *Oliver Cromwell*, 1934, p. 438.

CHAPTER XIX, Pages 170-180

1   Paul, *Lord Protector*, p. 294.
2   T.S.P., i, p. 384.
3   [M. Needham], *A True State of the Case of the Commonwealth*, 1654.
4   *A True State.*

5   *A True State.*
6   T.S.P., i, p. 641.
7   Ludlow, *Memoirs*, i, p. 435.
8   C.S.P.V., 1653–4, p. 164. See T.S.P., i, p. 641, for a report that the whole affair was 'publicly laughed at and derided.'
9   T.S.P., ii, p. 144.
10 T.S.P., i, p. 644; T.S.P., ii, p. 74.
11 O.P.H., xx, pp. 277–9.
12 T.S.P., i, p. 647.
13 Clarendon, *History*, Book xiv.
14 T.S.P., ii, pp. 9, 19; O.P.H., xx, p. 291.
15 Abbott, iii, p. 208.
16 Gardiner, *Documents*, p. 414.
17 Firth and Rait, *Acts and Ordinances*, ii, pp. 871–5; Terry, *Cromwellian Union*, pp. xlviii–li.
18 Firth and Rait, *Acts and Ordinances*, pp. 968–90.
19 E. Calamy, *Abridgement of Mr Baxter's History*, 2nd ed., 1703, p. 69.
20 J. Stoughton, *Ecclesiastical History of England*, 1867, ii, p. 204.
21 Abbott, iv, p. 368.
22 T.S.P., iv, p. 321.
23 Whalley remarked 'Doubtless, to say no more, they will bring in much wealth into this Commonwealth.' T.S.P., iv, p. 308.
24 Burton, i, pp. 168–73.

CHAPTER XX, Pages 181–189

1   T.S.P., ii, p. 445.
2   H. R. Trevor-Roper, 'Oliver Cromwell and his Parliaments' in *Essays Presented to Sir Lewis Namier* (ed. R. Pares and A. J. P. Taylor), 1957, pp. 1–48.
3   Trevor-Roper, 'Oliver Cromwell and his Parliaments', p. 28.
4   Gardiner, *Documents*, p. 410.
5   Gardiner, *Documents*, pp. 410–11.
6   Gardiner, *Documents*, p. 410.
7   Ludlow, *Memoirs*, p. 390.
8   C. Hill, *Oliver Cromwell*, 1958, p. 20.
9   Maseres, *Tracts*, ii, p. 632. Hobbes went on to comment that 'he knew not how lucky the same would be to the whole nation in 1658 at Whitehall.'
10 *The Life and Death of Stephen Marshall*, 1680, pp. 5, 7–10.
11 Abbott, iii, pp. 434–43.
12 O.P.H., xx, p. 348; Burton, i, pp. xxv–xxxii.
13 Burton, i, p. lxxxiii.
14 Trevor-Roper, 'Oliver Cromwell and his Parliaments', pp. 45–8.

15 The 'three colonels' were Mathew Alured, John Okey and Thomas Saunders. All were baptists. Their petition protested against a single-person command of the army. *Clarke Papers*, iii, pp. 10–11.

16 Burton, i, p. cxxxii.

17 T. Carlyle, *Cromwell's Letters and Speeches*, 2nd edn. rev., n.d., p. 566.

18 Abbott, iii, pp. 579–93.

CHAPTER XXI, Pages 190–202

1 Underdown, *Royalist Conspiracy*, p. 127.

2 Underdown, *Royalist Conspiracy*, p. 123.

3 Underdown, *Royalist Conspiracy*, p. 125.

4 *Clarke Papers*, ii, pp. 242–6.

5 Underdown, *Royalist Conspiracy*, p. 150.

6 O.P.H., xx, pp. 434–60.

7 O.P.H., xx, p. 441.

8 T.S.P., iii, p. 221.

9 Clarendon, *History*, Book xv.

10 Wentworth said, 'If you (the Protector) will command me, I must submit.' Abbott, iii, pp. 862–3.

11 T.S.P., iv, p. 274.

12 Burton, i, p. 315. Clarendon used the same phrase in 1641 to describe the Council of the North. Rushworth, iii, p. 231. See also Ludlow, *Memoirs*, i, pp. 405–6.

13 Abbott, iv, p. 112.

14 Hutchinson, *Memoirs*, pp. 370–1.

15 Hutchinson, *Memoirs*, p. 371.

16 Abbott, iv, p. 269.

17 T.S.P., iv, p. 719.

18 T.S.P., iv, pp. 449, 522–3.

19 Abbott, iv, p. 269.

20 Rushworth, i, Appx., pp. 12–17.

21 Gardiner, *Commonwealth and Protectorate*, iv, p. 249.

22 T.S.P., v, 299–300, 303.

23 *Clarke Papers*, iii, p. 68. See also T.S.P., v, p. 341, for a report that Sussex would have 'noe soldier, decemator, or any man that hath sallary'; and C.S.P.V., 1656–7, p. 87, for a similar report from Kent.

24 T.S.P., v, p. 230.

25 O.P.H., xxi, p. 2.

26 Pennington and Roots, *Committee at Stafford*, p. lix.

27 T.S.P., v, p. 365.

28 O.P.H., xxi, p. 23.

29 *Clarke Papers*, iii, pp. 73–4.

30   O.P.H., xxi, p. 26.
31   T.S.P., v, p. 453.
32   O.P.H., xxi, pp. 28–31; T.S.P., v, p. 456.
33   Abbott, iv, pp. 260–79.
34   Abbott, iv, p. 278.
35   Abbott, iv, p. 342.
36   *Clarke Papers*, iii, pp. 61, 76, 80.
37   Burton, i, p. 191.
38   Burton, i, p. 230. '*Col. Mathews*: The House is thin, much occasioned, I believe, by the observation of this day. I have a short bill to prevent the superstition for the future. . . . *Mr Robinson*: I could get no rest all night for the preparation of this foolish day's solemnity. . . . We are, I doubt, returning to Popery.' Burton, i, p. 229.
39   Burton, i, pp. 230–43.
40   Burton, i, p. 191; T.S.P., v, p. 472; *Clarke Papers*, iii, p. 85.
41   Burton, i, pp. 310–11, 315.
42   *Clarke Papers*, iii, p. 88.
43   W. H. Dawson, *Cromwell's Understudy*, 1938, p. 257.
44   *Clarke Papers*, iii, p. 87.
45   T.S.P., vi, pp. 20–1; Burton, i, p. 369.
46   *Clarke Papers*, iii, p. 88.

CHAPTER XXII, Pages 203–209

1   T.S.P., vi, p. 37; Burton, i, p. 371.
2   Abbott, iv, p. 417.
3   Abbott, iv, p. 264.
4   Abbott, iv, p. 368.
5   Gardiner, *Documents*, p. 416. Papists and prelatists might be adjudged, on political grounds if no other, potential peacebreakers.
6   Burton, i, pp. 24–5.
7   Burton, i, p. 50.
8   Burton, i, p. 154.
9   Abbott, iv, p. 366.
10   Burton, i, p. 275.
11   Burton, i, p. 278.
12   Burton, i, p. 282.
13   Burton, i, p. 249.
14   Abbott, iv, pp. 417–18.

CHAPTER XXIII, Pages 210–219

1   T.S.P., iii, pp. 75–6. 'Found in M.G. Overton's Lettercase'.
2   Usually ascribed to the Leveller Edward Sexby, who was also involved in the Sindercombe plot.

3   *Clarke Papers*, iii, p. 77.
4   T.S.P., v, p. 317.
5   Abbott, iv, p. 335.
6   Burton, i, p. 362.
7   Burton, i, p. 378.
8   *Clarke Papers*, iii, p. 89.
9   *Clarke Papers*, iii, p. 90.
10 *Clarke Papers*, iii, p. 91. See also T.S.P., vi, p. 74: 'The great man (i.e. Lambert) and some other considerable officers are against it. . . . I doe verily believe, that Lambert will if it can be done, put the army into a ferment. . . . There are great bussinges about towne, upon occasion of this debate.' T.S.P., vi, p. 93: 'Some of the army are unquiet. I doe not like the complexion and constitution of thinges. Settlement I feare is not in some men's mindes, nor ever will be.' *Clarke Papers*, iii, p. 105: 'Sword dominion is too sweet to be parted with, and the truth is (whatever kind of squeezines we may pretend to) that the single issue, the maine dread is, that the civill power shall swallow up the military. . . .'
11 *Clarke Papers*, iii, p. 92.
12 *Clarke Papers*, iii, p. 92.
13 Abbott, iv, pp. 417–19.
14 *Clarke Papers*, iii, pp. 281–2.
15 *Clarke Papers*, iii, p. 93.
16 This term is used by the author of *A Narrative of the Late Parliament* . . . , 1657, in *Harleian Miscellany* (1745 edn.), iii, p. 429.
17 *Clarke Papers*, iii, p. 98.
18 Abbott, iv, pp. 442–4.
19 T.S.P., vi, p. 106.
20 Paul, *Lord Protector*, p. 371.
21 T.S.P., vi, pp. 243, 261.
22 Burton, ii, p. 7.
23 Abbott, iv, pp. 512–14.
24 Burton, ii, p. 118.
25 Gardiner, *Documents*, pp. 447–59.
26 Gardiner, *Documents*, pp. 459–64.

CHAPTER XXIV, Pages 220–231

1 Gardiner, *Documents*, p. 462.
2 T.S.P., vi, p. 412. See also Abbott, iv, p. 569.
3 *The Grand Concernments of England Stated*, 1659, p. 61 (quoted in Firth, *Last Years*, ii, p. 5). Mrs Hutchinson says that 'they all like rated dogs, clapped their tails between their legs and begged his (Cromwell's) pardon, and left Lambert to fall alone . . .' *Memoirs*, p. 373. See also Baillie, iii, p. 358. 'In all men's eyes he (Lambert) was the heir-

apparent to the Protector's power, but the Kingship cutted him off clearly from that hope.'

4   Hutchinson, *Memoirs*, p. 372: 'The one was gallant and great, the other had nothing but an unworthy pride, most insolent in prosperity and as abject and base in adversity.'

5   T.S.P., vi, p. 609. See also T.S.P., vi, p. 648.

6   Ludlow, *Memoirs*, ii, p. 32. Yet Warwick married his grandson to the Protector's daughter, Frances. Fauconberg married Cromwell's daughter, Mary. Mrs Hutchinson comments: 'such pitiful slaves were the nobles of those days . . .', *Memoirs*, p. 371.

7   *A Seasonable Speech. . . . March, 1659*, in *Harleian Miscellany* (1745 edn.), iii, p. 470.

8   Ludlow, *Memoirs*, ii, pp. 31–2.

9   The full text is 'For ye see your calling, brethren, how that not many wise men after the flesh, not many noble, are called.'

10   Abbott, iv, pp. 705–8.

11   O.P.H., xxi, pp. 175–94.

12   O.P.H., xxi, p. 189. (My italics).

13   *Clarke Papers*, iii, p. 138.

14   Burton, ii, pp. 346–7.

15   Burton, ii, p. 423: '*Sir Arthur Haselrig*: I like your company very well, gentlemen; and do aspire no higher than to be a commoner of England.'

16   Burton, ii, p. 432: Mr Bodurda argued 'you must give them some name, "The other House" is an *individium vagum*. You must call them of House of men, or women, or something that have two legs. . . .'

17   Abbott, iv, pp. 741–2.

18   Burton, ii, pp. 419, 433.

19   Burton, ii, p. 390.

20   Burton, ii, p. 458.

21   Burton, ii, p. 416.

22   Burton, ii, p. 461.

23   Burton, ii, p. 408.

24   Burton, ii, p. 416.

25   Burton, ii, p. 375. *Clarke Papers*, iii, p. 134: 'Wee shall either sitt a great while, or rise very soone.' *Clarke Papers*, iii, p. 133: 'I dread the issue; here are very strange spirits come in amongst us, and here are dayly more flocking in; there are 206 sworne and likely to be a full House, but how longe lived I cannot say.'

26   Abbott, iv, pp. 712–20.

27   O.P.H., xxi, p. 205.

28   Ludlow, *Memoirs*, ii, p. 33.

29   Abbott, iv, p. 730.

30   Abbott, iv, p. 732.

31   Underdown, *Royalist Conspiracy*, p. 219.

32   Firth, *Last Years*, ii, p. 44.

33   *Clarke Papers*, iii, p. 141.

34 O.P.H., xxi, p. 205.
35 Baillie, iii, p. 357.
36 T.S.P., vi, p. 806; T.S.P., vii, pp. 4, 269, 295.
37 T.S.P., vi, p. 807; T.S.P., vii, p. 269; *Clarke Papers*, pp. 141–3, 145, 151; C.S.P.V., 1657–9, pp. 188–9, 226–7.
38 *Clarke Papers*, iii, p. 142.
39 *Clarke Papers*, iii, p. 143.
40 *Clarke Papers*, iii, p. 143; Gardiner, *Documents*, pp. 449–52.

CHAPTER XXV, Pages 232–241

1 Clarendon, *History*, Book xvi.
2 *Clarke Papers*, iii, p. 162.
3 *Clarke Papers*, iii, p. 162.
4 *Nicholas Papers*, iv, p. 148. Mrs Hutchinson noted some of Richard's parts but considered him 'a peasant in his nature', without spirit enough to 'manage such a perplexed government'. *Memoirs*, pp. 370, 376. See also the savage caricature reproduced as frontispiece to *Clarke Papers*, iii.
5 *Nicholas Papers*, iv, pp. 72–4.
6 T.S.P., vii, p. 387.
7 T.S.P., vii, pp. 454–5.
8 T.S.P., vii, pp. 387–8.
9 C.S.P.V., 1657–9, p. 238.
10 *Clarke Papers*, iii, p. 168.
11 T.S.P., vii, pp. 413–14.
12 *Clarke Papers*, iii, pp. 165–6, 168–9.
13 Commenting on the arguments Thurloe wrote of parliament as 'a thinge always usuall in the beginning of every prince's reign. The great necessities wee have for money, which cannot be supplyed but by parliament; the good opinion the people in generall now have of his highnesse; beside these, there be other reasons, which are more fitt to be told your excellency (the Lord Deputy, Henry Cromwell) then by this way.' T.S.P., vii, p. 546.
14 See Trevor-Roper, 'Oliver Cromwell and his Parliaments', pp. 42–5, and O.P.H., xxi, p. 246. But republicans like Ludlow, Vane, Weaver and Scott sat for small boroughs, too. Ludlow, *Memoirs*, ii, pp. 48–9. 'The Protectorate had no monopoly of small boroughs.' Davies, *Restoration*, p. 46.
15 T.S.P., vii, p. 541. 'Great striveinges there will be to get in and the commonwealth's-men have their daily meetings, disputeinge what kind of commonwealth they shall have, takeinge it for graunted they may picke and choose. . . .' See also T.S.P., vii, p. 550 'resolutions were taken how the buissness shall be managed in parliament' and Ludlow, *Memoirs*, ii, p. 50.

16   *Somers Tracts* (1748 edn.), iv, p. 527.

17   T.S.P., xvi, p. 7. See also *Clarke Papers*, iii, p. 179: 'this parliament consists as may seeme of various judgements, yett I am very hopefull they shall be found of sober spirits and that they will make itt their worke to fix and settle the present government, and not att all shake or weaken itt, whereby the spiritts of these nations will be much quieted, and the enemies of peace much disappointed'.

18   Burton, iii, pp. 2, 7–11; O.P.H., xxi, pp. 265–81; *Clarke Papers*, iii, p. 176.

19   Ludlow, *Memoirs*, ii, p. 55.

20   Burton, iii, p. 49: 'Col. Cromwell took exception that Sir Arthur Haselrigge should so often take notice that so many young men were in this House'. One of Haselrig's speeches lasted 'from nine to twelve'. 'If you go on at this rate', a member complained, 'to have one speech a day, the Dutch will give you 2,000 *l.* a day to do so.' Burton, iii, pp. 87–105, 117.

21   Burton, iii, p. 269. Some members objected to 'all the stories' (p. 113); 'long sermons' (p. 268); and 'stories by gentlemen of the late troubles .... not pertinent to our question' (p. 181). Haselrig's reply was that 'we came to serve God and our country, and not to make business of greatest concernment to be huddled over in haste. Let us lay foundations for posterity.'

22   *Somers Tracts* (1748 edn.), iv, p. 526.

23   *Clarke Papers*, iii, pp. 180–1. 'There is nothing yett done more than debates.'

24   Burton, iii, pp. 132–5, 146–8. 'the gentry do not now depend upon the peerage. The balance is in the gentry. They have all the lands' (pp. 335–6). See also Burton, iii, pp. 330–1, and iv, pp. 23–5.

25   Burton, iii, p. 144.

26   O.P.H., xxi, p. 317.

27   *Clarke Papers*, iii, p. 181.

28   Burton, iii, pp. 349–50, 354, 356, 358, 412, 514–19.

29   Burton, iii, p. 408.

30   T.S.P., vii, p. 661.

31   *Clarke Papers*, iii, p. 187; O.P.H., xxi, pp. 340–6.

32   *Clarke Papers*, iii, p. 189.

33   Baker, *Chronicle*, p. 641.

34   *Clarke Papers*, iii, pp. 193, 209–17; *Nicholas Papers*, iv, p. 122.

35   *Clarke Papers*, iii, p. 213.

36   *Clarke Papers*, iii, p. 194.

37   *Clarke Papers*, iii, p. 213.

38   *Clarke Papers*, iii, p. 213.

39   Baker, *Chronicle*, p. 642.

40   *Nicholas Papers*, iv, p. 122.

41   *Clarke Papers*, iv, p. 7; Baker, *Chronicle*, pp. 642–3.

42   Baker, *Chronicle*, p. 643.

43 *Nicholas Papers*, iv, p. 122.
44 *Nicholas Papers*, iv, p. 123.
45 O.P.H., xxi, pp. 367–8.
46 *Nicholas Papers*, iv, p. 135.
47 T.S.P., vii, p. 675.
48 *Nicholas Papers*, iv, pp. 148, 154, 160.

CHAPTER XXVI, Pages 242–250

1   *Nicholas Papers*, iv, p. 148.
2   *Nicholas Papers*, iv, p. 146.
3   *Nicholas Papers*, iv, p. 140.
4   F. Guizot, *Richard Cromwell and the Restoration*, 1856, i, p. 213.
5   *Clarke Papers*, iv, p. 18.
6   *Clarke Papers*, iv, p. 22; Baker, *Chronicle*, p. 648.
7   Ludlow, *Memoirs*, ii, p. 100.
8   *Nicholas Papers*, iv, p. 152.
9   Baker, *Chronicle*, p. 642.
10 James Harrington asserted in his *Political Aphorisms* (25 August 1659) that 'if Sir George Booth had prevailed, he must either have introduced a Commonwealth, or have restored a king'. (Aphorism no. LXI, p. 7.)
11 Baker, *Chronicle*, p. 562.
12 *Nicholas Papers*, iv, p. 165. The writer goes on to assert that Vane 'seems to have talked himselfe to jealousie and contempt in the house. He is outvoted by the Presbiterian members and sometimes for noe other reason but he shall take notice he is outvoted. . . .'
13 Baker, *Chronicle*, p. 655.
14 *Clarke Papers*, iv, pp. 59–60. Monk wrote to his subordinate commanders: 'You know it hath been alwaies against my way to signe any petitions at all, either to the Parliament or Generall, from the forces here, and I am still of the same judgement. . . .'
15 *Mordaunt Letter Book*, p. 54.
16 *Clarke Papers*, iv, p. 60.
17 O.P.H., xxi, p. 642.
18 Underdown, *Royalist Conspiracy*, p. 310.
19 Davies, *Restoration*, p. 156.
20 John Price, *Mystery and Method of his Majesty's Happy Restoration*, 1680, printed in Maseres, *Tracts*, ii, pp. 693–800. See especially pp. 726–7, 748.
21 *Mordaunt Letter Book*, pp. 155, 174.
22 Davies, *Restoration*, Chapters x–xvi.
23 *Clarke Papers*, iv, pp. 77–8.
24 *Clarke Papers*, iv, p. 126. 'If hee . . . but keepe Scotland hee will doe his worke.'

25   *Clarke Papers*, iv, p. 300.
26   *Nicholas Papers*, iv, p. 192.
27   *Clarke Papers*, iv, pp. 166–7.
28   *Nicholas Papers*, iv, p. 198.
29   *Clarke Papers*, iv, p. 300.
30   *Mordaunt Letter Book*, pp. 136, 138–9, 141. See *Nicholas Papers*, iv, p. 192, for a reference to 'interested and wary ones' waiting to see before acting.
31   *Nicholas Papers*, iv, p. 196.
32   *Clarke Papers*, iv, pp. 187, 215, 220.
33   Robert Wild, *Iter Boreale*, 1660, lines 240–1, 250.

CHAPTER XXVII, Pages 251–256

1   *Mordaunt Letter Book*, pp. 155, 174.
2   *Nicholas Papers*, iv, pp. 179, 194.
3   O.P.H., xxii, pp. 88–90.
4   Ludlow, *Memoirs*, ii, p. 219.
5   Maseres, *Tracts*, ii, p. 774.
6   O.P.H., xxii, p. 146.
7   O.P.H., xxii, p. 147.
8   *Mordaunt Letter Book*, p. xviii.
9   *Mordaunt Letter Book*, p. 139.
10   Maseres, *Tracts*, pp. 785–6.
11   Davies, *Restoration*, pp. 312–14, 340–1.
12   Sir Gyles Isham (ed.), *Correspondence of Bishop Brian Duppa and Sir Justinian Isham*, Lamport, 1955, p. 181.
13   O.P.H., xxii, p. 231.
14   C.J., viii, p. 8.

CHAPTER XXVIII, Pages 257–279

1   P.H., v, pp. 53, 55.
2   C.J., viii, p. 53.
3   J. Aubrey, *Brief Lives* (ed. A. Powell), 1949, p. 264.
4   P.H., v, p. 53.
5   *Statutes of the Realm*, v, pp. 231–3. Clauses xxxviii and xxxix exempted certain individuals including Sir Arthur Haselrig, 'onely of such paines, penaltyes and forfeitures not extending to life' (p. 232). Clause xli specifically excluded Vane and Lambert (p. 232). See also *An act for the attainder of several persons*. . . . *Statutes of the Realm*, v, pp. 298–90.
6   See below, p. 261.
7   Hargrave, *State Trials*, ii, col. 327.
8   Hargrave, *State Trials*, ii, col. 333.
9   P.H., v, p. 51.

10 Hargrave, *State Trials*, ii, col. 357.
11 Hargrave, *State Trials*, ii, col. 363.
12 Hargrave, *State Trials*, ii, col. 363.
13 Hargrave, *State Trials*, ii, col. 335.
14 J. Willcock, *Life of Sir Henry Vane the Younger*, 1913, p. 328.
15 Hargrave, *State Trials*, ii, col. 457.
16 The closing words of Hobbes' *Behemoth*. Maseres, *Tracts*, ii, p. 653.
17 Bray, *Evelyn*, p. 233.
18 Davies, *Restoration*, p. 355.
19 Underdown, *Royalist Conspiracy*, p. 330.
20 Ogg, *Charles II*, i, p. 329.
21 Hobbes thought that the assertion of royal control of armed force 'more instructive to the People, then any Arguments drawn from the Title of Sovereign, and consequently fitter to disarm the Ambition of all sedititious Haranguers for the Time to come'. *Behemoth* in Maseres, *Tracts*, ii, p. 652.
22 Ogg, *Charles II*, i, p. 448.
23 D. Defoe, *A New Test of the Church of England's Loyalty*, 1702, pp. 13, 33, 34.
24 P.H., v, p. 51.
25 C.J., viii, p. 8.
26 Ogg, *Charles II*, i, p. 163.
27 Gardiner, *Documents*, p. 466.
28 Davies, *Restoration*, p. 255.
29 Ogg, *Charles II*, ii, p. 508.
30 D. Defoe, *A New Test*, pp. 33–4.
31 J. Milton, *Areopagitica*.
32 J. Milton, *Areopagitica*.

Abbreviations

Abbott	W. C. Abbott, ed, *The Writings and Speeches of Oliver Cromwell*, 4 vols, Cambridge, Mass., 1937–47
Amer. Hist. Rev.	*The American Historical Review*
Baillie	D. Laing, ed, *The Letters and Journals of Robert Baillie*, 3 vols, Edinburgh, 1841
Baker	Sir Richard Baker, *A Chronicle of the Kings of England*, 9th ed (with *Continuation* by E. Phillips), 1696
Brailsford	H. N. Brailsford, *The Levellers and the English Revolution*, ed C. Hill, 1961
Bramston, *Autobiography*	Lord Braybrooke, ed, *The Autobiography of Sir John Bramston*, Camden series, 1845
Bray, *Evelyn*	W. Bray, ed, *The Diary and Correspondence of John Evelyn, F.R.S.*, n.d.
Brunton and Pennington, *Members*	D. Brunton and D. H. Pennington, *Members of the Long Parliament*, 1954
Bull. Inst. Hist. Research	*The Bulletin of the Institute of Historical Research*
Burne and Young, *Great Civil War*	A. H. Burne and P. Young, *The Great Civil War; A Military History*, 1959
Camb. Hist. J.	*The Cambridge Historical Journal*
C. J.	The Journals of the House of Commons
Clarendon, *History*	Edward, Earl of Clarendon, *The History of the Rebellion and Civil Wars in England Begun in the Year 1641*, 3 vols, Oxford, 1702–4
Clarke Papers	C. H. Firth, ed, *The Clarke Papers*, 4 vols, Camden Series, 1891–1901
Coates, *D'Ewes*	W. H. Coates, ed, *The Journal of Sir Simonds D'Ewes from the First Recess of the Long Parliament to the Withdrawal of King Charles from London*, New Haven, 1942
C.S.P.V.	The Calendar of State Papers, Venetian
Dalrymple	D. Dalrymple, *Memorials and Letters relating to the History of Britain in the Reign of Charles I*, Glasgow, 1766
Davies, *Restoration*	G. Davies, *The Restoration of Charles II*, Oxford, 1955

Econ. Hist. Rev.	*The Economic History Review*
E.H.R.	*The English Historical Review*
Firth, *Last Years*	C. H. Firth, *The Last Years of the Protectorate*, 2 vols, 1910
Firth and Rait, *Acts and Ordinances*	C. H. Firth and R. S. Rait, eds, *Acts and Ordinances of the Interregnum 1642–1660*, 3 vols, 1911
Gardiner, *Civil War*	S. R. Gardiner, *The History of the Great Civil War*, 4 vols, 1893
Gardiner, *Commonwealth and Protectorate*	S. R. Gardiner, *The History of the Commonwealth and Protectorate*, 4 vols, 1903
Gardiner, *Documents*	S. R. Gardiner, ed, *Constitutional Documents of the Puritan Revolution 1625–1660*, 3rd ed, Oxford, 1906
Gardiner, *History*	S. R. Gardiner, *The History of England 1603–1642*, 10 vols, 1883–4
Gregg, *Freeborn John*	P. Gregg, *Freeborn John: A Biography of John Lilburne*, 1961
Haller and Davies, *Leveller Tracts*	W. Haller and G. Davies, *The Leveller Tracts 1647–1653*, New York, 1944
Hargrave, *State Trials*	F. Hargrave, *A Complete Collection of State Trials*, 4th ed, 11 vols, 1776
Harleian Miscellany	T. Osborne, ed, *The Harleian Miscellany, or a Collection of . . . Pamphlets and Tracts*, 8 vols, 1744–46
Heylyn	P. Heylyn, *Cyprianus Anglicus*, 1671
Hist. J.	*The Historical Journal*
Hulme	H. Hulme, *The Life of Sir John Eliot*, 1957
Hutchinson, *Memoirs*	*The Memoirs of Colonel John Hutchinson*, by his Widow Lucy, n.d.
J. Econ. Hist.	*The Journal of Economic History*
J. Mod. Hist	*The Journal of Modern History*
Judson	M. Judson, *The Crisis of the Constitution*, New Brunswick, 1949
Knowler	W. Knowler, ed, *The Earl of Strafforde's Letters and Dispatches*, 2 vols, 1739
Laud, *Works*	*The Works of William Laud*, 7 vols, Oxford, 1847–60
Law Q. Rev.	*The Law Quarterley Review*
L.J.	The Journals of the House of Lords

Ludlow, *Memoirs*	C. H. Firth, ed, *The Memoirs of Edmund Ludlow*, 2 vols, Oxford, 1894
Maseres, *Tracts*	F. Maseres, ed, *Select Tracts Relating to the Civil Wars in England*, 2 vols, 1815
Mordaunt Letter Book	M. Coate, ed, *The Letter Book of John Viscount Mordaunt 1658–1660*, Camden Series, 1945
Nalson, *Impartial Collection*	J. Nalson. ed, *An Impartial Collection of the Great Affairs of State 1639–1649*, 2 vols, 1682
Nicholas Papers	G. F. Warner, ed, *The Nicholas Papers*, 4 vols, Camden Series, 1886–1920
Ogg, *Charles II*	D. Ogg, *England in the Reign of Charles II*, 2nd ed, Oxford, 1956
O.P.H.	*The Parliamentary or Constitutional History of England*, 24 vols, 1751–62 ('*The Old Parliamentary History*')
Paul, *Lord Protector*	R. S. Paul, *The Lord Protector: Religion and Politics in the Life of Oliver Cromwell*, 1955
Pennington and Roots, *Committee at Stafford*	D. H. Pennington and I. A. Roots, *The Committee at Stafford, 1643–45*, Manchester, 1957
P.H.	W. Cobbett, ed, *The Parliamentary History of England*, 36 vols, 1806–20
Rushworth	J. Rushworth, ed, *Historical Collections*, 8 vols, 1659–1701
Somers Tracts	*A Collection of Scarce and Valuable Tracts ... in Print and Manuscript ... from Publick, as well as Private Libraries, particularly that of the late Lord Sommers*, 16 vols, 1748–1751
Spalding	J. Spalding, *Memorialls of the Trubles in Scotland and England 1624–1645*, 2 vols, Edinburgh, 1851
Statutes of the Realm	*The Statutes of the Realm 1235–1713*, 11 vols, 1810–28
T.R.H.S.	*The Transactions of the Royal Historical Society*
T.S.P.	T. Birch, ed, *A Collection of the State Papers of John Thurloe*, 7 vols, 1742
Underdown, *Royalist Conspiracy*	D. Underdown, *Royalist Conspiracy in England 1649–1660*, New Haven, 1960
Walker, *History of Independency*	Clement Walker, *The History of Independency*, 1649

Whitelocke, *Memorials*	Bulstrode Whitelocke, *Memorials of the English Affairs . . . from the beginning of the Reign of King Charles the First to King Charles the Second his Happy Restauration*, 1722
Woodhouse	A. S. P. Woodhouse, ed, *Puritanism and Liberty Being the Army Debates 1647–1649 from the Clarke MSS.*, 1938
Yule, *Independents*	G. Yule, *The Independents in the English Civil War*, Cambridge, 1958

Bibliography

It has seemed unnecessary in a work of this nature to list all the numerous older sources, primary and secondary, used. Some are cited in the notes to each chapter. Others may be traced in the bibliographies listed in Section A. With a few exceptions the main Bibliography refers only to books published since the last war. The student may thereby appreciate on what topics recent published research has tended to concentrate and what has been neglected. The division into sections is a matter of convenience—many books mentioned might well appear under a number of headings. Place of publication, London, unless otherwise stated.

A   BIBLIOGRAPHIES

The standard bibliography is that edited by G. Davies, *A Bibliography of English History: Stuart Period*, Oxford, 1928. A new version is in preparation. It may be supplemented by:

(i) W. C. Abbott, ed, *A Bibliography of Oliver Cromwell*, Cambridge, Mass., 1929. (See also P. H. Hardacre, 'Writings on Oliver Cromwell since 1929', *J. Mod. Hist.*, xxx.)

(ii) P. Zagorin, 'English History 1558–1640, a Bibliographical Survey', *Amer. Hist. Review*, lxviii.

(iii) F. W. Bateson, ed, *The Cambridge Bibliography of English Literature*, 4 vols, Cambridge, 1938, with *Supplement*, Cambridge, 1957, ed G. Watson.

(iv) J. W. Fortescue, ed, *Catalogue of the Pamphlets Collected by George Thomason*, 2 vols, 1908.

(v) A. W. Pollard and G. R. Redgrave, eds, *Short Title Catalogue of Books . . . 1475–1640*, 1926.

(vi) D. Wing, ed, *Short Title Catalogue of Books . . . 1641–1700*, 3 vols, New York, 1945–51.

(vii) C. R. Gillett, ed, *Catalogue of the McAlpin Collection of British History and Theology*, 5 vols, New York, 1927–30.

(viii) C. L. Grose, ed, *Select Bibliography of English History 1660–1760*, Chicago, 1939.

(ix) E. S. Upton and G. P. Winship, eds, *Guide to Sources of English History from 1603 to 1660 in Reports of the Royal Commission on Historical Manuscripts*, Washington, D.C., 1952.

(x) A. T. Milne, ed, *Writings on British History, 1934*, 1937 (with annual volumes for subsequent years).

B   GENERAL

The fullest narrative is that of S. R. Gardiner, *The History of England 1603–1642*, 10 vols, 1883–4, *The History of the Great Civil War*, 4 vols, 1893, and *The History of the Commonwealth and Protectorate*, 4 vols, 1903. This is continued by C. H. Firth, *The Last Years of the Protectorate*, 2 vols, 1910, reprinted 1963, and G. Davies, *The Restoration of Charles II*, Oxford, 1955. Gardiner's account of the period 1637–1647 has been supplemented, modified, corrected but not superseded by C. V. Wedgwood, *The Great Rebellion*: (i) *The King's Peace, 1637–1641*, 1955, and (ii) *The King's War, 1641–1647*, 1958. Two stimulating general surveys are C. Hill, *The Century of Revolution, 1603–1714*, Edinburgh, 1961, with a miniscule narrative, and G. E. Aylmer, *The Struggle for the Constitution 1603–1689*, 1963. G. M. Trevelyan, *England Under the Stuarts*, first published in 1904, is still in print. A volume in Longmans' *History of England* entitled *The Stuart Era* is in preparation by Ivan Roots. There are two relevant volumes in the *Oxford History of England: The Early Stuarts* by G. Davies, 2nd ed, 1959, and *The Later Stuarts* by G. N. Clark, 2nd ed, 1955. (Both contain useful bibliographies.) D. Ogg, *England in the Reign of Charles II*, 2 vols, 2nd ed, Oxford, 1956, is witty and erudite.

Valuable collections of essays on many aspects of the period are contained in:

(i) W. A. Aiken and B. D. Henning, eds, *Conflict in Stuart England*, 1960, published in honour of Wallace Notestein, doyen of American historians of Stuart England. (Of particular interest are W. H. Coates, 'An Analysis of Major Conflicts in Seventeenth-Century England'; M. F. Keeler, 'Some Opposition Committees 1640', and W. L. Sachse, 'English Pamphlet Support for Charles I November 1648 to January 1649'.)

(ii) F. J. Fisher, ed, *Essays on the Economic and Social History of Tudor and Stuart England*, Cambridge, 1961, in honour of R. H. Tawney. (Includes essays by R. Ashton, 'Charles I and the City', and D. H. Pennington, 'The Accounts of the Kingdom'.)

(iii) J. H. Hexter, *Reappraisals in History*, 1960. (See especially 'The Myth of the Middle Class', 'The Storm over the Gentry', and 'The Problem of the Presbyterian Independents'.)

(iv) C. Hill, *Puritanism and Revolution*, 1958. (See especially 'The Norman Yoke', 'Recent Interpretations of the Civil War', and 'The English Revolution and the Brotherhood of Man'.)

(v) T. Aston, ed, *Crisis in Europe 1560–1660*, 1965. (Most of the essays, reprinted from *Past and Present*, a valuable journal, are ostensibly concerned with 'the general crisis' of the seventeenth century, which E. J. Hobsbawn sees as 'the past phase of the general transition from a feudal to a capitalist economy', and H. R. Trevor-Roper as 'a crisis in the relations between society and the State'. Other relevant essays are mentioned elsewhere in this bibliography.)

(vi) H. R. Trevor-Roper, *Historical Essays*, 1957.

(vii) H. E. Bell and R. L. Ollard, eds, *Historical Essays 1600–1750*, 1963, in honour of David Ogg. (See especially essays in puritanism in Wales by C. Hill and on Scotland and the English Revolution by H. R. Trevor-Roper.)

(viii) J. S. Bromley and E. H. Kossman, eds, *Britain and the Netherlands*, 1960. (See J. P. Cooper, 'Differences between English and Continental Governments in the Early Seventeenth Century'.)

(ix) G. Davies, *Essays on the Later Stuarts*, San Marino, 1958.

C   BIOGRAPHIES

(i) *The Rulers*. J. P. Kenyon, *The Stuarts*, 1958, is a harsh judgment on the dynasty. D. H. Willson, *James VI and I*, 1956, is solid and reliable. There is no satisfactory biography of Charles I. E. John, *King Charles I*, 1933, reprinted 1952, is slight. E. Wingfield-Stratford's three-decker (1949–50) commemorating the execution is prolix and tendentious. C. V. Wedgwood, *The Execution of Charles I*, 1964, illuminates the royal martyr's character. C. Oman, *Henrietta Maria*, 1936, does justice to his consort. H. Chapman, *The Tragedy of Charles II in the Years 1630–1660*, 1964, is full but inaccurate and ultimately unconvincing. The restored monarch awaits his biographer. For James, Duke of York, see L. Sells, ed, *The Memoirs of James II*, 1962, and the early chapters of F. C. Turner, *James II*, 1948.

For the first Lord Protector see especially W. C. Abbott's magisterial *The Writings and Speeches of Oliver Cromwell*, 4 vols, Cambridge, Mass., 1937–47. There is a full commentary. Recent biographies of value include M. Ashley, *The Greatness of Oliver Cromwell*, 1957, R. Paul, *The Lord Protector*, 1955, and P. Young, *Oliver Cromwell*, 1962 (stronger on the military aspects), but the best life is still that by C. H. Firth, 1900, available since 1953 in the *World's Classics* series. A pamphlet by C. Hill, *Oliver Cromwell*, 1958, provides a stimulating commentary on the whole career. (See also D. H. Pennington, 'Cromwell and the Historians', *History Today*, viii.) R. W. Ramsey, *Richard Cromwell*, 1935, is the latest life of the second Protector. It is unimaginative. (Ramsey also wrote lives of *Henry Cromwell*, 1933, and of Oliver's son-in-law, *Henry Ireton*, 1949.)

(ii) *Their Subjects*. R. E. L. Strider, *Robert Greville, Lord Brooke*, Cambridge, Mass., 1958, is an uninspired study of a leading aristocratic puritan. D. Grant, *Margaret the First*, 1957, is a pleasant literary life of the Duchess of Newcastle. C. D. Bowen, *The Lion and the Throne*, 1957, a discursive 'life and times' of Edward Coke, is slight on legal and constitutional matters. For these see S. E. Thorne, *Sir Edward Coke*, 1957. B. H. G. Wormald, *Clarendon*, Cambridge, 1951, is not a biography but an examination of the political thinking of the great historian and unfortunate politician. In tackling *Sir John Eliot*, 1957, Harold Hulme missed some of the irritating excitement of his character. M. A. Gibb's *The Lord General*, 1938, provides a fair account of Thomas Fairfax. An egregious careerist is anatomised in A. Upton's *Sir Arthur Ingram*, Oxford, 1961. H. R. Trevor-Roper, though unsympathetic, has written the best biography of *Archbishop Laud*, 2nd ed, 1962, and is particularly convincing on his social outlook. John Lilburne has found two competent female biographers, one, M. A. Gibb, stressing *John Lilburne the Christian Democrat*, 1947, the other, P. Gregg, stronger on the political aspirations of *Freeborn John*, 1963. W. H. Dawson, *Cromwell's Understudy*, 1938, rather weakly holds the field for John Lambert. Milton has numerous students, admiring or derogatory, few neutral. J. H. Hanford, *John Milton, Englishman*, 1949, is a lively introduction. Donald Nicholas, *Mr. Secretary Nicholas 1593–1669, His Life and Letters*, 1955, plods. An attractive life of one of Charles I's courtiers has been written by a descendant, G. Huxley, *Endymion Porter*, 1959.

John Pym has so far eluded the biographer, but J. H. Hexter, *The Reign of King Pym*, Cambridge, Mass., 1941, offers insights into his character. S. Reed Brett, *John Pym*, 1940, is very slight. W. Lamont, *Marginal Prynne*, 1963, is a solid investigation of the life and monumental writings of an ardent controversialist at all stages of the rebellion. B. Ferguson provides a soldier's view of *Rupert of the Rhine*, 1952. In 1961 C. V. Wedgwood published 'a revaluation' of *Thomas Wentworth, First Earl of Strafford*. A comparison with her earlier *Strafford*, 1935, shews strikingly how estimates of this remarkable man have changed in the last three decades. (See also the study of Strafford in Ireland by H. F. Kearney and the article on the same theme by T. Ranger mentioned below, p. 308.) D. L. Hobman's *Cromwell's Master Spy*, 1961, tells us little or nothing about John Thurloe. Frank Jessup's *Sir Roger Twysden*, 1966, is a pleasant account of the trials and tribulations of a misunderstood 'neuter' during the Interregnum. P. Verney, *The Standard Bearer*, 1963, a life of Sir Edmund Verney, is a work of family piety. John Wildman is one of the few Levellers apart from Lilburne to attract a biographer, M. Ashley (*John Wildman, Plotter and Postmaster*, 1947). (But see the excellent brief account of Col. Thomas Rainsborough in H. R. Williamson's *Four Stuart Portraits*, 1948.) M. Ashley has also outlined the careers of *Cromwell's Generals*, 1954. *The Dictionary of National Biography*, by now much out of date in spite of a few odd revisions to be found in *The Bulletin of the Institute of Historical Research*, remains the best starting point for investigation of many individuals mentioned in *The Great Rebellion*. It is a matter of regret that there are no recent biographical studies of, among others, Lord Broghill, Arthur Haselrig, Denzil Holles, Henry Marten, George Monk, Sir Philip Stapleton and Bulstrode Whitelocke.

D POLITICAL AND CONSTITUTIONAL (*Practice and Theory*)
The standard modern collection of documents was made by S. R. Gardiner, *Constitutional Documents of the Puritan Revolution*, 3rd ed, Oxford, 1906, often reprinted. It stresses conflicts and largely ignores routine. J. P. Kenyon, *The Stuart Constitution 1603–1688*, Cambridge, 1966, may supersede it.

M. Judson, *The Crisis of the Constitution*, New Brunswick, 1949, considers judiciously matters of accord and disagreement in the political and constitutional thinking of Englishmen between 1603 and 1645. (See also D. Wormuth, *The Royal Prerogative*, New York, 1939, and *The Origins of Modern Constitutionalism*, New York, 1949.)

M. Ashley, *Magna Carta in the Seventeenth Century*, Charlottesville, 1965, is a brief commemorative commentary. (See also F. Thompson, *Magna Carta 1300–1629*, Minneapolis, 1945.) G. E. Aylmer, *The King's Servants*, 1961, investigates minutely the Caroline Civil Service. It casts piercing glances at other aspects. H. E. Bell, *An Introduction to the History and Records of the Court of Wards*, Cambridge, 1953, is very useful, but there is need for a study of the court in its last decades on the lines of J. Hurstfield, *The Queen's Wards*, 1958. Apart from H. G. I. Phillips, 'The Court of Star Chamber 1603–41', *Bull. Inst. Hist. Research*, xviii, there has been little recent work on the closing years of Star Chamber or Council of the North. For the Council in the Marches of Wales see *Studies in Stuart Wales* by A. H. Dodd, Cardiff, 1953, and P. Williams, 'The Activity of the Council in the Marches of Wales under the Early Stuarts', in *Welsh History Review*, i.

D. Brunton and D. H. Pennington, *Members of the Long Parliament*, 1953, is complemented by M. F. Keeler, *The Long Parliament 1640–1641, a Biographical Study*, Philadelphia, 1854. J. D. Eusden's *Puritans, Lawyers and Politics in Early Seventeenth Century England*, New Haven, 1956, is insipid. The ideas of *The Classical Republicans* are searchingly probed by Z. Fink, Evanston, Illinois, 1945. Probably the best study of *The Levellers* is that by J. Frank, Cambridge, Mass., 1955, but H. N. Brailsford's massive *The Levellers and the English Revolution*, ed C. Hill, 1961, is passionate, human and stuffed with information and notions. Excellent selections of Leveller writings, with able introductions, are to be found in W. Haller and G. Davies, eds, *The Leveller Tracts*, New York, 1944, and D. M. Wolfe, *Leveller Manifestoes of the Puritan Revolution*, New York, 1944; they are complementary. J. W. Gough, *Fundamental Law in English Constitutional History*, Oxford, 1955, casts light on a dark subject. Rather slight, but not lacking in insight, is P. H. Hardacre's *The Royalists during the Puritan Revolution*, The Hague, 1956. (Cross-currents among the King's adherents in exile and at home are traced in loving detail by D. Underdown in his *Royalist Conspiracy in England, 1649–60*, New Haven, 1960. See also A. H. Woolrych, *Penruddock's Rising*, 1955, a brief but well-informed pamphlet.)

J. H. Hexter's *The Reign of King Pym*, Cambridge, Mass., 1941, pioneered critical study of the politics of the Long Parliament in the early stages of the Civil War. (Recent articles by L. Glow—'Pym and Parliament—the Methods of Moderation', *J. Mod. Hist.*, xxxvi; 'The Committee Men in the Long Parliament August 1642 to December 1643', *Hist. J.*, viii, and 'The Committee of Safety', *E.H.R.*, lxxx—focus attention on the committee-rooms rather than on the floor of the House of Commons. A stimulating book may be expected.) Old views of Strafford's aims and achievements in Ireland—and incidentally elsewhere—are impugned with vigour by H. F. Kearney in *Strafford in Ireland*, Manchester, 1959. Kearney errs perhaps in making the Lord Deputy out to be a typical seventeenth-century political careerist. Criticism by T. Ranger, 'Strafford in Ireland: a Revaluation', *Past and Present*, xix, reprinted in T. Aston, ed, *Crisis in Europe, 1560–1660*, 1965, is very pertinent. (See also J. P. Cooper, 'The Fortune of Thomas Wentworth, Earl of Strafford', *Econ. Hist. Rev.*, 2nd series, xi.) Ireland after Strafford is considered in T. Coonan, *The Irish Catholic Confederacy and the Puritan Revolution*, New York, 1954. C. B. Macpherson, *The Political Theory of Possessive Individualism*, Oxford, 1962, is confidently original on Hobbes, Harrington and Locke, and offers an important re-consideration of the Leveller franchise. W. M. Mitchell, *The Rise of the Revolutionary Party in the House of Commons 1604–1629*, Oxford, 1957, is assiduous but unconvincing. Simpler accounts of the role of the City in the early sixteen-forties are demolished by V. Pearl in *London and the Outbreak of the Puritan Revolution*,

Oxford, 1961, which also suggests some lines of approach to the problem in the latter part of the Interregnum, a period in this connexion, as in so many others, unduly neglected. P. Zagorin, *A History of Political Thought in the English Revolution*, 1954, is brief but fairly comprehensive. It may be supplemented by W. K. Jordan, *Men of Substance: Henry Parker and Henry Robinson*, Chicago, 1942; F. Raab, *The English Face of Machiavelli*, 1964; J. H. M. Salmon, *The French Wars of Religion in English Political Thought*, Oxford, 1959; and essays in K. C. Brown, ed, *Hobbes Studies*, Oxford, 1965. There is no recent edition of Harrington's *Oceana*, but P. Laslett has edited Sir Roger Filmer's *Patriarcha*, Oxford, 1949, with a lively introduction. In the same series of *Political Texts* Hobbes's *Leviathan* has a provocative analysis by M. Oakeshott, Oxford, 1955. For the Diggers there is G. Sabine, ed, *The Works of Gerrard Winstanley*, New York, 1941, and L. D. Hamilton, ed, *Selected Writings of Gerrard Winstanley*, 1944.

Among numerous articles on aspects of political and constitutional history the following may be mentioned:

G. E. Aylmer, 'Office Holding as a Factor in English History 1625–42', *History*, n.s., xliv, and 'The Last Years of Purveyance', *Econ. Hist. Rev.*, 2nd series, x.

G. Davies, 'Elections for Richard Cromwell's Parliament 1658–9', *E.H.R.*, lxiii.

J. W. Gough, 'The Flowers of the Crown', *E.H.R.*, lxxvii.

J. R. Jones, 'Booth's Rising of 1659', *Bulletin of the John Rylands Library*, xliv, and 'Political Groups and Tactics in the Convention of 1660', *Hist. J.*, vii.

B. S. Manning, 'The Nobles, The People and The Constitution', *Past and Present*, ix, reprinted in T. Aston, ed, *Crisis in Europe 1560–1660*, 1965.

C. R. Mayes, 'Sale of Peerages in Early Stuart England', *J. Mod. Hist.*, xxi.

G. B. Nourse, 'Law Reform under the Commonwealth and Protectorate', *Law Q. Rev.*, lxxv.

C. Russell, 'The Theory of Treason in the Trial of Strafford', *E.H.R.*, lxxx.

V. F. Snow, 'Parliamentary Reapportionment Proposals in the Puritan Revolution', *E.H.R.*, lxxiv; 'Essex and the Aristocratic Opposition to the Early Stuarts', *J. Mod. Hist.*, xxxii, and 'The Concept of Revolution in Seventeenth Century England', *Hist. J.*, v.

H. R. Trevor-Roper, 'Oliver Cromwell and his Parliaments', in R. Pares and A. J. P. Taylor, eds, *Essays Presented to Sir Lewis Namier*, 1956.

D. Underdown, 'The Independents Reconsidered', *Journal of British Studies*, iii.

C. V. Wedgwood, 'Intervention of the Scottish Covenanters in the First Civil War', *Scottish Historical Review*, xxxix.

C. C. Weston, 'The Theory of Mixed Monarchy under Charles I and After', *E.H.R.*, lxxv.

A. H. Woolrych, 'The Good Old Cause and the Fall of the Protectorate', *Camb. Hist. J.*, xiii, and 'The Calling of Barebone's Parliament', *E.H.R.*, lxxx.

E   SOCIAL AND ECONOMIC

M. P. Ashley, *Financial and Commercial Policy under the Cromwellian Protectorate*, new ed, 1962, first published in 1934, has yet to be replaced. R. Ashton provides guidance to royal finances before the Civil War in *The Crown and the Money Market*, Oxford, 1960. M. Campbell, *The English Yeoman under Elizabeth and the Early Stuarts*, New Haven, 1945, new ed 1959, is solid on an often sentimentalised social grouping. M. G. Davies considers in detail an important aspect of social policy in *The Enforcement of English Apprenticeship 1563–1642*, Cambridge, Mass., 1956. M. Dobb, *Studies in the Development of Capitalism*, 1946, offers a Marxist view. C. Hill, *Society and Puritanism in pre-Revolutionary England*, 1964, is more subtle. This provocative work, based on a wealth of contemporary material, chiefly 'literary', cannot be separated from Hill's other studies mentioned elsewhere in this bibliography. M. James, *Social Problems and Policy During the Puritan Revolution*, 1930, 2nd ed, 1964, was a pioneer work, still of use. (Much the same may be said of E. M. Leonard, *The Early History of English Poor Relief*, first published Cambridge, 1900, with a new impression, London, 1965). W. K. Jordan has been making a thorough investigation of English philanthropy from the fifteenth to the mid-seventeenth centuries; among several volumes so far published *Philanthropy in England 1480–1660*, 1959—a general introduction and methodology—and *The Charities of Rural England 1480–1660*, 1961, are outstanding. The sociological approach of P. Laslett in *The World We Have Lost*, 1965, though irritating in its brash generalisations, should not be ignored. D. Mathew, *The Age of Charles I*, 1951, taken with *The Jacobean Age*, 1938, *The Social Structure in Caroline England*, Oxford, 1948, and *Scotland under Charles I*, 1955, offers a curiously oblique analysis, often arid, but with flashes of brilliance. W. Notestein, *The English People on the Eve of Colonisation 1603–1630*, is scrappy but not so elementary as it seems at first reading. It is based on enormous reading. Notestein was obviously more at ease in *Four Worthies*, 1958, percipient studies of individuals rather than types. J. U. Nef's *Industry and Government in France and England 1540–1640*, Philadelphia, 1940, is a short essay, at once thoughtful and enterprising. G. D. Ramsay should be read on *English Overseas Trade during the Centuries of Emergence*, 1957.

L. Stone, *The Crisis of the Aristocracy 1558–1641*, Oxford, 1965, is a vast, ambitious work which will take a long time to digest. (See the review by G. E. Aylmer in *Past and Present*, xxxii.) Stone has also edited *Social Change and Revolution in England 1540–1640*, 1965, a short selection of first-hand materials with well-chosen extracts from books and articles by recent historians. It is a helpful introduction to the theme, illustrating the multitudinous, often flatly contradictory, attitudes towards the problems of the period. There is a solid but not exhaustive bibliography. A. Simpson, *The Wealth of the Gentry 1540–1660*, Cambridge, 1961, is narrower in scope than the title suggests. It deals with a few case histories in East Anglia—a group of 'perdurable' gentry. W. Schenk, *The Concern for Social Justice in the Puritan Revolution*, 1947, offers a catholic view. *English Travellers Abroad 1604–1667*, 1952, by J. W. Stoye considers what Englishmen looked for on and learned from tours in Western Europe.

B. Supple, *Commercial Crisis and Change in England 1600–1642*, Cambridge, 1959, is searching on both economic theory and practice and has valuable comment on social policies. R. H. Tawney, *Business and Politics under James I*, Cambridge, 1958, investigates the career of Lionel Cranfield, one of the ablest servants of the Stuarts, inevitably a victim of impeachment. C. V. Wedgwood has written in *The Common Man in the Civil War*, Leicester, 1958, a brief, sympathetic pamphlet. *Profit and Power* by C. Wilson, 1957, illuminates the Dutch Wars. Wilson's volume in Longman's *Social and Economic History of England* entitled *England's Apprenticeship 1603–1763*, 1965, is an informed synthesis of recent work, strengthened by his own wide-ranging researches.

There are numerous important articles in this field. The collections noted above (in Section B) by C. Hill and J. H. Hexter offer contrasting points of view, notably on the presence of a middle class and the problem of the gentry. Hill also contributed to F. J. Fisher's collection of essays in honour of R. H. Tawney (see Section B). Tawney's 'The Rise of the Gentry 1540–1640', *Econ. Hist. Rev.*, xi, sparked off the controversy that grew heated with H. R. Trevor-Roper's *The Gentry 1540–1640*, Cambridge, 1953, an essay published as a supplement to the *Economic History Review*. Tawney's reply was 'The Rise of the Gentry: a Postscript', *Econ. Hist. Rev.*, 2nd series, vii. Other comments, direct or oblique, are quoted or listed in Stone's *Social Change and Revolution*. (See also Ivan Roots, 'Gentlemen and Others', *History*, n.s. xlvi, a review-article.)

Other relevant articles of value are:

J. P. Cooper, 'The Counting of Manors', *Econ. Hist. Rev.*, 2nd series, vii; D. C. Coleman, 'Labour in the English Economy of the Seventeenth Century', *Econ. Hist. Rev.*, 2nd series, viii; M. Curtis, 'The Alienated Intellectuals of Early Stuart England', *Past and Present*, xxiii, reprinted in T. Aston, ed, *Crisis in Europe 1560–1660*, 1965; H. J. Habbakuk, 'Public Finance and the Sale of Confiscated Property during the Interregnum', *Econ. Hist. Rev.*, 2nd series, xv, and 'Landowners and the Civil War', *Econ. Hist. Rev.*, 2nd series, xviii; E. Kerridge, 'The Movement of Rent 1540–1640', *Econ. Hist. Rev.*, 2nd series, vi; E. Mercer, 'The Houses of the Gentry', *Past and Present*, v; G. D. Ramsay, 'Industrial Laissez-faire and the Policy of Oliver Cromwell', *Econ. Hist. Rev.*, 2nd series, xvi; J. Simon, 'Social Origins of Cambridge Students 1603–1640', *Past and Present*, xxvi; J. Thirsk, 'Sale of Royalist Lands during the Interregnum', *Econ. Hist. Rev.*, 2nd series, v, and 'The Restoration Land Settlement', *J. Mod. Hist.*, xxvi; and P. Zagorin, 'The Social Interpretations of the Puritan Revolution', *J. Econ. Hist.*, xix.

G   RELIGION

H. Barbour, *The Quakers in Puritan England*, New Haven, 1964, is a fresh, lively study. (See also A. Cole, 'The Quakers and the English Revolution', *Past and Present*, x, reprinted in T. Aston, ed, *Crisis in Europe 1560–1660*, 1965.) R. Bosher's *The Making of the Restoration Settlement*, 1951, is in fact confined to the Church. It stresses the role of the Laudians. *The Activities of the Puritan Faction in the Church of England* by I. M. Calder, 1957, considers the schemes and fate of the 'lay feoffees' of the early sixteen-thirties. N. Cohn, *In Pursuit of the Millennium*, 1957, has some useful comments on the sectaries. The background to the Scottish National Covenant is given a critical reappraisal by G. Donaldson in *The Making of the Scottish Prayer Book of 1637*, 1954. Allen French, *Charles I and the Puritan Upheaval*, 1955, makes its exciting subject rather dull. C. Hill has written extensively on the social aspects of puritanism. His *Economic Problems of the Church from Whitgift to the Long Parliament*, Oxford, 1953, is a careful study, extended and modified by books and articles mentioned elsewhere in this bibliography. (R. Ashton examines critically some of Hill's ideas and assumptions in 'Puritans and Progress', *Econ. Hist. Rev.*, 2nd series, xvii.) W. Haller, *The Rise of Puritanism*, New York, 1938, has been continued in *Liberty and Reformation in the Puritan Revolution*, New York, 1955, 2nd ed, 1963. Both volumes are marked by learning, historical imagination and humanity. Haller's *Foxe's Book of Martyrs and the Elect Nation*, 1963, has much that is relevant to Stuart England. M. J. Havran, *The Catholics in Caroline England*, Stanford, 1962, is a useful general study. More detailed work needs to be done on recusants in the localities. *The Development of Religious Toleration in England* was investigated in four solid volumes by W. K. Jordan between 1932 and 1940. It seems unlikely that this work will be displaced. A. G. Matthews, *Calamy Revised*, Oxford, 1934, and its companion piece, *Walker Revised*, Oxford, 1948, provide reliable information on clerical ejections.

Ecclesiastical jurisdiction in the diocese of York is minutely examined by R. Marchant in *The Puritans and the Church Courts 1560–1642*, 1960. G. Nuttall has written copiously and eloquently on puritanism as a religious phenomenon, notably in *The Holy Spirit in Puritan Faith and Experience*, Oxford, 1946, and *Visible Saints*, Oxford, 1957. *The Religious Foundations of Leveller Democracy* have been picked out, perhaps a little too sharply, by D. B. Robertson, New York, 1951. C. Roth has reconsidered *The Resettlement of the Jews in England*, 1960. R. Schlatter, *Richard Baxter and Puritan Politics*, 1957, is a thoughtful study of a prolific and resilient controversialist, just a little bit of a bore. Leo Solt draws attention to the authoritarian side of puritanism, not unknown to previous students, in *Saints in Arms*, Oxford, 1959. F. E. Stoeffer, *The Rise of Evangelical Pietism*, Leiden, 1965, has some stimulating chapters of English Puritanism. A. Simpson, *Puritanism in Old and New England*, Chicago, 1955, seems rather sketchy, as does G. Yule, *The Independents in the English Civil War*, Cambridge, 1958. The detailed local studies the latter suggests remain to be done.

The following articles may be noted:

C. H. George, 'A Social Interpretation of English Puritanism', *J. Mod. Hist.*, xxv; C. Hill, 'Puritans and the Dark Corners of the Land', *T.R.H.S.*, 5th series, xiii; M. James, 'The Political Importance of the Tithe Controversy in the Puritan Revolution', *History*, new series, xxvi; K. V. Thomas, 'Women and the Civil War Sects', *Past and Present*, xiii, reprinted in T. Aston, ed, *Crisis in Europe 1560–1660*, 1965; H. R. Trevor-Roper, 'The Fast Sermons of the Long Parliament', in *Essays in British History*, edited by himself, 1964; M. Waltzer, 'Puritanism as a Revolutionary Ideology', *History and Theory*, iii; A. Whiteman, 'The Re-establishment of the Church of England 1660–63', *T.R.H.S.*, 5th series, v.

H MILITARY

The Great Civil War by A. H. Burne and P. Young, 1959, is firmly 'a military history' with most of the politics left out. Col. Burne included Civil War engagements in his *Battlefields of England*, 1950, and *More Battlefields of England*, 1952. Brigadier Young also looks at the Great Rebellion again—this time with John Adair—in *Hastings to Culloden*, 1964. A. H. Woolrych, *Battles of the Civil War*, 1961, is selective, stresses politics and is well illustrated. J. R. Powell is useful on *The Navy in the English Civil War*, Hamden, Conn., 1963.

I LOCAL STUDIES

The importance of local studies for the understanding of the period is now generally appreciated.

T. G. Barnes, *Somerset 1625–40*, Oxford, 1961, is a solid, perceptive examination of a large county in a difficult period. C. W. Chalklin, *Seventeenth Century Kent*, 1965, is comprehensive but dull and not always accurate. E. M. Everitt, *The Committee of Kent*, Leicester, 1957, and *Suffolk and the Great Rebellion*, Ipswich, 1960, are thoughtful studies of contrasting communities. (His *The Community of Kent and the Great Rebellion*, Leicester, 1966, has appeared too late for consideration.) *The Great Civil War in the Midland Parishes* by D. R. Guttery, Birmingham, 1951, is inadequate. Difficulties in the relations of central and local government in wartime are explored by D. H. Pennington and I. A. Roots in *The Committee at Stafford, 1643–5*, Manchester, 1957. B. N. Reckitt, *Charles I and Hull*, 1952, considers the significance of this vital port. W. B. Willcox, *Gloucester: a Study in Local Government 1590–1640*, New Haven, 1950, is valuable.

J MISCELLANEOUS

A. Barker, *Milton and the Puritan Dilemma*, Toronto, 1942.

D. Bush, *English Literature in the Earlier Seventeenth Century*, 2nd ed, Oxford, 1962.

M. Curtis, *Oxford and Cambridge in Transition 1558–1642*, Oxford, 1956.

D. C. Douglas, *English Scholars*, 2nd ed, 1951.

B. Ford, ed, *From Donne to Marvell*, 1956.

313

L. Fox, ed, *English Historical Scholarship in the Sixteenth and Seventeenth Centuries*, 1956.

J. Frank, *The Beginnings of the English Newspaper 1620–1660*, Cambridge, Mass., 1961.

F. Smith Fussner, *The Historical Revolution*, 1962.

C. Hill, *Intellectual Origins of the English Revolution*, Oxford, 1965.

H. F. Kearney, *Origins of the Scientific Revolution*, 1965. (See also his 'Puritanism, Capitalism and the Scientific Revolution', *Past and Present*, xxviii.)

J. G. A. Pocock, *The Ancient Constitution and the Feudal Law*, Cambridge, 1957.

W. A. L. Vincent, *The State and School Education 1640–1660*, 1950.

C. C. Wedgwood, *Poetry and Politics under the Stuarts*, Cambridge, 1960.

M. Whinney, and O. Millar, *English Art 1625–1714*, Oxford, 1957.

D. M. Wolfe, *Milton in the Puritan Revolution*, New York, 1941.

Index
